WELL MET

WELL MET

Renaissance Faires and

the American Counterculture

Rachel Lee Rubin

NEW YORK UNIVERSITY PRESS
New York and London

NEW YORK UNIVERSITY PRESS
New York and London
www.nyupress.org

The title of chapter 3, "Shakespeare, He's in the Alley," is from Bob Dylan's "Stuck Inside of Mobile with the Memphis Blues Again," Blonde on Blonde, Columbia, 1966.

References to Internet websites (URLs) were accurate at the time of writing. Neither the author nor New York University Press is responsible for URLs that may have expired or changed since the manuscript was prepared.

Library of Congress Cataloging-in-Publication Data
Rubin, Rachel.
Well met : renaissance faires and the American counterculture / Rachel Lee Rubin.
p. cm.
Includes bibliographical references and index.
ISBN 978-0-8147-7138-9 (cl : alk. paper) -- ISBN 978-0-8147-3810-8 (ebook) -- ISBN 978-0-8147-6385-8 (ebook)
1. Renaissance fairs--United States--History--20th century. 2. Counterculture--United States--History--20th century. I. Title.
GT4603.R83 2012
394.609730904--dc23
2012024955

New York University Press books are printed on acid-free paper, and their binding materials are chosen for strength and durability. We strive to use environmentally responsible suppliers and materials to the greatest extent possible in publishing our books.

Manufactured in the United States of America

10 9 8 7 6 5 4 3 2 1

For Ann and Derek, with love and admiration

CONTENTS

ACKNOWLEDGMENTS

If I were to do a proper job of it—naming every person who helped me with this project—the acknowledgments would likely be as long as the book. I'll have to be content, then, with what I can accomplish efficiently on the page—but please know that inside, I am singing the praises of many people at length.

My first thanks must be to the scores of faire patrons who generously used their precious faire time, or their "mundane" time, to talk to me: in person, on the phone, by email, or by answering a quick question or two while they waited in line. I simply could not have understood the faire with any kind of adequacy without your insights, analysis, and storytelling. I deeply appreciate your opening your lives for me to peer at.

I cannot adequately express my gratitude to all the Rennies, past and present—performers, crafters, boothies—who let me in, sharing their experiences and stories (and, in some cases, their food and floor space). I spent most of my research process floored by your talents, skills, and knowledge. Your generosity moved me constantly and pushed me along by making me yearn for this book to be what you deserve. I am particularly grateful to Trent Anderson, Don Coviello, Ann Curtis, Deb Fischbach, Ernie Fischbach, Tim Furst, Steven Gillan, Peter Jelen, Joe Kudla, David Ossman, Will Spires, and Derek Weaver, who entertained my phone calls, shared photographs and materials, made introductions, and patiently brought me up to speed in their areas of expertise.

To Kevin Patterson, who was willing to act as both source and resource from the project's beginning to its end, this project is deeply indebted.

I am grateful to Les Blank for digitizing and sharing his footage of the 1964 Renaissance Pleasure Faire with me. Getting a glimpse of the early faire advanced my understanding in ways both practical and ineffable.

I have been blessed with inspiring colleagues at UMass Boston, both within the American Studies Department and across the university. I am especially thankful to Paul Atwood, Philip Chassler, Aaron Lecklider, Arthur Macewan, Bonnie Miller, Marisol Negrón, Patricia Raub, Lois Rudnick, Heike Schotten, Judy Smith, Shirley Tang, Lynnell Thomas, and Susan Tomlinson for providing me with company, support, encouragement, and above all, superb models of what it means to be a teacher and scholar. There is no facet of my job, period, that I could carry out without drawing upon the knowledge, competence, and generosity of Shauna Manning. Executive Committee and rank-and-file members of the Faculty Staff Union constantly help me understand why the work of the academy matters—as do my students, graduate and undergraduate, from whom I learn so much. I am also grateful to have received financial support for this project from UMass in the form of grants from the Office of Sponsored Projects and the CLA Dean's Office.

For intellectual guidance and insightful commenting on early drafts, I am grateful to Judy Smith, Jim Smethurst, Paul Wright, and Jeff Melnick. This book is so much better because of you.

To Jacob Rubin, who notices everything, thank you for pointing me in the right direction on more than one occasion. Thanks also to Lily Corman Penzel for pulling my coat about the faire on television.

I am lucky to have an extended family that has cheered me on (and put up with my occasional silences as I worked); thanks to Larry Rubin, Nora Cannon, Julia Cannon Rubin, Iris Swimmer, Len Swimmer, Deb Melnick, Dan Melnick, Dave Melnick, Hillary Kramer, Tasha Kramer-Melnick, Jaden Kramer-Melnick, Jewel Prell, Ludlow Smethurst, and Bill Smethurst. I owe so much to all of you. I have relied upon my dear friends every single step of the way—for encouragement, advice, political solidarity, raucous laughter, cultural arguments, and (sometimes) their ability to notice and communicate when I am going at something wrong-headed. Cindy Weisbart (my real sister), Judy Smith, Susie Ringel, Lisa Hershey, Geoffrey Jacques, Marcus Ranum, Napoleon Abdulai, Alex Liazos, Beth Boyer, Andy Levine, Sandra Haley, and Kostya Ustinov—I am so fortunate to know you.

Finally, I am deeply grateful to my "J" crowd—Jim, Jessie, Jacob, and Jeff—each more curious, opinionated, and outspoken than the next. Jim

Smethurst, your influence on my mind and heart runs deep. Jessie Lee Rubin, I aspire to your level of relentless thoughtfulness and brave nonconformity. Jacob Rubin, since your birth you have given me a nonstop moral, philosophical, and intellectual education—and you show no signs of stopping. And Jeff Melnick, your companionship in so many endeavors sustains and inspires me every day, as does your compassion, sense of humor, and smarts. Thanks, you guys, for jam, singing, movie suggestions, and breakfast scones, respectively, and thanks to you all for the many ways you contribute not only to what I do but to who I am. You mean the world to me.

NOTE ON INTERVIEWS

For each interview or survey I conducted, whether in person, by telephone, or in writing, I asked the interviewee how she or he preferred to be identified: by first and last name, by first name only, or with a pseudonym (which I have indicated by placing the pseudonym within quotation marks).

Introduction

Faire Grounds

If theme parks, with their pasteboard main streets, reek of a bland, safe, homogenized, whitebread America, the Renaissance Faire is at the other end of the social spectrum, a whiff of the occult, a flash of danger and a hint of the erotic. Here, they let you throw axes. Here are more beer and bosoms than you'll find in all of Disney World.

—Neil Steinberg, *Chicago Sun-Times*

"This is our ethnic background!" William Shakespeare tells me, gesturing at a Southern California fairground filled with visitors and workers. Together we study the crowd for a moment. Some sightseers are wearing street clothes in the variety of trends and statements that make up Los Angeles style. Many others, however, are wearing some form of costumery; this "garb," as it is popularly called, encompasses a range of degree of elaboration and historical reference (velvet cloaks, high leather boots, drawstring money pouches), as well as some fantasy-inspired elements (satyr horns, wings, leather masks). A performing "guild" of Scotsmen in kilts is visible, practicing some kind of formation with pikes in hands. A group of Pilgrims wanders by, sneers etched on their faces, Bibles in hand, and several young women in bodices and skirts pause to flirt outrageously with them, enacting a sort of erotic version of the tradition of trying to make the guards at Buckingham Palace smile.

Functional paradox is the stock-in-trade of the American Renaissance faire, and this knowledge helps me appreciate what Shakespeare—a performer named David Springhorn who is playing the Bard at the forty-seventh annual Renaissance Pleasure Faire in Irwindale, California—wants me to understand. Those who have been devoted to the faire for a period of years—craftspeople and entertainers, patrons and volunteers—frequently use the language of relatedness to describe their community: tribe, family, clan. Indeed, an anthropologist could find much to study here, using Springhorn's deliberately improvised version of "ethnicity." Faire workers, often referred to by the shorthand "Rennies," celebrate their own holidays. Both regular visitors and faire employees use the term "faire family" or "faire-mily" to define their networks. The faire has its own traditional cuisine, best emblematized by the turkey legs sold at every faire regardless of where it takes place; these will be mentioned or pictured in pretty much all media coverage or publicity material. There were no turkeys in Renaissance Europe, but the turkey legs are traditional cuisine nonetheless: traditional to the Renaissance *festival*, rather than the Renaissance.

Standing with Shakespeare, I muse upon the festivals I remember from growing up in a big city during the "ethnic revival" of the 1970s, while scouring the Renaissance faire for evidence of kinship of spirit. In addition to the turkey legs, there are traditional handicrafts being sold. There are recognizable items of clothing that mark Renaissance faire "folk" distinctly. There are rituals of storytelling particular to the faire. There is a sense of generational continuity and a number of ceremonies and rites. There is even "ethnic humor"—both the mocking kind from outside and the self-identifying kind from inside. Certainly, there are linguistic particularities, including both specialized vocabulary ("garb" for period-specific clothing, "mundanes" for people in non-Renaissance apparel) and an extensive language system that novelist Peter S. Beagle has affectionately dubbed "castle talk": words and formulations that invoke Elizabethan English to the American mind without necessarily hewing to its rules of grammar, pronunciation, and social convention ("Well-met, Milady," and "Gramercy!"). There are first-, second-, and third-generation faire folk, who readily identify as such.

Renaissance faire adherents such as David Springhorn and the many others I have spoken to have given their own meaning to the term "usable past," a framework introduced to the examination of American history, and historiography, by Van Wyck Brooks in 1915. However, in the instance of these outdoor depictions of European village life, both "usable" and "past" take on doubled meanings. There is, unquestionably, more than a little to be learned about the history and culture of the European Renaissance (and, increasingly, the history and culture of other continents during the same time period) through historical performance, and the founding family of the faire, as well as a large number of its longtime participants, emphasize the educational payoff as the most important "use" of the faire's romance with the past. Indeed, school buses continue to transport students to the faires in groups, indicating that a considerable number of educators agree with this premise. In 1994, Teacher Created Resources produced a guide for teachers, *Renaissance Thematic Unit* (Larson); this pamphlet offers suggestions for creating a faire as the culmination of studying Renaissance history and culture.

But although the Renaissance faire founders have been invited over the years to share their expertise with several "living museums"—such as Plimoth Plantation and Old Sturbridge Village in Massachusetts and Colonial Williamsburg in Virginia—the Renaissance festival has never been limited to "straight" reenactment. ("There's reenactment and then there's Ren faire," pronounces a costumed member of the faire's "Scottish guild" who happens to be passing by while I am speaking to his guild chief. He hands me a very welcome wooden mug of cold water and continues on his way.) Indeed, the remarkable success of the Renaissance faire in the United States begs a larger, more slippery, and ultimately more interesting question: to what concrete personal, political, and cultural uses can a group of Americans put a past that, for the most part, is *not* their own?

Those uses, of course, have changed over the course of the faire's four-decade run, as the meanings of the faire have been contested, revised, updated and, in some cases, co-opted. In many ways, the Renaissance faire is a mainstream, family affair in the twenty-first century, a largely corporate institution whose "brand" extends far beyond California, where the faires originated, to almost every state in the United States.

Most faires set aside play areas for kids, with attractions such as pirate ships for exploring, games, swings, juggling lessons, pony rides, and storytellers. As if to emphasize the faire's turn toward the saleably "wholesome," the children's television show *Reading Rainbow* filmed a rather sweet episode there in 1987 ("Rumpelstiltskin"), and Mattel introduced a "Renaissance Faire Barbie" in 2011.

But in the early 1960s, as the faire first began to establish itself, it functioned as a resounding slap in the face of 1950s conventions of Cold War bellicosity, compulsory female domesticity, stifling anticommunism, and narrow ideals of nuclear family. From a historical perspective, this is not surprising, given that the faire's birthplace was Laurel Canyon, a neighborhood located in the hills above the center of Los Angels and long known by the time the first faires took place for hosting bohemian types: Louise Brooks, Orson Welles, and David Niven lived there, and Laurel Canyon was where film noir actor Robert Mitchum's infamous marijuana bust took place in 1948. During the 1950s, the neighborhood was known as a sanctuary of sorts for movie industry victims of the infamous Hollywood Red Scare (Ossman interview).

The faire's founders, Phyllis and Ron Patterson, moved to Laurel Canyon in the late 1950s as a young couple and found among their neighbors the talented cultural workers who helped them give the early festivals their recognizable character. Then, just as the very first faires were being imagined in the Canyon, the musicians (and their followers) who were to make up Los Angeles's high-flying rock-and-roll scene flocked there in the mid-1960s; included in this number were members of the seminal folk-rock band The Byrds, who shortly thereafter recorded (in 1967) "Renaissance Fair," a valentine to the sights, smells, and sounds that those earlier Laurel Canyon dwellers created:

> I think that maybe I'm dreaming
> I smell cinnamon and spices
> I hear music everywhere
> All around kaleidoscope of color
> I think that maybe I'm dreaming
> Maids pass gracefully in laughter
> Wine-colored flowers in their hair

Last call from lands I've never been to
I think that maybe I'm dreaming
Sun's flash on a soda prism
Bright jewels on the ladies flashing
Eyes catch on a shiny prism
Hear ye the crying of the vendors
Fruit for sale, wax candles for to burn
Fires flare, soon it will be night fall
I think that maybe I'm dreaming

In the 1960s, when The Byrds were there, the Renaissance faire presented an intriguing mix of countercultural antimodernism and sophisticated avant-garde; it quickly became known as a locus for challenging the staid suburban ideal. "Renaissance Pleasure Faire—Why the Establishment Howled," shrieks the headline of a 1967 issue of *Adam*, a soft-core girlie magazine (Rotsler, front cover). Through its willful turn to the old, the Renaissance faire became a place to experiment with the new—new sexual arrangements, new ways of understanding and enacting gender roles, legal and illegal drugs (with LSD included in the "legal" category at this point), communal living, and ideals of art taken directly to the people. "A new way to relate to each other" is how Kevin Patterson, the first but not the last baby to grow up at the faire, puts it (interview).[1] "The early faire," pronounced influential faire musician Bob Thomas, "was given by one branch of the freak community for the rest" (Zekley, "Preston"). Hippies gravitated there, to take in the show, to be part of the show, to attend soon-to-be legendary after-hour parties—and, as in the case of Los Angeles "freak-scene guru" Vito Paulekas and his self-styled troupe of "freak dancers," to dance with abandon.[2] Aspiring artists arrived, finding in the faire a rare place to earn a living from their craft. Celebrities came, to be seen as well as to see. Vietnam veterans participated in large numbers, recruiting each other with the promise that the faire was a good and safe place for them in particular, as they returned to the United States dragging the heaviest of baggage.

The history of the American Renaissance faire—what went *into* creating it and how it has evolved over its more than forty-five-year lifespan—yields fascinating and sometimes astonishing insights into the

[5]

construction of the American counterculture. Excavating the faire's layers, its geological formations, as it were—from the perspective of labor, education, aesthetics, business, the opposition it faced, the key figures involved—reveals the way the faires immediately established themselves as a pioneering and highly visible referendum on how we live *now*—our family arrangements, our relationship to consumer goods, and our corporate entertainments.

Equally important, though, is what came *out* of the faire—the transforming gifts bestowed by the faire's innovations and experiments on the broader American culture, obscured as these roots often are in the twenty-first century. This book, therefore, is also concerned with the ways in which various forms of cultural expression "tried out" first at the faire became recognizable staples of American social and cultural life, even as their Renaissance faire pedigree has retreated from view. In this way, my framing of the faire reveals the role it played in creating what we have come to call the "Sixties." When we speak of the "Sixties"—in journalistic accounts, fashion rhetoric, academic histories, and so on—we often mean to call attention to a period of time that stretched from, say, late 1963 (with John F. Kennedy's assassination) through April 1975—when Saigon "fell." But here, I am less interested in concrete dates than I am in conventional wisdom and cultural memory. These reside, in part, in the shorthand signposts we use to invoke the "Sixties"—the flower in the rifle, Jimi Hendrix genuflecting over his guitar, the young woman weeping at Kent State—that obscure as much as they reveal. My goal here is to push past those acts of ritual summary by putting the Renaissance faire back at the center—as one point of origin—of much of the cultural activity that has contributed to our definition of the period.

In short, the Renaissance faire, I argue, helped to invent the Sixties—so much so that Tom Brokaw, in a 2008 television appearance, used his attendance at the faire as shorthand for his youthful gravitation toward the counterculture despite his "square" job and background:

BARBARA WALTERS: When I met you 40 years ago you were pretty square.
TOM BROKAW: Well, of course I had come out of the 50's. I was kind of a weekend hippy. I would take my kids, you

know, my daughters. And on weekends, Meredith and I would, I'd put on my bell bottom trousers and my sandals, and we'd go off to the Renaissance Faire outside of Los Angeles...

JOY BEHAR: Oh my God.

ELIZABETH HASSELBECK: Are you serious? Tom!

BROKAW: ... and hang out there, and then on Monday mornings I'd put on my white button down shirt and my narrow tie and my jacket and then I'd go off and be a network correspondent and I looked like that. (Qtd. in McCarthy)

Once we put the faire back in its place (at the heart of the narrative of how the American counterculture transformed *all* of American life in the 1960s and 1970s) it will be much easier to see how it acted as a bridge between the Old Left of the 1930s (and 1940s and 1950s) and the emerging New Left of the 1960s and 1970s. Standard histories of the transition from Old to New Left have neglected thus far to trace out the faire's influence, and in doing so they have given short shrift to all the cultural energy donated to the surrounding culture by all these sexual noncomformists, these truly antibourgeois "freaks," all the *women* who were the denizens of this new polity. More particularly, I examine several important phenomena that began at the faire: the so-called underground press of the 1960s and 1970s; experimentation with "ethnic" musical instruments and styles in popular music; the craft revival of the 1970s; the Americanization of mime and other comic performance styles. Here, I also use interviews and oral history to "track" central figures who began or came into their own at the faire and then went on to have a lasting impact beyond the faire gates: among them are the mime Robert Shields (later of Shields and Yarnell), the comedy group Firesign Theater, the musical group Golden Toad, the countercultural journalist Art Kunkin, and the performance artist Rachel Rosenthal.

This book also plumbs the meaning of the faire to its devoted participants, both workers and visitors, across almost fifty years of its history and in its present articulation. Many people who earn their living from the faire "travel the circuit" to work at more than one festival because each one's season lasts only a couple of months; indeed, some of these have no home base at all beyond the various faire sites. I draw on interviews with dozens of performers, crafters, booth workers, and food providers to explore what values and lifestyle choices have made "Rennies" of them: attracting them to some degree of communal life and leading them to develop their own culture, traditions, and—in the preferred locution of many of them—"tribal units." The faire's dedicated visitors, similarly, attend the faire every weekend it is open (buying season passes where they are offered), piece together elaborate costumes at great expense of time and money, and do their best to extend their faire-going experience through online communities, Renaissance faire publications, and their own treks (sometimes hundreds of miles) to visit other faires. Dozens of these dedicated faire visitors—"playtrons," in faire parlance—shared with me accounts of their involvement that ranged from moving to hilarious, and I allow them to speak for themselves as much as possible, as their testimony tracks both marked shifts in who has found the faire most useful—and why—and the ways in which the faire has enabled (perhaps paradoxical) strategies of resistance to the very forces of corporatism and cultural centrism that have inexorably resituated it in the American expressive landscape.

I also look at two other important ways in which the meaning of the faire has been established and codified: through the ways it has been pictured in literature, movies, and television shows, and through motivated opposition to it ranging from serious political attempts to block its opening to "haters" who publicly satirize the faire in ways that are more *self-defining* than anything else. Following an initial chapter that traces the founding and establishment of the first faires in California—up until their growth beyond these roots spawned a national "faire circuit" that performers, craftspeople, and other employees began to travel—the book is organized thematically, in order to highlight the faire's constituent elements: what their originary impulses were made of and how they changed with the faires over time. In all these ways, the deliberately pot-stirring "meaning" of the Renaissance faire remains in evidence while imagining a world outside the commercial marketplace becomes increasingly difficult, even as a lingering popular fascination with the 1960s indicates a continued, if distant, longing for an alternative.

1

"Welcome to the Sixties!"

The faire brought the lefties, the artists, the longhairs and the eccentrics out of the woodwork to play together under the trees.

—Alicia Bay Laurel

John Waters's 1987 movie *Hairspray* takes place in 1963, the same year in which the first Renaissance faire was held. In a key scene, the movie's protagonist, Baltimore teenager Tracy Turnblad, convinces her mother to update her old-fashioned hairstyle. Leaving the salon with her now-groovier mother, and gesturing expansively, Tracy exclaims, "Mama, welcome to the Sixties!"

A history of the Renaissance faire must naturally pivot, as does Waters's movie, on changes brought by the year 1963. But any genuine understanding of the meaning of the faire must also grapple with what came before. In other words, what cultural conversation did the faire enter? On whose shoulders did it stand, and what transformations did its trumpets and banners herald? Or, to use the framework of Waters's rebellious teenager, how did the Renaissance faire say to thousands of Californians, "Welcome to the Sixties"?

In a historically urgent way, the most dead-serious thing about the Renaissance faire was, from the very beginning, its sense of whimsy. This whimsy, along with related qualities of spontaneity, surrealism, and irreverence, came to characterize the counterculture of the 1960s and

1970s as exemplified by the name of the group around author Ken Kesey, who called themselves the "Merry Pranksters." The poet Allen Ginsberg embraced and elaborated a range of cultural practices he felt make use of these qualities in a speech he made to a group of Unitarian ministers in Boston in 1965; the title of that address was "Renaissance or Die."

The American Renaissance faire was from its earliest days well situated to marshal a sense of motivated whimsy to serve an antiestablishment agenda. "There was a playfulness and a liberation about the faire," recalls David Ossman, whose involvement in the faire started in 1963, when he was the drama and literature director at public radio station KPFK, and ultimately powered his founding of the influential comedy troupe Firesign Theater (interview). Indeed, Kevin Patterson asserts that getting people to "play" was the Renaissance faire's strategy for effecting social change (interview).

This privileging of playfulness remains a hallmark of the faires nearly half a century later; faire participants use the verb "play" more often than is common in American English, with concrete and professional connotations. "I love being a street [wandering] performer because you can play with people," more than one cast member explains to me, and in many instances, faire-set fiction penned by actual faire participants (as opposed to that written by relative outsiders) can be identified as such by this usage alone. In the 1960s, commentators were well aware that "play" could function as a rather direct repudiation of the status quo. Warren Hinckle, writing in 1967 in the New Left publication *Ramparts* about the generation of youth becoming known as "hippies," claimed, "Running around the outside of an insane society, the healthiest thing you can do is laugh." Hinckle insisted that this laughter can operate as a powerful refusal "in a climate dominated by Dwight Eisenhower in the newspapers and Ed Sullivan on television" (17). Mime Robert Shields, who began his career at the Southern California Renaissance faire and went on from there to become famous as half the duo Shields and Yarnell, chooses an image resonant with Hinckle's claim to describe his youthful reaction to seeing the faire for the first time: he compares the world outside the faire to the television show *Mad Men*, set in an advertising agency in the early 1960s, while inside the faire gates, "everything was 'yes!'" (Shields interview). In 1975, visiting Soviet/Russian writer Vasily Aksyonov recognized the faire as successfully using play to upend *all* cultural identities. "This fair," he wrote a year later, "even with all its charm, humor, and chivalry, seemed something like a revolt to me" (131). Seen in this light, the playfulness of the Renaissance faire takes on heft and deliberation, becoming what Kevin Patterson calls an "artistic manifestation of a protest gathering" (interview). But first the faire had to make the unlikely leap from backyard children's program to hipster affair located centrally in the counterculture.

From Nebraska to Backyard Commedia

The common sense and irreverence of the commedia is a public service.
—Peter Jelen, leatherworker

Although the faire has always been a strikingly collective production, dependent on the talents and involvement of hundreds, longtime participants trace its genesis to a visionary founder: high school English teacher Phyllis Patterson. Patterson was born in 1932 in Nebraska, where she remembers developing an interest in what she calls the "pioneer spirit," as manifested in literature by works such as Willa Cather's 1918 novel *My Ántonia*.[1] But she came of age in Memphis, Tennessee, during World War II. Patterson's father, Eldon Carl "EC" Stimbert, served as the superintendent of the Memphis public school district, eventually become state superintendent of schools; he held these leadership posts from 1957 to 1971, when the schools began the process of racial desegregation following the 1954 *Brown v. Board of Education* decision. Patterson recalls bringing her new husband home for holidays to a house protected by security details during this time.

Patterson graduated from high school a year early, giving her what she refers to as "a year to waste." So, in her words, she "wasted it in television": hosting a Memphis program called *Phyl's Playhouse*. *Phyl's Playhouse* was a modest yet highly imaginative variety show that introduced some new ideas to a new form; as Patterson tells it, "I can't say that I was brave or that I was a visionary or anything like that. I just had this idea for a television show that was very simplistic. It had to do with reading poetry on television and reading stories on television. . . . I actually had the first television show that was done by a woman, I'm sure, in any of the smaller cities" (interview). *Phyl's Playhouse* ran for two years, with a show broadcast every Saturday. Meanwhile, Patterson attended Memphis State College. For the "acts" on the show, as well as aspects of its production, she drew heavily on her college friends.

Although it seems like a far distance between the technological advances of television in the 1950s and the antitechnological structure of the Renaissance faire in the 1960s, Patterson is certain that her work on the television show mattered to the faire. This is because of the show's educational bent and its focus on culture, which contained, according to Patterson, "the essence of what the Renaissance faire was": "Because this is in miniature what I later made into large—they didn't have PBS yet. This was a real preparatory to that. . . . What I wanted to do was to teach through the arts. I didn't say it that way then. But as I look back, that's exactly what I was doing. You don't stray very far from your original passions, not really" (interview).

Patterson ultimately quit doing the show just as it was reaching a new level of success and attracting a sponsor; she realized, she explains, that her work on the show was coming at the expense of her college education. At that time, she was imagining a future in television, but she had particular ambitions for this new medium. She aimed to produce educational content:

> I realized that I had to make a clean break and I had to finish my college education if I wanted to really go on and do education on television. I then didn't see that this [the *Phyl's Playhouse* program] could have been that vehicle. I just didn't see that. . . . So I went away to Denver University and worked on my master's. And then I worked on my MRS. And I got my MRS. And then twenty years later, I got an MS.[2] (Interview)

Patterson moved with her husband, Ron, to the Laurel Canyon neighborhood of the Hollywood Hills in Los Angeles, and she began teaching high school English. She felt devoted to teaching, but after the birth of her first child, Kevin, in 1960, she decided not to return immediately to the classroom. Rather, she pursued employment that would allow her to make use of her teaching skills while caring for her new baby. In her new neighborhood, she came across a neighborhood newspaper called the *Canyon Crier*, which "somebody put out to just give want ads and what was going on in this little community of mainly actors, . . . nothing very serious about it." She learned from the paper that the neighborhood had a youth center, a nonprofit established in 1949 for the purpose of providing Laurel Canyon's children with recreational theatrical activities. The youth center was looking to hire someone to teach drama to the children enrolled in its program. Immediately, Patterson approached the listed contacts—and had a meeting with them that impressed her mightily:

> [The notice] said, "Wonderland Youth Center Hiring Director for Children's Theater." So I went right away to the house of Doris Karnes and Bob Karnes, [to] this incredibly beautiful, Danish-designed house that was two levels. The living room was two levels with a balcony around it. So it was awesome to go into. The woman who came to the door had long red hair almost down to her knees. I'd never seen that before either. (Interview)

At the end of that meeting, Patterson had the job. (The beautiful house was sold to Mickey Dolenz of the Monkees within a handful of years.)

In Patterson's own accounting, she was so delighted to be hired that she did not ask many questions about what the job would entail. Instead, she just assumed that she would be teaching older children, of the high school and junior high school age with which she was experienced. She envisioned a classroom-sized group of about twenty. In short order, however, she learned from Bob Karnes that she had been mistaken: "He said, 'Oh, there are eighty of them. And they range in age from six to thirteen years old.' I had never taught elementary school! I had no idea how to teach elementary school!" (P. Patterson interview).

This abrupt obligation to teach young children posed a great challenge to Patterson's teaching acumen. The challenge paid off historically, though, because Patterson insists that if she had been correct in her assumption—if she had ended up teaching a small group of high schoolers—then there would never have been a Renaissance faire. "I had to organize these kids into something that they would enjoy," she explains. "But I did figure it out. I knew how to teach history; I knew how to teach theater." So Patterson devised the idea of using snippets of plays to teach the younger children about the history of theater. She began to hold the classes in her backyard—"you'd better have classes in your backyard if you have a small baby"—and the cost of a run of eight sessions was two dollars a class, enough to pay a part-time babysitter for her son Kevin, born in 1960, and his brother, Brian, born in 1966 (P. Patterson interview). (Both sons spent much of their childhood at the faire and continued their involvement into their adulthood, Kevin as a producer and Brian as a puppeteer.)

Patterson divided the children in the classes into smaller, more manageable groups, so that no child had to "be a tree or a bush or something and not say anything or just stand there and hold a banner," and the groups were given different historical theatrical forms to work with. The youngest performed as the earliest storytellers, dressed in ragged "caveman" costumes. Others acted the part of a Greek chorus. One of the most popular theatrical forms with the children was the commedia dell'arte.

Commedia, a "lowbrow" form of popular entertainment, evolved during the Italian Renaissance, when traveling troupes of professional actors performed it outdoors. In the words of cultural historian Martin Green, the commedia "belonged to the world of entertainment—to circus and carnival, not to the high arts like tragedy" (xvii). Its history, Green and coauthor John Swan tell us, is difficult to delineate, because commedia "was such an unofficial or antiofficial phenomenon" (1). It used stock characters to develop satirical social plots, often calling social hierarchy into question or inverting it the way Shakespeare would do in his plays when the Renaissance reached England.

Teaching children the style and narratives of commedia dell'arte was, of course, exactly the combination lesson in history and theater that Patterson was shooting for. But many elements of the comic form were also well designed to capture the imagination of squirmy children, which was necessarily Patterson's primary goal. As it turned out, the child actors/pupils were delighted by commedia's privileging of improvisation, its use of masked fools, its acrobatic tricks and music, its plots of intrigue. They learned about the character Arlecchino, who carried two sticks tied together which he struck to make a loud noise—giving birth to the word *slapstick*—while experiencing the usual children's glee with pratfalls and loud noises.

Because so many residents of Laurel Canyon worked in the film industry, they had skills to donate to the children's theater classes, and connections to get other things that were needed. Doris Karnes, for instance, worked with the children's parents to make some eighty costumes for the performances. Dancer Connie Spriestersbach, who had spent time in China, contributed her knowledge of Chinese theater. Noted folk artist (and music-playing buddy of Woody Guthrie) Ed Mann, whose twin boys were in the program, built a cart to invoke the traveling nature of the commedia; the performing troupe would be transported from town to town in a cart, which would also serve as a makeshift stage. There was professional equipment, borrowed from various places, but the homemade cart was more lasting:

> And then when that summer was over, by that time, the father of one of the kids had built a cart for the commedia play. So that made that the most traveling theater. Because the stage that was loaned to us by NBC got taken back to NBC. The lights went back to CBS, wherever they went back to. I mean, we had all this stuff, but we didn't get to keep it. . . . Several years later, kids who came up to my backyard said, "You know that cart? We want to do that cart again." (P. Patterson interview)

The kids did get to "do that cart again," at the request of the American National Theater and Academy (ANTA), which invited the group to stage its commedia the following year at a festival in Los Angeles. Conceived of as a national, self-supporting theatrical alternative to for-profit Broadway theaters, ANTA had been established by Congress in 1935 at the same time as the Federal Theatre Project. ANTA began to develop in earnest after World War II and in 1955 had issued a statement that "ANTA's primary task is to bring the best plays, interpreted by the best actors, at minimum cost to the nation." Obviously, Patterson's young performers were not professional actors, but they did exemplify community involvement in region-based theatrical activity, and their performance was a success:

> The kids loved to do that. . . . Nobody else was here out of that whole group of eighty kids, just these ten. And they got to feel a little important. And

they thought that we should just take that cart, and we should go around the schools. And they kept bothering me and bothering me about it. And if those kids had not done that, there would have been no Renaissance faires. Because I wasn't trying to do that again. I was just trying to teach in the backyard. (P. Patterson interview)

As the Renaissance faire became well established, Ron and Phyllis Patterson drafted a sort of retrospective "vision statement" of their own, which now hangs in Kevin Patterson's office; in the statement, Ron and Phyllis noted how the faire flowed naturally out of these experiments with commedia:

The idea didn't come on us in full bloom. It grew originally from the fact that Phyllis was doing Commedia dell'Arte with children. Improvisation on a travelling players-cart was great fun and we imagined it could be even more fun surrounded with jesters and jugglers, tumblers and pipers, pie-men and other 16th Century entertainers, to more fully re-create the festivity of that time.

As we began to get caught up in the idea it seemed more and more important to be authentic. We imagined everyone in costumes and no microphones or other 20th Century mechanical devices. Perhaps it could develop into a *real* fair! And perhaps other people who still believe in personal involvement would help create it.

The commedia dell'arte was to set the artistic tone of the Renaissance faire in a lasting way; elements of it still flourish at the twenty-first-century faire. Faires' "street characters," actors who wander the faire site and interact with visitors instead of performing on stages, harken back to the use of improvisation to create social narratives in conversation with audiences. From both street characters and onstage performers, visitors see descendants of the commedia's Harlequin/Pierrot figure, the most lasting one to come out of commedia, enacting their ridiculous parody in the open air; the famous mime Robert Shields, who got his start at the Renaissance Pleasure Faire in Northern California, began by playing the Harlequin in a homemade costume.

In addition to these commedia-influenced performances, crafters' booths still sell artwork that invokes commedia dell'arte. For instance, mask maker Peter Jelen creates leather masks intended to be worn by stock commedia characters. Unlike the common flat masks, he explains, the commedia masks do not resemble the face underneath; instead, they transform the wearer into the archetypal caricatures they represent. As is the case with many Renaissance festival crafters, Jelen is very aware of the art history behind his craft, having done his own research about commedia before he began selling the masks.

Jelen considers it a "natural" thing for him to make commedia masks, because "there is a free-spirited and rebellious nature to renfairs [*sic*] in the same way that the commedia troupes were the sacred fools of their day. Both are definitely theaters of the people. Even as a vendor at the festival I find the atmosphere much more free in how I deal with the customer than in other venues" (Jelen email). Here Jelen is underscoring the defining qualities of commedia that led Martin Green and John Swan to praise it as "illegitimate theater" (9).

Jelen is correct that the commedia's overall rowdiness and deliberate flouting of respectability contributed much of the Renaissance faire's spirit, which made the faire a natural haven for the counterculture but immediately raised the hackles of cultural conservatives (and, indeed, continues to do so). As I will discuss, this has caused some practical difficulties and occasional consternation for faire organizers and participants, but this hackle-raising has always been a point of commedia, accounting, according to Martin Green, for its influence on cultural figures ranging from director Federico Fellini to musician David Bowie to comedian Charlie Chaplin. (Perhaps not coincidentally, another actor who got his start at the Renaissance festival, Billy Scudder, has made a career of playing Charlie Chaplin.) In Green's account, the images of commedia, both in its original moment and in its various survivals,

all represent a recoil from our society's dominant respectable values, and attack them by nonserious means. This last point distinguishes the commedia form from other forms of radicalism, political or artistic. It may have fostered culturally significant entertainment enterprises and inspire in us a genuine aesthetic response. But there remains something nonserious in its intentions, something defiantly frivolous or sullenly crude, which distinguishes it from other forms of protest. (xvi)

Green does not seek here to diminish the moral, political, or artistic intentions of commedia, or their historical import, by calling them "nonserious." On the contrary, he uses commedia to show how consequential nonseriousness can be. The early history of the Renaissance faire upholds this contention, and Green's locution "defiantly frivolous" is an apt way of describing the early Renaissance faire.

Forty years later, Peter Jelen's own relationship to crafting for the Renaissance faire mirrors this combination of glee—what he describes as a pleasurable fantasy of imagining Renaissance-era artisans making masks for the original commedia—and awareness of the "labor history" of festival work. The Pattersons' statement, quoted earlier, makes the same connection between commedia's gleeful, impious organizing principles and a collective approach to art. If the Pattersons needed to find people who "believe in personal involvement" in order to take the faire beyond their own backyard, they initially did not have to look very far. They found cultural allies among their neighbors in Laurel Canyon.

Laurel Canyon, 1959

> Laurel Canyon has what the oenophiles call *terroir.*
> —Michael Walker

When Phyllis and Ron moved to California, they found a house in the hills of Laurel Canyon, between West Hollywood and the San Fernando Valley. Although the neighborhood officially became part of Los Angeles in 1920, there was no bus service to the neighborhood when the Pattersons lived there, contributing to a self-enclosed feeling. Like Topanga Canyon, the Laurel Canyon neighborhood had long been known for attracting artists and bohemians, claiming, in the words of screenwriter and journalist Michael Walker, "longtime status as a haven for freethinkers" (10). Among this number were a good number of people who worked in the movie industry in one capacity or another.

What Walker called "freethinking" did not find the 1950s a hospitable decade, and when the anticommunist blacklist came to Hollywood, among those caught in its nets were residents of Laurel Canyon. Blacklisted actor Peter Bracco, for instance, lived in Laurel Canyon for more than forty years. During the anticommunist hunts of the postwar era, several hundred film-industry workers were "named" at congressional hearings between 1947 and 1951; they were then unable to work unless they provided so-called friendly testimony themselves. Some of these industry workers (writers and the like whose "delivery" of their labor did not depend on personal contact) could use "fronts" to continue working under assumed names or borrowed identities; in the past decade or so, in fact, there has been a move in Hollywood to restore credit to them for their work. But others, actors in particular, could not work if they were on the blacklist. There was also a larger category dubbed the "graylist" of actors who were never named at hearings but who were refused employment nonetheless; this could happen if an important sponsor decided someone was not patriotic enough for whatever reason and used its influence (generally, this meant threatening to pull its sponsorship) to get the actors removed from the set.

The Pattersons themselves had encountered a new level of Cold War anticommunism immediately upon moving to California. When Phyllis Patterson wanted to work as a teacher in Los Angeles, she recalls, she was asked to sign a loyalty oath. "I didn't know about the loyalty oath in Memphis, Tennessee. There wasn't any loyalty oath. We weren't important enough; we weren't going to make any news in Memphis," Patterson says. But as history has shown, it was a different story in and around glamorous Hollywood, a prominent site of activity on the part of the House Committee on Un-American Activities (HUAC), its Senate counterpart, and the state's own legislative equivalent. California's loyalty oath, which educators from primary school up through professors at the University of California's campuses were required to sign, was written into the state's constitution by amendment in 1952. It not only asked signers to pledge to uphold the state constitution; they were also required to deny membership or belief in organizations (including communist ones) that advocated the overthrow of the U.S. government.[3] Since no one who would not take the oath would be hired, by the state or any of its agencies, the oath was recorded literally millions of times. As a school-teacher, Patterson felt herself torn between the desire to refuse to sign at all and the "sign, stay, and fight" (Blauner 128) position that would allow her to continue to be a presence in the school. Either position took a toll on educators,[4] not to mention a toll on academic freedom and pursuit of knowledge.

In Laurel Canyon, recounts Patterson, Doris and Bob Karnes had gotten into trouble for opposing fascism in Spain and supporting of its civil-war refugees—the same charge that was leveled against singer/actor Paul Robeson, Albert Maltz of the Hollywood Ten, novelist Anna Louise Strong, and others. Actor and Wonderland Youth Center president John Anderson, known for his uncanny resemblance to Abraham Lincoln, "got investigated for something he donated money to": "I don't know what it was. But what happened in Laurel Canyon was it turned out to be a fight between the cowboy actors and the classical actors," Phyllis Patterson recalls, describing her impression of a neighborhood split that resulted from the blacklisting.

Doris Karnes (identified in the press as "a part-time actress") and four other Canyon residents were called to testify before HUAC in October 1959 about an alleged Communist infiltration of the Youth Center, which was soon to hire Patterson. Karnes testified behind closed doors, accompanied by ACLU lawyer Hugh Manes, who defended many who had been victimized by HUAC. Representatives of HUAC described the investigation as targeting a plan on the part of the Communist Party to convince former members to carry on their organizing even though they were no longer officially members. Two years later, HUAC issued a report supposedly detailing "how a group of alleged Communists and fellow-travelers infiltrated the Wonderland Youth Center in Laurel Canyon and seized control" ("How Alleged Reds" 2). Karnes and nineteen others were alleged to have been identified as Communists or members of so-called Communist front organizations by the sworn testimony of those who cracked under the pressure of the witch hunts and "named names." Many other members of the Youth Center, claimed the HUAC report, had taken part sporadically in Communist activity. In a move common to HUAC's witch hunts, refusing to offer self-incriminating testimony by citing the Fifth Amendment was presented as a sign of guilt.

The backlash against Laurel Canyon's Hollywood residents splashed over to Patterson's theater program for children as well, and she found herself facing virulent opposition. The degree of the hostile response to her work startled her, because of the wonderful support she had found for the children's program among the Laurel Canyon artists. "All I knew is they were not wanting me to teach those children," she muses. "And it was *very few* that were the 'bad guys,' *very few* that were the shouter-downers and that were you've-got-to-sign-a-loyalty-oaths" (interview). Patterson herself ended up going door-to-door in the neighborhood, telling parents that the "very few" had been trying to make it seem as though all the other parents in the group had already voluntarily signed loyalty oaths and were supportive of a proposed amendment to ban Communists from joining the center—and had, according to Patterson, stolen letterhead from the theater group to use for that purpose. "And so there were all kinds of demonstrative, incredibly inspiring town hall meetings" on HUAC's investigation of the Youth Center, Patterson recalls. "And they were led by the guy who was suddenly not going to play Abraham Lincoln after all. You know, I mean it was a very thrilling time and a very scary time to be alive" (interview). The amendment barring supposed Communists from the Youth Center was resoundingly defeated at one of those town hall meetings.

Patterson insists, "That whole thing [the anticommunist hysteria] helped guide what I did next. What happened to their lives and mine intertwined" (interview). She is emphatic in her conviction that the Renaissance faire was able to flourish thanks to the Hollywood blacklist, because the blacklist had the effect of making gifted and skilled people, many of whom were left-wing activists, available to lend their talents first to the backyard classes and then to creating the full-scale faire—thereby fostering an understanding of the connections between politics and culture for a next generation.

But, she adds, the origin of the Renaissance faire is inextricably linked to a few different things and thus difficult to pinpoint to any one moment or credit to any one person. "You can't say when I started the Renaissance faire," Patterson explains, because of the way it came out of, and culminated, several historical threads: the children's theater classes, the anticommunist blacklists, the Laurel Canyon "scene" in which two generations of activism and cultural activity began to overlap at the very moment she lived there.

How was the history of political activism legible in the early faires? One answer lies in the centrality for the faire of the resurrection of commedia dell'arte, with its deliberate flouting of respectability and its unruly inversion of social hierarchy. The faire's reinvigoration of commedia was contemporaneous with—and kindred in spirit to—the San Francisco Mime Troupe's exploration of the same form as a way to bring "movement" theater into public spaces in raucous, satirical performances that came to be called "guerrilla theater" (a term coined by SFMT writer and prominent anarchist Peter Berg in 1963). Both faire performers and SFMT performers were able to "tweak" commedia's stock characters, its bag of tricks, as it were, to comment on the present.

Overall, socially edgy parody permeated the first faires, as is audible in the coverage of the first faire by David Ossman and others. This humorous broadcast repeatedly invoked current political events, making explicit connections to the social movements that had begun to transform American society:

> Puritan agitation broke out in Leeds today. Rev. William Penn, leader of the East Middlesex Christian Leadership Conference was arrested for leading a sit-in demonstration at Leeds Cathedral. Mastiffs were released against those holding signs saying "We shall not be removed" and "Ban the Longbow." A Scotland Yard official says, "You can tell they are skilled Spanish agitators by the way they wear their hair." ("Fairest of the Faire")

In this way, the faire positioned itself within a Renaissance-era tradition of political pageantry, exemplified by the "pope-burning" processions that arose during the reign of Queen Elizabeth.[5]

The early faire organizers were constructing a sturdy vehicle for the politics of pleasure, as traces of these parodies can still be found in Renaissance faire humor. "Any cross-bow weddings?" asks a cast member playing a visitor to "Revel Grove," the fictional setting of the Maryland Renaissance Festival, during Sarah Palin's 2008 vice-presidential campaign. "I hear they still have them in Alaska." During the summer of 2010, performers of the Sturdy Beggars Mud Show at the Bristol Renaissance

Festival in Wisconsin deplore the audience's weak clapping in rapid-fire dialogue:

"I can't go on!"
  "Why not?"
  "This audience has no rhythm!"
  "Maybe that's why there are so many little kids here! [*glaring at unresponsive section of the audience*] I don't have time to explain everything to non-Catholics!"

Alicia Bay Laurel, who attended the first faire as a fourteen-year-old, makes a connection between the faire's chosen setting and the political struggles faced by the older Laurel Canyon residents. Laurel avers, "The Faire . . . was the first gathering of alternative types that I knew of in Los Angeles, and it had a[n] intellectual focus on the history of an era of awakening from the Dark Ages in Europe (as we were awakening from the Dark Ages of McCarthyism in the USA)" (email). Laurel's observation also gives a glimpse of how the Renaissance faire came to function for many people as a visible bridge between generations of activists—the "Old Left" that had been under such assault during the McCarthy era and the "New Left" that emerged in the 1960s and 1970s. Another relatively new California institution that increasingly formed a similar bridge between generations was Pacifica Radio, the country's first experiment in listener-sponsored radio. Pacifica's Los Angeles radio station, KPFK, was a natural partner for the Renaissance faire in its next stage of evolution.

KPFK/Pacifica: An Experiment in Listener-Sponsored Radio

Pacifica was the only game in town . . . for a basically free-thinking audience.
—David Ossman

Many of the Laurel Canyon residents were supporters of Pacifica Radio. The station had been founded by a group of pacifists and antiwar activists, most notably Lewis Hill. During World War II, Hill—a Quaker since his college days at Stanford—had served in the Civilian Public Service as a conscientious objector and organized on behalf of conscientious objectors—a decidedly unpopular undertaking in the middle of the supposed wartime consensus. Hill's wartime peace work led him to believe, increasingly, that the cause of pacifism could not be advanced unless it became less of an "outsider" philosophy. At the same time, he took at job as a radio announcer in Washington, DC, in 1944. The idea grew in his mind to start a pacifist radio station, which he envisioned as a modest educational institution that would give voice to a full range of viewpoints and, by doing so, would help to engage Americans in the civic process. When the war ended, Hill moved with his wife, Joy, to San Francisco, where he founded the first Pacifica station, KPFA-FM, in 1949. Ten years later, in 1959, the Los Angeles station, KPFK-FM, was added, just about the time the Pattersons moved to Laurel Canyon.

Hill's dream of making pacifism less "outsider" ran smack up against the legacy of McCarthyism, and the radio stations, according to Pacifica historian Matthew Lasar, gradually came to define themselves "primarily as a haven for unpopular ideas" (xv), rather than as hosts for the mass dialogue among people of different backgrounds that Hill and his colleagues had intended. The radio station became mostly associated with dissent from the politics and cultural mandates of the 1950s and early 1960s. The result, according to Robert Dawidoff, "would eventually serve as a template for the cultural and ideological history of the American liberal left in the post–World War II period" (vii). Dawidoff calls the early Pacifica stations a "grab bag of utopia," a name that, looking at the testimony of its participants, emerges as a good descriptor of the Renaissance faire as well (vii). Given this kindred spirit, it is not surprising that the very first public Renaissance faires were fund-raisers for Pacifica.

Led by Laurel Canyon friends, Phyllis Patterson decided to pitch the first "real" faire as a fund-raiser for Pacifica because, she says, the station was founded on "many of the political ideas I cared about" (interview). In January 1963, she met with the board of KPFK in the station's North Hollywood offices. Patterson described the idea: a festival of arts and entertainment, modeled on the open-air festivals of medieval Europe (with a place for the beloved commedia cart). A lawyer on KPFK's board reportedly objected on the grounds that human rights in medieval Europe were few, so Patterson swiftly suggested calling it instead a "Renaissance Faire" (Sneed n.p.). The radio station's board gave its approval: Phyllis and Ron Patterson, along with the volunteers they would round up from the Laurel Canyon neighborhood and beyond, would organize the faire from the "outside," while KPFK would publicize the faire over its airwaves.

In order to produce the first festival, volunteers were needed far beyond those who had been involved in the children's theater performances. As the many tasks became concrete, Patterson describes, "It dawned on me what I had announced. Because the only deal I made with them was, 'If you will give me some publicity on the air, I will do a radio show once a week to gather people who are subscribers to come out and help us build this.' Now most of the people who showed up were Laurel Canyon people" (interview). The Laurel Canyon volunteers made up "the nucleus of the 500 people who were ultimately to plan, develop, and successfully deliver the first Faire" (Sneed n.p.).

Joining the Pattersons were figures who came to shape the faire in important ways and who remained involved for years to come. Legendary session drummer Milt Holland (who played on literally hundreds of jazz, folk, and pop records) and his wife, Mildred, lived in Laurel Canyon and had had two children, sons Robert and Richard, in Patterson's backyard class. Their involvement with the faire spanned decades: they helped to fund some of the early faires, and Mildred Holland served as "Mistress of the Box Office" for more than thirty years. According to Kevin Patterson, without the Hollands, the Renaissance faire would not have survived past the 1970s.

Preston Hibbard, an artist, carpenter, and puppeteer, contributed greatly, along with Doris Karnes, the faire's art director, to creating the faire's distinctive visual economy. (Hibbard was soon featured in an article in the *Los Angeles Times*, humorously titled "Attention Pasadena— Bohemia in Your Midst" [Seidenbaum A7].) They worked (together with dozens of artists) on constructing the faire's sixty booths, painting murals, and crafting masks, parade props, and banners; according to Hibbard, the whole construction was done with scrap lumber and cost $150 ("Fairest of the Faire"). This work, declares Kevin Patterson, served as a veritable "farm system" for dozens of artists who went on to Hollywood jobs or careers as teachers and professional artists (interview). Influential musician Bob Thomas (as I will explore in detail in chapter 3) introduced styles and instruments from around the world to younger musicians beginning to construct the "counterculture."

Period costumes were contributed by NBC, and the faire site was donated by Oliver Haskell, who allowed the organizers to use his Ranch for Girls and Boys in North Hollywood. The event was broadcast by Pacifica commentators operating out of a KPFK booth; among them was David Ossman, who recalls the excitement and pomp of the first faire's opening:

> I had no idea what the event would be like. I knew the Pattersons from Laurel Canyon, where I lived on a street above them. . . . We had arranged to broadcast live from there. [The faire] started live with the opening, the grand entrance [of the cast]. There were movie stars there; there was a certain edge of Hollywood glamour. I was wearing a coat and tie. Phyllis saw me and said, "No, no, no!" She put me in a shirt and slouching hat. That was my first Renaissance costume. Ultimately, there was a costume workshop before the faire to teach people about what they should wear, and my daughter made the costumes for years and years. (Interview)

The KPFK broadcast of the first faire day was a humorous amalgam of news coverage, cultural program, marketing, and social commentary. The commedia dell'arte wagon is described, with young players dancing around it. Snippets of music can be heard, such as a slightly off-color song performed by balladeer Donna Burl, about a "young maid" whose "maidenhead is lost." A participant is interviewed about how she came by her beautiful dress. An auctioneer calls for items to auction off, declaring, "I am going to get pottery. . . . I am going to get pot, too!" The "Pacifica Crier" reads several satirical news items, including one about a grommet manufacturer's claim to make superior grommets to those made by "Dynamic Grommets General" and that using lesser grommets in the sails of Her Majesty's fleet "would weaken us vis-à-vis the international heretical Spanish conspiracy" ("Fairest of the Faire").

As part of the broadcast, Ossman introduces Phyllis Patterson as the "lady of the hour" whose idea led to the faire. He comments on the faire's "incredible spontaneity," and Patterson responds glowingly that the faire was exactly what she hoped it would be. In their exchange, glimmerings of early countercultural values are present: "It's very beautiful that people can have such lovely feelings toward each other," gushes Patterson, joy evident in her voice. "Nobody looks as bored as they usually do" ("Fairest of the Faire").

According to the testimony of many participants, the first Renaissance Pleasure Faire and May Market surpassed their expectations in a variety of ways. First, it attracted more visitors—more than three thousand people visited each of the two days it was open (Sneed n.p.). Food merchants and crafters did brisk business. And the faire was a very successful fundraiser for KPFK, netting the radio station something on the order of $6,000 (according to 1966–1967 station manager Paul V. Dallas) to $15,000 (in Richard Sneed's account). The station quickly put the chunk of money to good use, "remodeling and equipping a studio for live programming of the arts" (Sneed n.p.).

The Pacifica archives show that the faire almost immediately became central to both the work and structure of KPFK—which quickly began promoting itself as "a renaissance in radio" (Ossman 4). ("A Renaissance faire for a renaissance in radio" seems to have developed as a slogan by the second annual fair.) In March 1964, Ron Patterson was asked to design a special full-month issue of KPFK's folio, a paper program booklet usually mailed biweekly to the station's subscribers. The occasion of the extralong folio was the station's Shakespeare festival, organized to mark the four hundredth anniversary of Shakespeare's birth. The programming included thirty of Shakespeare's plays as well as musical programs based on Shakespeare's themes (KPFK). The programming for the Shakespeare festival was done by Ossman, who played the village herald in the second faire and, as such, led the faire's parade.

The lettering that Ron Patterson developed for use in the faire's program and other written materials, used in the folio (see fig. 1.1), became central to the establishment of the faire's distinctive "look." Even more striking is the way Ron Patterson's arresting and idiosyncratic creation, characterized by fluid, crowded characters (see fig. 1.1), quickly became an important forerunner of, and inspiration for, the lettering style that came to typify psychedelic rock-and-roll poster art, album covers, and the like; a compelling example is the record covers for the sunshine-pop band The

Hobbits (see fig. 1.2). Patterson's influence is especially strikingly visible in the squirmy, melting lettering that artist Wes Wilson produced beginning in 1966 (which *Ramparts* writer Warren Hinckle dubs "18, 24, and 36 point Illegible" [24]; see fig. 1.3) and that of multidisciplinary artist Peter Coyote beginning in about 1967 (fig. 1.4). This style of lettering remains emblematic of the era, a recognizable visual "wink" when invoked in the twenty-first century, as evidenced, for instance, in cover of Michael Walker's 2007 book about Laurel Canyon (fig. 1.5) or the publicity poster for the 2009 movie *Taking Woodstock*.

Fig. 1.1. Ron Patterson's artwork for the KPFK folio publicizing the first faire in May 1963

Fig. 1.2. The cover of The Hobbits' 1968 album *Men and Doors*

Fig. 1.3. Ron Patterson's fluid, crowded style of lettering became iconic of countercultural poster and album cover art, as seen in the poster art of Wes Wilson (1966).

Fig. 1.4. A 1967 poster by Peter Coyote

Fig. 1.5. This lettering style has come to function as a common shorthand invocation of the 1960s, as demonstrated by common usage in packaging books or movies about the period, such as in the cover art of Michael Walker's 2007 book about Laurel Canyon.

In the KPFK folio, a full-page notice invites subscribers to a series of "pre–Renaissance Faire pleasantries," called "April Eves: frolics and benefits for KPFK" to be held each Sunday evening in April. The events offered live music as well as drinks and food, most notably soup in a bread bowl, which became not only a Renaissance faire staple (still being served there in the twenty-first century) but a popular food to serve at other open-air events and even restaurants such as the popular chains Au Bon Pain and Panera. The bread bowl also represents another element of "Renaissance faire" traditional food, since it is unknown in England. The folio also seeks to round up the eager volunteers who had come together to put on the first faire, calling for workers who "canst build or paint or trim a book or sell a ticket or a pie, forsooth" (KPFK 30).

In short order, the faire became an annual event for KPFK. In the months following the first faire, the Pattersons formed Theme Events, Ltd., which was intended to function as the parent organization of the Renaissance Pleasure Faire, running the faire and giving a portion of its profits to the radio station. A larger site was located; as with the Girls and Boys Ranch, its use was donated by the owner. The faire doubled in size during its second year of operation, and the amount of money raised for KPFK doubled also.

With the second faire, the organizers and producers tried to grapple more consciously with the faire's relationship to Renaissance history. They began by organizing around a specific historical precedent: the Old Woodbury Hill Fair in Dorset, England. That fair most likely developed well before the year 1200, and by the time of the period focused on by the Renaissance Pleasure Faire, it had grown to be the largest fair in the south of England. It waxed and waned in size and prominence but continued to run until 1951, little more than a decade before the inaugural Pleasure Faire took place. This turn to more concrete historical precedent was brought directly to visitors, with early program booklets offering brief histories of English fairs such as the Old Woodbury Hill Fair. In addition to trying to invoke the Woodbury fair's combination of vendors and entertainment, the second Renaissance Pleasure Faire arranged for actors to depict historical and quasi-historical figures at the faire—Queen Elizabeth I, Sir Francis Drake, Sir Walter Raleigh, and others.

The Meaning(s) of Authenticity

What's real has become a freak.
—Swamp Dogg (1970)

The introduction of concrete historical reference added richness of detail to the faire; at the same time, it upped the intensity of the Renaissance faire's "functional paradox," in which attempts at historical authenticity act as commentary not on the past but on the present. This dynamic is evident in a "reminiscence" of the 1964 Pleasure Faire and May Market written in *FM & Fine Arts* by R. R. Witherup, who describes an authentically attired "monk in full beard and hooded robes" hawking papal indulgences and calling to fairegoers: *"Let me absolve you of the punishments and everlasting torments of commercialism!"* (8; italics in original). As the monk's humorous call indicates, the notion of authenticity at the Renaissance faire has always been complicated and has never been simply literal: he seeks to present "authentically" in some ways but not others, and the sense of authenticity he does create is largely intended to create a kind of pointed frisson with its current context. Instead, for many Pleasure Faire participants, invoking historical authenticity served an oblique, deeply symbolic purpose. As sociologist Richard Peterson clearly articulates in reference to country-music production and reception, "Authenticity is not inherent in the object or event that is designated authentic but is a socially agreed-upon construct in which the past is to a degree misremembered" (5). This does not mean that people seeking greater authenticity in the production of the faire were not careful researchers or that the pursuit of authenticity served no educational purpose. But authenticity—what constituted it, what it was "for," how desirable (or achievable) it was—quickly became a central debate that has remained constant while many other things about the faire changed.

Of course, as the work of Lionel Trilling and others has shown, the elevation of authenticity is a familiar expression of antimodernism. (T. J. Jackson Lears's study of antimodernism in middle-class culture at the turn of the twentieth century even unearths a fascination with the Middle Ages.) It cannot be denied that some manifestations of the early counterculture of the 1960s, the Renaissance faire included, did exhibit antimodernist values—though as Adrian Franklin has posited, the growing counterculture's early antimodern turn arguably represented "a very radical move against the hegemonic and heroic modernism of the 1960s" (201).

Nonetheless, to chalk the faire's impulse up to an anxious antimodernism is too reductive. In the first place, as Thomas Frank and others have pointed out, hippies were always suspicious of tradition, even amid their searches for authenticity. Even more important, though, is the fact that in the case of the faire, determining what "authenticity" has meant has never been uncomplicated or straightforward. Obviously, "authenticity" in regard to the faire did come to mean—especially during the 1970s—attempting to carefully re-create certain things about Renaissance-era England. However, for some attendees during this same period of time, "authenticity" meant the countercultural ideal of "being real" as opposed to fake—which had a lot to do with emotional truths or anticonsumerism and almost nothing to do with historical exactitude. "Be real, baby, be real," sang Doug Sahm in 1970, melodically voicing that particular countercultural credo. "For us, the faire was very, very real," insists musician Will Spires, who began performing at the faire in 1964, when he was twenty-one years old. "It wasn't some fantasy. It was one of the most real things we were ever in" (interview). For still others, what mattered most was a kind of "realness" that on the face of it represented the *opposite* of authenticity: a "realness" that hinged on theatricality and performativity. For this group of participants, the faire's contrast with the world outside its gates—which one could arguably call its *unreality*—allowed them to disregard certain societal expectations that required them to conduct themselves in ways that felt less true to themselves than did the faire's gleeful otherworldliness. Poignantly, for some, that which was "inauthentic" felt more "real" because "authenticity" enforced painful limitations or was not possible as a way to get along in society. The glittery, costumed world of disco during the faire's second decade tells the same story: singer and drag performer Sylvester's huge hit "You Make Me Feel Mighty Real" in 1978, accompanied in the single's music video by a remarkable number of sometimes cross-dressing costume changes, or Cheryl Lynn's hit from the same year, "Got to Be Real," which formed a defining moment in disco history and was then used in 1990 in the soundtrack to the movie

Paris Is Burning, Jennie Livingston's documentary about gay and transgender ball culture in New York City. At least in some part, the Renaissance faire needs to be considered alongside these other examples of groups of people seeking an important kind of authenticity through performance, through recognition that all self-presentation is a kind of drag—so you might as well choose the costume that suits you.

Authenticity as an overarching goal did not come immediately to the Renaissance Pleasure Faire and was not fully taken up, as I will detail shortly, until the 1970s, when its requirements earned it both approbation and condemnation. However, there has not been a year when the word "authentic" has not found its way into discourse about the faire: in marketing, praise or criticism, or insider debate. In the fifth decade of Renaissance faires, historical authenticity characterizes them, and their participants, unevenly. While a crafter at the Southern California Renaissance Pleasure Faire, looking at some booth workers wearing tails on their belts, remarks to me, "At some faires, those tails would be snipped off you," most performers adopt a more playful approach, like the lute player who weaves the guitar line from Black Sabbath's "Iron Man" in his music or the magicians who tell their audiences, "The magic I am about to perform is *not real.* If it were real, I'd be burned at the stake!" thereby making a joke about the real and the fake, the authentic and the inauthentic, that operates on at least two different levels. Indeed, mime Bill Irwin, commenting on his experience working at the Northern California Renaissance Pleasure Faire in 1970, recalls both artistic possibility and restraint in authenticity as a functional *idea*:

> One of the big questions always was the level of anachronism one wanted to employ—or resort to, as the case may be. I was all over the map, as I recall. Sometimes the purity of staying within some sort of historic context—very elastic, fairly amateur, but an attempt—seemed the right course. Sometimes poking fun at the whole operation and its attempt at historic recreation was too good to pass up. Depended on the context. (Email)

In this account, "authenticity" (and its complement, "anachronism") is not a fixed or transparent thing-in-itself; rather, it is a tool wielded variously by the deft performer.

It is overly simplistic to conclude that the impulse or desire at work in constructions of authenticity is a longing to return to the past, to become a citizen of it. Rather, as performance scholar Tavia Nyong'o puts it, "reenactment seeks a *presencing* of the past" (46). Taking all this into consideration, it seems as though the question of authenticity at the faire may well be most important as just that: a chance to talk about authenticity. In short, the argument itself might well be what really matters, rather than static positions within it. Anthropologist Charles Lindholm reminds us that the meaning of reconstructed historical sites is ultimately a subject that remains contentious and cannot be neatly "solved":

> There are heated academic disputes about the validity and even the morality of making such claims for places like Williamsburg or New Salem, which must necessarily reach compromises in order to market comfortable, politically correct, touristically appealing, hygienic reproductions of yesteryear. Are these presentations liberating because they permit visitors to supply their own meanings or are they replacing reality with a "sanitized and selective vision of the past?"[6]
> Both of these perspectives are correct and both are inevitable. (47)

Thus, even as shifts have occurred in which demographic and subcultural groups are most prominent as faire attendees, people have continued to be drawn to this argument. ("History is an argument about the past," declared British historian Raphael Samuel (430). It is an argument about the present also.) The conversation about what counts as "real," apparently, has been *useful* to decades' worth of Renaissance faire enthusiasts—and likewise to its detractors. Most recently, participants and observers have struggled mightily to understand the nature of the faire's significance to a generation defined by the growing amount of time it spends in cyberspace and at a moment when marketing experts cite the "new consumer" as one who seeks some kind of "authentic" experience in each purchase.[7] But as the faire grew beyond Pacifica's backyard, the question of what made it "real" began to reverberate as a central philosophical question, one that could never fully be settled. For discussions of the faire, "authenticity" was quickly established as what historian Patricia Nelson Limerick considers it to be: a "maddening term" that continues to bemuse and even infuriate (272).

From *Faire Press* to Freep

> The Mona Lisa is a common wench.
> —*Faire Press*, 1964

By the faire's second year, it had already acquired a reputation not only as an opportunity for KPFK but also as a place of expansive countercultural possibility more broadly drawn. When Art Kunkin, a thirty-nine-year-old socialist machinist from New York, began in 1964 to discuss his plans to found a weekly bohemian newspaper, modeled after New York's *Village Voice*, a friend proposed that he create a "pilot" issue for the second Renaissance Pleasure Faire. On a budget of fifteen dollars, Kunkin quickly put together an eight-page mimeographed tabloid-style paper he called the *Faire Press*; together with his young daughters and some college-student volunteers, garbed as "Robin Hoods and 15th Century peasant girls, . . . [they] gave their papers away as wandering peddlers, attracted a lot of sympathy and a little support" for what was to become the country's first "underground" newspaper, the *Los Angeles Free Press* (Brackman 83).

This first issue of the newspaper had on its front page articles that exemplified the spirit of the faire itself: creatively and humorously using the Renaissance setting to speak to the current moment. The "lead" article was about Shakespeare being arrested on obscenity charges; inside was a story (which, when the paper was refolded for distribution outside the faire, became the lead) about the work of avant-garde filmmaker Kenneth Anger, one of the United States' first openly gay filmmakers, whose *Fireworks* faced those obscenity charges. The *Faire Press*'s inside pages carried, among other things, an article by Seymour Stern, best known as the biographer of D. W. Griffith, about the Pacifica radio station being investigated for its radical affiliations. Those "radical affiliations" would have included Kunkin himself, who was at the time very active—including a stint as chair—in the Southern California Socialist Party, where he worked with German social psychologist Erich Fromm and six-time

Fig. 1.6. Art Kunkin distributes the first issue of the *Los Angeles Free Press*—then dubbed the *Faire Press*—at the 1964 Renaissance Pleasure Faire in Southern California. (Courtesy Art Kunkin)

presidential candidate Norman Thomas; Kunkin had a weekly program on KPFK debating longtime Communist Party activist Dorothy Healey (who became one of the most well-known American ex-Communists when she left the party in the 1970s). Kunkin's path to Pacifica, then the Pleasure Faire—and the *Free Press*—is fascinating in the way it locates the faire centrally in the politics of its moment.

While working as a machinist, Kunkin had enrolled in junior college with dreams of becoming a history professor. As he tells the story, while he was there, a group of students approached him about putting out a Mexican American newspaper because they knew he had experience in writing. He agreed and was soon writing for a small Mexican American weekly, the *East Side Almanac*, which had eight pages and a circulation of five thousand copies, under the name "Arturo" because he was only non–Mexican American on the paper's staff. In the summer of 1963, shortly after the first Pleasure Faire finished its run, Vice President Lyndon Johnson was to come to Los Angeles to address the Mexican American Education and Employment Committee, which was composed of "representatives of various community groups around California, including the GI Forum, LULAC [League of United Latin American Citizens], the Community Service Organization, and the Mexican Chamber of Commerce" (Pycior 130). The vice president's involvement was heralded as part of a campaign to prevent discrimination in hiring in the form of the President's Committee on Equal Employment Opportunity.

But on August 9—the day before Johnson was to arrive—the *Los Angeles Times* published a story casting doubt on whether Johnson would attend the meeting. In the end, the vice president did appear, but Kunkin's coverage of the event took a sudden turn:

> I was writing up this conference, and someone from City Hall called to tell me why Johnson almost didn't come. He tells me that [local Democratic Party leader] Roz Lyman and [California State Treasurer] Jesse Unruh . . . didn't want Johnson's sponsors to get credit. So they began a series of calls saying he shouldn't come, because he would get picketed over the *bracero* program. My contact gave me a record of all the phone calls and telegrams from City Hall to Johnson. I wrote this up as though all my information came from Sacramento, to protect my source. (Kunkin interview)

To Kunkin's surprise, his story was picked up by the *New York Times* and the *Wall Street Journal*. In his words, "for a couple of days I was a hero in East L.A. . . . Then I went back to writing about garbage collections—my usual" (interview).

Johnson returned to Los Angeles on November 14 of that year, to attend the Regional Conference of Community Leaders on Equal Employment Opportunity. Volunteers from Kunkin's weekly handed out copies of the paper at Johnson's hotel. Kunkin says that two members of Johnson's staff told the volunteers that Johnson did not like the article about his last visit: "He thinks you're a bunch of communists" (Kunkin interview). Nonetheless, Kunkin wrote up Johnson's second visit for publication in the *Almanac*. But before the article was published, Kennedy was assassinated, leaving Johnson as president. Kunkin's second article about Johnson, therefore, was about the *president*—and a president who was, Kunkin observes, "very sensitive" about press coverage. This made the columns in the little *East Side Almanac* stand out despite the fact that, Kunkin insists, "these articles were not slanderous; . . . [they were] very sober articles" (interview).

Kunkin's second article appeared in the first week of December. During the first week of January 1964, he recounts, he received a visit from the FBI in the form of two agents—"one rough, one friendly"—who showed up at the door of his apartment in East Los Angeles. "I had been advised never to speak to FBI without a lawyer," Kunkin relates. "I did keep them on my doorstep, so I could end the interview if I wanted. They asked, 'Are you a Communist?' I say, 'I was in the Socialist Party. I am not a terrorist. I have been an anti-Stalinist *always*.' They gave me names [of people they wanted information about] including Dorothy Healey's. I said, 'I will talk about myself but nobody else.'"

At the time of the visit, Kunkin was enrolled in evening college at the two-year East Los Angeles College and was working in a machine shop during the day. The next day, when he arrived at work, the foreman informed him peremptorily that he was fired. The three owners of the shop, relates Kunkin, would not speak to him at all. Instead, the foreman handed him two paychecks: one for the week and one for his vacation pay. He had been working at the shop for exactly one year and, he emphasizes, was an unusually valuable employee because of his ability to make parts that were no longer available. But the shop received an occasional government contract, and the owners, therefore, were more than a little nervous about the FBI visit.

As the organizers geared up for the second Renaissance Pleasure Faire, then, Kunkin found himself out of work. Because it was his newspaper columns that had attracted the president's attention in the first place, he determined that with his newly free time, he would start a newspaper.

As anyone with an organizing history would do, Kunkin began by "talking to people." Among these was the theater editor of *FM & Fine Arts* magazine, who told Kunkin, "If you get me a list of writers who could put out something like the *Village Voice*, I will help you start a paper. I will help you raise $10,000 dollars" (Kunkin interview). The *Voice* was at this time just under a decade old and in a few years was to become the best-selling weekly paper nationwide; founded by Norman Mailer, Dan Wolf, and Ed Fancher, it is widely recognized as the first of the "alternative press." It had quickly become known for its arts coverage, its quirky local reporting, and its occasionally inspired, often adjective-laden personal ads. In 1964, though, the *Voice* was considerably surpassed by the *Faire Press/Free Press* in the area of gay rights, because the *Voice* hosted no openly gay writers, no coverage—except for occasional unsympathetic coverage—of gay culture or politics, and no gay personal ads.

While Kunkin was thinking about his conversation with the *FM* editor, he continued to spend time at the KPFK studio. One day while he was there, the program manager came rushing through the hall in a panic. Someone had failed to show up for a program, and he had an hour of airtime unexpectedly free. Needing to cover that time, he asked those who were present, "Are there any takers?" Kunkin raised his hand and went into the console booth:

> I am talking into this microphone—I don't even know who is listening— about the paper I would like to run, how L.A. has all these communities, and we could use a paper to tie things together. I left the booth *high*. I was totally enthusiastic. I called up Phyllis Patterson. [I told her that] I thought it would be great to start a paper at the faire and asked her if I could have a card table at the faire to hand out a leaflet about the paper. (Kunkin interview)

Patterson replied with a counterproposal: she herself had been planning to produce a newspaper for the faire, but perhaps Kunkin could do it instead. Kunkin was intrigued; he recalls, "I put on a wool suit and went out to faire construction site. I was terribly uncomfortable." Like David Ossman, Kunkin remembers feeling discomfort in a suit, while nonetheless feeling that it was compulsory to wear one; this turned out to be a common—and significant—refrain among men involved in the earliest faires, as I will discuss in chapter 4. Patterson told Kunkin what she would like to see in a faire newspaper, and they agreed he would try. Later, Kunkin confesses, "She told me . . . that she had no expectation that I would do anything" (interview).

Kunkin was able to round up volunteers from his acquaintances at East Los Angeles College to help him write and produce one issue of the paper. At the same time, he made telephone calls to advertisers in KPFK's *Folio*, its publication for radio subscribers, letting them know he would be producing a faire newspaper. He budgeted and mailed out two letters: one to prospective writers and one to prospective advertisers, both drawn from the KPFK Rolodex. By the end of the week, he had raised $200 in advertising commitments. For production, he was able to return to a little print shop he had previously owned to lay out the paper on their equipment. He spent $125 printing five thousand copies of the first *Faire Press/ Free Press*.

When faire arrived, Kunkin traded in his wool suit for a rented costume with a long feather in his cap. He dressed up his two daughters, then aged ten and six, and brought them along to help. In his accounting, they sold a thousand copies at the faire, raising a thousand dollars: "Two weeks after the [KPFK] broadcast, I had a thousand dollars in my pocket" (interview).

Money in hand, Kunkin approached a coffee shop called The Fifth Estate, which ultimately gave its name to the publication considered by many observers to be the longest-running anarchist publication in North America. He was able to get the shop to give him office space in the basement while he distributed the newspaper—refolded so that the Kenneth Anger story was the lead and the Renaissance-faire-themed stories were inside—and tried to find out what kind of support there would be:

I was going around to art fairs and such and passing these out and selling them. I had no idea if I was going to come out with a second issue. I would sell subscriptions on the basis of "I will then pay" at rate of five bucks a year, when and if [the paper] comes out. By the end of that month, I had collected another thousand dollars in promised subs. I raised $600 from two friends, and I put out a second issue, which cost another $125. And I never missed an issue for the next ten years. (Kunkin interview)

Building on the support drummed up at the Pleasure Faire, the *Faire Press* turned into the *Los Angeles Free Press* (often called "the Freep"), generally considered to be the first mouthpiece of the new "underground press" of the 1960s and 1970s. According to Robert J. Glessing, in his 1970 academic study of the underground press,

The *Freep* soon gained the reputation of being *against* police brutality and President Lyndon Johnson's Great Society, and *for* acid heads, rock music, classified mating game sex advertisements. The classified ads which were mostly "for girls to share housekeeping with lonely studs" have been quoted widely in writing on the underground press and aptly reflected a segment of the diverse, casual, permissive Southern California life style. (18)

By 1968, the *Free Press* was threatening enough that Long Beach vice mayor Robert Crow was arrested for—and admitted to—removing all the copies of the paper from its corner boxes and destroying them (Neiswender). A year later, the paper made national news when it was sued for printing the names and addresses of some eighty state narcotics agents. The *Free Press* greeted the 1970s as a fifty-five-page weekly publication with ninety-five thousand paid subscribers and a per-issue budget of $15,000, sold at more than six hundred outlets and known for "open[ing] its columns to so many different groups on the Left—Women's Lib, Chicanos, black militants, gay (homosexual) liberationists, conservationists, doctrinaire Leninists, mystics and Maoists, revolutionaries, rock bands, cultural guerillas" (Glessing 18, 88; see also Foley).

The Pleasure Faire contributed more than fund-raising to the development of the *Free Press* and the world of underground publishing. Distributing papers at the faire, Kunkin met sixteen-year-old Alicia Bay Laurel, who had been at the first year's faire, lute-shaped guitar in tow. Laurel, who had read her mother's copies of the *Village Voice* (and already precociously aspired to live in a bohemian community like Greenwich Village), hung around the Press's booth until Kunkin gave Laurel her first job: doing layout for the Freep. A few years later, Laurel wrote a letter to the editor of the *Free Press* that became an influential piece of underground press writing, because it was chosen by Joan Didion as an exemplar of what the underground press had to offer.[8]

"The Faire brought the lefties, the artists, the longhairs and the eccentrics out of the woodwork to play together under the trees," says Laurel. "There and then I realized that how I wanted to live—out in nature, in a creative community with other artists" (email). In 1968, she moved to the Wheeler Ranch commune in Sonoma County, where she "never wore clothes, did Yoga, gardened, and felt wonderful" (McKinney). She also went on to write and publish (in 1970) a groundbreaking guide to sustainable bohemian living, *Living on the Earth*. The book was picked up the following year by Random House and became the first paperback on the *New York Times* best-sellers list—all by the time she was twenty-two years old.

Pointed Shoes and Bells: Dressing for the Faire

My robin-hood hat took over.
—R. R. Witherup, *Los Angeles FM & Fine Arts*, on 1964 Renaissance Pleasure Faire

By the second year of the faire, large numbers of visitors were arriving in costume, capturing the eye of a young film student named Les Blank, who shot footage of the faire that year (and soon went on to become an important American film documentarian, particularly of American ethnic musics). Indeed, some of the earliest faire participants date this practice to the second day of the first weekend of the first year, and David Ossman, in his broadcast of the first day, encouraged visitors to arrive wearing at least some costuming. The practice has continued unabated up to the present time and in fact has become the most common defining characteristic of Renaissance faire participation, leading writer Jerry Craven, in his children's book about folk pageants, to include the Renaissance faire along with Native American pow-wows, Hawaiian luaus, and quilting bees as examples of the phenomenon; in his simple breakdown, what qualifies the festival is that nonprofessional people wear costumes. In 1964, the garb was still being pieced together from homemade and repurposed items; one early participant remembers a man wearing a swimsuit over tights in order to approximate Renaissance-era clothing.

The wearing of garb significantly blurred the boundary between performer and audience, as well as contributing to the Pattersons' ideal that the whole faire should be the stage. Malcolm Boyd, radical Episcopalian priest, writer, civil rights activist, and gay rights activist, describes this effect in his brief 1971 account of the Southern California Renaissance Pleasure Faire, noting, "People milled around or sat on bundles of hay observing others" (70). But of even greater historical import was the *meaning* of dressing up in the context of the early 1960s. "Think of the 1950s!" says David Ossman. "Being dressed up was a black suit. The idea of taking that off was very symbolic, for men and for women. Your legs were in tights, in silks. Women could go braless, which was very liberating" (interview).

Attending in garb so quickly became a key aspect of experiencing the faire that by 1967, the Renaissance Pleasure Faire program included instructions for piecing together garb for faire visitors. "Increase thy pleasure at Pleasure Faire," urges the back cover of the program book. "Do-It-Thyself: Make for yourself a peasant or pleasant costume to wear to next year's Faire." Below this invitation are six boxes with sketches of garments by Ron Patterson. Each box contained instructions for a different category of makeshift period garb: "Laborers, Hunting Costume, Ladies Dresses [*sic*], Herdsmen and Hoods, Gowns for Musicians, and Travelers and Pilgrims." Along the same lines, publicity for the faire in newspapers and radio broadcasts informed would-be faire patrons that they could request a pamphlet by mail on how to make a Renaissance-era costume.

The Renaissance Pleasure Faire marked the earliest moment when people involved in the California counterculture began regularly wearing "fancy" clothing, a style that quickly became associated with hippies, from the elaborate apparel of musicians such as Jimi Hendrix (think of his ruffled shirt and velvet jacket at Monterey Pop) and Rolling Stones guitarist Brian Jones (a prominent hippie "dandy") to the more modest velvet bell-bottoms and thrift-store finery that became popular with many young people.

"The faire got people ready to be gaudy," declares Ossman. "People began to get out the old clothes" and wear them not only to the Renaissance faire (interview). Ossman is not the only architect of the counterculture who points to dressing up at the Pleasure Faire as the originary moment for the psychedelic dandy style. At the very least, faire garb predated, and resonated with, the countercultural sartorial sensibility of whimsy, gender bending (in style if not, sadly, always in personal politics), and rearranging of sensory input—particularly color and texture—to indicate a "blown mind" and also to separate the wearer from "squares." For instance, Peter Coyote describes attending the Human Be-In in 1967 "dressed in outrageous costumes" (75) as part of the event's visual manifesto. Jefferson Airplane vocalist Marty Balin recalls "talking to a guy at TIME magazine when it was just hitting and Haight Street was like a tourist attraction and people were dressed in colorful costumes like you see at the Renaissance fair [*sic*]" (qtd. in Morgan 183). Photographs of these early faires show efforts to achieve authenticity through period clothing, but they also show beaming faire visitors attempting to get into the spirit of things through a variety of colorful and fanciful adornments. Boyd offers a touching example, writing of what he did to attend the faire: "I retrieved a bright blue fourteenth century French chasuble from a trunk where I had long ago packed it away," adding that he "wore it, with a matching stole, over an open-necked plain shirt and Levi's" (68).

Booths that sold items of clothing quickly became the most popular ones at the faire. Alicia Bay Laurel remembers attending the first faire with her mother (a KPFK supporter), who helped her piece together her first Renaissance outfit. After that, she designed and sewed her outfits herself; by age eighteen (in 1967), she had her own booth at the faire selling items of clothing and accessories, all made by hand. "My invention was costume parts you could put on over whatever you were wearing that would transform it into a Renaissance outfit: tunics, long skirts, corsets, billowing gauze sleeves with elastic at wrist and armpit, pointed hats, belts and scabbards, and so forth," Laurel remembers (email).

Besides the faire's almost immediate bestowal of hip cachet and easy accessibility to fancy dress, the individual most often credited with popularizing and making accessible the hippie "fancy" or "dandy" style was a Laurel Canyon resident, like Phyllis and Ron Patterson, who was known to have attended the first faires. That is Szou Paulekas, the wife of sculptor and dancer Vito Paulekas. Szou Paulekas was born Sueanne Schaeffer in 1943; she moved with her husband to Laurel Avenue in the Canyon, where the two of them, along with their friend Carl "Captain Fuck" Franzoni operated Los Angeles's first "crash pad."

Although Vito became known as the "freak guru," Szou became a central figure in her own right in the "freak" scene. She opened a store called the Freak Boutique above her husband's clay studio, where she sold refurbished antique clothing and redesigned Hollywood finery to the young women of the emerging counterculture who hung out on the Sunset

Fig. 1.7. In a photograph published in the *Los Angeles Times* in 1966, a crowd watches a Robin Hood show. In the center of the photograph is "freak guru" Vito Paulekas, holding his child.

Strip. Vito's Freak Dancers, who were linked to Frank Zappa's Mothers of Invention (at whose performances they would dance and "freak out") provided built-in advertising for Szou's fashion creations—all of this during the time period when Szou and Vito Paulekas were attending the Pleasure Faire.

A number of rock-and-roll album covers, of American bands but also of English and other Europeans (and even Brazilians) in the years following the first few Renaissance faires, stand as wonderful illustrations of the mainstreaming of "fancy" garb. In addition to Hendrix's well-known penchant for velvet jackets (one of these is housed in the Rock and Roll Hall of Fame in Cleveland, while a replica of another can be bought on eBay), David Crosby of The Byrds wears a Renaissance faire tunic on the cover of *Turn! Turn! Turn!* (1965); the Beatles wear elaborate, shiny, military-styled jackets on the cover of *Sgt. Pepper's Lonely Hearts Club Band* (1967); the British band Kaleidoscope wear luxurious silks and jewelry on the cover of *Tangerine Dream* (1967) and cloaks, long coats, lace, and fantasy-tinged makeup on the cover of *Faintly Blowing* (1969); while the American band Kaleidoscope (which, as I will discuss shortly, had actual Renaissance faire connections) dressed as "dandies" to one degree or another on all of their albums for Epic Records between 1966 and 1970. The Beau Brummels referred to the "dandy" style in their name, and Sly and the Family Stone increasingly adopted a collage of "psychedelic fop" styles starting with their first album, *A Whole New Thing*, in 1967. Indeed, the front and back cover art of Heart's 1977 album *Little Queen* (famous again after the song "Barracuda" from the album was played at the 2008 Republican National Convention) looks as though it might literally have been shot at a Renaissance faire.

The fashions showcased by popular musicians have long been an important way in which styles have circulated in American culture, and following the issue of the earliest psychedelic records, the garb-inflected "fancy" countercultural style quickly became a national concern, moving from Southern California to all of the United States. From there, this clothing inevitably "trickled up," as celebrities adopted elements of the style and "high" fashion designers also began to imitate them. Indeed, "Laurel Canyon style" is still invoked in the twenty-first century by boutique owners, clothing and jewelry designers, and fashion writers to

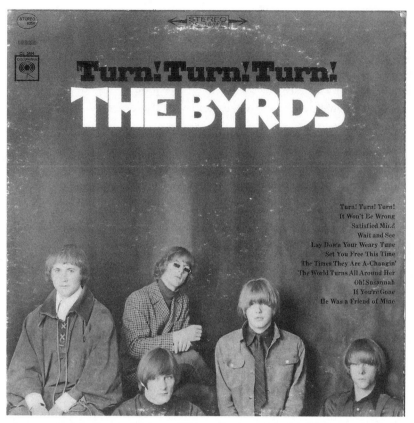

Figs 1.8 and 1.9. The countercultural "fancy" style of dress found at the early faire soon came to characterize "hippie" culture. On these record covers, David Crosby of the Byrds (*above*) (1965) and the Isley Brothers (*right*) (1969) wear Renaissance-inspired clothing.

describe current manifestations of the "dandy" aesthetic introduced by the Pattersons to the Southern California "hippie" scene.

With the faire's influence on the nascent counterculture steadily growing, it moved again in 1965 and again doubled in size; this time the location was a site the faire would use for decades (with a one-season break): the Paramount Ranch in Agoura. Paramount Ranch consists of twenty-seven hundred acres located between Malibu and the San Fernando Valley. It had been purchased in 1927 by Paramount Studios, which built several large-scale movie sets there. Paramount and other studios bought up large, undeveloped tracts of land as a matter of practice at this time,

as a way of obviating the need to film on location outside of California. Such filming was expensive for the studios, because in addition to travel expenses, union contracts required that they pay extra for movie production work if the filming took place more than thirty-five miles from the studio itself. The sizeable "movie ranches" allowed studies to achieve the cinematic scope that filming in large open spaces allowed—without incurring the extra expenses. As Los Angeles developed and its real estate became prime, most movie ranches were swallowed up in urban sprawl, though the Paramount Ranch still functions as a tourist attraction where people can visit a "Western town" that is still occasionally used for filming.

The May 1966 issue of the radio magazine *Los Angeles FM & Fine Arts* published a cover story on the 1965 faire, with articles penned by KPFK's David Ossman and *Los Angeles Free Press*'s Liza Williams, accompanied by photographs, lettering by Ron Patterson, and information about buying tickets to the current faire. Ossman and Williams both emerged as important architects of the counterculture, Williams through her writing for the Freep and Ossman through his writing and performing as a member of the Firesign Theater.

For many participants, the Paramount Ranch represents not only the best and most important location of the Southern California faire but also its best years. "[In the Paramount Ranch years] the faire scene was a love-in; now, it's a business," declares actor Billy Scudder. Scudder describes walking up the road toward the Renaissance Pleasure Faire's "village" for the first time and thinking, "Why does it feel like I'm at home?" (interview). Mime Robert Shields recalls, "There was no place like it. Your soul would just go, 'Oh my God'" (interview). Thirty years later, they still feel inspired: a group calling itself Friends of the Paramount Ranch has devoted itself to organizing events and reunions at the old site, as well as maintaining a website for photographs, stories, and memories of the faire in those days.

After the Renaissance Pleasure Faire's first season at the Paramount Ranch site, it ran for three annual stints, twice for one three-day weekend and then for two two-day weekends in the third year. By this time, it was generating approximately one-fifth of the annual income of KPFK. Despite its success as fund-raiser and as cultural event, though, the faire's relationship with Pacifica was becoming contested; the conflict came dramatically to a head during the short tenure of KPFK general manager Paul Dallas.

Dallas had been the host of a fifteen-minute weekly commentary on KPFK called *Thinking Allowed* when he became the station's general manager in 1966, a position he held for approximately one year before he was fired. His firing was both cause and effect of painful divisions within KPFK's supporter community. Ultimately, the embattled Dallas's chief legacy at the station was sorting out—for better or for worse—the relationships among Pacifica, the Pleasure Faire, and the Pattersons.

Understandably humiliated, Dallas was eager to express his side of the story after his abrupt dismissal in 1967. To that end, he immediately published a scathing exposé about the station, titled *Dallas in Wonderland*, with the stated purpose of "accent[ing] the incredible lack of logic which prevails" (iv) in the way the station was run. Since the Renaissance

Pleasure Faire had quickly become central to Pacifica's survival, bringing in volunteers, publicity, and audience as well as a significant amount of funds, it is not surprising that Dallas focuses on the faire in his typewritten account, which is written in painstaking detail and includes supporting matter such as legal agreements, internal memos, and financial reports.

Dallas presents his early months at Pacifica as ones in which he learns of the station's financial instability and dependence on the Pleasure Faire. He is forthright that he came to the position disapproving of events like the faire, hyperbolically suggesting that both fund-raisers and grants from foundations "threaten the integrity" of independent programming (11). No doubt amplified by his anger at being fired, Dallas laces the account with an unfortunate titillation and elitism, as he makes up the "study of hermaphroditism" as a supposedly ridiculous example of topics that Pacifica might be forced to take up in order to attract foundation money and allows that he, Dallas, fears the idea of a mass audience because that would mean bad programming, as the masses only respond to mediocrity. Nonetheless, despite the fact that Dallas's account reads like a rant, with a considerable helping of petulant self-justifying, the book provides a fascinating account of the first serious impediments confronted by the Pleasure Faire and the beginning of the faire's separation from KPFK.

Because of Dallas's motivations for writing the account, there is no way to be sure how much of the resentment he expresses is retrospective following his firing and how much he actually experienced during the run of the faire. Dallas does seem to have taken umbrage at the Pattersons all along, even though the 1966 faire brought a much-needed influx of funds to the station. He is eager to separate himself from the main organizers of the faire, pointing out, for instance, that he is a more presentable person because he does not have long hair and a beard like Ron Patterson. Dallas's more substantive struggles with the Pattersons were over control and ultimately ownership of the faire. They mark an interesting and important moment in the growth of the faire: whether it should "belong" to KPFK or the Pattersons.

Dallas questions the idea that the Pattersons were putting on the faire as outside organizers of a benefit and instead asserts that the faire's many volunteers were under the impression that it was Pacifica to which they were donating their labor, meaning that either the faire belonged at least partly to Pacifica or that KPFK should bill the faire for anything it put in: publicity, staffing, construction. It is certainly true that by the second faire, huge numbers of people were eager to work as volunteers. Many of these were enthusiastic supporters of Pacifica radio. Many of them also recall being willing to work for free just so that they could attend the faire for free—or, even more important, be on site to attend the after-hours parties.

During Dallas's second May as KPFK general manager, in any event, it is clear that the 1967 Pleasure Faire arrived with KPFK more than eager for the expected influx of funds and with every reason to expect them. A much bigger new site had been located in Ventura County, and a thousand or so volunteers had been lined up. Craftspeople had laid in stock, and performers had been auditioned. Food vendors had bought up supplies of turkey legs and pastries. Hippies and members of Los Angeles's theatrical community had bought tickets and gathered their garb. A requisite number of Hollywood's more glamorous denizens had arranged to attend. And then, unexpectedly, the faire encountered its first organized opposition.

Reds Wearing Red Tights

They conjured up visions of sin and debauchery.
—Paul V. Dallas, *Dallas in Wonderland*

According to Dallas, the new faire site "had been fraught with problems from the very beginning" (155). After the landlords agreed to lend the site for the faire, they had gotten in touch with the Malibu Division of the Los Angeles Sheriff's Department to request a report from that office on the 1966 faire. The report provided to them was, Dallas writes, "defamatory, slanderous, libelous, scurrilous, and untruthful" (156). Among other things, the report maintained that "a carload of narcotics" had been confiscated at the faire, without indicating a single drug-related arrest having taken place. The landlords changed their minds and announced that they would not allow their land to be used.

KPFK and the faire's organizers had to react quickly. First, says Dallas, he organized some of the station's more influential supporters to call the landlords and vouch for the character of the faire's workers. Then he and Patterson visited the landlords again, bringing with them scrapbooks of newspaper and magazine clippings of favorable coverage of the event. The landlords again reversed their position and signed papers promising that the site would be donated for the mounting of the faire and would furthermore be available for the next five years.

With that first roadblock overcome, preparations for the faire continued, and any attempts to find an alternative site were abandoned. Then, about two to four weeks[9] before the 1967 Southern California faire was to open, the Pattersons were notified by the Ventura County Sheriff's Office that all crafters who would be selling their wares would have to report to the Sheriff's Office for fingerprinting. Further, they were told, this fingerprinting had to happen by the following night, or they would not be allowed to collect money at the faire.

For some participants, this presented a practical problem: many crafters did not have a way to make the trip out to Ventura County in time to meet this deadline. The Pattersons were able to deal with this problem by hastily arranging bus service. But for others, there was a political or philosophical question as well; the fingerprinting felt, as Phyllis Patterson puts it, "absurd" (interview) or worse: an encroachment on their civil rights. Nonetheless, the majority of crafters decided that they would submit to the fingerprinting rather than be barred from participation. (For one thing, they would have lost a lot of money.)

Some of the Pattersons' Pacifica partners were more resistant to the requirement. At a station staff meeting, Pacifica employees decided that at their own KPFK booth, they would not agree to or require the fingerprinting (Dallas 160). Station manager Dallas further delivered a talk on the air on the subject of fingerprinting twelve days before the faire was due to open. In this talk, he addressed the question of fingerprinting as an attack on the expression of the faire itself but also on the radio station and its ideals. Dallas emphasized in his broadcast that the Pattersons did not "intend to take this edict lying down" (xvii) and that they were planning to mount a legal battle to have the law either rescinded or made inapplicable to the Renaissance Pleasure Faire. Further, he announced that what small gestures as could be made would be carried out. For instance, a crafter who had dissented from the policy, and refused to be fingerprinted, might pair with a crafter who had given his or her fingerprints. The dissenting crafter would then be present at the faire to discuss his or her wares, but the partner would be the one to handle the money.

Following the fingerprinting, the faire faced a second obstacle that proved even harder to overcome. Although the owners had granted use of the land, and the fingerprinted crafters had been given permission to sell, a permit was necessary in order for the faire to open legally. This "special use permit" had to be obtained from the Board of Supervisors of Ventura County. Further, without this permit, other necessary permits, such as a liquor license, would not be given. When the Pattersons applied for the permit through regular bureaucratic avenues, they learned that "a group of conservatively oriented people, including some fundamentalist ministers" had come together to block the awarding of the permit (Dallas 162).

Patterson does not like talking about the early opposition to the faire by name, because she does not "want them to come out of their hole in the ground and bother anybody or get them activated in any way" (interview). But she does specifically mention radio talk-show host Joe Pyne. Pyne (1924–1970) is known for having pioneered the now-common confrontational style of interviewing, in which he would hang up on callers, berate guests on the show, and toss around trademark insults such as "go gargle with razor blades." A particularly well-traveled (and most likely apocryphal) story about Pyne has him attacking the musician Frank Zappa (who moved into the Laurel Canyon neighborhood in 1968 and connected there with Vito and Szou Paulekas). In the story, Pyne asked Zappa, "Does your long hair make you a woman?" Zappa retorted, "Does your wooden leg make you a table?" Pyne frequently invited guests like Zappa on his show because they were such good targets for his vitriol; in addition to Zappa, Zappa's friend Vito Paulekas, freak guru, was a repeat visitor.

Pyne was famous for ridiculing hippies, homosexuals, and women's libbers, and he saw all of these involved with KPFK and the Renaissance Pleasure Faire. He took on the faire, and Patterson remembers him being colorfully dismissive: "He said, 'You know, those people, they're just

Reds over there . . . because they have a lot of red flags out there, and a lot of people come wearing red tights. So you know they're Reds" (interview). Pyne's line is hilariously compact in its evocation of the twin major objections to the faire, both established in the 1960s and thriving in the 2000s: communal habits on the part of people working the faire, and men in tights. (I discuss these anxieties further in chapter 5, on Renaissance faire "haters.")

Although there are comical aspects to Pyne's rants, he was able to attract a certain amount of attention, and the result was some fairly sophisticated organizing against the faire. The conservative group coalesced around a well-known name, that of Ruth Brennan, the wife of character actor Walter Brennan (1894–1974). Walter Brennan, a three-time Academy Award winner, was also well-known by then for his political conservatism, having made numerous appearances in support of Barry Goldwater's campaign for the presidency in 1964 and having supported American Independent Party candidate George Wallace over Richard Nixon in the 1968 election because he believed Nixon was too liberal.

The group led by Ruth Brennan was able to convince the Thousand Oaks Planning Commission to recommend that the faire be prohibited. Looking back on the campaign the following year, the *Oxnard Press-Courier* summed up the simple—yet effective—argument they made: "Right-wingers said the fair . . . attracted hippies and left-wingers" ("Pleasure Faire"). But the Planning Commission had no power to function in any role other than an advisory one; the real decision had to be made by the Thousand Oaks City Council. The City Council overturned the Planning Commission's recommendation and voted to allow the faire to open in Ventura County. However, this decision was subject to appeal to the Board of Supervisors, and Brennan's group immediately filed the appeal, just days before the faire was due to open.

Following a strategy meeting at KPFK, the station's lawyer went to court and obtained an injunction saying that the faire could open pending the appeal. As a result, the first weekend of the faire happened as planned at the new, bigger site and was a huge success in terms of participation and money raised—not to mention star attendance. Paul Dallas notes that Mort Sahl and Peter Falk were present on the opening day. Several days later, the appeal was heard. The Board of Supervisors decided to uphold the appeal, and the faire was barred from opening for its second weekend. Various attempts to pursue solutions through legal avenues failed.

Although organized conservatives succeeded in shutting down the Pleasure Faire, Patterson's assessment is that to some small degree, she was able to prevail nonetheless. In her account, this was because coincidentally, the United States Information Agency wanted to film the faire in that same year. The USIA, which was established in 1953 and lasted until 1999 (when it was integrated with the Department of State), was an "independent foreign affairs agency supporting U.S. foreign policy and national interests abroad" (USIA), in part through informational programs about American culture. Nancy Snow has thoroughly demonstrated that the USIA had Cold War origins; in particular, the USIA's international public relations campaign was intended to counter and compete with what it perceived as the Soviet Union's superior instruments for international propaganda. In 1958, the Thirteenth Report of the United States Advisory Commission on Information posited,

> The United States may be a year behind in mass technological education. But it is thirty years behind in competition with communist propaganda . . . each year sees the communists increase their hours of broadcasting, their production and distribution of books, their motion pictures and cultural exchanges, and every other type of propaganda and information activity. . . . We should start planning to close the gap in this field before it widens further. (Qtd. in Snow 85–86)

Prominent examples of the USIA's programs include the radio broadcast Voice of America and Radio Free Europe. In 1961, the Mutual Educational and Cultural Exchange Act, or the Fulbright-Hays Act, further expanded the ways in which the USIA could promote U.S. culture abroad. The film of the 1967 Renaissance Pleasure Faire was to be broadcast abroad as an example of an American cultural event.

In Patterson's account, she suggested that the USIA representative make his request to film the faire at another time, because the faire site was under threat from developers who wanted to build a golf course as well as from Ruth Brennan's conservative group, and she had her hands full. She told him, "'Well, right now I'm having problems. And I don't want you going overseas portraying that this is a faire that doesn't have people that are trying to knock it down over something it isn't.' I think I said to him, 'If you're going to tell the whole truth, then you could film the faire.' Well, he wasn't going to do that. Because that's not what his job was. His job was to make it look like everything was very democratic over here and nobody hurt the arts" (interview).

The way Patterson sees it, she was able to put the USIA in an "embarrassing position," because they did not want the press to pick up on their report that "[the faire] is closed because of the Birch Society"[10] (interview). Because the faire site was zoned for filming, the faire opened in a limited way for one day of the second weekend: no sales were made, but the participants came for a picnic in costume so that the faire would live even if the public was excluded. Patterson sees this one-day opening as a triumph against right-wing opposition, although it was obtained at great cost: "And it opened for just the filming. And we all—I mean, craftspeople, caterers—all lost a lot of money. We just did this private faire for us. And we never got to really open the other real faire [for the scheduled second weekend]. We were open one weekend. That wasn't enough to pay the bills. Because we had [counted on] a two-weekend faire" (interview). Paul Dallas, in his exposé, also recounts the story of the second weekend of the 1967 faire—the historically fascinating collision of the developers' encroaching on the site, the conservative group's red-baiting the faire and Pacifica in a successful effort to shut down the faire, and the United States Information's Agency's bid to film the faire for an overseas program. Attempting to capture the strain these events put on the faire's crafters, he writes,

> Serious craftsmen and artisans . . . had created a large supply of goods they expected to sell. Hours of toil and desperate money had been invested in their wares. They paid their entrance fees, thus financing a good portion of the Faire's building. They hand-built their own booths. Suddenly they were dragooned to the Sheriff's office to register their fingerprints which would thereafter nestle in the files of the FBI. It is customary that the second weekend of the Faire is the one during which most sales are made, and this was the one they missed. Finally, they were asked to come and romp

with jolly mien in front of cameras recording an event closed by County officials at the behest of conservative constituents in order to present foreigners with an example of fun and freedom in the United States. (170–171)

Here Dallas effectively captures the striking confluence of domestic politics, foreign-policy-making, the development of Southern California, and the faire's various economies.

The story of Patterson's and KPFK's confronting these obstacles and figuring out how to approach municipal and state bureaucracy is fascinating for what it reveals about the development of the faire into the huge event that it is today. Further, the nature of the opposition reveals much about the cultural landscape of the 1960s and also the character of the faire itself. But the story of the faire's confronting of these details is really a much broader one in import. Patterson did not know it at the time, but as she scrambled around trying to arrange permission for the faire to run, she was breaking new ground. The Renaissance Pleasure Faire and May Market formed one precedent for the type of event that perhaps most represents 1960s culture in the popular imagination: the huge outdoor rock-music festival. The first of these music festivals (on the scale of the faire) was the Monterey International Pop Music Festival in Monterey, California, in June 1967, and Monterey Pop, in turn, was considered to be the template for other festivals that followed, most notably the Woodstock Music Festival in August 1969 and the tragic Altamont Speedway Free Festival in December 1969—both of which, like the Renaissance Pleasure Faire, had permit problems just days before the show, resulting in a shift of venue at the last minute. Both Woodstock and Altamont took place years after the Renaissance faire dealt with these issues; as these festivals all drew hundreds of thousands of people, they also had to deal with similar issues of traffic planning, sanitation, and security.

Even as these roadblocks were being faced and, in some cases, circumnavigated, the festival's relationship with Pacifica was changing. Since being named KPFK station manager in 1966, Paul Dallas had been embroiled in a struggle with the Pattersons over ownership and artistic control of the Pleasure Faire. Ultimately, with the support of the KPFK Board of Directors—and with testimony in their favor from Pacifica and Pleasure Faire participants such as David Ossman—the Pattersons were able to retain legal control of the faire as "a name, an organization and a community activity," as board member Stuart Cooney put it (qtd. in Dallas 154). But the relationship of the Pleasure Faire to the radio station had become, in the eyes of many observers, painfully contentious even before the antifaire organizing forced the early closure of the 1967 faire.

When KPFK lost money due to the canceling of the faire's second weekend, Dallas blamed the structure of the faire's relationship with Pacifica for the loss, holding Phyllis and Ron Patterson specifically responsible. At Dallas's urging, KPFK broadcaster Elliot Mintz publicly raised questions about the operation of the faire on his show over a series of days. During one broadcast, he invited the Pattersons to appear on the show, along with their business manager, their secretary, and David Ossman.

In the eyes of Dallas (and, presumably, Mintz) this represented an open and honest "airing of the issues" (Dallas 172). According to the Pacifica Board of Directors, however, Mintz's broadcast represented divisiveness, public bickering, and deliberate sabotage at a time when the station could not afford it. To bring a close to the matter, the president of the Pacifica Foundation, Lloyd Smith, wrote a speech that was to be broadcast twice on May 21, 1967. In it, he apologized for Mintz's broadcasts to all the Pacifica listeners—and also to the Pattersons, Mildred Holland, and David Ossman by name. Dallas, however, was recalcitrant. On June 7, he took to the air in what was his last KPFK broadcast, once again detailing his objections to the Pattersons and the faire. Ultimately, he was fired as station manager following this broadcast. And in Los Angeles, the Renaissance Pleasure Faire would no longer be associated with Pacifica Radio—even as a contract for the first Renaissance faire outside of Los Angeles had just been signed by Al Pattridge, general manager of Pacifica's Northern California Station, KPFA. Although the first faire in the Bay Area was a success for all involved parties in the fall of 1967, the Renaissance Pleasure Faire had outgrown Pacifica.

Beyond Pacifica: The Faire Goes National

The Renaissance Pleasure Faire, after ending its formal association with Pacifica and helmed by the Pattersons, continued to grow quickly in both

Northern and Southern California: in range and quantity of offerings; in number of visitors, workers, and volunteers; and in ambitiousness of production. Patterson imagined a long future for the faire and, seeking to establish it as a stable offering, requested a ten-year zoning exception to continue holding the event on the grounds of the former Paramount ranch. Some members of the Chamber of Commerce and some residents of the area near the ranch immediately voiced objections, citing concerns about traffic. Patterson was not buying it. She had talked to police and fire officials about the faire, she insisted, and they had raised no objections (Burleigh 6). Patterson insisted that the opposition to the faire was politically motivated, as it had been the previous year when Ruth Brennan's group had charged that the faire had "immoral aspects" (Burleigh 6).

Patterson remained adamant that there was no basis to the charges that the faire constituted any danger to the community. Any accusations about previous years were "all hearsay," she repeated. Of the early closing of the 1967 faire, Patterson avowed, "Nothing happened that first weekend. There was one suspected narcotics arrest out of 24,000 people. They closed it on the theory that something might happen" (Burleigh 6).

But the faire became a front in a broader cultural clash despite Patterson's efforts, with faire opponents citing "fears of a hippie invasion" ("Agoura Pleasure Fair"). Herbert Grosswendt, who was president of the Agoura Valley Chamber of Commerce, asserted, "The basic premise of the Faire is fine, but it lures too many weirdies—all kinds of undesirables—to our locality." Grosswendt then elaborated on the supposed danger to his community posed by the roving lifestyle of the countercultural "weirdies":

> Your people come to our area for three weeks and have your fun and then go away. The weirdies don't stay on the Faire grounds. They roam. They move into shacks about the section and stay there. They scrounge after food. At many of our homes they are considered a threat. . . . If the faire comes, I'll either have to employ police protection, or I'll have to close my winery for the three weekends the faire is scheduled. (Schaffer)

Patterson, hoping to quell the opposition, denied the charges brought by Grosswendt and others. "This is no hippie happening," she testified at a public hearing at the Agoura Civic Center. "The fair attracts a very tranquil crowd" ("Agoura Pleasure Fair"). Patterson also pointed out that the Pleasure Faire would no longer be raising funds for Pacifica—another point of contention with its political opposition.

The faire was not forced to close a second time, but its next few years were not entirely tranquil in terms of opposition either. High-profile defense lawyer Leslie Abramson recalls in her 1997 memoir, *The Defense Is Ready*, working in the Malibu County Public Defender's Office during the Southern California Renaissance Pleasure Faire's 1970 season. The faire was being policed by the Special Enforcement Bureau (SEB), an elite group of sheriff's deputies. As the faire progressed, reports of enormous numbers of arrests for drugs were coming out—as many as a hundred a day. The police reports, writes Abramson, all sounded remarkably similar:

> They claim people are throwing the drugs out the window as they drive down the road. (What, they suddenly decided to just say no?) Or they claim the pot is out in the open (the roach-in-the-ashtray ploy) where it can be seen. Or, their favorite, they smell the aroma of marijuana coming from the car and, therefore, they stop and search it. . . . These cops have thrown the rule book away. They are making illegal searches and illegal arrest and I'm determined to prove it. (97)

In addition to the fairegoers who were arrested, many more were hassled, even "humiliated and violated," adds Abramson (97)—to the extent that the judge was also worried about the number of cases. But before long, a student protest near the University of California's Santa Barbara campus resulted in the burning of a Bank of America building. The SEB officers who were making the arrests at the faire were called to assist the police in Santa Barbara County. They beat the protesters so brutally, and generated such terrible publicity, that eventually the whole division was disbanded. Meanwhile, the judge threw out any arrest he ascertained was an SEB case from the faire.

The intense policing of the faire did not end, though, and it was not limited to Southern California. Fairegoers came to expect it and even to work a commentary on the policing into their Renaissance faire "play."

Fig. 1.10. As the faire has become increasingly mainstream, some tensions have arisen over the limiting of certain performers' bawdy material. On some faire sites, such as the Southern California Renaissance Pleasure Faire, pictured here, certain stages are designated for more "adult" material. These performers, a musical act called the Poxy Boggards, comment slyly on the policy by adapting the Parental Advisory Sticker placed on music CDs. (Photo by Madison Rose)

Bagpiper James MacDonald Reid recalls that at the 1968 Northern California faire, "When a police helicopter flew over the Faire area, people started shouting out, 'Dragon! It's a dragon!' and everyone ran for cover until it had passed" (email).

Such public controversy swirling around the faire in these years illustrated that it had become, for better or for worse, a prominent cultural flashpoint, attracting not only conservative detractors but an ever-increasing number of people who wanted to take part. (Whether this constituted a "hippie invasion" remained a judgment call.) The California faires were certainly gaining national attention; both evidence and vehicle of this was an ABC television variety special *Fol-de-Rol*, a puppet show set at the Renaissance faire that piloted on February 27, 1972. The show was based on the live puppeteering of Sid and Marty Krofft and featured a star roster of human talent as well: Robert Shields (who used mime to set the scene), Mickey Rooney, Ricky Nelson (playing a wandering minstrel), Cyd Charisse (who performed a butterfly dance), Howard Cosell, Ann Sothern, and Totie Fields (playing, somewhat provocatively, both a Mother Superior and a Goddess of Love). But the faires' raised profile was visible in many smaller, more scattered places: a band from suburban Billerica, Massachusetts, calling itself Renaissance Fair in 1967; a Renaissance-themed dance organized by the Ontario, California, Elks clubhouse in 1970; a one-day event borrowing the Pleasure Faire's name in 1971—in Salt Lake City, Utah; a high school Renaissance faire in Lawrence, Wisconsin, in 1973. The list continued to grow, picking up speed throughout the 1970s.

No doubt because the Patterson faires were doing so well, indeed perhaps inevitably, a few faire admirers, possessing the requisite entrepreneurial mind-set coupled with a fanciful spirit, began to develop bona fide faires in other parts of the country. (Renaissance faires appeared before long in other countries as well, though that is beyond the scope of this book.) The first full-scale non-California Renaissance faires in the United States were established in other states by hands-on individual owners, beginning with the Minnesota Renaissance Festival in 1970 and the Texas Renaissance Festival in 1974. The important figure in the history of these two faires is businessman George Coulam, who helped to establish the Minnesota faire before moving to Texas and designing what has grown to the largest Renaissance faire site, now boasting twenty-one stages and more than 350 vendors on fifty-three carefully landscaped acres. By all accounts, Coulam—an eccentric known locally for advertising that he would pay an annual salary for a woman willing to marry him for a two-year stint—is still an active presence at the Texas Renaissance Festival, living adjacent to the faire site, continuing to develop the grounds and the performances year after year, and accruing a reputation as an idiosyncratic, persistent visionary. Coulam has a somewhat freer hand in developing the faire—or, in the eyes of some of his employees, ruling somewhat tyrannically over it as "King George"—because he owns, rather than leases, the land on which it sits.

Whether tyrant or visionary—or both—Coulam was undeniably successful at taking the Renaissance faire concept beyond its initial geographic and social location. Just five years after the Minnesota faire was founded, when Minnesota Public Radio reporter Margaret Moos did a broadcast there, it was clearly already well organized and well-known as a place where "men [*sic*] who spend their work week farming, or selling insurance, or working in a factory" ("1975: Renaissance Festival") could symbolically redefine the time they inhabited, thereby marking it as separate from the time their employers "own" so much of (much in the way that historian Roy Rosenzweig showed leisure to represent important antiwork time for the urban working class at the turn of the twentieth century).

Before long, the Minnesota and Texas faires themselves inspired further imitators. Through the rest of the 1970s and well into the 1980s, important faires followed in Maryland, Kansas, Colorado, Michigan, Florida, and Georgia, until by the turn of the twenty-first century, there were more than two hundred of them across the country, in nearly every state of the United States. (The number can be tallied as reaching much higher, when one-weekend festivals, festivals at universities, and related festivals, such as those organized explicitly around fantasy, are counted.) A further innovation arrived in 2008, with the founding of Faire a la Carte, a faire-for-hire venture designed to bring a portable version of the faire to any location.[11] But the Minnesota and the Texas festivals remain among the most important—as well as the largest—Renaissance faires nationwide, boasting by 2008 more than 280,000 visitors and over 400,000, respectively, over the course of an eight-weekend season.

While some faires, notably those in Texas and Maryland, are still operated by individual, on-site owners, during the 1990s, large corporate entities bought many of them. The first of these, Renaissance Entertainment Corporation (later Renaissance Entertainment Productions), a for-profit publicly traded entity, acquired its first faire in 1989: King Richard's Faire in Bristol, Wisconsin, which it renamed Bristol Renaissance Faire. This traceable network of business deals on the part of motivated individuals, with their own artistic vision and, later on, aggressive corporations methodically consolidating their holdings, is as important to the story of the faires' expansion across the country as is the spread of countercultural values or theatrical innovation.

But not surprisingly, the eventual transformation from Pacifica fundraiser to for-profit industry has not been painless. When the Renaissance Entertainment Corporation acquired the original California faires in 1994, the process so transformed the meaning of those faires in the eyes of its original participants that it continues to be arduous for some of them to talk about REC at all. REC launched an explicit and fairly aggressive consolidation plan, acquiring the New York Renaissance Faire and opening some new faires as well, such as one in Virginia that was founded in 1996 and closed in 1999.

For many participants, these corporate purchases underlie a shift in the meaning of the faires from experimental happening to commercial entertainment of precisely the sort to which the earliest faires were intended as opposition. The Kansas City Renaissance Festival, for instance, operated for twenty-three years primarily as a benefit for the Kansas City Art Institute before being purchased by Mid-America Festivals; this changing of hands correlated with a change in priorities as well as management style. Longtime faire performer Ray St. Louis writes, "I have seen the fairs change a lot over the years. Most have become more commercial, adopting more rules and regulations governing festival participation, requiring more insurance, charging more in the ways of fees for camping and the like. Every aspect of the Renaissance festival participation seems more controlled, more businesslike" (vii). Across the country, this shift has deeply rankled some of the faire's longtime adherents. "I don't go [to the faire] anymore. I don't like the visuals now: it's too commercial," admits actor Billy Scudder, who recalls with ecstasy his years miming at the Southern California faire during the 1970s (interview). "The community has gotten less alternative over the last ten to fifteen years," laments Katrina Ranum, a booth worker and longtime attendee at the Maryland Renaissance Festival, adding, "This has become more of a family show, and *unfortunately* what is considered 'family' is a man, a woman, and two kids" (interview). Performer Rush Pearson, who plays a character named "Billy Billy von Billy" in the Sturdy Beggars Mud Show, agrees, remarking that over the course of his twenty-odd years of involvement in the faire, shifts in its character did not happen in a vacuum but instead mirrored shifts in prevailing national priorities:

> The whole country went more family oriented. When I joined the faire, you still felt connected to the Sixties. You still felt connected to possibility, to freedom. And the crafters were all real characters. As everything became a business, you had more of a puritan work ethic [at the faire]. Which is fine. Because if the audience isn't number one, you don't make any money, and if the money isn't number one, you don't get an audience. The two go together. But I knew a lot of people before who were following the beat of a different drummer, and that added a lot of color. (Interview)

As Pearson's analysis hints, faire workers mostly do acknowledge the need for a higher level of planning and organization as the size of the faires increased. But a huge number of them—even ones who continue to work at the faires—still feel that an excessive level of rationalization and a policy of playing it safe so as not to alienate the "lowest possible denominator" (as one dedicated visitor puts it) has had a high cost in terms of creative values and spontaneity and has turned some faires into "shopping malls with entertainment," a phrase that came up often enough to cause one to wonder how commonly, and through what media, it is circulating. Pearson, for his part, reminded me that a more anarchic, less regimented philosophy is what allowed the faire to develop into the financial success that brought mandates of increased regimentation to it: "I don't think any owner came in with the idea for everything at the faire," he maintains adamantly. "There were a lot of crazy crafters and crazy performers who created what became the industry standards at the different faires. Now, it's a lot more premeditated, and it's really hard to get your foot in the door" (interview).

In the business world, though, providing entertainment in order to draw in shoppers represents sound and admirable practice, and as such, the faire has been taken up as an industrial model, even as others have come to see the faire as an educational model or theatrical model. B.

Joseph Pine and James H. Gilmore, authors of *The Experience Economy: Work Is Theatre and Every Business a Stage,* call the Minnesota Renaissance faire an "outdoor shopping mall" that charges admission—and advocate for retails stores and malls to follow suit. "The history of economic progress consists of charging a fee for what once was free," write Pine and Gilmore, adding that it was a particularly savvy business move for the company producing the Minnesota faire to extend its brand by adding Halloween- and Christmas-themed events in the same location (67), a development that certain faire participants are inclined to see as so schlocky that it spills over and erodes the integrity of the faire itself.

In addition to hastening changes in ownership and management, the faires' grand success both in and beyond California also rather emphatically brought to the forefront when it came to the old argument over authenticity, as both the new faires and the two original ones in California had to consider seriously what would matter the most to them and, in the case of the two Pleasure Faires in California, what would distinguish them from what was promising to become a large mass of followers. In order to ensure consistency of planning and vision in a time of rapid growth, the California faires established a full-time staff in 1970, firmly plunking down their flags on the side of greater historical accuracy. In 1972, Phyllis Patterson began holding instructional workshops, tutoring participants in period-appropriate dress, social conventions, and speech, and producing take-away guides in the form of illustrated booklets on those subjects. John Compton, who sold plants at a booth called The Queen's Herb Garden at the Northern California Renaissance Pleasure Faire in 1972, recalls that Patterson would

> go through [the faire site] with a clipboard making notes for people: "No, I don't like your sign—the calligraphy isn't correct, please change it." I was a nut. I lived twenty minutes from the faire, so I went out and built a stucco building. I built a little Tudor building. I actually went out by the highway and cut tall grass and hand-thatched a roof. I built something that had to be bulldozed down [when the faire moved]. (Interview)

The grown-up Pleasure Faires also began to cultivate institutional relationships that would further the goal of greater historical authenticity. In 1976, the faire's staff created the Living History Centre (LHC), a statewide nonprofit educational foundation. (The Centre soon branched out to developing programs that presented other historical periods as well, including early California.) Through the LHC, the faire's organizers sought to align the faire philosophically with the tradition of open-air museums or "living history."

The practice of living history is generally considered to have been initiated in the United States with Henry Ford's Greenfield Village, which he established in Dearborn, Michigan, in 1928. Currently this tradition is perhaps most commonly associated with Colonial Williamsburg in Virginia, which opened in 1934—and where the Pattersons, after the impressive success of the early faires, were invited to visit as consultants. Organizations devoted to living history can now be found across the country, frequently associated with an experiential philosophy of education; open-air museums presenting rural settings, military posts, industrial centers, and other sites are located in many states. Historians Roy Rosenzweig and David Thelen have convincingly shown that many Americans feel alienated from book-oriented history, which they associate with schools, museums, government, and media—institutions they assess as elitist and disciplining. Practices of experiential history, then, such as living history, offer an opportunity for them to forge intellectual and emotional links to the past in ways they find more relevant. Thus, as easy as it has been for certain observers—accurately or not—to criticize or even to ridicule the faires' uneven attempts at authenticity, for many attendees, the faire provided a way for them to take on an engagement with history in an empowering way. It is worth remembering in the twenty-first century that for every educated stickler, there are others who genuinely feel that the faire has enriched them by encouraging an interest in another time and place.

Through the Living History Centre, Renaissance faire practice crossed paths with the practices and values of other "historymakers," in the useful coinage of Rosenzweig and Thelen: reenactors, preservationists, genealogists, and collectors—all important roles through which Americans have sought to create a workable relationship with historical knowledge. The LHC's work quickly ramped up the Pleasure Faire's educational claims and goals, offering "workshops in the woods," similar to the instructional sessions organized for participants, to thousands of schoolchildren. The LHC also sought—and was able to obtain—grants to facilitate its educational work. To promote the faire's educational potential, organizers commissioned publicity videos that underscored the event's connection to seasonal celebrations in Renaissance-era England: the coming of spring for the Southern California faire and the harvest for the Northern California faire. Further, the California owners, in order to protect their brand and their vision for what a Renaissance faire should look like, copyrighted the name "Renaissance faire"; for this reason, the faires founded after it are officially called "Renaissance festival" instead, although they are all popularly called "Renaissance faire," frequently contracted to "Ren faire" or just "faire" by their most loyal visitors.

Those who participated seriously in the California faires during the 1970s were, unsurprisingly, deeply divided over the question of the increased weight being given to authenticity in California. Some participants refer disparagingly to "RINO" faires—"Renaissance In Name Only"—that compress historical references willy-nilly with fantasy or fairy-tale elements thrown in for good measure. In this perspective, the jettisoning of authenticity is inextricably linked to a for-profit mind-set and an increasing "cheesiness" that is emblematized by plastic swords and generic polyester "princess dresses" marketed to parents with the calculated knowledge that parents will spend money more quickly on their children than on anything else.

Taking a contrary view is Howard Patterson (no relation to the family of Phyllis Patterson), a juggler whose troupe the Flying Karamazov Brothers (FKB) became one of the best-known acts to spend its early career at the faire. The FKB stopped performing at the faire altogether as soon as other performance opportunities allowed them to do so in the late 1970s, feeling that the attention to authenticity had become compulsive, with the result that it was stifling the untrammeled, creative composting that constituted the early faires. "What was problematic for us was that they [the faire management] had very specific regulations about what was authentic and what was not," explains Howard Patterson, adding that owners and staff members policed for authenticity and challenged performances that they deemed insufficiently authentic (interview). Howard Patterson feels strongly that acts containing contemporary political references are actually more in keeping with the *spirit* of Renaissance-era street performance, which likewise would have contained contemporary political satire, than are performances in which such anachronisms have been excised.

For a noteworthy group of performers and crafters, Howard Patterson among them, the more freewheeling approach that characterized the first California faires came to be typified by the Oregon Country Fair, an annual three-day affair established in 1969 as a benefit for an alternative school. This fair, described by seamstress and performer Avery Watts as a "hippie spin-off" of the Renaissance Pleasure Faire (interview), was in fact known as the Oregon Renaissance Faire from 1969 up through 1976, when it changed its name in response to the Living History Centre's copyright of the name "Renaissance Faire." The new name, which participants say suits it better, was meant to invoke the back-to-the-land movement, which was strong in Oregon (Prozanski 182). The Country Fair continues to be held annually outside Eugene, Oregon, with a particular focus on ecology and a whole range of performances including some varieties cut out from the California faires because they were anachronistic, such as drum jams.[12] (Some key performers continued to work at both the Country Fair and Renaissance faires.) Unlike the training required of Renaissance Pleasure Faire participants, "you just needed to show up" to take part in the Oregon Country Fair, says Watts, noting with a chuckle that as far as costuming was concerned, "as long as your genitalia are not actually showing, anything goes" (interview).

Although the faire's individual participants have always distributed themselves across a full spectrum of interest in authenticity, the institution's approach to authenticity as a defining goal has fallen into three rough historical periods, at least in California: first, the faires were somewhat loosely defined countercultural "hippie" events; beginning in about 1972, they were cast as educational in intent, as "living museums" or even reenactment; finally, they became commercial enterprises run by businesspeople according to business plans, owned as "chains" by corporations starting in 1989. Of course, this is not to say that any of these categories are mutually exclusive. On the contrary, they have always coexisted, and most participants readily find some advantages (or disadvantages) in all three orientations: the educational value of the more authentic focus versus the sense of whimsy of the less structured approach, or the family-friendly nature and financial stability of the more commercial enterprises versus the less straight-laced nature of the earlier ones. But the emphasis did shift over time and geographic distance, with a certain amount of controversy following in the wake of the changes.

The Faire Circuit

As the faire spread nationally, it became increasingly viable as a primary means of support for the various people who worked at it—performers, crafters, and booth staffers. Kevin Patterson contends that the faire quickly evolved into "a counterculture economy that supported young people—and middle-aged people—who were looking for another way to make a living, and not support the military-industrial complex. They [his parents, Phyllis and Ron Patterson] did that consciously" (interview). As early as 1967, the first year that the Northern California Renaissance Pleasure Faire was held, faire participants (both workers and visitors) traveled within California to take part in both the Northern California and the Southern California faires in tandem, with campers and vans converging on the faire sites annually as people organized their lifestyles around working at the faire. Traveling—and further, traveling light—became an iconic part of the countercultural ethos, emblematized in the hitchhiker, the Volkswagen minibus, and the crash-pad, and for many people, working the faire's newly developing circuit dovetailed nicely with this ideal.

Avery Watts, an early faire performer and seamstress, hitchhiked away from her parents' home near Kalamazoo, Michigan, after graduating from high school in 1968. Merely months after leaving home, she was "a hippie in the Haight" (interview). In a turn of events that efficiently sums up the faire's entwinement with the growing counterculture, Watts says that she first heard of the faire when drivers who picked her up hitchhiking would ask her if that was where she was headed. Soon enough, she was regularly attending both California faires.

As the faire spread to other states, traveling the circuit allowed performers and crafters to earn more of their income through their art (as opposed to day jobs) and allowed other faire adherents to incorporate the faire into a pursuit of an idealistic, countercultural lifestyle. Each faire is open on weekends for somewhere between eight and twelve weeks, and whereas now enough faires are held nationally to occasion some overlap, for a long time, the runs in different locations took place at different times, with the overall faire season lasting roughly from February through October (excluding small, local one- or two-day festivals).

Traveling performers and crafters alike became adept at retooling their vehicles to transport their materials or props—and, like as not, to provide living space; mime Avner Eisenberg, for instance, used a converted postal-service truck with a bed he could sleep in, store costumes and props underneath, even use as an impromptu stage if necessary by propping open the back doors. At the end of one faire's run, the crafters, performers, and booth workers pack up their wares, their props, their garb, their personal belongings, and an occasional cat and, in many cases, hit the road for the next faire. This constitutes the life "on the circuit" that still dominates the working world of the Renaissance festival.

On the permanent faire sites—which means that buildings and other structures need not be torn down at the end of the season so that the land can be repurposed—many booths now have sleeping lofts above, where the craftspeople live during the run of that particular faire's season. Others live in campers and tents in designated areas. (On occasions when faire owners have done away with camping for faire workers, either of their own volition or because regulatory laws caught up with faire practice, it has been a serious hardship for year-round faire workers.) Those who follow the circuit and move from state to state according to the schedule of faires call themselves "Rennies." The term is used by some to refer to devoted patrons, but its primary reference is to faire workers. One crafter, a mask maker named Shane Odom who paints and designs leather masks in animal and fantasy forms, tells me about a faire insider's joke that you cannot call yourself a Rennie unless you "wake up six months of the year looking at plywood" (interview).

Nomadic life, even at its most rewarding, is stressful in many ways, particularly within a larger culture that values the homestead. It brings with it a whole variety of sacrifices—on top of those already familiar to the self-employed. Some crafters—even among those who travel the circuit—maintain off-season homes that operate as anchor and haven. Others, though, completely refuse to focus on the value of accumulating property; but without permanent homes or consumer objects, they all too frequently find themselves to be marginalized and made the subject of scorn both in person and in popular culture. A crafter relates a story of two female Rennies shopping for groceries before the start of a season and being told at the checkout that they must be connected to the Renaissance faire because they had "long skirts, long hair, no bras" (Curtis interview). (That cashier, speaking in the 2000s, was enacting an incredibly neat—and revealing—overlay of old stereotypes of "hippie" with "Renaissance faire.") Many crafters and other faire workers insist that the cultural scorn that sometimes greets the faire—which I focus on at length in chapter 5—stems from the fact that its workers are a kind of migrant labor.

And migrant labor has it particular challenges. Living above a booth with extremely limited space and no plumbing takes careful managing but is comparatively cozy. But there have been many circumstances when living in booths has not been possible, such as during the faire's earliest years, in locations where the faire site is not permanent, and for those who do not own booths. "It was sleeping bags under a fabric tent at first," recalls costumer Steven Overstreet of the faire's first decade (interview). After the economic collapse in 2008, many crafters began to muse on whether their lifestyle would remain viable at all, since the cost of fuel was so high that sometimes they were worried about whether they could even get themselves to their next location. Richard Copeland, a Texas native with no permanent home, explains, "It takes everything I have to get from California to Colorado, with car repairs and gas. Many people now spend all they have to get to the next place. It's getting harder—maybe we can't do it anymore, what with the cost of travel" (interview).

But for many Rennies, for whom the attraction of vending at the faire goes far beyond a functionalist appreciation of someplace to sell their work or perform their acts, this pared-down traveling life is part of the point. In some cases, the attraction is a straightforward love of moving around: finding new places, new people, and a way of life outside mainstream consumer culture. Writes a participant in one of the Rennies' self-published newsletters, "When I became a 'Rennie' over twelve years ago, I did so because I was impressed with the community spirit and the efforts that individuals put forth to create beauty and support the func-

tions that made the circuit an alternative to the soul-less mind numb-
ing traps of modern living. The circuit was the antithesis of such a mundane existence" (Rook 37). "We were looking for a way not to punch the
clock" is how Derek Weaver, of Masquerade Lifecasting, sums up his own
gravitation to the faire circuit (interview). Weaver does have a permanent
home base in Texas with his partner, faire craftswoman Ann Curtis, but
he is no exception to the rule that even faire folk with houses are still not
generally measuring their progress in life as a linearly measured acquisi-
tion of property. The fact is, they visibly do prefer the handmade and the
offbeat, nurturing an irreverent sensibility and deliberately taking themselves largely outside the consumer system. For a good number of Rennies, this impulse became stronger rather than weaker as the heyday of
the counterculture gave way to the so-called greedy eighties. "I'm sure
that, to many, the Renaissance festivals looked like a good place to hide
and ride out the eighties and Ronald Reagan," wrote Renaissance faire
novelist and longtime performer Ray St. Louis in his 2006 novel *Road
Dog Diary* (53).

Vince Conaway, a hammered-dulcimer player in his midthirties who
grew up in Lorain, Ohio, has been traveling the faire circuit for ten years.
He is one of the dedicated circuit workers who currently does not have a
permanent home. I asked him to tell me his performance schedule from
January 2008 to January 2009. The telling took some time, and the number of trips and moves makes it completely unsurprising that Conaway
had to pause at times, unsure if he was getting his own chronology right.
The only way to do justice to Conaway's itinerary—the complexity of
which is not unique to him but cannot really be summarized by someone
else—is to let him speak:

> Last January, I had the month off; it's not a very big time for festivals.
> At the end of January, I went to Europe and street-performed in Italy
> for three months until the very end of April. Then in May and June, I
> was performing at the Greater St. Louis Renaissance Faire. After that,
> I performed for a one-week medieval festival for the SCA [Society for
> Creative Anachronism] in Kansas City, Missouri. And then I think I
> had a week or two off. I don't remember what exactly was going on at
> the end of June. Then it was the Sterling Renaissance Festival in upstate

New York, north of Syracuse. I performed at Sterling for five weekends. Also during Sterling, I was doing a commute to the big SCA event in Pennsylvania. I was spending weekends at the festival and then driving five hours and spending Monday through Friday for two weeks north of Pittsburgh. And then I went to the Michigan Renaissance Festival for two weeks. And that brought me here to King Richard's Faire [in Massachusetts], where I've been for the last seven weekends. And then I've got a weekend off during which I'm going to fly to Seattle to visit friends basically for a long five-day weekend. And then I'm going to spend six weeks in Louisiana for the Louisiana Renaissance Festival, which is on the north shore of Lake Ponchartrain. That brings us to mid-December. I'll probably spend an extra week or so there [in Louisiana]. I have a friend in the French Quarter. I tend to spend a lot of time down there whenever I can. And then I will spend the holidays in Cleveland, basically [with] family. (Interview)

Conaway adds that because he has a good number of years performing at the faire under his belt, he has been able to "trim the fat" in his schedule as it pleases him to do, resulting in a schedule that is less packed with traveling than it has been in previous years, when he was less experienced. He recognizes that at first, his parents were worried about his ability to support himself in this way, but "suddenly it went from being 'I'm really scared about what you're doing' to being 'Look at what my kid can do!'" (interview).

A sizeable number of Renaissance faire loyalists see direct connections between the Rennies' countercultural ideals and the public excoriating they are accustomed to taking. Brianna Smith, a college student who grew up working at the faire and following the circuit with her family, says that she recognizes that people "like to make fun of migrants." She compares disrespect of Rennies to that of seasonal farmworkers, traveling carnies, freight-train hoppers, and youthful hitchhikers. "We're so far outside 'regular' culture," she acknowledges (interview). Smith posits that there are two categories of Rennies who attract the severest scorn from outsiders: hippies, who are defiantly rejecting a more structured life, and educated adults, who are perceived to have given up something better to work at the faire.

Brianna Smith is the daughter of a food crafter, Victor Smith, who homeschooled her for all twelve years of her primary and secondary education, taking her to museums in Washington, DC, for instance, when he was working at the Maryland faire in Annapolis. Her family's schedule was also complex and did not involve a permanent residence for the first half of her life:

> Until I was twelve, [my parents and I] did Scarborough Faire [Scarborough Renaissance Festival in north Texas] and then Sterling [Renaissance Festival in New York State]. Then my mother did Kansas [Kansas City Renaissance Festival]. I went with her, and my father did Maryland [Renaissance Festival in Annapolis]. We stayed on the Texas site during the winter. When I was twelve years old, we got a house in Ithaca, where we stayed in the winter months. (Interview)

On her college application, Smith listed four hometowns.

Growing up at the faire for Smith did not merely consist of being dragged around by her parents. When she was old enough, she worked too: first for her father as counter help, then at a game booth. Later, she had her own food cart, selling pickles and pretzels at the Maryland and New York faires. She retains some ambivalence about her migrant upbringing, but after enrolling at Tufts University—a year early—and declaring a triple major in German, psychology, and political science, she states without hesitation that the faire has prepared her well: "I am a lot better socialized than most people at school. I spent my entire life dealing with thousands of people every weekend. And—maybe this is a working-class thing—people at Tufts complain about having to find a job. Everyone I know has had to work. I had friends selling their possessions so they could get fuel to get to the next job" (interview). On the downside, though, she comments that in college, she found it hard to stay comfortably in one place: she simply misses moving around.

Smith is too analytically inclined to romanticize the faire entirely. She had ideas of her own about what people "gave up" to work at the faire, and some of those things, frankly, she might have preferred to keep. "So much in our society is set up for people who stay in one place," she explains. "For instance, I studied martial arts since I was eight but never really advanced." This reality was especially poignant, Smith says, as she entered her teenage years, because among traveling faire families, "there is more of a social life for the younger kids. This is because most people stay in one place to go to school by high school age." She hastens to add that the close friends she had at the faire were people she "hung out with all the time" because of the tight-knit nature of the faire culture. Still, she says, "I'd get involved in a community, and it would be starting to come together, and then it would be time to go" (interview). Smith's observations about what the social cost of constant moving for young people call to mind the somewhat parallel situation faced by children in military families.

Longtime Renaissance faire performer Ray St. Louis has written a "true life novel" (vii), *Road Dog Diary*, about his thirty years' worth of involvement with the faire as the founder and director of the Sticks and Stones Stilt Dancers, a troupe he worked with starting in the early 1980s. The book is a work of fiction and, as such, often enough lists toward the sensationalizing (if not the salacious)—but St. Louis's description of the end of a year's circuit affectingly conveys, in its melancholy portrayal of Rennies' seasonal farewells, both the gifts of circuit life and its costs:

An early November autumn chill . . . was in the air as the rapidly dwindling army of Rennies slowly filtered out of the campground and site of the Texas Renaissance Festival. Vans, busses, pickups pulling trailers, station wagons, old converted hearses and limousines, cars with roof racks overloaded with suitcases held down with bungee cords—a veritable stream of itinerant Renaissance show people—fanned out in all directions. . . . All headed for home, or for whatever substituted for home. All participants in the annual fall Diaspora. (502)

2

Artisans of the Realm

Crafters at the Faire

Observe ye the Potters at their Wheels, Weavers at their
Looms and divers other Craftsmen creating their wares in
their Self made Stalls.
    —Renaissance Pleasure Faire and May Market program
book, 1967

In 1991, countercultural publisher (and religious founder and leader)
Kerry Thornley wrote an essay looking back on the phenomenon in
California's history that "has since been characterized as the Love Generation, the Hippie Movement, the Counter-culture and Flower Power."
Rejecting all of these terms as both inadequate and externally imposed,
he attempts to convey more accurately what he says really mattered to the
people walking that new cultural and philosophical path before it came
to by known by those now-familiar names. In order to do so, he describes
the Southern California Renaissance Pleasure Faire:

> Every year near Thousand Oaks, California, was something called a Renais-
> sance Faire. As a custom it survives even now, but before the media discov-
> ered the hippies it was not the same. That it was less commercialized was
> only part of the difference. What could be gathered about the people who

came there to peddle their wares was significant. Self-sufficient individuals who lived by means of their craft, whether it was leather carving or pottery or one of a dozen other skills, they were bearded and long haired in the years before anyone employed by a corporation was permitted to look so outlandish. Self-styled gypsies who lived in the canyons and foothills and desert areas up and down the coast from Los Angeles, they were tanned, wiry and weathered. In their conversation they were knowledgeable without seeming pompous.

In Thornley's retrospective vision, the crafters at the faire, both "significant" and "outlandish" in that moment, were bringing much more than saleable items to the faire-as-marketplace.

The English country fairs on which the first Renaissance Pleasure Faire was modeled occurred at the marketplace; practically speaking, they were seasonal celebrations organized around commerce. This precedent, coupled with the fact that the earliest faires were fund-raisers for KPFK, meant that there was never a question that items would be for sale at the faire, alongside the performances that the Pattersons found to be period appropriate, either directly or evocatively. From the beginning, the faire's organizers imagined selling not only food and drink that would be different from the usual limited offerings at outdoor events but also handmade crafts. And although the faire's origins may have been in performance, this craft vending quickly turned out to be not only one of the most popular aspects of the faire but also one of the most influential and central to its self-conceptualization.

Indeed, potter Stephen Bennett, who began selling his ceramics as a teenager at the Southern California faire, insists, "The first festivals were craft festivals with entertainment" (interview). Bennett, now in his sixties, still travels to faires; he recalls selling his pottery at every season of the Southern California faire's earliest decades except the first two, which means he has been working the circuit for more than forty years. Bennett's retrospective assessment of the early faires echoes the much earlier observation of Steven Roberts, the Los Angeles Bureau chief for the *New York Times*, and his wife, Cokie Roberts, then a television producer and freelance writer, who jointly wrote about the same faire for the *New York Times* in 1972. "The focus of the Faire is the craftsmen," pronounced

Fig. 2.1 Renaissance faire crafters build the booths in which they sell their wares and sometimes live during the faire's run. (Courtesy of Joy Photography, 2009)

Roberts and Roberts. "This year more than 150 of them will be making and selling their products. . . . There are dozens of potters, jewelers, and leatherworkers, a sprinkling of glass blowers, carpenters and print makers. And a swordsmith."

Nonetheless, when the very first festival was being mounted, finding crafters to sell their wares was a challenge for the faire's organizers. The Pattersons intended for all wares to be handmade, using no modern materials—especially not plastic. And the items for sale were to be reminiscent of goods that might have been found at a Renaissance marketplace. Today, there are thousands of permanent and temporary craft fairs and both brick-and-mortar and online craft shops, as well as dozens of craft-oriented magazines. In 1963, though, there was no visible supply of crafters from which to enlist artisans—even in California, which was soon to become known as the center of a handicraft revival. Within a handful of years, the Renaissance festival became vital to that revival, providing one of the surest ways artists could earn income from selling their creations. However, the Pattersons had to work hard to find crafters in the faire's earliest days.

One way they did this was through direct recruiting. Phyllis Patterson recalls that a cobbler whom she occasionally visited for shoe repair had sandals that appeared to be handmade hanging in his shop. She drove over to visit him and learned that he made the sandals himself, as a sort of hobby or labor of love. "I asked him, 'Would you be willing to come and sell your sandals at the faire?'" she recalls (interview). In this ad hoc manner, she and her husband began to line up vendors.

The Pattersons hit pay dirt in an artists' commune in Santa Barbara that they had visited with their then-infant son Kevin. The Mountain Drive Community was an experiment in unconventional living founded by writer Bobby Hyde and his wife, Florence "Floppy" Hyde. In the early 1940s, the Hydes bought fifty acres of land in the hills above Santa Barbara. They were able to do this cheaply because the rugged, hilly landscape had been blackened by fire shortly before. After World War II, the Hydes began to invite like-minded family and friends to live on that acreage with them, producing much of the food and other goods they needed and developing their own customs and rituals. There were no building codes in the county yet, so the residents built their own (sometimes quite quirky) homes, eventually sparking a broader interest in adobe home construction.

Mountain Drive residents owned their land individually but developed a close and rich community life, adopting elements of European bohemianism which many of the community's founding members had experienced firsthand during World War II: communal living, unconventional sexual arrangements, radical political philosophies, and principled appreciation of the carnivalesque. According to reminiscences of community members (collected by Elias Chiacos into a self-published collection of oral history and photographs), the glue holding this bohemian community together was the set of annual celebrations that developed over the years: Twelfth Night, the birthday of Scottish poet Robert Burns, Bastille Day. In particular, an annual wine stomp became a cherished custom. As Chiacos recounts,

> As the community grew, the celebrations and annual wine stomps became more elaborate. A wine queen was chosen each year amid great pageantry. The Queen began the stomp by climbing into the vat adorned only with a wreath of grape leaves spray-painted gold. Wine tasting became a high

point and wineries from as far away as Napa Valley and even New York State sent bottles to the Mountain Drive club for evaluation. (27)

Chiacos's book includes beautiful photographs of garlanded and naked residents stomping grapes in tubs; although such group nudity was considerably rarer in the American context than in the European bohemian communal experiments, the joy on their faces is unmistakable.

For the invention of the Renaissance faire, the Mountain Drive custom that came to matter the most began just one year before the faire, in 1962, with a combination of serious intent and impious whimsy that was characteristic of the community's self-defining rituals. This was an annual event that came to be called the Pot Wars, and its originary impulse sheds light on the Pattersons' difficulty in locating crafters: the Wars were conceived in response to the fact that there were very few venues where crafters and potential customers could come together.

The concept behind the Pot Wars was developed by two Mountain Drive potters, Bill Neely and Ed Schertz. These two decided that they needed a way to sell what they made to people outside Mountain Drive, so they conceived of a fake rivalry—the "pot war." The stakes were as followed: whichever of them sold more could claim to have won the war. To attract buyers, Neely and Schertz publicized the "war" in Santa Barbara and set about creating a festive atmosphere. Mountain Drive residents dressed in fancy garb, some of which prefigured the Renaissance-inspired costumes that became so visually important at the Renaissance festival. There was music at the event, including "Renaissance" music, as well as food and drink. The two combatants devised ways to make their war exciting for shoppers: one filled all his pots with wine; the other declared he would smash anything not sold while hopping on one foot (Chiacos 92).

These events at Mountain Drive inspired the imagination of the Pattersons, particularly the jocular atmosphere, the outdoor setting, and the ways in which the artists themselves became part of the entertainment. The Pot Wars attracted thousands of people at their peak and were ultimately shut down because they interrupted the flow of traffic too much. But the Pattersons had taken note early on that here were craftspeople successfully selling what they had made themselves—the way they might have in a Renaissance market. The Mountain Drive Community became an important source of the faire's first craftspeople, and the craftspeople in turn contributed more than just their wares to the festivals. They also imparted a fanciful spirit, a bent for the performative, an emphasis on collective values and anticonsumerism, and perhaps above all, a sense of play.

The Pleasure Faire visitors were receptive to the anticommercialism of the Mountain Drive Community artists. And many artists and would-be artists were, in turn, immediately thrilled by the way the faire provided a noncorporate marketplace that welcomed the handmade. Before the faire, "there was no craft revival," Stephen Bennett says. "If you wanted to sell your art, you did it at the Ren faire" (interview). Steven Overstreet, a costumer with more than forty years of Renaissance faire experience, emphasized the same point. "Back then, there weren't craft shows. The faire was like the first. . . . The faire was our ticket into the craft" (interview). As Lee Nordness and others have pointed out, interest in the "hand arts" began to pick up a little steam following World War II, with the founding in 1956 of the Museum of Contemporary Crafts and the forward-looking orientation of the American Craftsman's Council, tracing in its house journal a gradual changing of attitudes about craft (Nordness 11–20). But it was hard to imagine young crafters either making a living from their work or gaining widespread acknowledgment as artists. The first Renaissance festival was held a year before the World Crafts Council, with its stated mission to further "the establishment of a craft movement to provide a better future to the craftspersons of the world," held its first meeting at Columbia University in June 1964. But the number of artists available to the festival's organizers grew quickly as interest in handmade objects for use and decoration was revitalized across the country, with California in particular emerging as a hotbed of craft, during the same years in which the faires emerged as a lasting proposition.

Revival

Through crafts, a man can rebel and say, "I am powerful in my own world."

—Paul J. Smith, director, Museum of Contemporary Craft

"A revival of pottery, weaving, woodworking, and metalworking is taking place everywhere throughout the U.S.," excitedly declared *Life* magazine in 1966 in a lavish photo-essay on artists working in a variety of media ("Old Crafts" 34). By 1972, *New York* magazine was taking this accelerated interest in handcrafts as a given, citing California as the place where the handcraft scene was strongest. Where *Life* was celebratory, *New York* was dubious, with its columnist Barbara Rose doubting that "counter-culture dropouts" had the "discipline" to create a legitimate artistic movement out of what she saw as inchoate impulse (72). Still, both of these articles and many others make it clear that a popular discovery of crafting was indeed taking place.

With this discovery supplying both artisans and eager customers, the number of crafter vendors at the faire grew quickly, and within a decade, there were about 150 of them, with three times that number applying for slots. The *Los Angeles Free Press*'s Liza Williams, writing in *FM & Fine Arts* magazine about the 1965 Renaissance Pleasure Faire, captures the synergistic relationship between the faire and the swelling interest in crafting as something well established by the faire's third year: because the Renaissance Pleasure Faire, she writes, was "created with a respect for authenticity, the craftsmen of California will find a setting worthy of their labours" (6). In her description of the faire's offerings, Williams explicitly links its emphasis on crafting with the countercultural anticorporatist, anti-mass-production values that came to characterize the decade:

> [Children] pull boats on strings, wave small flags, run through the grass with windflung pinwheels, and all the painted, plastic, Mickey Mouse vinyl, squealing, battery-operated world of their years vanishes in the delight of the simple, workable and colour-bright of handmade toys. . . .
>
> If you remember dishes that broke when you dropped them, or were irregular in shape, that did not have five-year guarantees, nor were made of dehydrated milk mixed with the coal tar derivatives, then you will enjoy seeing potters working at the Faire. . . .
>
> Come see the reality of things being born, not out of clanking, antiseptic machines that have no pride, but from the probing, sensitive fingers of artisans for whom each creation is his pride's identity. Come to the Pleasure Faire and May Market! (7)

The early Renaissance faires were very influential on the revival of crafting—encouraging both those who were moved to create objects themselves and those who were interested in observing those objects being made and purchasing them at the faire.

A forty-eight-hundred-word article in the January 28, 1968, issue of the *Los Angeles Times* on the development of craft business in and around Los Angeles describes the concentration of craftspeople "between San Diego and Santa Barbara" as being "greater than in any other part of the country"; the author, Jane Wilson, then hails the development of a crafting entrepreneurship as an outgrowth of the faire, in particular the season canceled in response to organized conservative opposition:

> Fortunately, the craftsmen [*sic*] are getting together to open their own shops. In the Silverlake and Echo Park areas, where rents are low and where many independent young people live, something of a "guild" feeling has grown up around a new shop called Jabberwock at 3202 Sunset Blvd., one of 12 in the Other End of Sunset Association. The project for this shop began last May, when the second weekend of the Ventura County Renaissance Pleasure Fair was canceled and many craftsmen were left with quantities of unsold work. So Judy Frank (clothing and jewelry) and Richard Yasskin (sculpture and leatherwork) opened Jabberwock as a clearing house for all this work, and then as a permanent sales center for the products of about 150 craftsmen, most of them from Silverlake and Echo Park. (B19)

"When I started working at it," toymaker Terrie Sullivan told Roberts and Roberts in 1972, "it was so hard to be a craftsman. . . . People weren't into handmade things so much and they didn't want to pay. Now it's the groovy thing to buy handmade things." A book-length guide for young people published by the *New York Times* in 1973, *Guide to Adventure, Travel, & Study, U.S.A., for High School and College Students,* uses a report on the Renaissance faire to open its section on craft, succinctly capturing the mutually constitutive relationship between the Renaissance faire as an institution and the swell of interest in craft: "Ten year ago a crafts marketplace in California called the Renaissance Pleasure Faire and Market had to scrounge for 60 craftsmen to fill its booths. Today, 500 craftsmen flock to its door, ranging from potters, glassblowers, woodworkers, and silversmiths, to toy-makers and swordsmiths" (Rowland and Rowland 151). In fact, several years before the authors of the guide for students had singled out the Renaissance faire as both emblem and engine of a swift, nationwide growth of interest in craft, craft-oriented publications such as *Ceramics Monthly, Fine Woodworking, Goldsmith's Journal,* and others had begun touting it as a place where crafters could find appreciative markets for their work.

The resurgence of American craft production that arose congruently with the faire's establishment has come to be referred to by the somewhat ungainly phrase "craft revival of the 1960s and 1970s." To be sure, there had been earlier waves of intense attention to American crafts; each time, the newfound interest developed because the world of handcrafts was able usefully to host a cultural conversation that helped Americans understand, and respond to, their concrete historical situations. Perhaps the best-known "craft revival" in U.S. history is the American participation in the Arts and Crafts movement, a revival that initiated in Europe and reached its peak at the turn of the twentieth century (though it continued to be influential through the 1930s). The Arts and Crafts movement grew out of the writings of the English socialist artist and writer William Morris, who advocated a return to traditional crafts in the face of what he considered to be the impoverishing effect of industrialization on the decorative arts. In the United States, a variety of artists committed to using craft in the service of enriching the experience of industrial consumption through expressive design, which has led some historians to consider the movement to be an aesthetic counterpart to Progressivism.[1] The Arts and Crafts movement was a powerful precedent for the craft revival of the 1960s and 1970s, prompting art historian Marion Nelson to call the latter "a *second* general arts and crafts movement" (37; italics added).

The periodic "discovery" and subsequent marketing of crafts has formed a complicated cycle in U.S. history, as (for example) historian David Whisnant has compellingly demonstrated in his work on outside attention to Appalachian culture. Above all, this "discovery," regardless of intentions, cannot be understood outside the context of the power dynamic that characterizes the counterposition of "folk" art to "high" art. Further, over the course of American history, "discovery" of crafting has corresponded and given expression to hugely consequential social and economic shifts: anxiety over the loss of rural spaces, desire to claim ethnicity versus the desire to claim Americanism, impulses to promote a certain vision of the "folk" through missionary interventions, feelings about contested categories such as racial "purity" or nationalism. For this reason, contemporary writing about craft and crafters (in addition to the crafts themselves) has the ability to shed light on a variety of political movements, from the Old Left assertions during the 1930s of the revolutionary potential of "the folk" to the advocacy of a return to African and African-influenced art forms on the part of activists and intellectuals in the Black Power movement of the 1970s.

In the 1960s, the acceleration of the return to crafting was, in no small part, a powerful reaction—both symbolic and practical—against the previous decade's popular idealizing of the machine-made, the polished, and the plastic. "Color Flyte, the greatest name in Melmac dinnerware," trumpeted an advertisement from the 1950s for plates and bowls. "Color-flyte is modern, . . . it has style, . . . it has color, . . . it has durability" ("Plastic Product Brochures"). Along with other anticommercialist endeavors of the era, such as the back-to-the-land movement (bleakly pictured in the 1969 movie *Easy Rider*), the faire was widely received as being in dialogue with the values of Fordism; of the Northern California Renaissance Pleasure Faire, the *San Mateo Times* reported in 1969, "The Renaissance Pleasure Faire, as a showplace for handcrafts, is especially important in the twentieth century when so much individuality is lost in mass production" ("Hie Ye Back").

The lost individuality in question refers not only to the standardization of the product but also to the expectations for conformity on the part of the populace. Speaking to Cokie and Steven Roberts at the 1972 faire, Patterson articulated the idea that the craft revival manifests, at least in part, a desire to recuperate an expressive voice squelched by the mandates of industry. "Maybe we went farther than anybody should go with the machine age," she is quoted as commenting. "To get something made off a machine was where it was at in the early 1900's. But then machine goods got so removed from anything human that people began to say, 'I'm here, too.'" Howard S. Rowland and Beatrice L. Rowland, authors of the *Times* guide for high school and college students, share Patterson's perspective. Declaring, "There is no doubt that crafts are 'in' for the '70's," they offer the following explanation:

> Today the increasingly look-alike quality of housing, clothing, and belongings, and the increasing routinization and fragmentation of jobs into mechanical functions have eroded the individual character of most people's lives and work. Many young people look at adults as simply interchangeable ciphers in some incomprehensively intricate and dehumanizing mechanism. And they want no part of it. For them the machine-made environment has grown stale and they welcome the idea of putting their hands to work. (150–151)

By 1964, the nascent counterculture had begun to use "machine" as political metaphor, as when Berkeley Free Speech Movement activist Mario Savio declared in what was to become his most famous speech,

> There's a time when the operation of the machine becomes so odious— makes you so sick at heart—that you can't take part. You can't even passively take part. And you've got to put your bodies upon the gears and upon the wheels, upon the levers, upon all the apparatus, and you've got to make it stop. And you've got to indicate to the people who run it, to the people who own it that unless you're free, the machine will be prevented from working at all! (Qtd. in R. Cohen 178–179)

In the case of crafts, literal and metaphorical meanings of "machine" merged during this period, which had the potential to politicize the production, distribution, and reception of even the most utilitarian craft objects.

While a thorough history of the craft revival of the 1960s and 1970s remains to be written, curators and critics have generally agreed with these contemporary observers that the growth in studio crafts during this time corresponds to a broad rejection on the part of the counterculture of the conventional and reproducible. This rejection led to a privileging of the unusual and idiosyncratic as well as the handmade—qualities increasingly at home at the Renaissance faire. "I think of things I want to see made" is the way a crafter at the Southern California Renaissance Pleasure Faire explains her creative process in 1972 (Roberts and Roberts).

This elevation of the quirky meant that American artists' "drive toward self-expression has eroded the idea that the craft object must always be functional," remarked *Newsweek* writer David L. Shirey with conviction in a 1969 article about the craft revival (62). Shirey's observation was validated by author-collector Lee Nordness in his important 1970 book *Objects USA*, in which he identified a difference between "production" crafters, those dedicated to creating utilitarian crafts using a certain mold or prototype, and "non-production" crafters, who sought to make unique crafts, suited to special situations but not following a recognizable mold. For the latter group, Nordness coined the term "object makers." Although the objects themselves flowed from a wide variety of aesthetic styles and artistic intentions, and although they might be useful as well as purely ornamental, the "non-production" crafts fashioned in the craft revival of the 1960s and 1970s formed an increasingly important part of the counterculture's expressive culture.

The craft revival of the 1960s and 1970s supported a holistic philosophy in which the production of art was a central, but not singular, aspect of a chosen lifestyle. Writing about the resurgence in woodworking during this time, critic Michael Stone remarks,

> Just as Arts and Crafts styles protested the mechanical mass production of Victorian ornament, so Crafts Revival styles of the 1960s and 1970s may be read as a high-minded reaction against the color and gloss of the then-fashionable Pop and High-Tech styles of decoration. But parallels between the two movements are not confined to aesthetic attitudes. The lives led by many Arts and Crafts workers were shaped by a desire to escape from the industrialized Victorian world, and many American craftsmen in the 1960s and early 1970s engaged in a similar search for "alternative lifestyles." (xi)

What Stone dubs a "search for 'alternative lifestyles'" appeared to be at the core of the way many new crafters self-identified as artists. Writing about the craft revival of the 1960s and 1970s in a 1972 article in the *Los*

Angeles Times, under the headline "Artisans Mold Lives into New Forms," newspaper staff writer Mary Barber fancifully spins a countercultural fairy tale:

> Once upon a time there was a handsome young editor in a major publishing firm who wanted to be living the good life and knew he wasn't.
>
> Now Dick Fitz-Gerald, bronzed and smiling, jeans-clad and long locks whipping in the breeze, knots rope into massive hangings and spends his time at Fiesta de Artes and the like.

Not surprisingly, Barber's portrait of lives changed by the craft revival includes a born-again crafter—a jewelry maker named Margaret Kartalia—who sells her creations in a booth at the Southern California Renaissance Pleasure Faire.

Observers from a variety of vantage points (and the benefit of hindsight) have tended to concur that the craft revival of the 1960s and 1970s was about changing lives as well as producing objects. Fine woodworkers Kevin Rodel and Jonathan Binzen comment, "Like the original Arts and Crafts movement, the American craft revival of the 1960s and 1970s was as much concerned with social philosophy and lifestyle as with aesthetics" (214). Art historian Marion Nelson explains that the revival "was a reaction against mass culture . . . because it removed the presence of the human hand from objects of everyday use and reduced the possibilities for self-expression even among members of the larger society" (37). Potter, lecturer, and collector Julie Hall notes, "The problems of postindustrial society have been met by craftsmen in many different ways. Aware of the runaway materialism of our culture, the artists . . . have committed themselves to a search for personal iconography that recaptures the elusive potency of spiritual energy in art" (154).

For many observers, the craft revival was not only about personal lifestyle: it was part of the wider cultural politics of those decades, in which music, theater, literature, and object making were harnessed as a medium for activism, and needs to be considered in the context of the civil rights movement and the subsequent "roots" movements of the 1970s as well as the movement against the war in Vietnam. This relationship to politics was not limited to narratives of content but rather related to the work of craft production itself. Writing about "folk" art in Minnesota, Marion Nelson writes, "By taking the production and distribution of everyday objects out of the hands of big business, one was no longer supporting its military interests" (37–38). Nelson adds that the craft fairs that were beginning to take place in the 1960s and 1970s "were permeated by a peace and civil rights movement atmosphere" (44n. 44). Of a group of San Francisco crafters working in a style dubbed "Funk," Julie Hall writes, "Funk was more than an art style: it was a social movement that heckled the sacred and ostracized the conventional" (104)—a turn of phrase that could easily characterize the Renaissance faire in the eyes of both its adherents and its detractors.

While the impulse for returning to crafting was located for many commentators in the politicized counterculture, the Pattersons expressed hope that the faire would continue to spread interest in crafting beyond bohemians—and that crafting would attract people to the faire who were not part of "the artsy intelligentsia." Both Pattersons told Roberts and Roberts that "folk arts are where you can communicate": "'Many of the craftsmen have long hair, but if you put them in a costume it's all right,' Phyllis says with a grin. 'Well, Robin Hood had long hair. I've seen little old ladies who if they saw the artist on the street they'd walk clear over to here to avoid him. But at the Faire they're in earnest conversation with the guy with long hair and a beard and they're not even noticing it.'" The notion of communicating through (and about) craft was clearly articulated by early observers of the faire. The greatest new opportunity being presented to visitors at the faire by crafters, writes Liza Williams in *FM & Fine Arts* magazine in 1965, was not that their goods were available for purchase but rather that fairegoers could have the opportunity to "speak to the craftsmen who are happy to explain their techniques and to know that you appreciate their efforts, even though you do not always buy" (7). Almost immediately, craft demonstrations became a faire staple.

Glassblowing in particular emerged early on as particularly well suited to on-site demonstration: the process is visually striking, immediately gratifying to watch, and dramatically outside the everyday experience of most spectators. Not surprisingly, then, as the craft revival and the Renaissance faire as a phenomenon spread across the country, hand-blown glass emerged as one of the faires' most characteristic craft offerings until not only did glassblowing characterize the faire, but the faire came popularly to characterize glassblowing. "Blowing glass is a true art form, usually found at a Renaissance faire," (over)claims Trent Hamm in a 2009 self-help book, *1001 Ways to Make Money If You Dare* (200). "You may have seen them at work in historical restoration sites or Renaissance fairs, blowing glass at the end of a long pole much like you'd blow a big bubble of gum from a pipe," assume Alecia T. Devantier and Carol Turkington in a similarly themed book, *Extraordinary Jobs for Creative People* (50). In addition to glassblowing's performative potential, there is a concrete historical reason that it also became closely associated with the Renaissance faire: the festivals came of age simultaneously with what came to be known as the studio glass movement.

Glassblowing was one of the first crafts to be thoroughly industrialized, and through the 1950s, glassblowing in the United States was a factory affair produced under the circumstances that Karl Marx would have called "alienated labor"—by teams working together and each performing a single task. The American Craft Council's Lake George Conference in 1959 raised the possibility of glass as medium for individual artists rather than factory teams. Artist Harvey Littleton was the central figure in the rise of art glass as he set out to wrest glassblowing from being a "cog in industrial machinery," as the first president of the American Federation of Labor, Samuel Gompers, put it in 1916 (qtd. in Littleton 17). Due to the efforts of Littleton and a few other key figures, in September 1962—less than a year before the first faire—the University of Wisconsin became the first school to introduce glassblowing into its graduate art curriculum. By 1971, over fifty American colleges, universities, and schools offered instruction in glasswork. Among the most influential of these were the programs at San Jose State University and the University of California, Berkeley.

A mutually constitutive relationship quickly grew between the new studio glass artists and the Renaissance festival, which perhaps is fitting given that during the Renaissance, glass pieces were made by individual artisans in the manner that Littleton and his colleagues hoped to revive. Since California was an early center of the studio glass movement, the faire was able to develop a close relationship with budding glassblowers in the 1960s and early 1970s.

The craft demonstrations, a novelty to audiences during the faire's earliest years, were even more trumpeted during the faire's "authenticity"

period and have lasted into the twenty-first century. At some faires, crafters willing to conduct demonstrations will have certain fees waived, and
"demonstration crafts" in a variety of media—not only glassblowing but
also blacksmithing, metalworking, candle making, weaving, wood carving, and leatherworking—are marked with signs so that patrons can seek
them out. Further, building on the success of the demonstrations, by 1970
the Southern California faire had hired a coordinator of crafts instruction and was proactively marketing the faire as a chance for visitors to
"dabble in ancient arts and crafts" themselves ("8th Annual"). "Participation crafts" joined "demonstration crafts," and faire visitors were offered
instruction in puppet making, molten-lead sculpture, Middle Eastern folk
arts, American Indian crafts including beading and sand art, and making
true-to-life face masks from castings.

Ironically, although the increased attention to crafting in the 1960s and
1970s for which the faire was an engine is commonly termed a "revival,"
crafting at the faire was never only about reviving the arts of bygone days.
The countercultural prizing of both the antimodern *and* the experimental
produced a set of values that allowed not only nonutilitarian craft objects
but some wholly new craft forms as well to be exhibited at the faire. A
fascinating example of this craft innovation is "hippie marbling," a form
of paper art developed by an artist named Don "Cove" Coviello, who
worked out the process in the back of his Volkswagen bus.

Coviello was born in Waterbury, Connecticut, in 1942. After graduating from the University of Connecticut, he lived in New York City. But
this got "too heavy," so he "bought a fifty-dollar ticket on Greyhound
and moved to San Francisco" (interview). There he lived for a while in
a commune on Haight Street, before moving to Berkeley with a friend.
The friend soon introduced Coviello to the Renaissance faire. He began
his association with the faire by creating candles and selling them there
(interview). But he soon switched his focus to marbled paper, which he
called "Fabrianos" ("Fabs," for short) after an Italian town known for
the production of artistic paper, and invented a character named "Count
Fabriano" for the purpose of vending them (Clark). A "perfect storm" of
interest in handcrafts and popularity of psychedelic design meant Coviello's creations were well received in the 1970s. The artist would float mul-
ticolored swirls of paint on the top of a fifty-gallon vat of water. Keep-

ing the paint constantly moving, he would then submerge large pieces of paper, measuring as much as forty square feet, in the water, and the wavy, colorful designs made by the floating paint would transfer to the paper, which he would then remove and hang dry. (A five-minute eight-millimeter film shot in 1972 shows Coviello demonstrating his technique.) The patterns resembled the marbled paper traditionally used in bookbinding, but whereas conventional marbling occurs in repeating, symmetrical patterns, Coviello's pieces are each unique in the combination of colors and the shape of the waves of paint. According to an article based on a 2005 interview with the artist, Coviello's career of hippie marbling peaked during the mid-1970s, when he was commissioned to make "large marbleized star maps for the first Star Trek conventions, and a 15′ by 30′ Fab that served as a background for a Grateful Dead and Jefferson Starship free rock concert in San Francisco's Golden Gate Park" (Clark).

Now in his sixties, Coviello states that he spent "many *wonderful* years" at the Pleasure Faire, working there through the 1970s. Eventually he became what he calls a "Fair-ever," meaning that he had participated for so long and with such dedication that even after he stopped working at the faire, he was always welcome to come in for free. Looking back at his experience as a crafter, he emphasizes how important the faire was in creating a market for crafts. "There was no ready market, no galleries for that kind of stuff," he says, echoing other crafters who also sold at the faires in the 1960s and 1970s. "But in addition to that, crafting at the faire encouraged artistic excellence, because of the high level of crafts" that other vendors were producing. For a while, Coviello lived with his wife, Maya Blue, on the faire site year-round. His involvement was multifaceted: he moved on from selling marbled paper and other crafts to running a food booth, and from there he crossed over to acting (interview).

Making a Faire Living

Conformity isn't always possible for these people. They're so different. They can't go to a gallery and try and sell. Where else are they going to go to make this happen?

—Ann Curtis, craftswoman

As the Renaissance faire spread across the United States, its craft "staples"—those reliably found at any of the faire's locations—became firmly established, and calls for crafters' booth applications began to enumerate which crafts would be considered. In 1979, Writer's Digest Books began producing in book form guides to the craft market; Renaissance faires around the country were included in the books, along with lists of desireable crafts. The Sterling Renaissance Festival in Sterling, New York, for instance, invited "batik; candlemaking; ceramics; decoupage; dollmaking; glass art; sculpture, soft sculpture; weaving; woodcrafting; block printing; scrimshaw; dried flowers; and musical instruments" (Lapin 562). As more faires were founded, the process was aided by the branching out of some artists' businesses to encompass more than one shop operating at a time (as opposed to moving from faire to faire as the season changes). An example is Ron Peckham, a jewelry maker out of Sugarloaf, New York, who operates a Renaissance faire business with his wife, Fa, called Moon Angel. The Peckhams have booths at three faires: one in Michigan, one in New York, and one in Maryland. These three faires have seasons that overlap, necessitating the hiring of a booth manager at one of the faires and giving a kind of miniature chain-store effect.

But if the staple crafts of the Renaissance faire became more and more codified as the faires spread, during the 1970s and 1980s a certain amount of variation also developed from faire to faire, some of it geographically determined. A number of the southern faires, for instance, including those in Georgia, Louisiana, and North Carolina, showcase spinning or weaving demonstrations. In addition, because apparel sells extraordinarily well, the number of booths selling clothing or footwear has mushroomed dramatically, so that wearable items have come to dominate other forms of crafts at all the major faires. And occasionally, the standard faire crafts are joined by more unusual offerings: body casting, found-object sculpture, kaleidoscopes, wind chimes, tapestry, wheat weaving.

Even during an era when craft fairs, classes, and shops (online or brick-and-mortar) have become ubiquitous, crafters still readily attest that Renaissance faires present them with unusually good business prospects. Leatherworker Pete Jelen declares,

For the crafters, for me, it's an absolutely wonderful opportunity to sell your items. Because, coming through the gate, you are guaranteed that people will have an interest in your product. It's a targeted audience. . . . Basically, you are getting about twenty-two thousand people a day in past your product. They are already a group that likes that kind of thing, culled out from the general populace. All you need is a percentage of that percent to make a fairly decent living. (Interview)

The trick, though, is to score a booth at the faire in the first place. Unlike at many current craft fairs, to which artists willing to pay the admission or "booth" fee are automatically admitted, the crafts at the Renaissance faire are both juried and regulated (so that one form cannot dominate) by a craft director. Jumping the admissions hurdles of a desirable faire can be difficult, but even after that is accomplished, the fees charged by the faire management, whether they constitute a percentage of sales, a booth fee, or a "frontage fee," can be high.

Ann Curtis creates true-to-life ceramic sculptures, with glazes and ornamentation, from plaster casts she makes of patrons at the faire, ranging from babies' bottoms and children's faces to lovers' clasped hands and full torsos. With decades of experience, she speaks of the faire's development from countercultural carnival to big business in terms of its meaning for artists' livelihoods. "It used to be a place where, if you were a poor, starving artist, you'd make some money," she says. "Now, in order to even do the shows, you've already got to be a successful artist" (interview).

In some states, the faire's transformation into corporate venture has resulted in a fair amount of tension over what is sold; mostly this takes the form of resentment on the part of crafters that certain faire owners allow too much "buy and sell," which is how crafters refer to the practice of importing goods that are not handmade. Derek Weaver, who with Ann Curtis runs Masquerade Lifecasting, admits, "Watching the steady flow of cheaply manufactured goods into our world saddens me" (4). Some faires, such as the one in Maryland, have the reputation for trying to hold the line against goods that are not handmade, albeit with certain exceptions (such as for souvenir T-shirts or performers' CDs or DVDs). At the Georgia Renaissance Festival, on the other hand, which features a relatively high level of "buy and sell," handblown art glass sits side by side with hanging ornaments in the shape of mooning witches and T-shirts emblazoned with slogans about vodka.

"I'm one of the diehards: I still make all my stuff," potter Stephen Bennett tells me with some bitterness in 2007 (interview). The handmade crafts are necessarily more expensive to buy, and the crafters know they sometimes lose out if there is cheaper merchandise available. More often, they feel that the hawking of mass-produced objects serves to devalue their art. I saw this in action on more than one occasion: in Maryland in 2007, for instance, two young men stood side by side drinking beer from mugs they had procured and comparing their purchases. One held a handmade item by Bennett, glazed in his characteristic rich blues and purples, the other, a mass-market affair emblazoned with a dragon and the words "Maryland Renaissance Festival." The man holding Bennett's mug was expressing jealousy because he had not bought the "official souvenir." This is not to say that the crafters advocate that sales at the faire be strictly limited to what would have been available during the Renaissance—"that would be boring," confesses mask maker Shane Odom (interview)—but among crafters there is a pronounced valuing of the handmade and the unique. What has changed, though, is that crafters not infrequently complain that faire owners no longer share this value with them.

The Rennie Tribe

> They walk into your booth. And they say, "Wow. You people are so creative." They're not just buying our art from us; they're buying a little slice of our lives.
> —Shane Odom, crafter

With the advent of the faire circuit, discussions of labor conditions for crafters (and performers, too) have always been complicated by the overlay of "workplace" and "home place" that the faire constitutes for them. In some quite literal ways, the booths are cottage industries, with crafters living in the same space where in some cases they produce and in all cases they sell. But they are cottage industries with bosses, whose interests sometimes coincide with those of the crafters and sometimes, by definition, cannot. "It's feudalism," states Pete Jelen with deliberate historical appropriateness. "If the owners don't like you, you're in trouble. They can throw you out. They don't have to justify it" (interview).

Many of the crafters have a profound emotional attachment to the faire as an institution, one that can sometime clash with or even override their financial interests. Most crafters will say that what is most important to them about their jobs is the powerful sense of community and the non-judgmental atmosphere that characterizes the workplace. A very particular, tight-knit culture exists among the faire's craftspeople, a culture that developed very early in the faire's countercultural history and has been nurtured since the 1960s by the closeness of communal or semicommunal living, shared experience, and mutual reliance, not to mention a sort of chosen "outsider" status. The craftspeople, especially those who travel the most, talk about themselves frequently as "a tribe" or "tribal unit."

On an everyday basis, the faire operates, if not quite as a commune, then as a kind of bohemian intentional community: Rennies eat together, share expertise and time on tasks, raise money for unexpected expenses, shop in town as necessary together, socialize (and sometimes hook up), swap artwork and skills, and in general spend their days and nights within feet of each other in campgrounds and booths. "A craft-based barter society" is how former Renaissance faire performer Avner Eisenberg sums up the lifestyle of those who live at the faire all week (interview). This group ethos makes the Rennies' otherwise marginal social life feel "safe," so that many identify a sense of safety as what attracts them to the Rennie lifestyle, challenges and even hardships of that lifestyle notwithstanding.

The Rennies' references to the faire as a place of safety has roots in the Vietnam era, when the word invoked not only the community support encountered inside the gates but also the ravages of violence encountered outside them. One longtime crafter who describes himself as drawn to that sense of safety over the course of four decades was John Schulps, who sold artisanal knives and pottery at the Southern California Renaissance Pleasure Faire until his death in 2010. Schulps landed at the faire as a crafter after a life packed with enough interesting chapters to fill its own book. He grew up on a cattle ranch, where he made his first knives at age nine. From the ranch, he headed off to college at UCLA to study architectural design. In 1964, Schulps was drafted by the Minnesota Vikings, for whom he played offensive tackle for three years. (He subsequently played two years for the New York Giants, too.) Inevitably, he was drafted once again, this time to serve in the Marines in Vietnam—returning, as he puts it, "scarred—a lot of vets came to [work at] the faire because it's a good place for the scarred" (interview).

According to Schulps, former Marines of his generation were considered to be very desirable as police officers, so when he came back, he joined the force, until a friend introduced him to the Renaissance faire in 1969. (Schulps also reported that because he was a former police officer, other cops frequently asked him to report on the goings-on at the faire.) Out of all of these occupations—rancher, student, athlete, soldier, cop—crafting at the faire is what "stuck," and Schulps, who was sixty-nine years old when I met him, had been selling his creations at the faire for more than forty years by that time. He also found time along the way to create fresco murals for the Disneyland Hotel and the Independence Bank in Encino. "I raised my kids in this," he informed me, gesturing expansively to include the whole faire (interview). Considering himself too old to travel much at the end of his life, he lived on a small ranch in Northern California and sold his pottery and knives only at Southern California's Renaissance Pleasure Faire and a small Renaissance faire run cooperatively by artisans (as well as at the Patterson family's other annual event, the Dickens Christmas Fair, founded in 1970 and still run by Kevin Patterson in the San Francisco Bay Area).

In addition to creating craft objects and vending them at the faire, Schulps taught art at local junior colleges and was an astute theorizer of the craft revival in which he was participating. In 1972, in a puff piece about the faire in a local newspaper, the *Van Nuys News*, Schulps compared the pottery being produced in California to that made in Europe. In the few words attributed to him in the article, Schulps rejects a purely nostalgic and retrograde attitude about the new interest in crafting, concluding that the work produced in the revival was "much freer and less tradition bound than European crafts" (Keating).

Schulps was an artist who, like many other Renaissance faire crafters, found the faire to be a rare environment that allowed him to contemplate making a living from the art he had been creating as long as he could remember. Steven Overstreet similarly affirms that the permanent establishment of the faire circuit meant "you could do what you love to do full-time" (interview). But for another group of artists, the appeal of the faire's atmosphere was what generated the desire to learn a craft in the first place.

Cora Hendershot, a wheat weaver, recalls going to her first faire in Southern California when she was seventeen years old. "I thought, 'I want to do this!'" she recalls about that first visit (interview). Thereafter, she apprenticed herself to a master artist in the historic art of wheat weaving, an ancient harvest-based practice that is found worldwide, although the designs vary from culture to culture. When the master artist retired, Hendershot took over his Renaissance-faire-based business plaiting and weaving straw into hats, fans, wall hangings, and wedding crowns. She has been "doing" the faire for decades, crisscrossing the country in step with the faire season and nurturing her craft in the off-season by attending such events as the international wheat weaver's conference.

The faire's environment has continued to attract artists from subsequent generations. A body painter named "James," still in his twenties, speaks of atmosphere as the primary factor in his decision to work at the faire. Although the world outside the faire gates is more materially comfortable, "James" finds it taxing. The faire is "a respite from the mundane," he tells me, using the term that both patrons and employees in the faire community use for ordinary clothing and activities from outside the gates. But more important, "James" emphasizes, is the extremely open-minded character of faire society. "If you are a misfit [outside], in here you're a hero. Whoever you are is accepted—we've had gutter punks, we've had cowboys," he remarks. (Mischievously he adds, "Also, I like to smoke a lot of pot, and here no one bothers me.") "James" has been working at the faire since he was in high school. Recently, though, he has reluctantly agreed to do less traveling at the request of his more settled family (interview).

Indeed, the opportunity to live where "no one bothers" you (or as more Rennies put it, "off the grid") and (to varying degrees) communally continues to draw Renaissance faire crafters as much as the desire to make a living off a handicraft. Reaching for words to capture this dynamic, costumer Steven Overstreet speaks in sort of Rennie chiasmus: whereas once the Renaissance faire was artists' "ticket into the craft," he maintains, soon enough for many, the craft became the "ticket into the lifestyle." Most crafters lovingly build their booths by hand, although fire codes and building codes have regulated this aspect of faire-site life considerably. In the faire's early days, though, Overstreet was able to follow his inspiration when he built onto his booth a little back room with a four-poster bed facing trees and a stream—and the animals he and his wife kept: peacocks, ducks, goats. "In time," Overstreet allows, "we [crafters] created a fabulous lifestyle" (interview)

As soon as the faire became a regular event in California, the "fabulous lifestyle" Overstreet recalls quickly became associated with wild parties that took place after hours—parties that were so legendary that a good number of faire employees were willing to work only so that they could remain on the grounds for the parties. Craftswoman Buffalo Larkin went to her first Renaissance faire in 1968, as a patron. "I thought it was glorious good fun," she reminiscences. "And it wasn't until about 1975 that I realized that the real fun was had after hours when the parties are happening. So I started my funny hat business at the faire—not to make a living, but so I could go to the big parties all the time" (Zekley, "Preston").

Most Rennies who were around during the years of those wild parties recall them with the sort of nostalgia reserved for something whose time has passed. Paper artist Coviello rhapsodizes, "Ah, the after-hours! That part was incredible. I will always remember that time. The whole thing was magic. It was like summer camp for hippies" (interview). Potter Bennett reminisces, "After doing the [Southern California] faire for five or ten years in the mid-1970s, I hadn't seen the campground. And then a woman took me back there—it was wild! He [mime Jack Albee] had a tree house, you had to climb a rope to get up there. That was his camp. It was funny. There was a lot of craziness, beyond most people's experiences" (interview). Overstreet recalls that the early Rennie night life revolved around music: singing along to someone's guitar or watching "X-rated versions of a lot of the shows" put on by the entertainers and illuminated by the headlights from someone's car for the "boothbound" who could never see the shows during faire hours. "And some of us had sex out there," he mused with genuine lyricism (interview). Derek Weaver is succinct about the attraction of the faire's camping lifestyle during this time: "It was all about fucking and drugs" is how he puts it—without a trace of sheepishness (interview).

These wild parties have calmed down, in no small part because of outside regulation from corporate owners or government bureaucracies—though one still hears about "clothing optional" parts of certain Rennie campsites or moonlit parties on site during the week. But Rennies still hold after-hours events for themselves, and in those events, bohemianism and countercultural mocking of "straight" culture are still in plain evidence. One such event is the Funky Formal, a dance in which crafters and performers wear fancy dress that is neither the sort of clothing to be found at a "mundane" black-tie event nor the Renaissance-oriented garb that, after all, forms a sort of work uniform for them. Another is the Erotic Food Contest, a sort of X-rated pot-luck in which judges award prizes for dishes that are decorated and shaped in a variety of semipornographic ways. The Monday after each faire weekend, crafters (along with a few performers and booth workers) hold a "Bizarre Bazaar," when they sell to each other—things they have made, garb they do not need, and assorted garage-sale-type offerings—at low prices.

Traces of the after-hours wildness remain, and the reputation for wildness certainly does, with the most devoted faire patrons still highly valuing the opportunity to stay on site after hours. But because so much attention has been focused on the parties, going back all the way to the accusations of "hippie happenings" at the California faires in the 1960s, some faire workers are skittish about any kind of outside attention to their after-hours lives. During my research process, two people—a hair braider and a craft-booth worker—decline altogether to talk to me about their experiences working at the faire because, they apologize, they feel too hurt by salacious coverage of their culture, mostly in local newspaper and magazine articles. One of the two seeks me out to explain her refusal and to express regret, because, she says, she really wants to help let young people know that the Renaissance faire is a way they can earn a living from their art—she is just afraid that the message will be twisted by titillation. The other will not talk to me at all because, some of her fellow Rennies explain, she is engaged in a messy divorce and custody process, and her ex-husband is trying to use the fact that she works at the faire against her in court.

Many of the crafters I spoke to connect the importance of their tight-knit Rennie culture to this sometimes-inhospitable attitude on the part of the surrounding culture. Bill Jezzard, who makes and sells hair jewelry along with his wife and crafting partner, Debbie Jezzard, says that the closeness of the crafters, and their markedly irreverent style, has managed to create "a little bohemian enclave" around the site of the Texas Renaissance Festival, which is held near Houston in an area where, Jezzard noted metonymically, a politically and socially conservative majority voted overwhelmingly Republican in the 2008 presidential election. At the Texas faire, a group of crafters writes and publishes its own newsletter under the organizational name Benevolent Order of Scurrilous Monks. "I'm Brother Get-the-Hell-Off-My-Lawn," Jezzard tells me, invoking a satirical meme that held presidential candidate John McCain to be a grumpy old man (interview).

Leatherworker Peter Jelen contends that those who make their living from the faire do, in fact, have "a different value system than most of America. Mainly, it's because art and ingenuity are respected more than money," he says. Jelen grew up in rural Ohio, where "if you don't have something or it breaks, and you're far enough out [from the city], you either have to fix it or invent it"—an approach he connects to his life as a self-taught crafter, making shoes, bags, and other whimsical, mostly wearable items. Jelen found his way to the faire after retiring from the Green Berets, where he says that he learned to consider *all* kinds of clothing to be "psy-ops."[2] At the faire, according to Jelen, "You can dress in velvet and tights as a guy, and nobody looks twice at you. If you did that on the street, well, you know, you'd probably get a couple second looks. They'd probably cast aspersions on your manhood" (interview).

Food as Craft

If you want to jump right into the full Renaissance spirit, then grab a giant roasted turkey leg with all the fixings, and wash it down with a fine English ale.
—*Explore: Your Complete Guide to Silicon Valley and Surrounding*

Victor Smith, sitting in his booth at the Maryland Renaissance Festival below a colorful hand-lettered sign advertising stuffed jalapeno peppers, introduces himself. "I'm a food crafter," he informs me; his striking turn of phrase is instructive not only about how he conceives of his own occupation but also about the role of food at the faires (interview). It is a phrase worth adopting: while certain fare, most notably turkey legs and ale, have become so associated with the faires that they operate as met-onym in both advertising and parody of it (see chapter 5), Smith and others who run food businesses at the festivals are continually creating new recipes for unusual comestibles that can be successfully produced in large quantities and consumed on site, sometimes at picnic tables but just as often while walking around.

Generally speaking, food sells briskly at the faire even when economic constraints hobble the profit turned by other attractions. In fact, according to Don Coviello, who ran a food booth for most of the 1970s at the North-ern California Renaissance Pleasure Faire, he could make so much money through food concession at the faire that it was "tempting not to report" all of his sales, since his contract provided that he pay the owners a share of his take (interview). Coviello's experience is not surprising: early newspaper coverage of the faire seems rather dazzled by the food offerings, enumer-ating the products for sale in stylized language; for instance, a 1969 article in the *San Mateo Times* gushed, "The 'fun and frolick' of the Pleasure Faire is further enhanced by the vendors of tasty tarts, fruit and meat pies, roast beef and fowl, fresh breads and gladdened by the purveyor of cheese and sweetmeats" ("Hie Ye Back"). Words and phrases in many articles about the faire during the 1960s seek to call the reader's attention to the distinc-tiveness of the faire's food offerings through renaming of familiar items, such as "sweetmeats" and "cow's milk."

For a significant number of faire visitors in all three of the faire's peri-ods—countercultural "happening," Living History production, and cor-porate pastime—food at the Renaissance faire has always gone beyond the purchase of treats as the fancy strikes; rather, it is the primary draw to the faire in the first place. Organizing the first faires, the Pattersons worked to make the food evocative and out of the ordinary, if not authen-tic to the period, and coverage of the faire, beginning with the original KPFK broadcast of the first one, spotlighted it. Kevin Patterson avers that faire food seemed so special because when the faire got its start in 1963, outdoor food purveyors had not figured out yet how to make more com-plicated offerings work:

Even the creators of Disneyland befriended my mother. And they'd come out, and she'd walk them around, and they would talk with her about her design philosophy. And they'd say things to her like, "Our staff tells us that we can't have any food at the park that isn't 100 percent consumable." Well, they do now. They figured it out. But the Renaissance faire was absolutely the groundbreaker for all of those. (Interview)

Kevin Patterson is correct that when the faire was conceived, food traditionally sold at outdoor events was long recognizable to attendees. Brett Witter and Lorelei Sharkey's semiserious *Carnival Undercover* (2003) offers a history of the standard fare of outdoor concession, ranging from popcorn and cotton candy to hot dogs and hamburgers; they even offer a "carnival food pyramid" to organize the familiar offerings into categories. Notably, giant turkey legs—the signature food offering of Renaissance festivals since 1968—soon found their way to food carts at Disneyland.

Actress Camryn Manheim, who spent four summers as a teenager working at the Southern California Renaissance Pleasure Faire in the 1970s, recalls that she belonged to a category of workers who were paid in food tickets—and that this was an attractive enough proposition. "That food was incredible!" she says. "Those big turkey legs—they were serious meals! People would walk around eating those with a thing of ale" (interview).

Under corporate ownership, despite the "mainstreaming" of some aspects of the faire, the food sold there has become, if anything, more sophisticated (although mobile carts and wandering vendors sell simpler treats such as pretzels and pickles). At the huge Texas Renaissance Festival, Victor Smith reveals, he texts over two hundred people (who have requested this service) with information about the menu he will be preparing the next day. "Over the course of that faire, I do over eighty different pastas," he tells me (interview). The run he is talking about lasts about eight weekends.

The Texas Renaissance Festival is decidedly large, and Smith is decidedly ambitious. But the elaborate menu he describes is not anomalous. (Nor is Smith the only food crafter at a given faire. His brother Vince, for instance, operates a German-food booth in Texas.) At the Bristol Renaissance Faire in Wisconsin, the following foods were among the offerings sold in 2010, along with the de rigueur turkey legs and beer: shepherd's pie, beef ribs, iced chai latte, roast beef sandwiches, fish and chips, bangers and mash (with an option of portabella bangers), vegetable tempura, ice cream crepes, gelato, artichokes, fresh baked goods, Cornish pasties, mushrooms in garlic sauce, and cheese fritters. As with the handicrafts, there is variation based on geography, with crabs being sold in Maryland and rice and beans being offered in Texas. All faires offer various edibles "on a stick"; the custom began with "steak on a stake" and a quest for foods that are convenient to eat while walking around and has moved into the realm of inside joke and challenge. Smith, for instance, sells macaroni and cheese on a stick.

Smith has been working at the faires for more than thirty years, raising his children as "faire brats." Much of this time, he traveled the circuit without a permanent home base. (His daughter, Brianna Smith, is quoted at length on this subject in chapter 1.) "I really like to cook," Smith says simply; but it is more than cooking that drew him to his "food-crafting" occupation. Like leatherworker Pete Jelen, Smith claims to take satisfaction from the way the faire's craft culture encourages him to turn his ingenuity to a whole host of tasks, making the sale of food an extremely holistic process for him, and he stresses that working at the faire allows him to avoid the alienation of performing only one task in the food-making process—much as glassblowers in the studio glass movement sought to reclaim glassblowing as the occupation of an individual artist, rather than a process performed by teams in factories. In addition to developing recipes or novel ideas for food presentation, Smith does his own food prep and his own cooking. But he also likes to do construction and has himself built and wired the buildings in which he cooks, vends, and sleeps at night. He repairs and maintains his own kitchen equipment. He enjoys teaching and considers that part of his job. He runs a full bakery at the faire and takes pride in his ability to decorate cakes (including wedding cakes, for which he likes to use edible flowers). He is also loud and therefore a good hawker. "I'm a generalist," he explains (interview).

In addition to being an early purveyor of gourmet food in outdoor settings, the faire also led the way in introducing certain beverages to American drinkers. The early Renaissance faire was significant as the first venue where English ale was widely visible in the United States. In 1963, when the first faire was held, the brewery business in the United States was in the middle of several decades of intense consolidation: there were fewer than 250 operational breweries then, and the energy in beer production was being put into the marketing of convenience or perhaps expedience: pop-top cans (first introduced in 1962), "lite" beer (first introduced in 1967). Imported beers were a truly minor presence during the whole decade.

The Renaissance faire entered the history of beer in the United State as an early location where dark beer, ale, and mead were sold and, for almost all visitors, tasted for the first time. (Exceptions would almost exclusively be those people who had traveled to Europe and tasted the beverages there.) To do this necessitated having the beer shipped directly from Sussex, England, to the faire, a fact that is singled out by much local newspaper coverage during the 1960s. According to these newspaper accounts, soda was not sold at all at the Southern or Northern Renaissance Pleasure Faires, but nonalcoholic drink was offered in the form of cider.

No matter what else has changed about the faire, beer has been given a lot of stage without interruption, with five to six varieties typically being offered and many faires hosting tastings. Of course, the types of beer introduced at the faire have become considerably more familiar. From the end of the 1970s and straight through the 1980s, home brewing grew in popularity as a hobby and eventually served as the engine of a microbrewery "boom"; by 2009, there were more breweries in the United States than in any other country, with "craft brewing" still rising.

Early introduction at the Renaissance faire has more recently powered a growing awareness of honey mead. Speaking of this spike of interest in the 2000s, Becky Starr, co-owner of Starrlight Mead in North Carolina, declares that the drink "isn't just for the Renaissance fair anymore" (Breed). Similarly, the "foodie" review website Chowhound uses the faire as a sort of standard for judging mead, praising one variety as being "a cut above the Renaissance faire" (Anderson). This is not to say that the Renaissance faire no longer plays an important role in introducing patrons to mead: many meaderies, including Starr's, maintain booths at Renaissance faires (a fact they use in their advertising). A fascinating historical evolution has occurred wherein certain faire patrons first tasted mead at the faire, imported from England, and were impressed by it. They were inspired to start producing mead in the United States. The fact that they can now sell their mead at the faire means that organizers no longer have to import it directly from England, which is how the mead makers tasted it in the first place. Thus, although it is true that mead is having a moment of prominence outside the faire (though it is too early to tell if this will be lasting or turn out to have been a brief novelty), the mead makers are still deeply connected to the faire's imaginative economy, and the drink, as Redstone Meadery in Colorado declares on its website, "generally evokes images of Chaucer, Beowulf and the friendly neighborhood Renaissance Fair" (Cioletti). Through food and drink, the faire's crafts have found their way into patron's refrigerators as well as their closets, moving by doing so from novelty to mainstream offering.

3

"Shakespeare, He's in the Alley"

Performing at the Faire

Such hi jinks appear almost nowhere else except at the Renaissance Faire.

—*Novato Daily Review*, September 21, 1971

Onstage at the Bristol Renaissance Faire in Kenosha, Wisconsin, juggler Rob Williams, a.k.a. One Flaming Idiot, gathers an audience to his stage by calling, "Come to see One Flaming Idiot, on this stage in five minutes! It's the best show you'll see at the faire . . . except for the Tortuga Twins . . . and the Swordsmen . . . and the Sturdy Beggars Mud Show . . . and Christophe the Insulter. . . . Odds are I'll only get ten or fifteen people, and then I'll only give it one-half of my attention. . . . You shouldn't come now! Don't come!"

Comic reverse psychology aside, by the time the show starts, Williams has gathered a sizeable crowd. Onstage, he slings knives and sarcastic cultural observations with equal dexterity. He cracks a whip to sever a cigarette held in an assistant's mouth. He juggles sharp objects while balanced on a board set atop a medicine ball. He makes a sandwich (bologna, bread, mustard) using only his bare feet before handing it to an audience member to eat, comparing himself to "our primate cousins" while loudly apologizing to "anyone from Kansas" for the comparison. Along the way he engages in near-constant self-ridicule, lampooning his own costume, relatively short stature, and willingness to engage in seemingly dangerous activities.

As Williams's performance builds to a fast-moving, politically and culturally topical, vaudevillian hilarity, he looks outward, to his audience, for comic inspiration. He forces one member of the audience to recite lines from Monty Python, and when the young man is able to do it, he calls "my nerdy friend" onstage for further participation-cum-teasing. He cajoles and coerces "volunteers" onstage, where he gets them to engage in his sometimes risqué, sometimes fear-inducing antics. (The more off-color lines are intended to fly neatly over the heads of any children in the audience.) Any passive audience members are scolded, as a sense of almost transgressive glee builds. One result is that audience members spend a fair amount of time looking around at each other, which, coupled with the improbable tricks Williams performs, creates an atmosphere of what might be described as collective, jovial mayhem.

Williams has been performing on the Renaissance faire circuit for his entire adult life. Watching him, it is clear that one of his goals precisely is this pushing at the audience, inching them outside their comfort zones, just as much as it is to continue refining what many faire performers consider the last bastion of vaudeville. In his vision, this approach to audience involvement separates the faire from more common corporate entertainments. "How many places let you dress up and play along?" he asks the audience rhetorically. "Not many! I went to Disney World dressed as Goofy—not welcome! They took me behind the castle and beat me like it was Gitmo."

Getting spectators to look in more than one direction is an organizing principle of Renaissance faire entertainment. The entire faire site is stage: wandering characters interact with visitors or play out scripted and improvisational dramas as they run through the faire. Patrons in garb— sometimes (often, really) as elaborate as what the cast wears—blur the boundary between audience and actor. Crafters in costume call to customers in faire language, in the early days learned from workshops or handbooks, and still present now, though in muted or at least evolved form. Musicians sit alongside the pathways and play period instruments—harp, hammered dulcimer, lute—and sing. And, of course, there

Fig. 3.1. The faire is organized so that the entire site operates as stage. Here, patrons in varying degrees of garb encounter cast members and other patrons as they stroll the faire's "street" at the Minnesota Renaissance Festival in 2009. (Photo by Amber Sunderbug)

are multiple actual outdoor stages of varying sizes, with benches (and sometimes hay bales) for the audience, though all the performances on these stages incorporate a large amount of audience participation.

In order to understand *how* faire performers do their work, then, one needs to picture *where* they are doing it. Of course, there is variation from faire to faire. The Texas Renaissance Festival is much larger than almost any others, and permanent faire sites look very different from temporary ones, where booths and buildings must be torn down and reerected each year. Further, the natural landscape makes a faire in California look different from a faire in Massachusetts.

But overall, the faires are impressive in their size, complexity, and organization. For instance, the site of the Bristol Renaissance Faire in Kenosha, Wisconsin, consists of thirty wooded acres crossed by dirt paths, and two ponds with walking bridges. The front gate is built as a castle, with balconies for performers who open the faire daily and greet visitors. There are more than ten stages with bench seating. In addition to these stages are other stationary performance sites: a mud pit, where the Sturdy Beggars Mud Show takes place; a maypole, where a dance and play occurs; a tavern, where musical acts perform—and also more off-color, adults-only acts such as the hugely popular Christophe the Insulter (whose act is pretty well summarized in his stage name); and a jousting field. Along the paths sit other entertainers: a harp player here, a story-teller there. Still other performers, known as "street characters," roam the site interacting with patrons and occasionally playing out more scripted dramas as they run from area to area. At scheduled times, a parade moves through the site, with all cast members participating, some on horses and some on foot, led by trumpets and banners.

The streets along which these characters—and faire visitors—move are lined with close to two hundred vendors, selling food (seventy-five different kinds), drink (alcoholic and nonalcoholic), and crafts. The booths are elaborate and whimsical, with "secret" nooks for gargoyles, turrets, stained glass, ivy on the walls, balconies, latticework and ginger-bread trim that suggests fairy tale cottages. For instance, one is shaped entirely like a ship, complete with mast, sails, and painted figureheads, while another is painted a rose color and surrounded by plantings of mul-ticolored flowers and has a second floor with round rooms, a shingled roof, and paned windows.

Some areas of the site are arranged with gorgeously ornate furniture, oriental rugs, and various ornamentation. Here, aspects of daily life that range from table setting to military exercises are enacted, and faire visi-tors and cast members may mingle. A chapel hosts weddings—more than one hundred since the faire's establishment (though not all of these wed-dings have been heterosexual or singular, and therefore "legal"). One area holds rides—all powered by human operators—and game booths, such as "Vegetable Justice," in which customers pelt soft tomatoes at a human target in response to—really, in exchange for—rapid and clever insults tailored to the pelter. (That particular game has a sign warning those who are easily offended to avoid playing, though occasionally customers still become genuinely irked at the insults.)

The faire sites, given this complexity and level of activity, are busy places. But busy as they are, the faires are not chaotic or confusing: on the contrary, they tend to demonstrate a remarkable visual continuity. According to Kevin Patterson, a great degree of planning goes into layout: figuring out where people will walk and what they will see from various vantage points. (Phyllis Patterson traces her own affinity for layout to her youthful days working in television.) Part of this is simply good crowd engineering—once the faire became as heavily attended as it did, large numbers of people needed to be directed safely and without too much bottlenecking.

The English use the term "immersion theater" or "promenade theater" to describe performances in which audience members are watching the drama unfold around them, rather than in front of them. In 2009, the English theater troupe Punchdrunk brought its form of immersion theater to the United States in a highly regarded tour of Shakespeare's *Macbeth*, in which audience members, themselves wearing masks, wandered on their own among multiple rooms and spaces, exploring the setting and watching actors in the order in which they encountered them. American critics have used the phrase "environmental theater" and "confrontation theater" to describe a theatrical performance that seeks to put all participants—actors and audience—on a stage (broadly construed). Examples of American theatrical companies known for this goal are the Living Theatre and the Bread and Puppet Theater.

The Living Theatre, generally considered to be America's oldest experimental theater group, was founded in 1947 as an alternative to commercial theater, and with fairly explicit goals of using drama as a medium for social commentary and social change; members created plays together and often lived together communally as well. Their best-known play was staged in the 1960s, as the faire was creating its own identity: *Paradise Now*, in which actors read aloud from a list of social taboos, breaking them as they went along. (Because one of these taboos was "nudity," and actors disrobed, the play led to arrests of cast members.)

Bread and Puppet Theater was founded contemporaneously with the faire, with initial performances dating to 1962–1963. Its members also often lived together communally, since 1970 in a farm in Glover, Vermont. Its enormous (ten to fifteen feet tall) puppets quickly became a fixture at antiwar demonstrations, and its series of "Cheap Art" manifestos express an ethos of bringing art directly to the people. For more than thirty years,

Bread and Puppet held an annual pageant and circus that were in many ways kindred in carnivalesque spirit to the Renaissance faire.

The earliest performances of the Renaissance Pleasure Faire in Los Angeles drew directly on the avant-garde theatrical tradition, recruiting performers from North Hollywood's Instant Theatre, an experimental acting company whose performers found the faire to be a congenial place for its interactive theatrical innovations. Instant Theatre was founded in 1955 by Rachel Rosenthal, who soon became a key figure in the Los Angeles women's and environmentalist movements and its developing art scene. Influential in the developing Southern California countercul-ture, this "underground" theater created "happenings"—improvisational, interactive gatherings that became iconic to representations of 1960s cul-ture—in which the element of chance was deliberately foregrounded. Rosenthal, after ten years as the artistic director of Instant Theatre, went on to form the Rachel Rosenthal company; that company's multiform performances (which incorporate video projection, spoken word, music and movement, and elaborate costumes, among other elements) seek to blur the boundaries between art theater and performance art, while using its performances to address social justice issues, much like the Living Theatre and Bread and Puppet.

The actors from Instant Theatre, including Rosenthal herself, whom Phyllis and Ron Patterson had met when they moved to Laurel Can-yon, were crucial to the conceptualization and development of the faire's improvisational street theater and its characteristic (and occasionally envelope-pushing) active involvement of audience. Performances at the early faires were striking in their deliberate reformulation of the mean-ing of theater—exploring the dynamic that theatrical innovator Richard Schechner invokes as the lessons of environmental theater: "what hap-pens to a performance when the usual agreements between performer and spectator are broken" (40).

Experimental theatrical pioneer Sam Blazer, in an early essay (1976) about the faire, emphasized this interactivity as a key to understanding the faire from a theatrical perspective. Blazer, who during the faire's early years was a member of several groundbreaking improvisational acting companies, writes, "The spectators are the component that gives the fair its *raison d'être*. They direct themselves as if they had been cast in a spectacle. . . . Interaction on such a massive scale cannot avoid being theatre" (37).

Among those who describe themselves as having been swept away by the early faire, the interactive nature of the performances is frequently what drew them in and separated the faire from other events they had experienced. However, there have always been those for whom the performers' deliberate shattering of the comfortable boundaries between audience and actor is upsetting. According to Schechner's study of environmental theater, this is par for the course. "Many people," he writes, "trained in the rigid reaction program of orthodox theater, are embarrassed by what they feel at environmental theater" (19). Schechner goes on to describe instances of audience members becoming "afraid and angry" at requests that they participate, and this is occasionally true at the Renaissance faire as well—especially given the boisterous nature of many of the performances. Such spectators sometimes turn their embarrassment back on the performers or on audience members who absorb themselves in the performance, as I will discuss shortly, by talking about how those active participants *should* be embarrassed.

Blazer insists that the faire must be considered as a total performative entity, cumulatively conceptualized and experienced; because it is impossible for a visitor to see all the events, he writes, "the events merge into a texture where richness is conveyed through sheer density and sensory overload rather than through direct experience; through the knowledge that so much is happening everywhere rather than through the effect of any particular occurrence" (36). From an anthropological perspective, Abner Cohen, in his book on urban cultural movements, similarly emphasizes the simultaneity of the faire's many performances—by artists and audience members alike—as key to understanding the meaning of what patrons see:

There was a great deal of eating, . . . and there was a great deal of ale drinking, of kissing, dancing, bawdiness, revelry and singing. Through all this the crowds moved from one type of activity to another, watching each other, playing, eating, resting, attending theatrical performances, strolling through the numerous kiosks, sampling handicrafts and watching craftsmen at work. Periodically through the day organised parades by bands of costumed men and women moved from one end of the town to the other. (140)[1]

This upending of the rules and the solemnity of the "official" is the way the carnival is theorized by Mikhail Bakhtin, which, not incidentally, he does through an exploration of Renaissance-era folk carnivals. Indeed, apropos of the debates on authenticity, it may well be by aiming to achieve a "temporary suspension of all hierarchic distinctions and barriers among men and of the prohibitions of usual life" (15) that the Renaissance faire initially achieved and still retains the most authenticity and energy.

Most important: there is no place or no one who is really off-stage. The early California faires, in fact, took "All the faire's a stage" as their slogan. For many people, this is deeply gratifying, because unlike theater, which Schechner says works to highlight hierarchy, the faire seeks to upend it. Schechner lays out the limitations and agendas of traditional, bounded stages:

> Have you ever thought how *stupid* the proscenium theater is architecturally?—most places disadvantageous to see or hear, first few rows you get shouted at and spit on, some seats "claustrophobic and acoustically murder"—others too far away. But this is no surprise. The proscenium theater was originally designed to emphasize differences in class and wealth. It was meant to have very good seats, medium seats, poor seats, and very bad seats. (31)

This interactive conceptualization of theater is what actors at the faire still love most about it. Paul Hudert, who performs on the Renaissance festival circuit as Paolo Garbanzo the Gypsy Juggler, speaks of that relationship with the audience as key: "[I love] the interaction and the anything-can-kind-of-happen live theater, you know. . . . And the people at the faire are ready for that. Even at an art festival like Arts in the Park or something like that, it's a big art festival but people aren't necessarily ready for oddball humor and the kind of thing [that takes place at the faire]" (interview). For some people, though, this is literally unbearable and accounts for the occasional snapping at performers by spectators

they have approached too directly; almost all performers have a few stories like that, though they have many more about artistic successes they
feel they have accomplished through these direct interactions.

The faire further destabilizes the category of "actor" through its craft
demonstrations, which turn the costumed crafters into performers.
Woodworker Don Weber describes how he was hired to perform the role
of a Renaissance-era woodcarver at the California faire in 1979. Although
the job put him in touch with others interested in handcrafts and allowed
him to explore his interest in working with ancient tools, he was technically hired as a performer (Birchard).

Even crafters who do not make their wares in front of an audience
are, in some consequential ways, performers as well as artists. Crafters
and their booth workers are required to be in garb, for instance, though
the degree of elaboration and historical authenticity varies from faire to
faire and crafter to crafter. They address patrons (at least initially) in some
variation of "faire talk" and hawk their goods in creative ways, from the
young Californian's deliberately silly distillation, "We have shiny things!"
to the Maryland body caster's invitation, "It's a fine day to get plastered!"
Management finds ways to encourage crafters to present their booths as a
kind of performance space, if not an outright stage, by offering incentives
that encompass both rewards (the Maryland faire owners offered a thou-
sand-dollar prize in 2010 for the crafter with the most "authentic" booth)
to sanctions (the same management chastised booth owners who hung
colorful Tibetan prayer flags above their booth in 2009).

As the faire's ideal of turning the whole site into a performance area
was being newly established, organizers had to recruit acts for both
onstage and off. For the first few years of the faire, the Pattersons saw their
major task as recruiting talent that matched up with the types of entertainers who might have been found at an English country faire. A juggler was located whose previous performance opportunity was children's
birthday parties, and a vocalist named Donna Burrow was signed on to
sing English, Irish, and Scottish folk ballads. These acts, all of which were
greeted by audiences with pleasure that is audible on KPFK's broadcast
on the first faire's opening day, reflected the early faires' mix of scholasti-
cism and nascent hippiedom. Onstage, for instance, a baroque ensemble
from the Immaculate Heart College performed, while an actress named

Sandra Lee Gross roamed the faire urging visitors to buy a "skeleton key for chastity belts" with the slogan, "For bad knights and good nights" ("Fairest of the Faire").

These performances quickly began to establish the Renaissance festival as a prominent manifestation of hip, as the performers brought countercultural cachet into the faire and then carried new artistic discoveries and interests back out. "All the poets, artists, and musicians of the underground of that period surfaced in the Faire!" recalls Rachel Rosenthal, adding, "And I, as the Queen, 'galloped' with a toy cardboard horse around my waist, and my feet in the mud! My husband, King Moody (his real name!), was Essex!" (email). Singer/keyboardist/songwriter Robb Royer agrees: "It [the Southern California faire] was part of the whole new hippie thing," he says (interview). Royer attended the early faires in Los Angeles before "stealing the name"—with its of-the-moment cultural capital—for his first musical act, the Pleasure Fair, a "sunshine pop" quartet consisting of Royer, vocalist Michelle Cochrane, bassist Tim Hallinan, and guitarist/arranger Stephen Cohn.[2]

The career of the pioneering comedy troupe Firesign Theatre models the way performers carried countercultural aspirations and affiliations into the faire and then turned around and carried new cultural energies and priorities back out. Its four members—Phil Austin, Peter Bergman, David Ossman, and Phil Proctor—met doing live radio broadcasts for KPFK/Pacifica. Through the station, the group's members first became involved with the shaping of the faire as individuals: variously conceiving it, publicizing it, and joining its cast. Shortly thereafter, they were able, as a troupe, to move comfortably from their first-ever performance at the University of California's Experimental Arts Festival (at UCLA's Student Union) to performing at the Renaissance Pleasure Faire a year later, bringing their avant-garde approach to comedy back to the faire in a show called "The Sword and the Stoned." Furthermore, after experiencing the faire's "density" and "sensory overload," as Sam Blazer puts it (quoted earlier), the Firesign Theatre developed its trademark layered recorded albums, on which background noises constitute their own narratives alongside the "foregrounded" ones, running gags create a texture reminiscent of the faire's, and deeply meaningful frivolity, irreverence, and upended hierarchy reign supreme.

The Firesign Theatre's stream-of-consciousness, drug-oriented comedic style turned out to be groundbreaking—even prophetic, in the opinion of cultural critic Greil Marcus (175). Certainly, it formed a sort of soundtrack to the "stoner" 1970s. Early Renaissance festival acts such as these pushed the performing arts along and, in many cases, succeeded in shaping the mainstream (as avant-garde culture often does) so emphatically that the countercultural roots have become deeply obscured. The faire's driving influence on the arts is nowhere more profound than in the arena of vernacular music.

Music and Dance at the Faire

[The faire] was the forefront of the ethnic and folk-music scene in both Northern and Southern California—same as with the Folk-dance and exotic ethnic dance scene of those days. It was an unparalleled event.
—Bob Thomas, bagpiper

Describing the musical acts at the California faires in the 1960s and 1970s is a bit like trying to describe a sweater by pulling on one loose thread. The point is the way they are all woven together, and teasing out one strand, even for the sake of clarity, not only misses the big picture; it risks destroying it. Partly this is because, as Richie Unterberger has insisted, bands that came to be known as "psychedelic," as did certain of the important early faire groups, are characterized above all by their insistent eclecticism (79). Musical acts from the 1960s and 1970s faires passed around styles, songs, riffs, instruments, instruction, gigs, and personnel so avidly that their edges blur, and even if one wanted to separate them out from one another, at times it is impossible to do so. Sometimes, as I will discuss shortly, musicians not only played together but also lived together, forming households that overlapped but did not entirely replicate bands—though composition of both households and bands often changed.

Occasionally, too, the difficulty in sorting out early faire musical acts is the product of a very practical dimension to the bands' shifting boundaries: periodically, reveals musician Ernie Fischbach, a band would get fired from the Renaissance Pleasure Faire. This might happen in pursuit of greater authenticity or as a money-saving strategy or following a work-place conflict. "We'd come back under a different name, playing a different kind of music," he laughs (interview).

As Unterberger wryly observes, the name chosen for the influential psychedelic band Kaleidoscope—one of whose members, Solomon Feldthouse, performed at the faire and lived in various arrangements with others who did—provides a visual model for the way the band and others of its cohort operated: though patterns are visible, the picture keeps changing because all manner of shapes (in the case of the music, traditions), along with a healthy measure of drug-influenced psychedelia, are captured and fused. For the present purpose, I would add that the name "Kaleidoscope" also provides a visual model for the early Renaissance faire's musical activity: the faire pulled in, and showcased, a host of different existing musical forms, then refracting them, combining and recombining them, and sending them back out as a new kind of art.

In short, it is not only difficult but inherently inadequate to craft the Renaissance faire's musical story in a linear fashion. Yet while some authors have managed to resist the linear—such as William S. Burroughs during his "cut-up" period—in the tracing of history, even cultural history, there remains something to be said for linear narrative. This section, then, attempts to identify, and discuss, several important "clusters" of musical activity at the faire during its first decade, as well as introducing the early faire's central musical figures.

Creating the Faire's Soundtrack

The Pattersons' earliest searches for performers yielded, almost by chance, a figure who was by all accounts to become central to the faire's musical identity: a young advertising artist named Robert Thomas. Thomas was born in 1939 in Hollywood; his father was a Welsh immigrant and teamster, while his mother, a native of Los Angeles, had taught in a one-room schoolhouse. Interested from his youth in both music and visual art, Thomas moved after high school to Washington, DC, where—already an accomplished performer on string bass and tuba and experienced in instrument repair—he attended the Navy School of Music, Georgetown University, and the Corcoran Gallery School. He then returned to California to attend UCLA and the Art Center School. On top of all these institutional affiliations, he was known as a driven *self-educator* and inventor. Musicians and others involved with performing at the faire during its first decade are emphatic, and seemingly unanimous, about Thomas's shaping influence on the Pleasure Faire—and in turn, on the hugely important developments in popular music that radiated outward from his artistic innovations there.

Thomas died relatively young—at fifty-five years old, in 1993. But he left an indelible mark first through visual arts as well as music, having designed the skull-and-lighting logo and two album covers for the Grateful Dead. According to Owsley Stanley, Grateful Dead sound engineer and good friend of Thomas's—who himself gave up ballet dancing in favor of countercultural pursuits—Thomas also create a new method of psychedelic painting that was the visual equivalent of the Dead's music:

> The swirls of color Bob used . . . have this almost sinuous look to them. Bits of color here and there. Swirls of red, blue, black and gold. When you look at it, you think: This is strange, it seems sort of messy . . . but if you take acid and look at the painting again you see all these highly complex patterns melt into each other. Magnificent shit. He had painted all the visual clues that you needed for that particular pattern set. All these odd looking smears and swirls were all meaningful. It was a composition in itself. All you had to do was take some psychedelics, and when you gazed at the painting, you would always see the same patterns. With any other normal painting you might experience while on acid, the patterns would vary. You would see certain patterns one time, next time you took acid, it wouldn't be the same patterns. But Bob knew how to "fix" the patterns so your mind would create the same visual patterns each and every time, as part of the painting's artistic statement.

Because Thomas's talents went in multiple directions, many of his friends and acquaintances at the faire jokingly refer to him as a "Renaissance man."

Thomas first learned of the faire from Ron Patterson, a fellow graphic designer, when they were both working in advertising agencies in Los Angeles (Brown). Patterson described to Thomas the fund-raiser for

KPFK/Pacifica Radio that he was involved in organizing and promoting; as Thomas was already a lute player, Patterson invited him to perform at the faire. Years later, in a 1979 interview in the Rennie publication *Buck and Mug*, Thomas says that he had readily agreed to take part in the faire because "it had been many years in Los Angeles since there had been any kind of gathering place for the artistic community, and this [the Renaissance Pleasure Faire] was the first emergence after the suppression of the coffee houses and the eviction of the beatniks" (Brown).[3] Explains Thomas's old friend and bandmate, fiddler Will Spires,

> In L.A. in 1960, 1961, there was a thriving coffeehouse scene. There were jazz coffeehouses, and poetry coffeehouses, and baroque coffeehouses, and chess coffeehouses. In 1962, the LAPD did everything they could to shut them down. The city told the cops, "You're doing this wrong. Get the Health Department [to shut them down] instead of saying, 'there's dope there,' or 'they're all Beatniks there.'" Afterward, the only place you could gather with people of your own stripe was at the midnight movies on Melrose Avenue near Sunset. And then ... there was the faire! (Interview)

Spires, who was born in 1944 in San Diego, first met Thomas when Spires was fifteen and in the process of "dropping out of high school into that coffeehouse scene." Spires adds that when Thomas first told him about the faire, he promised, "You'll love it. You'll see everyone you know!" (interview). Spires's recollection sketches the continuity between the activity of earlier cultural radicals (i.e., the beatnik coffeehouse scene) and the innovations of the faire's cultural workers.

At this time, no one had much more than a glimmer of suspicion that the faires would become a permanent event, let alone turn first into an important countercultural institution and ultimately into a multimillion-dollar corporate venture: because the first four faires were benefits for Pacifica, all labor was volunteer. "Bob was the first official music of the faire; Phyllis [Patterson] got him to play for free. Later he struck, in the first labor action of the faire," jokes Mickie Zekley, himself a leading Celtic musician out of the early faires who at times played in bands with, and lived in communal situations with, Thomas (interview). Spires relates, of his own first time performing at the 1964 faire with Thomas, "We passed the hat, and people threw money in it. We gave a lot to KPFK, and we kept some because we were broker than rats" (interview).

For Thomas and Spires, the faire's first few years constituted a time of immense creative ferment. Thomas and Spires lived together in Altadena, and every evening, they would take down some fifteen or twenty of the musical instruments that lined their walls and play "everything from medieval dance tunes to jugband music for several hours" (Spires 2). Owsley Stanley brought members of the Grateful Dead to join in, and Thomas began a long collaboration with them. During the faire's season, says Spires, "We'd drive to Agoura, down the freeway through miles and miles of Squareville—and then you'd start seeing folks in colorful costume" (interview).

In short order, Thomas became, in Kevin Patterson's words, "the flashpoint for all of these young people interested in experimenting with learning about the music of different cultures" and, before long, even beginning to think they could earn some money through it (interview). Ultimately, this position as "flashpoint" evolved into what Spires called an influence "as far reaching and long lasting as that of any single traditional musician active in California in the last half of the twentieth century" (Spires 1). Through Thomas and others, the faire exposed a couple of hundred thousand people each year to new instruments, rhythms, and styles, functioning as a kind of seasonal precursor to what came to be marketed as "world music." Bagpiper Alan Keith, who first attended the faire in 1969 in Southern California and thereafter performed at both California faires for eighteen years, describes the excitement of the faire's musical bounty, recalling that there one could hear

> all kinds of strange stuff that one did not hear or see on commercial radio or T.V. (and mostly still can't). There likely existed recordings of some of the stuff we heard there, but we didn't know about them, or where to get some. There was all kinds of European folk music, English madrigals, North African belly dance, Balkan [music], Gypsy music, ritual Tibetan horns and percussion . . . you name it. (Email)

Celtic musician Mickie Zekley similarly describes the faire (and Bob Thomas) as having broadened his musical horizons in its first years.

Zekley, who plays and teaches Celtic pipes and flutes as well as running a music camp, Lark in the Morning, was also introduced to the faire by Thomas and first attended it during its second year, in 1964. Zekley recalls first hearing about the faire when he was seventeen years old and being interested in honing a guitar act with his friend John. "I was banjo shopping in Pasadena, and I saw [Bob Thomas's] art gallery," he says (interview). The gallery, called the Catacombs, was an underground space that Thomas sublet to craftspeople and artists as well as hosting musical performance, poetry readings, and "all that the underground Sixties had to offer" (Spires 13). The day Zekley wandered in, there was a liquid light show on display in the gallery, which, he says, grabbed his attention because he had not seen anything like it before (interview). Indeed, while these light shows were to become popular and even characteristic of the late 1960s and early 1970s, 1964 was very early for someone to be hosting one.

Even more striking than the light show to the budding musician's eye was Thomas's large collection of unusual instruments, including lutes—which he had played at the first faire—and various pipes. When Zekley asked about the instruments, Thomas "spoke of the Renaissance Faire," Zekley says. "And my friend John and I—we just showed up to play. We didn't know much about costumes" (interview). The first few faires were freeform enough that Zekley and his friend could just pick a spot and busk without needed to audition, be hired, or even ask permission—a state of affairs to which Phyllis Patterson makes amused reference during the KPFK broadcast of the initial faire, commenting that she had performers she had only just met that day. Zekley eventually played at the faire in a more officially sanctioned capacity, with Thomas's most influential band, the Golden Toad, formed in 1965.

After Thomas's first, somewhat-by-chance, faire gig as a solo lutenist, he turned his attention to putting together musical ensembles to provide to the faire music that was not period specific in a narrowly focused way but rather suited the faire's social location and cultural goals. (I will discuss the faire's period-specific music—known as "early music"—shortly.) In the faire's second year, Thomas returned to perform with a small ensemble called Pro Arte Submarine Band; the core of the band was Thomas, his wife Julia, and Will Spires. According to Spires, they would show up with as many as thirty instruments to play, though Thomas focused on Portuguese bagpipes, Julia generally played drums, and Spires mostly played fiddle (having just been gifted with the instrument by his friend Charles Perry, who went on to become *Rolling Stone* magazine's first copy chief and the Haight-Ashbury neighborhood's historian). Thomas's explanation of the name was that "pro arte" referred to their motivation for playing the faire, and "submarine band" referred to a kind of jug-band blues (Brown). Spires—currently a folklorist—describes the band as "Dionysian with an Apollonian side" (interview).

Although Thomas was able to play many instruments, he developed a particular expertise on (and collection of) various kinds of bagpipes from around the world. Ultimately his knowledge base became so wide and deep that Kevin Patterson jokes that Thomas practically made his own pipes by killing the goat himself (interview). In fact, Thomas did invent ways to construct pipes himself, telling friends that he acquired the necessary lathe skills during a relatively short stint in jail following a drug bust that ended with his arrest in 1967, along with his friend Owsley Stanley, dubbed the "Acid King" by novelist Tom Wolfe for manufacturing the exceptionally pure LSD used in Ken Kesey and the Merry Prankster's "acid tests."

According to William Gilkerson, who was associated with the Golden Toad for several years, this expertise on the lathe had completely fascinating international ramifications. Gilkerson came across the Toad at the first Northern California faire; at the time, Gilkerson was working as an entertainment editor and columnist for the *San Francisco Chronicle*. In his accounting, he fell immediately in love with the Golden Toad's music: "Balkan music, North African, Indonesia, Tibetan, baroque and folk-medieval. . . . The music was exquisite, mind-blowing." Thomas began to teach Gilkerson to play the Spanish bagpipes, and Gilkerson "spent a year or two with them, learning how to play the bloody instrument": "They didn't have a rap man, so I performed those services for them. . . . I could supply the missing element of a voice with a poetically phrased explanation for all the wonders that the audience was hearing" (interview).

Gilkerson planned a trip to Europe while Thomas was incarcerated and, at Thomas's request, brought back drawings and measurements for the construction of the Swedish bagpipes, which Gilkerson says were newly "extinct" at that time, the last traditional player having died in 1949. He passed the drawings to Thomas, who was able to figure out how to make the pipes in the jail's woodshop. The pipes he made were then carried to the Swedish museum by instrument dealer Tony Bingham and promptly copied by other instrument makers (and popularized in particular by instrument maker Leif Eriksson, who began making them in the 1980s). In this way, says Gilkerson, "Sweden got its pipes back"—courtesy, one could argue, of the acid tests and the Renaissan faire (interview).

Nearly twenty years after Thomas's death, his level of influence as a piper is still plain from the way that other pipers in the United States and beyond—among them Alan Keith, James MacDonald Reid, and Oliver Seeler—name him as inspiration and mentor. Keith is not unique in how he credits Thomas: "Bob was instrumental in opening my eyes to the possibility of acquiring and learning to play other kinds of folk instruments, especially the many bagpipes of Europe. Because of his knowledge and talent as a musical historian/folklorist/performer, he literally became my primary mentor and an inspiration to many others" (email).

Psychedelic Folk: The Golden Toad and A Cid Symphony

The faire's discovery of sounds and instruments from many cultural traditions and geographic locations—the "strange stuff" Keith remembers hearing at the faire—was coupled by some of the faire's musicians with other sensory experiments of the 1960s (including but certainly not limited to LSD), feeding into the emergence of a new kind of music that came to be known, though not consistently, as "psychedelic folk" or "acid folk" (or sometimes "ethnic-psych" or "ethno-acid folk").[4] These musical explorations corresponded with attempts in other art forms—literature, painting, fashion—to model or encourage a sort of motivated rearrangement of sensory input as a way to achieve a new consciousness—or perhaps more important, freedom from an old one. But it was music that "brought psychedelic thought into the mainstream," as Jim DeRogatis points out in *Turn on Your Mind: Four Decades of Great Psychedelic Rock* (2), sowing a wide awareness in the second half of the 1960s. LSD was first specifically mentioned in a recorded song as early as 1960, by early rock musicians the Gamblers, in the title of their surf instrumental "LSD

25." It was trippy folk music, though, that first used the word *psychedelic* in a lyric: the Holy Modal Rounders' "Hesitation Blues," in 1964. Nick Bromell writes that psychedelic drugs and music were coupled so tightly in the countercultural imagination and experience because both offered a way "outta this place," as the Animals sang in 1965; the constructed otherworldliness of the faire, which for at least some participants involved both of these, could be said to offer the same thing: "The closely related phenomenologies of music and psychedelics help explain, I think, why millions of young people in the '60s turned to those experiences as a way to work through and beyond their conditions" (73).

The genre (or subgenre) of music that I hereafter refer to as *psychedelic folk* never really settled into a name, perhaps because it has received scant critical attention; according to some historians, this is because certain of the more well-known bands who may have started out closer to this aesthetic, such as the Grateful Dead, the Byrds, or even Bob Dylan—all of whom attended the Pleasure Faire in California at least sometimes—electrified, and their new format quickly overshadowed the folk roots. But a special combination of historicism, global reach, and contemplative instrumentation did become associated with the faire, as evidenced by David Browne's delightful description, in his book *Dream Brother: The Lives and Music of Jeff and Tim Buckley*, of a song of Tim Buckley's as "pure psychedelic Renaissance fair" (85). In a nod to this association, Sean Axmaker of *The Scarecrow Video Movie Guide* calls the LSD scene in Roger Corman's 1967 Peter Fonda vehicle *The Trip* "part psychedelic Renaissance fair" (58), and an online auction specializing in "psychedelic pop culture" such as posters, reading material, and musical recordings calls itself, simply, Renaissance Fair.

The instrumentation of psychedelic folk was generally acoustic, as music *always* was at the faire, with an emphasis on improvisation or jamming, atmosphere, open tunings, and world instruments. Of particular importance was the presence of drone instruments, such as the Tibetan horns that Keith mentions or the various kinds of bagpipes that Thomas and other musicians brought to the faire. On the drone's special function in psych-folk, Peter Bebergal writes, "The almost inverted notion of transcendence, a kind of thick and muddy immanence, is what many psych-folk musicians have found in using the drone" (1). Gregory Weeks, a contemporary musician who sees himself as building on the psych-folk of the 1960s, limns the drone's importance for both musicians and listeners of psych-folk:

> The drone is absolutely the fastest way to induce the drug phenomena or mindset within a straight listener or audience. It's also a very introspective experience, for player and audience alike if done well. Drones are so simple, one would imagine they'd grow incredibly stale after several minutes, but instead they increase in interest and intensity in many cases. That's because listening to a drone is like watching a fire take hold. Invisible frequencies manifest in the ear much like an elusive green flame appears amidst the oranges and yellows. A fire never gets old, there's something primal and pri-mordial about its engagement. Droning sonics are similarly primal in their appeal. They evoke strong responses, both emotional and physical, within the listener and player alike. (Qtd. in Bebergal 3)

Certain of the faire's musicians were able to be remarkably influential in conveying both intent and strategy for creating a musically generated altered consciousness (whether spiritual, political, or social depended largely on the listener). This is because many of them productively inhab-ited the border between the avant-garde and the popular in hippie music. If the faire, as the Firesign Theatre's David Ossman contends (see chap-ter 1), prepared people for the counterculture's visually striking sartorial turns, then two of the faire's earliest ensembles, Bob Thomas's Golden Toad and Ernie Fischbach's A Cid Symphony, drew from the well of the folk to prepare their ears for new cultural frameworks.

The Golden Toad had a huge impact on the revival of American interest in traditional "ethnic" music, taking the faire's styles and perfor-mances and projecting them outward. The Toad formed to play at the faire. No one quite remembers how the name was chosen, though there is general agreement that being high was part of the process. But in addi-tion to presenting dozens of instruments and song traditions at the faire to hundreds of thousands of listeners who had never heard them before, the Golden Toad was a fixture on the San Francisco streets, becoming, Zekley contends, "the first real buskers in San Francisco in its modern incarnation" (interview). Furthermore, as I will discuss shortly, the band

Fig. 3.2 Members of the faire's first ensemble, the Golden Toad, busk on a San Francisco street corner in 1969. From left to right are Will Spires, Deborah Fischbach, Bob Thomas, and Ernie Fischbach. (Photo: Robert Altman; courtesy Institute for Traditional Studies)

played a number of significant countercultural venues and institutions. Finally, members of the Toad carried some of what they had done in that band to other contexts in subsequent projects.

"A lot of people, they came to us, and we addicted them to all kinds of music," comments Ernie Fischbach of performing at the faire with the Toad. "They came to the faire, and they'd never heard it. Bob Thomas would give them a little history lesson with it [the music]," he adds. "He would say, 'This is from Afghanistan,' or wherever." In Fischbach's eyes, this was "the most important thing about the faire: anyone who came got to see a different world, maybe opened their eyes to the fact that there were these other countries" (interview). Zekley believes that Thomas's efforts with the Golden Toad are the reason "ethnic music became popular" in the 1960s (interview). The band's motto—both serious and joking—was, writes Zekley in a reminiscence, "We perform the music of your ancestors no matter where they were from" ("Adventures").

But although the band members were serious historians of the music—"the faire made us into music scholars," notes Fischbach—the band was not curatorial in its approach (or not only). "We took liberties," says Fischbach. "Music is amorphous. It grows. A Gypsy hears Mahler and makes a tune out of it. All musicians have a tendency to do that," Fischbach continues, cleverly reversing the familiar paradigm (and attendant power hierarchy) in which Mahler used folk tunes as raw materials for his supposedly more sophisticated compositions (interview). Spires, attempting to sum up this dynamic of constant multidirectional borrowing, maintains that the best description of the Golden Toad's music is "audacious" (interview).

The Golden Toad came into its own as a morphing, swelling San Francisco countercultural institution, known as an acoustic sister band to the Grateful Dead. It began, however, as a four-person, Los Angeles–based band: besides Thomas and Spires (who played fiddle), it included accordionist Jehan Paul and bass drummer Don Brown. Brown found his way to the faire after a youthful tragedy stemming from an arrest in his late teens after police found joints in his car. For what would now be considered a minor offense (and in some states not a criminal one), Brown was jailed in Los Angeles, where he was brutalized. The experience left him traumatized and addicted, but, recalls Spires, "he settled into the faire and did very well there. . . . He worked through all that." Soon, Brown founded a Turkish coffeehouse that Spires considers to have been "the beating heart of the faire, the crossroads for all faire subcultures" (interview). For decades, until Brown's death in 2009, the coffeehouse was the hub of after-hours socializing and performance.

Soon after the band formed, though, Thomas's Los Angeles gallery began to attract the attention of law enforcement agencies, and rumor of a planned bust reached him. Rather than despair, he seized on this as an opportunity, since his marriage had ended and he was, according to Spires, truly "weary of job-shop ad work" (interview). At the invitation of Thomas's close friend Owsley Stanley, both Thomas and Spires moved to Northern California, focusing on music while expanding their collection of antique and folk instruments.

Together, Thomas and Spires performed at the Berkeley Folk Festival. After that "official" performance, they headed on impulse up to Sproul Plaza to play there. The success of that venture led them to realize that street busking could be a source of income (Spires interview). The Golden Toad became one of the most visible street acts in San Francisco, inspiring other bands to try to earn a living—and reach an audience—this way. The size of the band changed accordingly, swelling to as many as eighteen or twenty with frequently changing personnel. The band acquired dancers as well, such as John Patterson (no relation to the faire's founding family), who had been one of the lead dancers for the San Francisco Ballet. Patterson came to faire, encountered the Golden Toad there, and promptly dropped out of the San Francisco Ballet and joined the Toad, performing such dances as the dervish. Although Thomas had seniority, the band, according to Thomas's partner, Wendy Newell, did not have a stated "boss" (email; the quotation marks are hers).

The Golden Toad also began to play in more institutional settings and events. Although this represents one of the very most important ways that faire culture spread, it began, according to Ernie and Deborah Fischbach, with characteristic informality. "We'd played as Acid Symphony for several years [at the Southern California faire]. Then we went to the Northern faire and played as Acid, and at the end of the faire we joined Golden Toad. Bob Thomas said, 'Anybody want to join Golden Toad? We're going to go on the road, and play county fairs'" (E. Fischbach interview). The Toad subsequently played at a number of more "mainstream" venues—the California State Fair, the San Francisco Zoo, a Bastille Day celebration in San Francisco, and a college appearance in Santa Cruz. Ernie Fischbach opines, "We weren't received very well at county fairs—they were afraid of us." But the band had great success in other places, where sometimes, Fischbach says, "the hippies . . . said they had been waiting for us" (interview).

In retrospect, Fischbach finds himself uneasy with that kind of hyperbole. But the group did find itself well matched with some of the most iconic countercultural venues. For instance, the band played (in several configurations) in 1969 at concerts organized by Family Dog Productions, an agency founded by countercultural music promoter Chet Helms. Helms is sometimes nicknamed "father of the Summer of Love"—an event in which more than one hundred thousand people converged on San Francisco's Haight-Ashbury neighborhood, thereby pushing the statements of the counterculture into great public awareness. Helms had arrived in San Francisco in 1962; in 1966, he took up with a commune calling itself Family Dog and organized the concerts for which the commune was known into regular publicized events at such venues as the Avalon Ballroom and the Fillmore Auditorium.[5] The Golden Toad played at least seven times at Family Dog events, sharing billing with the Grateful Dead, Timothy Leary, the Hells Angels Own Band, the New Tranquility String Band, and others.[6]

The Golden Toad also played several times in 1969 for the Floating Lotus Magic Opera Company, a commune and folk theater group based in Berkeley. In these performances, the band joined the roster of musicians and other artists who performed with the company along with the eager nonprofessional participants who composed the group itself. The company presented two "operas" from 1966 to 1969, under the leadership of poet Daniel Moore; in addition to functioning as a celebration of the "new consciousness" in the Bay Area, both operas were intended to counter "negative energy" (such as that emanating from the war in Vietnam) with "positive energy." Writing in the *Oakland Tribune* in 1969, John Rockwell (shortly to become the music critic for the *New York Times*) called the Floating Lotus Opera Company "a superb challenge to 'establishment' notions of what musical theater is all about'" (11). According to Stuart Hobbs, the Floating Lotus "illustrated the avant-garde influences on the counterculture (172)—much like the Renaissance faire itself during this period.

Many members of the Golden Toad consider the band's summary performance to have taken place in 1970 at Grace Cathedral, an imposing Episcopalian church sitting at the top of San Francisco's Nob Hill. William Gilkerson, then an editor for the *San Francisco Chronicle*, convinced the church's bishop to let the Toad play a summer-solstice concert there. (According to Zekley, the only limitation was that no one was allowed to pee on the altar.) Gilkerson provided voice-overs and narration, and seventeen members of the Toad performed on bagpipes, lute, oboe, bass drum, pipe, tabor, saz, sarod, cumbus, tamboura, and dumbek and did folk dances from Macedonia, Yugoslavia, Spain, and more. The concert prompted a television crew to arrive at Preston Ranch, where many band members lived together, to do a news spot on the Golden Toad. Oral testimony about the visit collected by Zekley has the band members somewhat resistant of this attention:

> "The hippies in the woods," Deborah Fischbach says with a chuckle. "They did it in the church. We were sitting in there and they would take individuals—like me or Wendy—and ask us dumb questions. When they were through with their filming, Bob and Elliott and Ernie got out the gazach horns. Bob said, 'We're going to play for you.' The gazach horns were these big long things—fake horns that MGM used as movie props. They sounded like horrible farting things. So Bob says to the TV crew, 'Do you want to hear our great trumpet fanfare?' And when they heard all these farting sounds with the gazach horns their faces dropped and they put away all their equipment and left." ("Preston")

Members of the Golden Toad were enmeshed in influential unrelated musical projects as well. Solomon Feldthouse, born in 1940 in Idaho but raised in Turkey, was a founding member of Kaleidoscope—incidentally, Led Zeppelin guitarist Jimmy Page's favorite band—and recorded four albums with them on the Epic label between 1966 and 1970. This venture is widely credited with introducing Middle Eastern percussion to American popular music of that time. Later members of the Toad, Brian and Marianne Steeger, went on to work with the United Farm Workers' El Teatro Campesino, a preeminent bilingual, experimental Latino theater company founded in 1965. Debbie and Ernie Fischbach, at Bob Thomas's suggestion, founded the Institute for Traditional Studies, whose mission is to research, perform, and promote education in traditional arts; ITS has taken on projects including presenting and preserving the music of early California, producing banjo instructional videos by Mike Seeger, creating a world music program for K–12 students, and providing a referral service for West Coast traditional musicians including players of bagpipes, steel drums, accordions, mandolins, Klezmer, salsa, Middle Eastern oud, saz, bouzouki, oboe, world rock, French folk dance, and more. Mickie Zekley founded Lark in the Morning, a world music adult and family camp described in the *New York Times* as "part music-and-dance academy, part freewheeling hoedown" (Rosen 24). Spires sums up this remarkable productivity with the words, "The faire taught us skills" (interview). After the Golden Toad dissolved as a band, some of its members ended their involvement with the Renaissance faire, while others, such as Ernie Fischbach, continued to perform there informally on and off.

The triple-signifyingly-named A Cid Symphony (sometimes written as A-Cid or Acid Symphony, in order to bring home the point) has confounded reviewers and documentarians trying to categorize the group's music.[7] "There is nothing remotely pop about the group," wrote allmusic's Stanton Swihart in a CD review. It is likely that the musicians would have been pleased with this description. The group was founded in Los Angeles in 1966 by Dustin Miller, a leader of the Berkeley Free Speech movement. Miller had some experience selling protest records to raise money for the student movement, and his intention was to form a "folk-and-ethnic" band (Miller); to this end, he pulled in his childhood friend Charles Ewing, who had studied flamenco and classical guitar in Spain. Ewing, in turn, knew Ernie Fischbach, a Glendale, California, native and already a multi-instrumentalist. Before long, Ernie's wife, Deborah Cleall, a former teenage model, joined the band as well.

With Miller as manager, A Cid Symphony played a variety of venues, mostly sponsored by the Students for a Democratic Society. Miller was associated with the Diggers, a Haight-Ashbury anarchist improv collective founded by Peter Coyote, Emmett Grogan, and Peter Berg and overlapping with the guerrilla commedia dell'arte company the San Francisco Mime Troupe. A Cid Symphony often followed the Diggers' tradition of feeding everyone who showed up for free concerts. They also lived together on a farm in Pauma Valley. In this configuration, A Cid Symphony played for a couple of years at the Southern California Renaissance Pleasure Faire.

By the following year, several important developments pulled the band into the Bay Area's countercultural music scene. First, they were written up in the *Los Angeles Times*, which, according to Miller, prompted them all to quit their jobs to focus solely on music. Second, Fischbach and Ewing became increasingly interested in East Indian music in particular and exploring non-American forms of music more generally. The band—Miller, Ewing, and Ernie and Deborah Fischbach—all moved to

Fig. 3.3. Deborah Fischbach plays the harp in a field at the 1966 Southern California Renaissance Pleasure Faire. (Courtesy Institute for Tradtional Studies)

San Francisco so that Ewing and Ernie Fischbach could study Hindustani music with Ali Akbar Khan at his music college in Berkeley; there they began to play at the Northern California faire. Soon after their arrival, the music columnist for the *San Francisco Chronicle*, Ralph Gleason, introduced Miller to Fantasy Records producer Max Weiss.

Weiss allowed the band to use Fantasy's recording studios, and the result was that, unlike the Golden Toad, A Cid Symphony—a much shorter-lived band—recorded one record: a self-titled triple LP, bankrolled by Miller's mother, pressed on colored vinyl (a different color for each LP), and released on the Thermal Flash Music label of Denise Kaufman, an original member of Ken Kesey's Merry Pranksters. Along with singing, yodeling, silence, and chanting, Ernie Fischbach and Ewing, joined by a couple of friends, play dulcimer, harmonica, flamenco guitar, steel-string guitar, and bells. The songs represent a fusion of ethnic traditions—country, blues, raga, flamenco, European classical. At one point, a guest vocalist sings "The Internationale" in English, but to an alternate tune. At another, sounds of a printing press interrupt the vocals.

With retrospective ears, Swihart calls A Cid Symphony a "harbinger of the times." Of the three-album self-pressed LP recording the group made in 1967, he writes that their sound captures "the kaleidoscope" (that word again) of cultural energy in the environment. He dwells on the band's use of a variety of folk instruments, noting their

> complete immersion in Hindustani and Middle Eastern music, with modal, raga-esque scale progressions and a discernibly mystical bent. . . . Ernest Fischbach's fluttering dulcimer is the basis of these songs, interspersed with Charles Ewing's flamenco-picked guitars. At times, alongside the Eastern underpinnings, the music is wholly evocative of front-porch Appalachian folk and blues, and the mixture of the two genres mostly works brilliantly, and at least much more successfully than it would seem possible. There are also elements of Native American ceremonial music, Spanish music, and a smattering of 12-bar acoustic blues.

However, if Swihart, looking back, saw that ground was broken by the album, others found that outside of its moment, it was too challenging to be gratifying. In *Fuzz, Acid, and Flower: A Comprehensive Guide to American Garage, Psychedelic, and Hippie Rock (1964–1975)*, Vernon Joynson throws up his authorial hands: "This was a three-LP set, with one album on green vinyl, one in yellow and the other in purple. Needless to say, this album is now rare and collectible. It's a very strange and personal project. A kind of private documentary on which music does not seem to be the most important factor" (9). It is certainly true that the album is profoundly unconventional, down to the track titles and artwork, the latter done by Les Shipnuck, whom Miller describes in liner notes to the 1999 CD reissue as "a crazed 60s artist." Shipnuck's cover drawing is of a colorful Arab tent in which A Cid Symphony frequently performed; Miller points out in the album notes that a photograph of that tent appears in the album booklet for the Beatles' Magical Mystery Tour. The track titles, says multi-instrumentalist faire musician (and sometime Fischbach collaborator) Joseph Pusey, were chosen after the fact: "From what Ernie told me, I gather that the A Cid Symphony record was a series of jams that they would stop afterwards and say, 'OK, what do you want to call that one?'" (Lundborg). Rereleased on compact disc in 1999, the album received a fair amount of attention among aficionados of psychedelia and in nonprofessional or semiprofessional online publications. One such blog, called Spaced2Savior, exemplifies this positive discovery of A Cid Symphony by people with historical interest in early psychedelic folk:

> Originally put out in . . . '67 as a fundraiser for th' free speech movement which was rapidly mutatin' into anti-nam militant peacenix in berkeley . . . its beatnik folk jams groovin' in a chemically active environment let this meander in trancy wiggedout spaces . . . a groovy lobeful that'll make any afternoon o' layabout inclination'n hooligan activity a mighty hep tyme . . . cats understandin' th'relative time'n space principal o' one minute sometimes bein' longer than a day will dig this from th'first moment . . . a worthy artifact o' different days . . . (spacedsaviour)

Following the release of the album, A Cid Symphony performed together for about another year. They collaborated with the Firesign Theatre (whose founding member David Ossman had told them about the faire in the first place) in both live performances and on one of their albums. They "crashed the Monterey Pop" (E. Fischbach interview), playing on the grounds but not the stage, and in doing so, met Ravi Shankar, whose performance there widely introduced him to American audiences and furthered the popularity in youth culture of Indian music, dress, names, and religious practices. And, of course, they performed at the Renaissance Pleasure Faire—sometimes with the Golden Toad and sometimes on their own—and when people approached them, eager to share the kind of music they themselves knew how to play, says Ernie Fischbach, "We'd hang out and try to figure out how to play along" (interview).

Middle Eastern Fusion

Arguably the faire's area of greatest musical influence, and one in which Ernie Fischbach was deeply involved, was in its contributions to the popularization of Middle Eastern music, dance, and instruments in the American context. The faire's musicians, many of whom traveled to study with masters in the music's countries of origins, rearticulated the music in a dynamic and complex way that simultaneously assimilated and undercut "exotic" visions of the "Orient" from American popular culture, while contributing to a thriving and adventurous celebration of non-Western musical and dance traditions and interjecting into the faire's collective narrative the story of Europe's commercial exchanges with Asia via the Silk Road. Elements of these performances were then carried back out of the faire into the broader American musical landscape, finding their way into other (and in some cases more commercial) musical configurations and forms, sometimes carried by the faire's musicians themselves in their nonfaire work and sometimes by other players they influenced.

The faire's establishment in Los Angeles and then in San Francisco coincided with a Middle Eastern restaurant and cabaret boom. In some ways, these clubs' navigation of the "authentic" and the "fake," the titillating and the artistically serious, paralleled Harlem clubs during the Harlem Renaissance, which often had décor or acts organized around "jungle" themes while simultaneously showcasing and promoting the music and dance of the black avant-garde. In looking at situations of creative ferment, particularly in stratified societies, purism is most often not possible, let alone useful.

Writing about the Bay Area's ethnic clubs in the late 1960s, ethnomusicologist Anne Rasmussen notes that this complex navigation brought musicians "unprecedented success" even as it enmeshed them in a racist economy. The clubs hosted modern, even experimental music and dance but deliberately constructed a context for the performances in which the music was presented as "primitive" and "raw" to American audiences (67). Further, because the clubs usually presented a generalized vision of the "Orient," regional and ethnic distinctions were elided as cultural traditions were combined in the service of this vision. Through this club-driven musical boom, "Orientalism," writes Rasmussen, "became a sort of ideological blueprint for a polyethnic, Middle Eastern music," while at the same time, musicians adapted Western instruments to their own purposes (69). Through their disregard of authenticity, the clubs' musicians were able to "play a music that was fresh and exciting to polyethnic audiences in American urban areas" (74).

These panethnic restaurants and clubs donated a great deal of artistic energy to the two California Renaissance faires in the late 1960s. A key engine of the faire's Middle Eastern musical evolution, a dancer named Jamila Salimpour, carried the hybridizing impulses of the club scene to the faire's stages, gathering musicians and dancers into her performances of what is generally called "belly dance" in the United States.[8] Belly dance has always been linked in the American imagination to an exoticized Arab sexuality; in the face of this association, Salimpour has consistently articulated that she intended to bring the form back to folkloric roots and away from the colonial harem fantasy with which it had been associated since Middle Eastern dance was first made widely visible in the United States, at the Chicago World's Fair in 1893.

Born in 1926 in New York City, Salimpour describes having been exposed to Middle Eastern dance by her Sicilian father, her Arab American friends, and the Egyptian movies she watched starting in childhood. By the time Salimpour was a child, Egypt had established itself as the center of the film industry in the Middle East, and dances were incorporated into nearly every movie (in a similar fashion to the way Bollywood movies today characteristically feature dance). From the early years of the American film industry, Hollywood presented its own vision of seductive belly dancers, and in a fascinating instance of the multidirectionality of global entertainment influence, Egyptian movies began to adopt and present the Hollywood version of Middle Eastern dance.

This Hollywood version held sway in the United States until the 1960s, when Middle Eastern restaurants began to hire dancers, generally a mix of local dancers and professional dancers from the Middle East. As a young woman, Salimpour, who had briefly joined Ringling Brothers Circus at age sixteen as an acrobatic dancer, was able to find work in those restaurant shows; as she had not studied formally (indeed, there were no belly dance schools in the United States yet), she largely improvised at that time, developing a vocabulary of gestures and forms in a nonsystematic way. But when she began teaching dance in 1965 while pregnant with her daughter Suhaila, who also went on to be an important belly dancer and dance instructor, Salimpour began to codify her mixed exposure to a variety of styles.

Echoing the story of other performers who first just "showed up" at the faire to perform, Salimpour describes attending the faire in 1967 to find that her students had arrived at the faire en masse and started dancing wherever they could. She arranged with the faire's entertainment director to put together a more organized show the following year. In Salimpour's accounting, the performance troupe she organized, Bal Anat, or "dance of the mother goddess," was "half real" and "part hokum":

> I created a variety show where each number was no more than three to five minutes long and represented a cross-section of old styles from the Middle East. We had two magicians, Gilli Gilli from Egypt, and Hassan from Morocco. I featured snake dancers, water glass dancing routines, and pot dances.... I had a student dance with a real Turkish sabre, balancing it on her head.... That was, I believe, the first time that the sword dance was seen in America. We had a Ouled Nail dancer from Algeria, Kashlama dancers from Turkey, a Mother Goddess mask dancers, a male tray dancer, and the list goes on and on. We even had a Greek math professor from UC Berkeley who knew how to pick up a table with his teeth, all the while balancing Suhaila on top. (17)

The more fictive elements of Salimpour's Pleasure Faire show drew inspiration from a variety of sources; these included "pictures of tribal groups from the *National Geographic*, orientalist paintings by Gerome, films such as *Justine* set in North Africa, and a photo from a Moroccan cook book" (Sellers-Young 284).

Salimpour's Northern California Renaissance Faire performances with Bal Anat went on to inspire a distinct school of belly dance, generally called American Tribal or Tribal Fusion. American Tribal was a combination of earnest attempt to reclaim belly dance's "ethnic" roots and a somewhat impressionistic pastiche of regional techniques and costumes, conveying, as Barbara Sellers-Young puts it, "a collective image of the professional dancers of Morocco, Tunisia, Algeria, Turkey, and Egypt in the (re)created environment of the Renaissance Pleasure Faire" (285). In doing so, Sellers-Young contends, the dancers detached masculinity and femininity from Western normative structures and "danced new gender identities in a process that reflected the contemporary interest in new sexualities and at the same time challenged prior constructions" (285).

American Tribal belly dance continued to evolve after Salimpour's involvement with the faire, with students of hers devoting their own professional lives to it. Among them are her daughter, Suhaila, the first belly dancer nominated for the Isadora Duncan Dance Award; Carolena Nericcio, founder of the Fat Chance Belly Dance company, whose stated purpose is to challenge the male gaze and promote size acceptance; and John Compton and Rita Alderucci, cofounders of the troupe Hahbi 'Ru. Compton was Salimpour's first male student; he describes himself as "the first traditional male dancer in the 'Khawal' since the Chicago World's Fair of 1893." He performed in area clubs during the 1970s as well as at the faire; a performance at the Egyptian consulate landed him on the cover of "the Egyptian equivalent of *Life* magazine" during his second year as a dancer (interview).

Salimpour describes being challenged in her quest to find appropriate music to accompany her dancers at the faire, but this challenge, she contends, led to more innovation. No recorded music or amplification was allowed, so she had to locate live musicians who were willing to play—as were the rest of the faire's musicians—largely out of desire to be part of the faire despite the relatively low pay and chaotic setting. She considered that A Cid Symphony's Ernie Fischbach had a decent "Middle Eastern flair" and hired him to be not only a player but also Bal Anat's composer, presenting him with old reel-to-reel tapes of Egyptian music and asking him not simply to transcribe the music but rather to create new compositions in the spirit of those recordings (E. Fischbach interview).

For many listeners, the music of Bal Anat became the faire's characteristic sound, introducing tens of thousands of listeners to Middle Eastern music each year and inspiring other musicians to study it themselves. Musicians also followed Salimpour's path back and forth from the clubs to the faires. Percussionist Mark Bell joined Bal Anat in 1972 (in typical early faire fashion, having started playing that same year):

> It was pretty mind boggling to play for *Bal Anat*. Darioush Sami was playing santour, with strings breaking and flying all over the place. The whole bunch of us hippy drummers was pounding away. Add the dancers with the cymbals and drums, and it was a very big sound. Jamila was in the center with her big drum, trying to control everything, marking the beat with one hand.
>
> It was also at the Ren Faire in '72 that Salah Takesh played one day. He came on stage and looked at the drumming crew and at me. "Play plenty of 'dooms' so I can trip out," he said. He wanted us to keep the basic beat so he could improvise over the top. We were reluctantly impressed. (Harris)

Bell went on to study percussion extensively throughout the Arab world, including with Mahmoud Hamouda in Egypt and Farhadman in Iran.

Like Thomas, Fischbach, and other faire musicians, Bell acquired from the early faire an interest in working in various musical traditions; like Jamila (in fact, sometimes with Jamila), he worked in the Middle Eastern nightclub scene as well as performing regularly at the faire. At present, he performs with a Bay Area Middle Eastern music and dance ensemble called Helm and teaches a variety of percussion instruments. He also performs with an Armenian group, Mirage; an Arabic/American fusion band, Light Rain; a Greek group, the Aegeans; a Turkish group, Tufan; and, occasionally, with a Balkan group, Panacea. Bell also won a Grammy in 2005 for his tracks on *Beautiful Dreamer—Songs of Stephen Foster* and has worked with Fat Chance Belly Dance. By carrying out and promulgating the deep study of international musical traditions, and the artistic fusion of those traditions, Bell demonstrates through his wide-ranging career the way the faire functioned as precursor and engine of the "world music" musical genre.

In addition to the musical influence that Bal Anat had in its own right, it also led to the creation of other Middle Eastern bands at the faire. After the Golden Toad broke up (when Bob Thomas went to jail on LSD charges), Ernie and Deborah Fischbach formed a Middle Eastern group called Zincali with their friend Chris Carnes, a flamenco guitar player. As Deb Fischbach relates, "Chris taught us flamenco and got us all into Moroccan music. Because when he was studying in Spain, he would go to Morocco for vacation. So he had all these tapes. He was a self-made ethnomusicologist. He would just record these sessions. . . . He had tapes from the Dancing Boy café" (interview). Zincali still performs, though not at the Renaissance faire; among other new members of the band is Melissa Fischbach, the percussionist daughter of Deborah and Ernie Fischbach.

The Fischbachs also played for years with Solomon Feldthouse, in a group called Kos-Kadas, founded by dancer John Compton. Kos-Kadas took faire-generated music into the musical mainstream, most notably when the band played a huge show in 1976 at the opening extravaganza for the King Tut exhibit at the De Young Museum in San Francisco. Further, Feldthouse's years performing at the Renaissance faire (and living collectively with faire performers and dancers—see later in this chapter) overlapped with years in which he was a key member of the psychedelic folk group Kaleidoscope, which recorded on Epic records between 1966 and 1970 and was known for using an unusually huge number of stringed instruments in its songs. The calling card of the group was its use of Middle Eastern instruments such as Feldthouse's oud and saz. David Lindley, who was the leader of Kaleidoscope—or as much of a leader as the group had, since its stated principle was not to have a leader—went on to become an influential sideman for Jackson Browne, Linda Ronstadt, Warren Zevon, and others, carrying the faire's hybridizing musical influences further into the mainstream of American popular music.

The Philosophy of Fusion: Lev Liberman and The Klezmorim

The giddying musical environment of the faire's first decade, summed up earlier by Ernie Fischbach's statement "we'd try to play along," had a somewhat surprising and concrete byproduct in the form of klezmer music. Klezmer, the instrumental tradition of Yiddish-speaking eastern European Jewry, traveled during the late nineteenth and early twentieth centuries to the United States, where it absorbed American influences: initially jazz and film music and, during its later revival, bluegrass and funk.[9] But as Jews culturally assimilated, the popularity of klezmer declined; in particular, the Jewish celebrations for which klezmer had been so important increasingly featured more "mainstream" American music.

In the 1970s, though, a klezmer revival started in the United States and became an international phenomenon, connected to a renewed interest in Yiddish language and culture. Widely credited with sparking that revival is a Berkeley group, The Klezmorim, founded in 1975. Although klezmer music as such was not featured at the faire, Lev Liberman, a cofounder of The Klezmorim, cites his experience as a faire musician as having helped him put together all the pieces that led him back to klezmer recordings. Liberman was born in 1952 and grew up in Oregon; while in college at Pomona, he became involved in radio drama and broadcasting and did some work at Pacifica's KPFK station—the station that had sponsored the first Renaissance faires as a benefit. There he learned about the Renaissance Pleasure Faire from Mario Casseta, a folk and ethnic music broadcaster. Liberman attended the Southern California faire, which he describes as "magical," and when he moved shortly thereafter to the Bay Area in 1974, he headed to that faire to busk. "I couldn't afford the ticket, so I snuck in with [accordionist] Nada Lewis's Balkan group, the People's International Silver String Macedonian Band," he admits, noting that the group's name—taken with its acronym—encapsulated the spirit of socialist collectivism in which most of the musicians operated, as well as their simultaneous self-mocking (interview).

One way that spirit of collectivism manifested itself, according to Liberman, was in how the musicians all played in each other's bands. "The best music happened after hours," Liberman recounts. "After hours, it was not about playing songs that people would know. You played for other musicians. You took chances. You played your most abrasive, most experimental music then" (interview).

Liberman played Balkan tunes at the faire but was in search of something else, a musical ground not yet staked out. "That was the zeitgeist of the time," he says. "You make the world you want to live in" (interview).

He grew up listening to Moses Asch's influential Folkways recordings, which were instrumental in the popularization of folk music and multilingual ethnic music. As a young musician, he says, he "walked around with Russian harmonies and sonorities" in his head all the time. As an aspiring jazz player, he found his way to the compositions of Jewish composers such as George Gershwin, and during a "Brecht phase," he encountered the radical European theater and the music of Brecht's frequent musical collaborator, Kurt Weill (Rogovy). With great chronological precision, Liberman reports that in 1971, he "deduced that a single unknown genre had linked Russian and Rumanian folk music to Depression-era cartoon soundtracks, early jazz, and the compositions of Gershwin, Weill, and Prokofiev" (Liberman). Liberman figured that the "missing link" must be Yiddish, because it formed a common denominator among these elements.

Liberman did not find his way to klezmer recordings for a few years, though—when he attended the faire's famous after-hours parties. There, the proximity of various kinds of music, the hybridizing that the musicians carried out as a matter of course—especially when jamming with each other—and the ethos of musical experimentation led him to what he narrates as a sort of epiphany:

> I attended a bacchanalian midnight after-party where Patty Farber performed her notorious Goat Dance, the single most salacious tail-twitch in the history of the world. Then Pitu Guli—a Bulgarian-themed UCLA Balkan supergroup featuring Stu Brotman, Stewart Mennin, Miamon Miller, David Shochat, and Ed Leddel—played Yiddish and Serbian tunes on sax, clarinet, trumpet, tuba, drums . . . and I was utterly enchanted as the music I'd been trying to wrap my brain around since 1971 seemed to emerge from the murk . . . a hidden treasure that, maybe, had been in my back yard the whole time. (Rogovy)

Shortly thereafter, Liberman recounts, he was able to "rescue" a box of klezmer records from storage and, together with violinist and Klezmorim cofounder David Skuse, begin to transcribe the songs on those records. "This was not a voyage of ethnic rediscovery" for him or for Skuse, insists Liberman. On the contrary, their musical intent was "to challenge sacred cows," and for this reason, their music did not immediately find a niche audience of Jewish Americans (interview).

With some thirty musicians joining them for various recording sessions and live performances, The Klezmorim released nine albums and a box set of their own and contributed tracks to half a dozen anthologies, as well as touring extensively in the United States and in Europe. And the klezmer revival soon spread—first to other U.S.-based klezmer groups and then to other countries as musicians began to track down not only old recordings but also still-living players in Europe. In 1985, radio producer and Yiddish-culture preservationist Henry Sapoznik founded KlezCamp, an annual music festival in New York State; in 1999, Sapoznik authored a book on the history of klezmer. Due to all these efforts, klezmer music again received the broad acknowledgment that had faded away (or been deliberately turned away) in the first decades of the twentieth century.

British Isles: Early Music, Morris Dance, and Celtic Music

The early faire's musical experiments with ethnic music and dance, not to mention with psychedelics, have at times been seen as departures from the more "authentically" Renaissance-era musical forms and instruments that have been present at the faire all along—such as Bob Thomas's lute playing or the madrigal singers who can be heard on KPFK's broadcast of the first faire in 1963. In fact, during the California faires' increased focus on authenticity in 1970s, as many of the faire's musicians point out, much of the more experimental music was eliminated, at least temporarily. However, twentieth-century revivals of "early music"—the bundling name used to refer to music from its earliest times up through the Renaissance—are themselves, music critic Harry Haskell contends, a countercultural formation, a registry of opposition to, or at the very least a comment on, the prevailing cultural and political landscape. As such, the cultural project of early music at the faire, especially during its first two decades, must be understood in tandem with the faire's ethnic, folk, psychedelic, and fusion forms.

The phenomenon of cultural revival has been inadequately theorized, but certainly, reaching back into history is an impulse born of feelings about the present or about certain historical developments that characterize the present. Take, for instance, *Los Angeles Times* columnist Jack Smith's self-described reaction to musical performance at the 1969 Southern California Renaissance Pleasure Faire:

> I wandered among the motley crowd. Most were attired in costumes of the Renaissance or medieval times. There was some magic in all this mummery. I felt the spirit. It could not possibly be 1969. Something inescapable in our own century was missing. But what?
>
> Suddenly it struck me. There was no electronic sound. No radios. No public address loudspeaker with its Big Brother bark. No squeak, no squawk, no siren blast. Just light melody on the breeze, as from afar.
>
> Then I strolled into the aura of a group of six musicians sitting on a rude wood stage under an oak bough. They were playing an Elizabethan round. Their instruments were the lute, the recorder, the flute, the viola da gamba. Nothing was plugged in....
>
> The sound floated out over the green dell only as far as its own life force would carry it, then sweetly died.
>
> It turned me on, man. (144)

Smith's anxiety about the present is couched in this column—which ends with the preceding praise of the faire—in terms of gender; he worries that men have been "robbed" of the sound of women singing as they do housework, adding that if they have been robbed of the sound of women talking, that is "not so great a loss" (143). His framing of the matter illustrates how an interest in historically informed performance symbolically expresses a reaction against an ideological present. The early music revival, then, hinges on the notion Smith states so clearly: that something has been lost and that a carefully re-created performance can bring it back, if only symbolically. His sardonic appropriation of countercultural slang in the column's final line—"It turned me on, man"—at once acknowledges and ironize the fact that the early music he is enjoying is brought to him courtesy of a youthful subculture.

Just as what constitutes "early music" has no clear historical starting or ending point, so the interest in historically informed musical performance—the "early music revival"—is impossible, Harry Haskell reminds us, to delineate with any chronological specificity. An interest in the music of the past, writes Thomas Forrest Kelly, has been "characteristic of a part of the musical world since the early nineteenth century—from about the time of the rise of museums" (1). In the United States, interest in early music was noticeable in the early part of the twentieth century (the revival got under way earlier in Europe): but this attention was largely located in the university, as it was tied to the rise of musicology as an academic field. In the second half of the twentieth century, though, early music was increasingly seen as nonelitist and participatory. Kelly compares the early music revival to the Arts and Crafts movement's reaction against industrial mass production, noting that in the 1960s, it took on "political overtones . . . fueled by a sense of return to the natural, a rebellion against received wisdom and enforced conformity, and a notion that early music was a participant's music as much as it was a listener's" (2). "It cannot be sheer coincidence," he muses, "that the early music 'movement,' as it is sometimes called, arose at the same time as a number of other popular and popularist movements" (3).

The early faire's performances of early music functioned as an important bridge between the academic associations of the early music revival and its subsequent more popular manifestations. During the faire's first years, the Pattersons recruited directly from area colleges and universities, and these musicians were gratified to find in the faire a way to broaden their own appeal beyond the academy. One such musician was Shirley Robbins, whose ensemble performed as the Shirley Robbins Consort at the Southern California Renaissance Pleasure Faire through most of the 1960s. Robbins, who died in 2008, was involved in the American revival quite early, having become interested in the music in the 1940s in New York. She moved to California as a young woman and became a significant figure in shaping the early music revival on the West Coast, performing and teaching medieval and Renaissance music for some five decades. Among other teaching activities, Robbins led the summer early music program at the University of Southern California's Idyllwild campus.

Robbins's daughter, Karen Robbins, who performed with her mother's faire ensemble as a child, situates her mother's enthusiasm about the faire in terms of this desire to broaden the early music revival:

It is increasingly clear as I have reflected on my mother's life . . . that the early music scene in Southern California was very, very nascent when she arrived [there]. It was lonely in many respects, to be out there trying to establish early music as a real, legitimate, meaningful musical genre. It was a very small slice of activity. . . . I think the faire did that, in the sense that it made this whole experience of the Renaissance so approachable and tangible to people. It was so much fun. It was not like the performers were up there all hallowed, you know: they were out there walking around; they were singing as they went. It was a very spirited, community-based thing, and I think that warmed her a lot. (Interview)

Many of the faire's early musicians began their involvement in early music in an academic setting as Robbins did, carrying their interest and expertise to the faire, where they developed it further in this more informal context and projected it outward. Marco Alpert, who performed Renaissance music at the Southern California faire in the late 1960s with the three- or four-person Unicorn Consort, first played with a recorder ensemble at UCLA, where he was an undergraduate student (interview). The Unicorn Consort then moved from the university to the faire to other distinctly countercultural contexts: a 1970 photograph in the short-lived but significant countercultural fashion magazine *Rags* shows the consort (consisting of Alpert, founder Charles Fischer, and a third musician) performing in faire garb at a wedding, while a similarly garbed-up guest eats a faire-inspired turkey leg—and a caption notes that all of the wedding food was served without utensils ("Earth Mother's Wedding"). Among other features, the photograph of the consort shares space in the magazine with a photographic profile of the San Francisco drag troupe the Cockettes.

The connections among the early music revival, the 1960s folk and ethnic music revival, and psychedelic musical experimentation are particularly plain in the performance catalog of Celtic folk ensembles. The Bay Area vocal ensemble Oak, Ash, and Thorn, for instance, which began performing at the faire in the early 1970s, sang madrigals as well as Celtic and Scottish folk songs. Meanwhile, some of these musicians and their repertoire crossed back and forth with the hybridizing groups such as the Golden Toad and A Cid Symphony.

A striking example of these interconnections is the career of influential Celtic performer, teacher, and instrument collector/purveyor Mickie Zekley. Zekley began playing the guitar as a teenager and offering guitar lessons at twenty. He performed in 1967 at the Elysian Park Love-In; in his account,

> The Elysian Park Love-In was quite an event. I played sitar on stage wearing my bejeweled velvet magician's robe just before Jim Morrison and the Doors did their most famous performance. Parachuting hippies, half naked barbarian women in leather, patchouli, incense, peace symbols, beards, long hair, the dusky odor of pot. I was playing guitar and sitar at another Love-In wearing my velvet robe once again and was photographed by a newspaper reporter only to find myself on the front page of the morning paper with the caption "King Of The Hippies." All of a sudden many of the mothers of my 46 guitar students called with one excuse or another quitting lessons but obviously they did not want the "King Of The Hippies" teaching their kids guitar. ("Adventures")

It might have cost him his guitar students, but it was countercultural activities that fed Zekley's musical interests. He developed an expertise on the Celtic pipes and flute, eventually opening Lark in the Morning, a summer music camp and musical instrument business named after a Celtic folk song.

In some cases, musicians from the early music ensembles crossed over with musicians from the ethnic folk ensembles and the psychedelic folk ensembles. Zekley, for instance, performed with the Golden Toad, while the Toad's Bob Thomas, Will Spires, and Ernie Fischbach provided musical accompaniment to English folk dancers. The Unicorn Consort's Marco Alpert describes the physical space of the faire as temporarily erasing, through agreed-on fantasy, some of the restrictions and divisions of the everyday city; for him, this included not only the social categories that people at the faire might occupy outside but also the different kinds of music that could be heard. He recalls wandering the faire when not onstage himself, taking in the sorts of music that others were playing. For people in the United States affiliated with a university, as he was, comments Alpert, an array of musical options was much more easily available than it was to those faire attendees who might otherwise not have encountered the faire's mix of musical styles and traditions (interview).

Along with musical performances, the faire's period-specific dance presentations embodied the ways in which countercultural interest in folk forms could encompass an interest in historically informed performance. Morris dance is a ritualistic English country dance tradition in which teams of dancers use their steps to create choreographed figures, sometimes wielding swords, bells, sticks, handkerchiefs, pipes, and other objects. Morris dancing at the faire, in addition to itself directing fairegoers' attention to early folk expression, also pulled together musicians from the other ensembles. The key figure responsible for bringing morris dancing to the California Renaissance faire was Richard Chase, an important collector of Appalachian and English-American folklore. Born in 1904, Chase was considerably older than most of the early faire's performers. But he came along to the faire after a chance meeting with Will Spires at a downtown Los Angeles bus stop, Spires attracting Chase's attention because he was carrying a lute. It turned out that Bob Thomas's wife, Julia, also knew Chase a little bit, so she and Spires invited him to join them there. Before long, Chase teamed up with Thomas to introduce morris dance to the faire's growing roster of performance.

Much about the early history of morris dancing remains in dispute, particularly regarding how old the tradition is both in England and in the United States.[10] Historian Daniel Walkowitz points out that the style was found in the United States at least as early as the mid-nineteenth century; this American iteration of an English rural tradition, Walkowitz writes, spearheaded a folk revival anxiously responsive to the influx of immigrants to urban areas, while simultaneously revealing the influence on the form of American cultural products such as the minstrel show. In the first half of the twentieth century, morris performances in the United States were largely limited to "high" cultural spaces and audiences. Toward the end of the 1960s, though, English country dance became part of what Walkowitz dubs "the modern country dance nation," which was often anchored by college dance departments (225).

Morris dancing spread to these new participants and audiences a little earlier on the East Coast than in California, taking a foothold in the broad folk revival and in the imaginations of such figures as Students for a Democratic Society organizer Carl Wittman, for whom, in the words of Walkowitz, English country dance became a "leisure-time passion and complement to the political activism that consumed him then" (231). Morris dancing and mummers plays were included each year in the popular performances of the Christmas Revels, seasonal productions invoking sixteenth-century and earlier English theatrical precedents. The Revels were begun by singer and educator John Langstaff in New York in 1957 and carried over to its longest running location, Cambridge, Massachusetts, in 1971 and subsequently to other cities as well.

At roughly the same time that the Revels productions in Cambridge were introducing morris dances to a growing—but still relatively small—nonacademic audience, on the West Coast, Richard Chase, drawing on his scholarly interests, founded a group called the Anglo-Folk Ballet, an informal constellation that met in a Unitarian church. This group learned morris dance as well as other English folk performance (as opposed to social) dance styles. Before long, Chase brought the Anglo-Folk Ballet to perform morris dances at the faire to live music, as part of what was, as Walkowitz convincingly demonstrates, an increasing visibility of folk dance in the counterculture (though Walkowitz neglects the Renaissance Pleasure Faire and the Christmas Revels as centers for folk dance *performance* that drew faire visitors to take up folk dance as a leisure activity). In 1973, the dancers organized into the Pipe and Bowl morris troupe, which in some configuration has been performing at the faire straight through to the present. Pipe and Bowl was followed by other morris dance troupes at other faires, such as Michigan's Hole in the Bog Morris and Mummers, Arizona's Black Wren Morris, North Carolina's Queen's Capers Morris, and Colorado's Maroon Bells Morris Dancers. At present, there are more than 150 morris teams dancing in almost every state; these teams, such as West Virginia's wryly named Hicks with Sticks, perform at other festivals, parades, and outdoor markets, as well as on stages.

The early faire's signature conjunction of early music, folk music, and psychedelic music paralleled, and in some cases contributed to, the development of a new genre in the 1970s and 1980s that is variously called medieval rock, medieval folk rock, or medieval folk (and sometimes derided as "pomp-rock" by detractors who find it to be overblown or pretentious).[11] Medieval folk/rock combined rock-and-roll or pop sounds with the instrumentation, tonalities, and sometimes vocal arrangements, lyrical themes, and tropes of medieval or Renaissance music. The genre was particularly strong in the United Kingdom, as heard in the work of such medieval folk bands as Incredible String Band (formed in 1966), Steeleye Span (formed in 1969), Pentangle (formed in 1967), and Fairport Convention (formed in 1967) and in the development of influential progressive rock bands such as Led Zeppelin (formed in 1968), King Crimson (formed in 1969), Jethro Tull (formed in 1967), and Yes (formed in 1968). But the genre flourished in the United States as well, providing an expansive context in which to understand the faire's own geographic as well as aesthetic combination of early music, psychedelia, and folk explorations.

The Byrds, for instance (formed in 1964) not only attended the faire but chose a name that not only can be understood as pseudo–Old English in its spelling but also invokes William Byrd, an English Renaissance-era composer. Their vocal harmonies and sometimes their repertoire ("Wild Mountain Thyme") seek to call up a kind of fantasy medievalism. Similarly, the supergroup Crosby, Stills, and Nash (formed in 1968), on such songs as "Guinevere" and "Cathedral," and much of the catalog of Styx (formed in 1970) feature classically influenced arrangements, elaborate harmonies, and story ballads. In this music, as Edward Macan points out, "fantasy landscapes and medieval or Eastern imagery come to represent the idealized society—close to the earth, based on mutual dependence and a strong sense of community, linked to the past—to which the hippies aspired" (73). The faire's prominence in hosting and encouraging these developments is clearly evident in a 1977 folk-psych album recorded by Southern Californian Joseph Pusey, *In My Lady's Chamber*, which Pusey says was inspired by his experiences working the Renaissance faires in Northern and Southern California. Reaching for a way to express the countercultural congruence of interest in psychedelia, folk music, early music, and fantasy landscapes and soundscapes, Pusey describes the album's cover art as having a "fantasy/psych look" (Lundborg).

The genre of medieval folk and rock declined by the end of the 1970s, though the influence of early music soon found its way into the tonalities and imagery used by heavy metal bands. But in a fascinatingly circular development, a number of bands emerged in the late 1980s that rely on the faires, formerly praised for their strictly acoustic sound, as performance venues for electrified Renaissance and medieval music. Among these are Blackmore's Night, formed in 1989 by Ritchie Blackmore, previously of the English art rock group Deep Purple, and his romantic partner, Candice Night; and the Medaeval Baebes, an all-woman English band with as many as twelve members. These bands are several musical turns removed from, but still significantly indebted to, the early music presented at the California faires during their early, countercultural period. They employ electric amplification and contemporary instruments that would not have been found at the faires during their most "authentic" period. And these bands command bigger crowds than any other musical acts at the faire.

Musical Communes

In addition to onstage and after-hours jamming, the key musicians at the Northern California Renaissance Pleasure Faire established several homesteads where they lived together communally. This style of living famously flourished in the countercultural 1960s and 1970s, but among musicians, it had a huge artistic payoff: living communally allowed them as much time as they needed to practice and play music together. Even more important, it provided for a great deal of cultural exchange, with players swapping not just songs but musical styles and rhythms as well. The communes contributed to the faires' characteristic musical hybridity, especially among forms of what could be loosely (but inadequately) described as "ethnic music." The results were then performed at the faire, and the faire, in turn, reshaped the hybridity, by encouraging participants, as the Golden Toad's Will Spires recalls, to have "awareness and respect for other people's . . . traditions" (interview).

Folklorist and folk musician Mike Seeger hailed this "musical ferment" in the liner notes to *Berkeley Farms*, an album he recorded 1967 on the Old Left–founded Folkways label. The album featured some twenty musicians from the Berkeley music revival scene; Seeger writes in his notes that the excitement and artistic significance of these musical interactions reminded him of the early days of the recording industry, when rural forms were first sought out and recorded. The album's notes, in addition to offering the usual biographical sketches of the musicians, also provided a list of places where musicians could find opportunities to meet each other and to perform in and around Berkeley; the Northern California Renaissance Pleasure Faire, which had just been established, was included in the list, along with the Old Time Fiddlers' Convention and Irish dances in San Francisco. The faire's period clothing is referred to as "super old-timey garb" (Seeger).

The first significant faire musicians' commune was on Colby Street in Oakland. Golden Toad members Eric Thompson, Will Spires, and Jehan Paul lived there in a house full of musicians, playing together in the Toad and other formations and exploring Cajun music, Irish music, and old-time string band music at the same time. The Colby Street House, as it was called, became "a focal point of musical activity in the 1960s (DeWitt 157), with other musicians frequently passing through and swapping songs, styles, and forms with the resident musicians. Fiddler Sue Draheim recalls that the commune "was the center of much music-making and the exploration of mind-altering elements characteristic of the era."

Two years after the first Northern California Renaissance faire in 1967, a group of musicians and dancers who performed at the faire moved together to Preston Ranch, a small group of buildings not far from the faire site. Preston Ranch had been established in the late nineteenth century by Emily Preston, a charismatic faith healer. A community grew up around her, ultimately "developing its own residential cottages, school, hospital, church, cemetery and even a large and imposing Victorian mansion." After the founder, the community took on the name "Preston." The community had dissolved by the 1940s, but the last of them, an octogenarian named Elisha Green, met Renaissance faire performer Ernie Fischbach in 1968. "He liked all of us hippies," Ernie recalls. "He thought we were cool. He loved our music" (Zekley, "Preston").

When Ernie Fischbach met Elisha Green, Ernie and his wife, Deborah, were living in a Volkswagen bus in Berkeley. But when Deborah got pregnant, she made what seemed to her at the time to be a somewhat conventional decision: she wanted to be living in a house when she had the baby (D. Fischbach interview). Elisha Green was still living at Preston Ranch in the house his parents had owned there; the Fischbachs asked Russell

Lee, the owner of the Preston Ranch property since 1967, to let them move into one of the other houses. They paid twenty dollars a month for their own little "shack," and shortly thereafter, Preston Ranch became the home for a large number of the faire's musicians and dancers—some permanently, some for smaller stints of time. In the words of fiddler and faire musician Cait Reed,

> Preston was a music colony, that's what it was. . . . If a person wasn't a good musician when he or she got there, he became one really quickly. Because that's all you did—every day. That's how we all got good so quickly—we were *immersed* in it. We couldn't get away from it even if we wanted to. Another reason was that there were no radio and TV sets. So every night we played music. (Qtd. in Zekley, "Preston")

Multi-instrumentalist Mickie Zekley declares that there was "a continual migration of artists" to Preston Ranch; by defining a resident as one who lived there for at least thirty days, though, he was able to make a list from memory of forty-five people. Most if not all of these were employed in some capacity by the faire ("Preston").

The strong sense of the collective and the communal, acquired from living at Preston Ranch and working at the faire, according to Deborah Fischbach, contributed positively to the education of the "faire kids":

> You never worried about your kids. Everybody watched them. . . . One time in school, my daughter was trying to get a scholarship. She had to make up units to be tested in, and they asked, "What will we do for history?" She said, "How about if I name instruments from different ethnicities? You show them to me or play them for me, and I'll name them." She got an A. . . . [The communal living] fostered creative thinking. Kids had a worldview instead of a one-town view or a one-family view. (Interview)

As artists circulated through Preston Ranch and other musical communes, the California faires were becoming known as a center of the countercultural folk music scene through both formal and informal publicizing. For instance, Sheila Weller describes Northern California singer-songwriter and general scenester Laura Allen, who performed at the Renaissance faire, taking part in a jam session with "Canyon-Lady musicians and singers" at Joni Mitchell's Laurel Canyon house (303). The quarterly folk-music magazine *Sing Out!*, founded in 1950 by then-Communist editor Irwin Silber, began reminding its readers about each California faire, Southern and Northern, both acknowledging and cementing this position. Of the faire's role in bringing musicians together, hosting their explorations, and introducing their music to a growing audience, Will Spires comments, "We were all musicians before faire and knew each other, but it coalesced at the faire and put it out into the world" (interview).

And following certain shocking events, those that are passed on as representing the death of the counterculture (the violence that erupted at the Altamont Speedway Festival in 1969, the attacks by police on demonstrators and community members at Berkeley's People's Park the same year), the faire's early musicians argue emphatically that the faire played a new role: providing continuity in what they still think of as revolutionary values, cultural and social. "It [the counterculture's experimentation] went underground. It didn't end, but it went underground, and the faire let it continue. The ideas were there, and the faire became the medium," insists Ernie Fischbach, looking back over his own history (interview).

Reinventing Physical Theater

> We believe in the seriousness of laughter.
> —New Old Chautauqua mission statement

What Peter S. Beagle called "castle talk" is probably the most caricatured element of Renaissance faire performance; this purposeful construction of a pseudovernacular language form attracts attention as a fascinating rhetorical gambit in its own right. But the majority of nonmusical Renaissance faire performance falls under the rubric of *physical theater*—meaning that the narrative of the performance is conveyed mainly through gestures and manipulations of the body. In other words, although most performances do include speech, the draw is likely to center on some physical skill. The framework of physical theater is broad, but it is helpful for understanding the performance world of the Renaissance festival, which comprises a wide variety of acts that furthermore tend to have an interdisciplinary cast to them, operating on the borders of different forms or involving bits from more than one style of performance.

A host of performance styles that fall under the umbrella of physical theater are found at the faire: mime, clowning, puppetry, commedia, acrobatism, and dance theater, among others. In keeping with the ideals of physical theater, all these performers devise their own work, individually or collectively, in advance or improvisationally, rather than working from a script that is already established or authored by someone else. (If a script is established already, they will monkey around with it.) Especially important for the Renaissance festival, in these performances the traditional passive-audience/active-performer dichotomy is challenged.

Twentieth- and twenty-first-century physical theater has its roots in some very old forms, with scholars drawing connections to ancient Greek drama, Renaissance-era commedia dell'arte, Japanese Noh drama, and Balinese theater. It also has roots in "high" literary theater, with influential theorists, such as Konstantin Stanislavsky, Antonin Artaud, and Vsevolod Meyerhold experimenting with physicality as a central mode of the theatrical experience as they moved away from the idea (or ideal) of emotional realism. Over the course of the twentieth century, physical theater has steadily grown in mainstream popularity and influence, with a number of universities offering MFAs in physical theater.

The kinds of performances that fall under this rubric were to be found in a scant handful of divergent places in the United States when the Renaissance faires were starting: in a few avant-garde political theaters such as the San Francisco Mime Troupe or El Teatro Campesino, in looked-down-on "children's entertainment" such as party clowns, in somewhat rarified if important work by contemporary dance companies or certain stage directors (such as Peter Brooks). Most spectators had not heard of these experiments before the faires, and many avant-garde physical theatrical artists not only popularized their acts at the faire: they used the faire to develop cutting-edge acts that in turn shaped the theatrical world.

During the faire's first decade, the type of physical theater that audiences were most likely to have heard of would have been mime. But when performers were being located for the earliest Renaissance faires, the term *mime* had different associations from what it conjures today, which is largely "street mime" performances organized around "invisible" objects or forces. In 1963, many Americans were aware of French mime Marcel Marceau, whose melodramatic stage and film performances arguably created a large, worldwide audience for mime as a form. Marceau, who was deeply influenced by screen pantomime artists such as Charlie Chaplin and Buster Keaton, strove in his own account to use his body to convey psychologically revealing universal types (Lust 90–95). Other performers under the mantle of *mime*, most notably the San Francisco Mime Troupe (whose circles intersected from time to time with the faire's) used the term to invoke spirit rather than form.[12]

Because of the Renaissance Pleasure Faire's evolution from the commedia dell'arte, with its emphasis on satirical mimicry, it did not take long for the faire's entertainment directors to discover in mime a fitting act; mimes, in turn, found in the Renaissance faire a congenial home from which to evolve into a recognizable form in the United States. In addition to the commedia dell'arte, antecedents of mime were found in Renaissance-era England, in the vernacular "mummers plays" that generally marked the changing of the seasons; these were performed in public places—in the street, in pubs, or house to house. Scholars of mime distinguish between these performances and other silent comedy, such as Charlie Chaplin's movies, in which the actors play a single character, who moves seamlessly through a continuous plot. Instead, they define mime as built around some degree of spontaneity and making use of short sketches and the artist's ability to "become" multiple characters (often based on real people) in quick succession.[13]

As early as during the Renaissance festival's Pacifica days, it came to be associated with a school of mime that it was instrumental in popularizing and developing, generally called "street mime." James Gousseff offers a somewhat fluid definition of the form in his book *Street Mime*: "What is street mime? 'Street Mime' is used here as a generic term to include any relatively spontaneous silent entertainment (neither dance nor silent acting), performed while mingling (at least partially) with an unexpecting (somewhat) audience in almost anyplace *except* a theatre" (9). Gousseff, writing in 1993 when the faire as an institution was thirty years old, cites the Renaissance festival as a place where street mimes could be found.

But the history of mimes at the faire goes much further back. The figures who taught the generation of mimes that Gousseff studied found performance opportunity and honed their craft at the early Pleasure Faire. Those innovators continue to feel the giddiness of possibility that the faire's first decades represented to them.

Billy Scudder and Robert Shields

Actor Billy Scudder, who, following years at the Renaissance Pleasure Faire, has built a career out of impersonating pantomime artist Charlie Chaplin, likes to point to a poem he wrote in 2001 about the faire as the best demonstration of what those early faires meant to him when he was a budding actor and mime. The poem connects the artistic possibility of the faire with the idealism of the early counterculture, declaring that the faire "came from a generation called Love." Scudder first attended the faire in 1968, when he was living in North Hollywood, trying to succeed as an actor while supporting his three children. At the time, the faire was held at the Paramount Studios ranch in Agoura Hills. Scudder recalls having been to the property much earlier, in 1959, when it held a car racetrack that had been built for the 1959 movie *On the Beach*. He describes what he saw when he returned to the ranch to attend the faire ten years later: "There was the village. It was like discovering Brigadoon. I knew there was a world like this somewhere. . . . The first day, I walked around in awe." Scudder went on to perform at the faire the next year, joining a mime troupe run by Jack Albee, of whom he laughs, "He was a complete anarchist!" (interview)

Jack Albee was the son of artists and a cousin of playwright Edward Albee; the character he played when he put on his makeup was so carefully developed that Patricia J. Campbell, in *Passing the Hat: Street Performers in America*, calls it a "literary construct" (154). Albee grew up in Paris, among "the absurdists and existentialists of the thirties" (155). Fascinatingly, Jack Albee's grandfather was the owner of several important vaudeville theaters, in which an earlier generation of pantomime artists performed. Developing his mime character, Albee "combined his early memories of the Fratellini clown act, the films of Giulietta Masina, and the early work of Marcel Marceau, and came up with a Pierrot-like character that was unique for that time" (155). According to Campbell, Albee carried his faire innovation directly and literally to the streets beyond:

> He again donned the makeup and costume to distribute posters for the first Renaissance Faire, and when his armful of posters was all gone, he continued to cavort in the street. Such a thing at that time was, of course, unheard of, but the decade was receptive to public craziness. Jack took his mime persona to San Francisco, where he performed to the accompaniment of a musical trio of violin, harp, and bass, and later joined forces with pioneer street-mime Robert Shields. (156)

Shortly after joining Albee's mime troupe at the faire, Scudder attended classes in Shakespeare and commedia dell'arte taught in Berkeley by Carlo Mazzone-Clementi at his Dell'Arte School of Mime and Comedy. Mazzone-Clementi, who grew up in Padua, Italy, played a paramount role in the revival of the commedia dell'arte form and the renaissance of Italian theater in the 1950s. When he was performing with the Piccolo Theatro company in the first Italian staging of Bertolt Brecht, Mazzone-Clementi met the American stage director and scholar of American theater Eric Bentley, who had come to Italy to direct the play; with Bentley's support, he toured the United States teaching mime and commedia. By the time he arrived in the United States, Mazzone-Clementi had worked with both Marcel Marceau and Jacques Lecoq, another French innovator in the theater of movement, and had come to assert that mime was the basis of all theater. Mazzone-Clementi liked to remind his American students that although the dramatic theater in the United States had been becoming more and more elitist and exclusive since the heyday of vaudeville, theater had once been a form of popular culture, and he urged that those popular forms—with their attendant ridiculing of officialdom—be reinvigorated. By training with him, the faire performers were schooled in, and subsequently themselves passed along, this radically populist view of theater.

After performing for three years in Jack Albee's mime troupe and training with Mazzone-Clementi, Scudder began performing commedia at the faire. His first new role was the character of the Fool, or Harlequin. Scudder likes to tell a story about his first costume to illustrate what he considers to be the nature of the 1960s faires: he made the Harlequin costume himself, from scraps of fabric of varying sizes donated to him by numerous other faire workers. This made the costume resemble the faire itself, according to Scudder: it was handmade, improvised, communal, and motley. Scudder recalls the faire's role in offering an alternative to mainstream values as vividly as he does its performances. "The first faires—we camped there," he rhapsodizes. "Everyone was on the same wavelength. We all worked for each other" (interview). The faire, says Scudder, thrived as a place where countercultural ideas about the nature and utility of performance were swapped and developed.

It was at the faire that Billy Scudder's path crossed with that of a very young Robert Shields. The teenage Shields had ahead of him a prominent career as one of the United States' most visible mime performers, most notably as part of the duo Shields and Yarnell, which he formed with his then-wife Lorene Yarnell. Shields, born in 1951, grew up in Los Angeles. He gravitated toward performance early on, working as a birthday party clown at the age of fourteen and demonstrating nascent miming skills as a performer at a wax museum, where he honed an imitation of a robot's movements as "Robbie, the Mechanical Man."

In 1968, Shields visited the faire and saw Scudder's silent mime performance. Immediately sensing a kindred spirit, he says, he approached Scudder to demonstrate how he could imitate a robot. Shields then asked in wonder, "What are you doing?" In response, Scudder, without breaking his silence, took Shields to his booth and put mime's traditional whiteface makeup on him. Both Scudder and Shields refer to this moment as a truly dramatic moment of conversion. Shields declares, "I was a little high school kid, and Billy [Scudder] turned me into a mime" (interview). Shields claims to have known right off the bat that the moment, symbolized by the silent application of mime's makeup, was life changing for him. "I hurried home to tell my father about the faire," says Shields as he describes his transformation. "I wanted him to know. I told him, 'Something has happened in my life!'" (interview).

The Renaissance faire and Shields turned out to be very good for each other. From 1968 to 1969, Shields played a Harlequin there, a stock character from the commedia dell'arte. Though he initially performed with Scudder and Scudder's miming partner, as part of a three-person troupe,

Shields quickly became the biggest act at the faire. "I was a jack-in-the-box," says Shields. "I developed my own act, drew giant crowds. This was the beginning of my career" (interview).

Forty years later, Shields is still effusive when he talks about what made the early Renaissance faire seem so special. He is adamant that the cultural importance of the faire stemmed from its countercultural-ism, from the utopian, anticonsumerist, anticonformist opportunities it presented in contrast to mainstream cultural values and practices that he found stultifying. "The most interesting part was coming *out* [of the faire]," he explains. "You couldn't wait to go back" (interview). Shields has remained rhapsodic about the thirty-odd times he entered the faire gates. "Everyone was in a *really good mood*," he emphasizes. "The food was amazing. There was no hype—we *made* everything. Now, the costumes are all shiny, they are bought—but then, we *made* our shirts. We made the ruffs for our costumes. . . . Outside, it was like the world of the show *Mad Men*. Inside, there was color, makeup, scented oils, raw avocado. There was no packaged stuff!" (interview). Shields remains celebratory about the experimentation and sense of newness that guided early faire culture. "Sure, we were doing drugs," he comments bluntly. "We were all young! It reminded me of Pinocchio's time at the fair. Everything went, everything was 'yes!' I had sex in a tree house!" (interview).

Despite the opportunities the faire offered, Shields moved on for two practical reasons, one of which was, paradoxically, his success there. "I left the faire because I was drawing such big crowds," he confesses. "From passing a hat, I earned $150 to $200 a day. At that time, there were very few mimes [in the United States]. So I left—I was trying to do this full-time. I wanted to make a living at it. I learned how to make a business plan." Further, says Shields, "I was hurting my knees. I wanted to wear kneepads, but they wouldn't let me because of the question of authenticity" (interview).

So, after some thirty faire performances, Shields sought out other stages. In 1970, the famous French mime Marcel Marceau invited him to be a student and guest at his home in Berchères, France. In 1971, Shields moved to San Francisco, where he became a well-known street performer in the city's historic Union Square, where, in keeping with the faire's strategy of putting everyone onstage, he developed an attitude that is "not 'look at me,' but 'look at you'" (Shields 13). One of San Francisco's earliest buskers, Shields occasionally landed in jail for jumping on buses, directing traffic, and otherwise making the public square his "stage"; these police efforts served to turn him into a citywide cause célèbre. In 1972, Shields began to perform in a variety of venues that ranged from hospitals to rock concerts, cementing his hipness in 1972 by opening for the Rolling Stones and contributing to *Rolling Stone* in the same year. That same year, he formed the mime duo Shields and Yarnell with Lorene Yarnell, whom he married. The two went on have their own television show, *The Shields and Yarnell Show*, which ran on CBS from 1978 to 1979, in addition to making hundreds of other television appearances. After all that, Shields insists, "My greatest routines were created there—at the Renaissance faire" (interview).

Following Shields's formative stint at the Renaissance Pleasure Faire, he became perhaps the most well-known American mime and certainly the country's first—and most successful—street mime (Gousseff 15–19). In other words, he was remarkably able to carry outside the faire gates some of what he is so eloquent about finding within them, and forty years later, the street mime is a familiar figure, and the American mime tradition has continued to evolve. (Shields currently lives in Sedona, Arizona, where he makes jewelry and sculpture.)

One particularly striking example of Shields's influence was the impression he made on the young Michael Jackson. By Jackson's own accounting, he intently watched Shields on television with his siblings while he was growing up in Gary, Indiana, in the 1970s. Not surprisingly given his own huge talent for performance, young Jackson was more than a passive viewer. He was fascinated by Shields and carefully studied his movements. Later, Jackson stated outright that he learned his robot movies from studying Shields, who performed a robot character, named "Mr. Clinker," on the show. (Yarnell played his robot wife, "Mrs. Clinker.") From Shields, Jackson also took his propensity to wear gorgeously elaborate military-style jackets, which became a trademark for him as it was for Shields (think of the black, sequined, military-style jacket Jackson wore in the *Bad* era) and sparkling white gloves.

Indeed, it is difficult to overestimate the significance of Shields's influence on black urban culture. Imitating a robot, or "botting," is a central practice in the breakdancer's repertoire and furthermore is the skill that underlies related practices such as bopping or popping. The more historically inclined dancers cite Shields, as Michael Jackson did, as an important teacher and inspiration. In other words, to understand fully the cultural significance of the Renaissance faire, it is necessary keep in mind the following linear development, striking in its straightforwardness: Robert Shields reports that his most important routines were devised at the Renaissance faire, where he furthermore was first introduced to mime. Shields then became an object of fascination, inspiration, and imitation for Michael Jackson, who came to be called the King of Pop and known to be the most successful entertainment artist of all time—as well as for a whole generation of urban black dancers.

Thus, when magician Penn Jillette—who also got his start at the Renaissance faire in the 1970s—jokes that the deliberate anachronism of the Renaissance faire performers can be summed up as "ye olde Michael Jackson" (Trillin 122), he is correct on levels that he is not intending. For that matter, many performers and crafters at the Southern California Renaissance Pleasure Faire recall Jackson visiting the faire in his late teens or early twenties when it was held in Agoura (dressed, somewhat idiosyncratically, as a modern clown)—bringing the faire's influence on him full circle in addition to literalizing Jillette's offhand jokes.

Both Shields and Scudder describe the faire's performing world as the last bastion of vaudeville, a description that the faire's performers—mimes and also jugglers, sword swallowers, dancers, magicians, acrobats, tightrope walkers, and comedians—have continued to use. "It's the new vaudeville, man!" is how Ray St. Louis describes the faire—and his novel *Road Dog Diary*—on the book's back cover. These performers are embracing the umbrella term for variety shows that developed and became popular from about 1880 to 1930, declining with the advent of motion pictures. Vaudeville shows presented some of the performance arts found at the Renaissance faire and others as well: a theater's bill would include a dozen or more acts, such as musical numbers, trained animals, comedians, celebrity appearances, and more, performed by different artists. The individual acts were unrelated to each other but tended to have in common an element of physical virtuosity.

Vaudeville was lastingly influential on American culture not only for its performance styles but also because of the wide audiences it entertained. The most popular form of entertainment in its heyday, vaudeville stages large and small attracted thousands of Americans, including new immigrants and the growing urban working class. In fact, vaudeville came to represent as well as speak to the new cultural diversity of the early twentieth century, bringing together material from a variety of cultural traditions. Thus, in terms of production and reception, vaudeville was the earliest entertainment form to cross racial and class boundaries. It also represented entertainment fully and successfully operating within the realm of the commercial without losing its artistic edge, making it a congenial model for some of the performers in the faire's latter corporate period.

One of the most popular current acts among these self-styled vaude-villians at the Renaissance faire is Johnny Fox, a magician and sword swallower. Fox was born in 1953 and became interested in physical stage arts at an early age, beginning his performance career as a sleight-of-hand magician in Florida. In a trajectory not unusual for faire performers, both those in physical theater and musicians, he began his career as a street performer before discovering the Renaissance faire as a hospitable environment for his act. Fox has been performing on the faire circuit since 1979; at his peak of traveling, he says, he performed at six or seven faires each year (interview).

It is hard not to wonder how Fox learned to swallow swords—he taught himself, he says, practicing five minutes before breakfast, lunch, and dinner each day—or why—he says that he needed an act that other performers could not easily copy. In his act at the Maryland Renaissance Festival, Fox swallows a twenty-two-inch sword, the handle of a metal spoon of the same length, a giant screwdriver, and a long balloon of the kind that clowns fashion into animals.

Fox is particularly historically minded and describes himself as deeply influenced by the popular vaudeville performers, as well as by the circus and sideshow performers who preceded vaudeville, such as Dan Rice. Rice, a multiform performer, reached his height of popularity just before the Civil War, becoming—as the Industrial Revolution allowed for mass production and dissemination of culture—a leader in the invention of

American popular culture. Rice was an important clown and, later, black-face singer; he became associated with parodies of Shakespeare that are similar in spirit to jokes and productions at the Renaissance festival, such as those by the Reduced Shakespeare Company, the Nickel Shakespeare Girls, and Shakespeare's Scum Players.

According to Fox, when he began putting together his act, "some vaudeville performers were still alive": "I would pick their brains. I also studied vaudeville and vaudeville-influenced performances on film, in print, in books, to give me the feel [of vaudeville styles]" (interview). Through the faire, Fox met other performers who were also studying vaudevillians, immersing themselves in the techniques of that genera-tion's burlesque and variety performers. According to an estimate Fox made in 1999, the number of working sword swallowers in the United States has grown since he began practicing the art, possibly supporting the argument that vaudeville styles are undergoing a resurgence (though if his estimation of the number—about two dozen—is correct, it is still not many; Louie).

Fox's historical interest in the content and contexts of vaudeville has taken him outside of his own performance, leading him to open a museum of curiosities, called the Freakatorium, which was located for five years in Times Square and now operates as the Museum of Unnatural History at the Maryland Renaissance Festival. Fox's museum was home of an important collection of some of the earliest sideshow memorabilia and was originally conceived as an homage to the Bowery dime museums of the 1890s, where magicians of the day got their start performing. The museum was presented in Victorian style (somewhat muted in its current Renaissance faire iteration), with the exhibits mostly dating from before 1912: a photograph of Jojo the dogface boy, for instance, perhaps the most famous sideshow performer of all, who suffered from hypertrichosis and traveled with P. T. Barnum's circus until his death in 1904, or a carving by Charles Tripp, armless woodcarver (and later in life, armless photog-rapher), who was one of Canada's best-known entertainers. "I want to get people to look at something they don't want to see," says Fox of his exhib-its, in a video on his website (J. Fox).

Like Johnny Fox, juggler Paul Hudert, who performs on the Renais-sance faire circuit as Paolo Garbanzo the Gypsy Juggler, identifies vaudeville as the style in which he works. Hudert's juggling skills are impressive, and a single performance will have him slinging knives, flaming torches, onions, and a variety of other objects. But at least as important to Hudert's act is his banter with the audience. In standard faire practice, he uses various techniques to push the audience outside their comfort zones: flirting stagily with men in the audience he judges as straight, bribing children to steal banners and signs from surrounding booths, giving impious interpretations of recognizable forms such as safety advice for children ("Kids, when you are at home, don't play with fire! Go to your friends' house to do it!").

Hudert locates the Renaissance faire at the forefront of what he says is turning out to be a reemergence of vaudeville: "The faire is the last bastion of vaudeville. Well, it *used* to be the last bastion of vaudeville. Now vaudeville's making a comeback, which is so strange," he comments, when I ask him to look back over his whole performance career (interview).

In bringing back the skills or vocabularies of vaudeville, Hudert and many other faire performers feel as though they are working to create a sort of populist theater of the kind Mazzone-Clementi promoted. Hudert finds this goal to be both gratifying and subversive, given the associations many Americans have of the theater with either an economic or educational elite:

> But the other thing about performing at this kind of venue . . . is the live audience. And I get shit for this all the time, but I said this in a TV interview. I said, "Renaissance faires are live theater without the stigma of live theater." And what I meant by that was that—okay, say, if I said the word "opera," you think of boring. You think of snobs. You don't want anything to do with opera. If I said, "Let's take in a show somewhere," again, elitist. But you can go to the Ren faire and drink your beer and look at tits and still end up having a theatrical experience. And so it's part of the subversiveness, I think, of the Ren faire. It's like, "Ha, ha. I just gave you theater." And that's what I like about it. (Interview)

Hudert's point about the assumptions many audience members carry in with them about theater points to a fascinating kind of double consciousness that exists about faire performances. For instance, most faires have some performances that are versions of Shakespeare. At the Georgia faire, for instance, the Nickel Shakespeare Girls approach patrons, ask them to name any play of Shakespeare's, and then perform something from that play—with clowning, gymnastics, music, fire eating, and general hollering. Many audience members howl with laughter at this, because seeing Shakespeare treated irreverently is satisfying to them. But the performers, backstage, comment that the off-color jokes, the juggling or acrobatics they have mixed in, and the topical political references are all entirely in keeping with the original tone of Shakespeare's plays, which worked at multiple levels in the same way that the more self-conscious vaudeville performers do at the faire.

The New Vaudeville

> Non-sexist, non-racist humor simply did not exist before that time. Before that we never had the 70s under our belt. The old joke books are filled with jokes that were useless . . . jokes based on sexist or racist assumptions that were now being questioned.
> —Tom Noddy, puppeteer and bubble magician

From Johnny Fox's sword swallowing to Paul Hudert's juggling, the range of faire performances called "vaudeville" make use of a variety of physical skills. They are unified, though, by a subversive self-consciousness and a purposeful goading of the audience outside its comfort zone. In the 1980s, some of these performers took the acts they were able to create at the faire and, with other kindred spirits, created a loose theatrical movement that came to be known as "New Vaudeville." The term *New Vaudeville* was coined by *New York Times* critic Mel Gussow, who began using it regularly in reviews by 1983. New Vaudeville emphasizes, in the words of Robert Knopf, "physical comedy, improvisation, and a direct relationship with the audience in the service of anarchistic comedy and irreverence" (148). New Vaudeville shares much with "old" vaudeville in terms of form; what distinguishes it the most is probably a certain self-awareness about intent, as practitioners consider themselves to be motivated not only by entertainment value but also by a desire to make political statements and social satire and to break through the traditional wall between spectator and performer.

According to theater historian Ron Jenkins, who profiles New Vaudeville artists—including three important acts that first flourished at the Renaissance faire—in his book *Acrobat of the Soul*, these performers are "linked by the ingenuity with which they subversively attack the oppressive elements of everyday life in modern America" (xii). Jenkins identifies several strands of performing influence that are also found flowing into and out of the Renaissance faire:

> Drawing on traditions of circus, commedia dell'arte, carnival, medicine show, vaudeville, and the experimental theatre collectives of the sixties, they have developed unique forms of popular entertainment that offer audiences an exhilarating blast of comic liberation. . . . The virtuosity of these comic performers is particularly compelling because it is presented not as an end in itself, but as a means of illuminating the conflicts between ordinary people and the forces that victimize them. (xii)

Jenkins locates these performers in a history of "American clowns pitting their skills against the forces of social oppression" (xv).

Mime Avner Eisenberg, who performs as Avner the Eccentric, is a member of this latter group. Eisenberg was born in 1948; he received a degree in theater from the University of Wisconsin in 1971 and then left for Paris, where he studied mime and movement with renowned movement instructor and physical theater innovator Jacques Lecoq at his École International de Théâtre from 1971 to 1973. Upon returning to the United States, Eisenberg taught at Carlo Mazzone-Clementi's school of commedia dell'arte (where many early Renaissance faire performers studied). In 1974, he moved to Minneapolis with a friend he had met in Paris to try to get bookings for shows of his own; there he met the entertainment director of the Minnesota Renaissance Festival, who recruited him to perform there the next year. In his own account, Eisenberg went from scrambling for stage time to performing six shows a day at the faire, no matter how tired he was or what the weather conditions were; because of this, he calls the Renaissance faire his "training ground" (interview).

Eisenberg credits the Renaissance faire with incubating many new vaudevillians. "It was the vaudeville of its day," he says. "The birth of New Vaudeville was at the Minnesota Renaissance Festival in a lot of ways" (interview). Like many faire performers, Eisenberg traveled the circuit according to its season. At the height of his involvement with the faire, he traveled to perform at three faires in a given year; this provided enough "stage time," he explains, to enable a performer to support him- or herself for a whole year. Eisenberg is emphatic that his experience at the faire was "essential" to his development as an artist (interview).

At the faire, Eisenberg's act was not assigned to a particular space. Instead, he would scout out locations where there were trees large enough and the right distance apart for him to set up a rope-walking act. Because the rope would be high up, and therefore visible from a distance, he would easily gather a good-sized crowd who would applaud wildly after he walked the rope. Thereupon, recalls Eisenberg, he would have nothing equally dramatic to follow up with. This situation prompted him to think about what really mattered to him about his own performance and what his goals and motivations were as an actor—in other words, what Avner Eisenberg wanted to put across as Avner the Eccentric:

> The wisdom at the time was you had to do danger: fire, swords. I wasn't interested in that. So I would start to tie the rope up, which would start to collect a crowd. I would practice these digressions. So, for me, in a theatrical or philosophical sense, it was about all the things we do to avoid responsibilities. I'd get distracted—I'd have a whole set of maybe a ten or twenty distractions that could happen, and I'd choose from them, depending upon who was in the audience. I'd have things that I did with various musical instruments, with things that people had bought at the faire, with baby strollers. And slowly, it became an act. (Interview)

At the Minnesota festival, Eisenberg met other performers who, after similarly developing trademark acts at the faire, using physical skills to comment on their own acts and on the modern condition, would also very shortly transition to perform at "legit" theatrical venues and receive acclaim in the theatrical world under the New Vaudeville moniker. Most significant among these were juggler/acrobat/comedians the Flying Karamazov Brothers, a troupe that formed in 1973 at the Northern California Renaissance Pleasure Faire, and the Asparagus Valley Culture Society, illusionists who later became famous as Penn and Teller.

The Flying Karamazov Brothers have, at present, been performing more than thirty years (with some changes in personnel along the way, including a short stint by Paul Hudert). The high-energy, fast-talking troupe has become well known for its exhibition of startling dare-devilry but just as much for the "brothers'" incredibly fast-paced banter, which juxtaposes "high" and "low" cultural references, political satire, and self-mockery, mostly without pausing to catch their own breath, let alone letting the audience catch theirs. (This is a literal observation: founding member Howard Patterson describes a style of speaking that the troupe developed in which the "brothers" take turns hollering out parts of the same line in tandem, so that one can breathe while the other finishes the thought, thereby allowing them to perform certain parts of their act without pausing for breath.) In the words of Ron Jenkins, the Flying Karamazov Brothers "take fragmented bits of American miscellany and juggle them into patchwork symphonies of visual jazz" (59).

The Karamazovs also became known for a couple of trademark acts. In one, called the "Terror Trick" (and renamed the "Danger Trick" for a couple of years after the September 11, 2001, attacks on the World Trade Center), they juggle an egg, a sausage, a lit torch, a frying pan, a cleaver, a pair of handcuffs, and a bottle of champagne—ultimately chopping the sausage and cooking it, with the egg, in the pan using the flame of the torch, whereupon two "brothers" wearing the handcuffs drink the champagne while another plays a chord on the ukulele. In another trademark skit, they invite audience members to come forward and present "the Champ"—for years, founding member Howard Patterson—with disparate items to juggle; those in the know come prepared with things they think would be hard to juggle because they are slippery or breakable or imbalanced: a raw chicken, a box of donuts, a head of lettuce, stuffed animals, items of clothing, or various household objects.

Penn Jillette and his performing partner, Teller (who has legally changed his name from the first-name/last-name combination he was given at birth to just "Teller"), are most frequently described as magicians. But this label is so inadequate to describe what they do onstage that Calvin Trillin joked, when they won an Obie for their Off-Broadway show, that it was awarded to them for "whatever it is they do" (101). They began performing together at the Renaissance festival in the mid-1970s. At that time, Teller was a high school Latin teacher who moonlighted as a magician. Jillette had studied at the Ringling Brothers Clown College after leaving high school early in Greenfield, Massachusetts, where he had begun performing as a juggler with classmate Michael Moschen. (Moschen went on to invent "contact juggling," receiving such rarefied praise as "sculptor of motion" and a MacArthur "genius" grant for doing so.)[14] Together with a third performer, a musician named Weir Chrisemer, Jillette and Teller began performing as Asparagus Valley Cultural Society. Teller took a year's leave from teaching to try it, and their first gig was the Minnesota Renaissance Festival. In the act, Jillette juggled, Teller did magic tricks, and Chrisemer played music.

During the 1970s and into the early 1980s, Penn and Teller honed an act in which Penn talks a mile a minute, Teller generally remains silent and uses pantomime for communication, and juggling was phased out. (They also split with Chrisemer along the way.) The duo prospered at the faire, earning several thousand dollars a weekend at their peak. While the faire itself was not as philosophically compelling to them as it was to performers such as Shields, they do consider the faire as having provided important performance opportunities that enabled them to develop their act—crafting a much grittier one than the type of thing Penn calls "circus schlock" (Trillin 115). Penn says, "Minneapolis was where I understood us to have created the show" (Trillin 120). Further, when a play that Penn and Teller staged closed almost immediately, devastating them emotionally and financially, they were able to take to the faire circuit to recover (Trillin 130).

More than thirty years later, the grittiness is still in evidence. Penn and Teller's tricks are often gory, using shock value to up the ante on Houdini-like escapes on the part of Teller. Characteristically, they discuss onstage the intellectual foundation of illusionism; their act has developed over the years increasingly to emphasize the exposing of fraud—including both the "fraud" they are perpetrating on the audience through their tricks and spiritualism of any kind. They have said that while they consider it insulting to the audience's intelligence to pretend that they have mystical powers, practicing a kind of self-debunking packs a much more powerful punch; in the words of Penn Jillette,

> Now if . . . I come out, I fan that deck of cards, and I say to you: "Bullshit. There's no fucking ESP. I'm not reading your fucking mind. I learn to do shit to be able to fuck with you in ways you ain't been fucked with before. And I'm going to tell you what that card is, and I'm going to tell you something else—I don't got nothing. I don't got nothing but the fact that I am going to cheat you, and I'm going to dick you around, and I'm going to yank you, until I know what that fucking card is." Now which one of these has more social and political repercussions. (Jenkins 163)

While Penn and Teller, along with Eisenberg and the Flying Karamazov Brothers, were in Minneapolis for the Minnesota Renaissance Festival, they were noticed by a local performance venue founded by, and named for, theatrical innovator Dudley Riggs. Riggs had pioneered a kind of theater involving audience input in New York, which he called "instant theater." Today this kind of performance is called "improvisational theater"—but at the time, the term *improvisation* was only recognized in reference to music, specifically jazz. Riggs's company performed in various locales across the United States before settling in Minneapolis, where it established a focus on satirical comedy revues under the name Dudley Riggs' Brave New Workshop. In the words of improvisational actor and director of improv theater Second City Michael Gellman, looking back in 2008 at the Brave New Workshop's history,

> The Brave New Workshop had been, since the late 1950s, a cutting-edge cabaret theater performing satire and comedy revues. For years the shows at the Brave New Workshop had been written (scripted) by four journalists who wrote by day for the *Minneapolis Star* and the *Minneapolis Tribune*: Mike Anthony, Dick Guindon, Irv Letofsky, and Dan Sullivan. Years later the slogan for the Brave New Workshop's twenty-fifth anniversary was "Twenty-five Years of Comedy, Satire, and Promiscuous Hostility." (xiii–xiv)

The Brave New Workshop booked Avner the Eccentric, the Karamazovs, and Penn and Teller to perform one-month runs in tandem. This, according to Eisenberg, provided the definitive transition for these acts to leave the faire. He explains, "I think what happened to all of us is we started doing theater shows, and we felt that we couldn't go to the faire and pass the hat anymore. We couldn't ask them to spend ten bucks to see us in the theater and then be begging for quarters" (interview).

Eisenberg worked out a way to stay at the faire for just a little while. "In my last few years of doing the faire, I negotiated a deal where they paid me a little more, but less than I would have made passing the hat. But at the time of the hat-passing speech—I made a little speech that the queen had been flogging the peasants, the coffers were full, and the show was a gift," he recounts (interview). The Flying Karamazov Brothers, on the other hand, had come to feel considerably less at home at the faire than Eisenberg did and, according to founding member Howard Patterson, were just as happy to move on. They point out the faire's role in the development of performance styles that did not have venues elsewhere, but in the context of their own labor, they were beginning to find it tough going. Longtime Flying Karamazov Brothers juggler Tim Furst describes a complicated tension between enjoyment of the faire's community and the realities of working conditions for performers who might be Rennies but were still working persons performing labor for other persons:

> In the early days, the faire gave the opportunity for people to perform types of things that there weren't other venues for, except [busking] on the street. For many, the atmosphere and fun of doing it mattered more than the money, although for people who performed there more than a couple of years, especially if they didn't have regular jobs, it was hard enough work that after a while they would be *willing* to do it—for the money. (Interview)

Howard Patterson, for his part, acknowledges that the faire "felt like a home" to many performers but remarks that he never felt quite the same level of comfort there. In his view, the Oregon County fair, which remained "more of a hippie fair," gave broader artistic license to comment on the postindustrial world, rather than donating energy to re-creating a preindustrial one (interview).

The Karamazovs' fellow New Vaudevillians Penn and Teller adopt a somewhat defensive stance about their years performing at the faire, with Penn Jillette saying that he "would do anything" to move into show business, and "one of those anythings on that list was a Renaissance festival" (Ken P.). Jillette's partner, Teller, expresses a similar sentiment in the foreword he wrote for the memoir penned by fellow faire performer Mark Sieve, who formed half of the vaudeville-style duo Puke and Snot with Joe Kudla; Teller sums up the faire's after-hours scene as "dirt, dope, and drumming" (Teller xii). Although it made professional sense for Penn and Teller to use the faire as a launching pad for their performance career, they were eager to leave the faire for other venues. But their friends Puke and Snot, whom Calvin Trillin described in the *New Yorker* as "the nonpareils of the Renaissance faire circuit" (123), continued to work on the faire circuit, becoming a favorite act and drawing crowds of hundreds. After Kudla (a.k.a. "Snot") died in 2009, he was replaced by John Gamoke (as "Snot, Jr."), and the new duo continues to work at the faires.

Soon after leaving the faire, Eisenberg, the Karamazovs, and Penn and Teller were doing stage shows exclusively, ultimately on Broadway, where, along with mime Bill Irwin, they were noticed by the *New York Times*'s Gussow and collectively dubbed as part of New Vaudeville. Irwin, whom Gussow described as "a brilliant clown, mime, dancer and prankster" (331), went on to perform in plays (winning a Tony award for his Broadway role in Edward Albee's *Who's Afraid of Virginia Woolf?*), television (including a long-running role on PBS's children's series *Sesame Street* as a character named "Mister Noodle"), and movie appearances. First, though, he performed at the Renaissance faire as part of a small troupe put together by fire eater Michael Mielnik, a.k.a. the Reverend Chumleigh, an old friend of the Karamazov Brothers and Avner Eisenberg (Mielnik email). Mielnik was "the closest thing to a hippie version of W. C. Fields," in the words of trapeze artist Rebecca Chace (6).

At an arts festival in Orange County, California, in 1975, Irwin met some performers who convinced him to hitchhike up north with them to perform at the Northern California Renaissance Pleasure Faire. Like many of his contemporaries, he recalls being drawn to the opportunity to "improvise in the thoroughfare areas—the streets," though eventually he did more performing on stages. Paid in food tickets and whatever he could garner from passing the hat, he could experiment with his act and "thread the needle . . . and stay clear of the realm of the day-job" (email).

The New Vaudevillians were fascinated by the history of American theater and the idea that theater could be a populist institution. Mielnik in particular poured a lot of energy into the project of revitalizing vaudeville-inspired performances. For a short while, he operated a small vaudeville theater north of Seattle, where he staged performances and showed old movies. (He no longer owns the building but still advertises a "16mm Historical Film Archive of the Classic and Offbeat.") The theater also housed Mielnik's collection of books and souvenirs pertaining to early vaudevillians (interview).

The Renaissance faire was one important route traveled by New Vaudevillians, along with the San Francisco Mime Troupe and the Bread and Puppet Theater in Glover, Vermont. Among them, these three major loci of 1960s radical theatrical traditions contributed to bigger stages for not only the Karamazov Brothers, Avner the Eccentric, Penn and Teller, Bill Irwin, and Reverend Chumleigh but also members of the Big Apple Circus, members of Cirque du Soleil, members of the Pickle Family Circus, and others. At the height of the Reagan era, they drew on 1960s-era political idealism as part of their performance stance.

Eisenberg is eloquent about the impetus and goals of New Vaudeville: "Among the elements of New Vaudeville is that it is nonviolent and nonracist, and it is a reaction to the kinds of theatre we don't like. . . . New Vaudeville did not grow out of Old Vaudeville. We reinvented theatre for ourselves. We reacted against TV and Hollywood movies. . . . We created a theatre that grew out of the streets and out of the political sense of the sixties" (Lust 209).

As many commentators have pointed out, a hugely important focus for the New Vaudevillians is direct interaction with the audience. This focus has several shaping functions on the content of the performances. Many New Vaudevillians routinely break the fourth wall, addressing audience members directly, bringing them up onstage, or, in the case of the Flying Karamazov Brothers, dramatically entering (by swinging overhead) the space of the audience. Along the same lines, many New Vaudevillian performers conduct a deliberate demystification of what they are doing onstage, with magicians revealing how their tricks work, jugglers commenting sarcastically on their own skills, or acrobats admitting, with faux bitterness, that jousters are going to "steal" their audience. Eisenberg, for instance, comments, "The way I used to see it, I had fifteen minutes of tricks crammed into a two-hour show" (interview). "Despite their avant-garde affinities," writes C. Lee Jenner in the canon-making *Cambridge Guide to American Theatre*, "New Vaudevillians forsake elitist aspects of experimental theatre for populist perspectives, and expose the mysteries of their entertainment specialties" (478).

In addition to these structural attempts to break down the hierarchy of traditional theatrical settings, New Vaudevillians thought deeply about the social meaning of their acts, down to the humor. Bubble artist Tom Noddy feels that this is, in large part, because of the way that these acts shared space with audiences and thus were pushed during the 1960s and 1970s to consider audience reaction to the implications of their jokes. It is this consciousness, he believes, that brought about the loose confederation of New Vaudeville performers:

> When I met the Flying Karamazov Brothers and saw their act, when they saw the act of Avner the Eccentric, when Avner saw Reverend Chumleigh and Magical Mystical Michael, . . . we knew that we were connected. Some of it was political, but not all. Some was a revival of old vaudeville skills or even actual routines refreshed, rewritten, and revived, but some were brand new and would not have worked in old vaudeville. When we all saw Polaris the Wizard (later called Alfredo Fettuccini of Laughing Moon Theater) we all immediately knew that he was one of ours. I believe that it was related to the fact that each of these performers made you laugh for long periods of time without once bringing up a sexist or racist assumption. Comedy was so tied to those old racial and sexual stereotypes that to do that at that time it was necessary for you to have consciously removed or rewritten the jokes that carried those assumptions. Maybe you took it out only to sharpen the pace of the act (by avoiding the hisses) or maybe you took it out because you cared about the issue . . . but the end result was non-sexist, non-racist humor. That conscious exclusion of sexism, like Tony Pastor's conscious exclusion of sexy material in an earlier age helped to shape a new kind of entity . . . a new kind of vaudeville. (2–3)

Tim Furst of the Flying Karamazov Brothers agrees that New Vaude-ville is consciously historically based but at the same time deliberately free of the cultural assumptions that shaped the original vaudeville per-formances: "It reminds grandparents of vaudeville acts that they might have seen seventy years ago, but minus the ethnic and gender stereo-types . . .not that it's entirely PC, but it doesn't depend on that type of humor. The sexual innuendo is not as heavy-handed as in the acts of bur-lesque comics who based whole routines on that" (interview). In this way, in the words of critic Rachel Shteir, the New Vaudevillians strive to "clown and fly and leap and hurdle and shout their way to a kind of staged democracy" (540).

Joust as Theater

"They've been doing it for hundreds of year, and we can do it too!" exclaims a jouster at the Maryland Renaissance Festival, by way of sharing the pro-cess that brought him to competitive jousting twenty-three years ear-lier. The jouster, a retired postal clerk who performs under the name Sir Barchan, was self-taught in the sport, having been inspired by a joust he watched in Wales in 1981. "We're the largest act at the faire," he says, stroll-ing around the faire site in ninety pounds of armor between jousts.

Equestrian jousting is by far the most popular performance at *any* Renaissance faire. In particular, many first-time and casual visitors—"mundanes," in faire parlance—consider it the backbone of the faire experience, whether because it is a kind of performance they are most likely not to have seen elsewhere or because the notion of bold knights on horseback is such an important part of romanticized European his-tory. Necessarily, a lot of space is given over to it; in addition to a tour-ney field with adequate room for horses to run, the horses need tack rooms, stalls, and tenders. The way to judge the status of the joust at the faire, though, is to look at the seating. Whether it is on the grass, as in Massachusetts, on rough wooden benches, as in Georgia, or on orna-mented stone benches, as in Texas, it is clear that hundreds of patrons are expected to watch each show.

European jousting came about during the Middle Ages, after the mil-itary cavalry introduced heavy use of the lance. As spectacle, it did not become really popular until the twelfth century; but it remained fashionable among English, German, and French nobility for the next four hundred years, losing its association with military exercise by the 1500s. (The sport was discontinued in France after King Henry II died from wounds received while jousting in 1559.) During the Renaissance era, combatants who were seen to have behaved honorably on the jousting field were rewarded both financially and in terms of reputation.

Jousting contests were held in the United States during the early colonial period, probably introduced by Cecil Calvert, Lord Baltimore. But they picked up in popularity after the Civil War, during the same time when interest in the sport declined in Europe. According to Robert Loeffelbein, who in 1977 wrote what is still the only history of American jousting, these American contests were equal parts sports and pageantry, with sideshows such as greased pole climbing or trick riding sometimes adding to the spectacle.[15] "Colored" tournaments became popular in many areas during the post–Civil War period, though markedly few black jousters rode in the twentieth century; jousting is, reports Loeffelbein, the only "unisex" national sport, crowning a single national champion who may be either a man or a woman (9, 33). From the turn of the twentieth century, jousting was largely kept alive through what Loeffelbein calls "family follow-the-leader" (6). These enthusiasts formed the Maryland State Jousting Association in 1950, and in 1962, when the state of Maryland became the first in the country to declare an official state sport, it named jousting.

Although the faire's innovations and conventions—its formulae, as it were—mostly spread outward from the original California faires, jousting was one of the few important elements introduced first in the East. The bigger, permanent Renaissance festivals all have jousting performances, but these might be scripted or unscripted, depending on the jousting company. At the Maryland Renaissance Festival, for instance, the performers are members of the Maryland State Jousting Association; their jousting displays are competitive and "full contact," and their aim is to resemble as much as possible the sport that lasted some four hundred years in Europe. At King Richard's Faire in Massachusetts, on the other hand, the jousting is scripted, and the riders are practiced stunt men and women with training in circus arts. Both versions of jousting require a great deal of training, and both are dangerous; tellingly, full-contact joust-ing has spread from the Renaissance faire context to the "extreme sport" context (Slater), where inherent danger is the point, not the side effect. Jonathan Simon and others have connected the growing popularity of dangerous or "extreme" sports to an emphasis on risk taking as healthy for individuals and societies.

Loeffelbein writes that Maryland's competitive jousters are too seri-ous about their sport to indulge in historical costumery, which he calls "foolish frippery" (42). However, unscripted faire jousters tend to care a great deal about the historical exactitude of their clothing, armor, and weapons, even those who entered the job through their participation in the sport. Furthermore, there are also jousters at the faire who entered the job through their interest in its paraphernalia, including clothing. Sir Barchan, for example, says that his desire to learn competitive joust-ing was fueled by his interest in historical reenactment: he belonged to a history club at the University of Maryland and already owned "all the weapons, all the costumes" before deciding to acquire the horse skills that would allow him to participate. By the time he and a friend were able to joust, in 1983, members of the Maryland Jousting Tournament Asso-ciation were performing at the Maryland Renaissance Festival. "When the jousters saw what we could do," he recalls, "wear full armor, hit each other, and take it and keep on going, . . . they hired me and my friend to joust professionally" the following year (interview).

But scripted jousts require that performers wear "full armor, hit each other, and take it and keep on going" as well. The faire's first scripted joust performers—or "theatrical jousters," as they call themselves—were those of the Hanlon-Lees Action Theater. With a background in physical the-ater and an interest in commedia dell'arte, these artists were, like other faire performers, deeply interested in historical performance styles. They named their troupe after a troupe of acrobats founded in the early 1840s, whose work they carefully studied (*Renaissance Men*). The early Hanlon-Lees owned a number of patents on magic tricks and technologically advanced stage illusion. In fact, the cofounder of the latter Hanlon-Lees troupe, Kent Shelton, says, "We not only took the name, but we took a lot of their ideas and made it into a jousting act of extravaganza theater" (interview).

Shelton studied dance and circus techniques, including juggling, unicycling, and stage combat, at the North Carolina School for the Arts. After he graduated, he headed to New York along with several classmates. There he took a job driving a horse-drawn carriage in Central Park and encountered performers from the New York Renaissance Faire:

> One day I was sitting there on my carriage, waiting for a ride, and this group of performers came parading up and did a performance right there on the Plaza. It was this New York Renaissance Faire that was doing PR. There were jugglers and sword fighters, and I said, "I can do all that." . . . So the next year, I found out more about it, and a couple of us from School of the Arts who were up there auditioned for it. (Interview)

Shelton and partner Robin Wood were hired in 1979 to do fight choreography and to perform as sword fighters. It was the faire's entertainment managers who raised the possibility of a joust during the rehearsal process. Having never done one—and without owning any horses—they agreed, warning the management that they would not be able to present a joust for the opening weekend. "Never mind," they were told. "Just keep working at it, and we'll schedule you for the third or so weekend" (Shelton interview).

So Shelton and Wood rented horses and set about figuring out how to stage a joust. They were able to perform, just the two of them, for the second half of that first summer. The following summer, they were joined by two other acquaintances, Taso Stavrakis and Steven "Omms" Ommerle, and with this expanded troupe, they performed several jousts a day as well as their own commedia skits. Their show evolved into a stylized narrative, complete with live musical accompaniment (which Shelton compares to the soundtrack of a movie), a cheating villain, stage blood, and a final "joust to the death." Shelton is quick to point out that in a crucial way, the jousting is real, if scripted: a dive off a horse is a dive off a horse, whether planned or unplanned.

Because of the presence of the horses, Sir Barchan explains, jousters need to keep to themselves a bit: "We have to be careful with people around our horses. Not that they would hurt the horses, but they could be hurt *by* the horses" (interview). Not surprisingly, the scripted jousters, whose background in theater preceded their presentation of jousting, tend to be much more tightly involved with the rest of the Rennies on the circuit. Kent Shelton, for instance, was married to a faire cast member who portrayed the queen at several faires before her death, and he uses the language of "family" common among those on the faire circuit. The jousters who entered the faire through a primary involvement in jousting, on the other hand, might "have no real interest in the rest of the festival," although there are certainly exceptions, such as Sir Barchan himself, who performs as a street character at the Maryland Renaissance Festival in between jousts (Sir Barchan interview).

More than thirty years after the Hanlon-Less performers were first asked to develop a jousting show at the New York Renaissance Festival, they are still presenting their theatrical jousts at the faire (though some founding members have retired). They hire some thirty people each year, including squires, grooms, and announcers. Other scripted jousting troupes, such as New Riders of the Golden Age (based in Sarasota, Florida) work the Renaissance faire circuit as well—as do the unscripted jousters. Taken together, these troupes present and represent a remarkable admixture of pageantry, sport, and circus theatrics. From an analytical perspective, perhaps what is most interesting about this mixture is that it hints that none of these pursuits is ever really quite empty of the others. Are organized sports, with their uniforms and sentimentality about history, a kind of pageantry? Or rather, with their emphasis on the extraordinary (and even the freakish), are they a kind of circus? Bearing all of these elements, jousting has, in 2011, arrived at a cultural location that also puts front and center the tension between scripted and unscripted: a reality show, to be called "Full Metal Jousting," has put out a casting call.

Street Characters

The audience is a character that you've got to play.
—Rush Pearson, performer, Sturdy Beggars Mud Show

While most stage performers at the Renaissance faire seek to interact with their seated audience, an important category of faire performers does not even set foot onstage. These are the "street performers"—members of the cast, credited in the programs, who wander the faire grounds in character, interacting with faire patrons in ways that befit the role they are playing. There has not been a time when faires did not depend on street performers to create the theatrical environment that distinguishes the faires from other forms out outdoor entertainment, though the overall orientation of these key cast members has shifted over the years. With their improvisational nature and avant-garde influences, street characters in the earliest years reflected the political cast of the faires as fund-raisers for Pacifica and as countercultural "happenings," such as the monk offering to absolve visitors of the sins of commercialism or the vendor hawking skeleton keys for chastity belts. During the period when the faires were most organized around the presentation of "authenticity," the street characters leaned toward the educational: they were trained to explain their job or station, to demonstrate how certain tasks were carried out, and to use props, dress, and language that were as accurate as possible. Traces of both of these orientations are still to be found in street characters now, after many faires have been bought by corporations, but visible concessions to popular cultural mandates are sprinkled in: fairies and dragons, wizards and princesses, and above all, pirates. At most faires, especially large ones with lengthy histories, street characters playing all three of these roles coexist. In 2010, for instance, the Bristol Renaissance Faire in Wisconsin had some forty street characters in its cast list. These cast members inhabited a variety of characters: sometimes actual historical figures, performing historically researched activities in careful staging, and sometimes popularly entertaining or mythological figures, such as Robin Hood or the Green Man.

In the opinion of many faire adherents, street performers are as important to their experience at the faire as are the most popular (and better-paid) stage performers. This is because the street performers play a huge role in transforming the entire site into a stage. The street performers, in turn, are no less serious about their roles than are the performers who work on the stage, and although they might be hired (or, in some cases, accepted as a volunteer) for a particular role, they definitely consider themselves to be the "authors" of their characters. At the Bristol Renaissance Faire, a longtime faire patron wrote an as-yet-unpublished mystery novel set at the faire. When he wanted to include particular characters in his book, he asked permission of the actors who developed them, as an acknowledgment that their characters are their intellectual property.

Street performers work hard to develop characters in a holistic way, rather than write a series of lines or speeches that they intend to deliver. They contend that the deeper they can sink into a character, following "rules" of personality that audience members might never even become aware of, the more successful their performances will be.[16] This is because they are always interacting one-on-one with audience members and must constantly be responding to "cues" given by those whom they engage.

Not only is every single exchange improvisational to some degree, but street performers must also figure out what kind of humor will be desirable, or even acceptable, with each patron or group of patrons. Amy Wachtell, who plays a courtesan at various festivals across the country, says that knowing how to "play" differently with different visitors is, in fact, a way of staying in character: "I have a hard time convincing the Carolina [faire] owners that she [the courtesan character] is really kid friendly. Little kids, they see a pretty princess in a pretty dress, with sparkly makeup and a lot of feathers. That's what they see. But even within this world, the courtesan as a person would certainly need to know how to comport herself in any type of company" (interview). Wachtell's strategy involves continual adjustment of her "act" to keep it in balance with what visitors are open to: "You throw something out there and see what comes back," she explains (interview). A performance guide for street characters working at the Florida Renaissance Festival in the 1990s, titled "Language Aids," phrases the strategy as cautionary in a section on insults: "Don't get punched for using the wrong phrase at the wrong time. Tact and judgment must rule."

Over time, most of the street performers develop not only characters but also serious performance goals and strategies to accomplish them. Tony Guida, who has been performing at the faire since the late 1980s, uses Renaissance conventions to enact commentary on the prevailing definition of morality. At the Maryland Renaissance Festival, he plays a priest named Sinius Lascivious Vice, whom he describes as "fictitious and accurate" (interview). This wholly irreverent character is in keeping with the Renaissance tradition of pope burnings but also in keeping with the

Renaissance faire's early tradition of using pseudoreligion to comment on the relationship between prevailing morality and state authority. Guida has invented for his character what he calls an eighth deadly sin: sluttony, which is a combination of the words *slut* and *gluttony*. On his shirt, he wears a button that says, "Go and sin some more."

Guida says that performing at the faire is liberating for him as a person, because it gives him a reason and an opportunity to perform himself, "released." He tells me with audible delight that as Sinius Lascivious Vice, "I can be gross and outrageous—as outrageous as I am interested in being." Guida repeatedly reaches for apparent contradictions to describe what he, as a performer, thinks is most important about his performances. They are "titillating and safe" and "dangerous and racy and safe." Nonetheless, he says, during a time when the faire was attempting to "Disneyfy"—water down its socially challenging performances in the service of a profit-driven corporate agenda—he was "cut loose" from the paid cast, though he still brings out his character for fun (interview). Guida's experience is illustrative of a key way in which street characters shape the meaning of the faire: their casting provides a useful window on who it is the faire management wants to attract. Gorgeously arrayed, nonthreatening characters who are largely occupied with posing for photographs with casual visitors and children do, indeed, recall the costumed characters at Disney's theme parks whose job it is to greet visitors and pose for similar photographs. At the same time, these more commercially conceived characters often share space with edgier performers and performances, of the kind that give the faire its reputation for bawdiness.

Tony Guida retains one specific official faire function: every year the owners hire him to do a mass renewal of wedding vows, and over the years, by his reckoning, he has married or joined in same-sex "handfastings" some two hundred couples at the faire. Indeed, he took the trouble to become ordained through an online "pay to play" service so that the ceremonies he performs would be legally binding (interview). He continues to go to the Maryland faire almost every day it is open, inhabiting and further developing his character. He says that he does this not only because he finds it enjoyable but also because of his deep admiration for the faire's stalwarts. "People here are trying not to be eaten by the machine, to take a path less traveled," he says. "There is an unequalled sense of community—an 'it takes a village' sort of community. There is a purity to people's interactions; people want to do well, but not by hurting someone" (interview).

Many street performers stress that their lack of a stage and the constant improvisation, coupled with the close mingling with the audience that they do as a result, allows their act to develop "organically," as Rush Pearson of the Sturdy Beggars Mud Show puts it (interview). Pearson is part of a somewhat rotating group whose shows are now tied to a mud pit that constitutes their stage. But the show began in 1979, when Pearson and some of his college friends from Northwestern University auditioned for jobs at King Richard's Faire (then in Illinois) and began to play beggars of the "streets" of that faire. At first, they would cling to a patron's leg and refuse to let go until she or he gave them a quarter. One day, there was serendipitously mud on the ground, and the mud seemed to be "a wonderful medium." What Pearson calls a "You Asked For It" show developed, one that was not in the program, in which the beggars would create a mud puddle, and patrons would give them money to do things in the mud. Nearby crafters would "motivate the audience to play with us," says Pearson, so that quickly, there would be hundreds of people bottlenecked by the gate, where the mud puddle was (interview). The show evolved to encompass other faire cast members, as the final parade led everyone out the gate at the day's end:

> A friend of ours who was the Archbishop would "baptize" us in the pond, to clean us up. My character was mute, so he'd perform a miracle: he'd give me speech. At this point, five hundred patrons, members of the cast, the whole parade, he'd have them all kneeling before the parade. It was really a wonderful organic piece of street theater. They'd all be silent. I'd palm some of the pond algae. It was like almost a neon green. I had it in my hand, and I'd open my eyes, pretend to sneeze, and I'd say, "Does anyone have a hanky?" And then, "Oh, my God! I can talk!"
>
> Next year, they told us, "You've got to have a mud pit; you can't be blocking the front gate." . . . We had to start developing a more structured show. That was the beginning. (Interview)

Even in this "more structured show," Pearson considers that the street performer's orientation around audience and environment still defines his act. "Can you imagine doing a stage show with bagpipes over there, not closed in a room?" he asks rhetorically. "Where all of a sudden you smell turkey legs? Where you can hear somebody laughing, but it's at a whole different show? . . . I don't define myself as an actor but as a performer," Pearson explains. "For an actor, when push comes to shove, the material comes first. For a performer, when push comes to shove, the audience comes first. In a perfect world, of course, it's both. But actors, they rely on their material, and try to bring it alive. Performers, they try to connect with the audience and through them bring their material alive" (interview).

The Sturdy Beggars Mud Show has a fairly high gross-out level; it is structured around various competitions that result in "losers" sliding various body parts through the mud, culminating in one person eating mud. The "competitions" provide a gentle sort of political satire based on "hating" others because they are across the aisle. (Pearson says that it was easier for the performers to wear their liberal politics on their sleeves and assume the audience was with them, before a shift to the right in the 1980s made it necessary to work harder to reach everyone.) But for Pearson, the most important part of the show is the hat pass at the end. "Our show makes no sense without the hat pass," he insists. "Without that, we're just a geek show." Every show ends with the same line: "What's more disgusting than us eating mud? The fact that you people gave money to see it." That, says Pearson, is "the string that you put in the sugar water for the crystals to grow on" (interview). He means that the Mud Show, ridiculous as it is, flashes a mirror on the audience and gets them to examine, if only briefly, their own spectatorial desires.

4

"A Place to Be Out"

Playing at the Faire

I'm given the chance to feed a part of me that has to hide out
most of the time.

—Dakota Scott-Hoffman, playtron

As the earlier chapters have hinted, attending the Renaissance faire was,
during the 1960s and 1970s, a sort of statement of purpose: of belong-
ing in some way to the counterculture, of resistance to consumerism, of
side-stepping—albeit briefly—the external constraints of social convention. Through the faire, people could demonstrate public participation in, and affirmation of, a new type of community that was resolutely
transnational, transhistorical, transcultural, and one of choice rather
than birth—of which the Human Be-In (1967), the Monterey Pop Festival (1967), and the Woodstock Festival (1969) were to become the
most remembered examples. In portrayals of the faire during this time,
it is plain that this statement of purpose was legible to both friendly and
unfriendly observers. Take, for instance, the 1967 issue of skin mag *Adam*,
which featured a spread filmed at the faire (Rotsler). (A note indicates
that the photographs were taken before the faire was open for the day.)
Adam, launched in the mid-1950s and lasting some three decades, was
one of many *Playboy* imitators eager to follow in the footsteps of—not

to mention cash in on—the most famous skin magazine's success at making pornography mainstream, even somewhat respectable and high class. Like Playboy, *Adam* featured fiction, cartoons, and advertising as well as nude photographs, the latter often featuring well-known models and, in a nod to "taste," tending to artistically cover the pubic area. The magazine's Renaissance faire feature is no exception to this: with a certain level of deliberate ridiculousness, the model is pictured at the faire among costumed cast members, in poses that would be ludicrously romantic (e.g., with a knight in armor kissing her hand) if she were not completely naked.

More historically interesting is the scanty text accompanying the pictorial. In the table of contents, the faire is described as "Hippies' Mardi Gras," promising to show "hippie flower-people frolic[king] in mad world of middle ages." Inside, the article's head note describes the faire's participants as "California's swingers" and comments that the response to the "gentle hippies" at the faire has caused "minor rumbles of discontent and discomfort from those in the establishment who can't believe that merriment can be had without booze and sin." *Adam*, however, gleefully invites its readers to participate in the "Hippie's happy festival of love" (Rotsler 23, 24).

The campiness of *Adam*'s coverage aside, for many attendees at the first California faires, part of the draw was a sense of sexual liberation and antiestablishment cultural politics. As early as 1966, coverage of the Pleasure Faire in the *New York Times* had a sense of humor about the faire's atmosphere of principled nonconformity. "Madrigals Lull the Bohemians at Faire in California Meadow," announced a headline, conveying appreciation and laughter in equal parts (Bart).

With none of the tongue-in-cheek undertones that *Adam* and the *New York Times* shared, Farida Sharan, in her 2000 memoir *Flower Child*, writes with undiluted admiration of the faire's bohemianism, situating it prominently in the imaginative economy of Los Angeles's counterculture. During the 1960s and 1970s, Sharan designed "Clothes for a World of Be-Ins, Love-Ins, Freak-Outs, and Freedom" (99); her creations were worn by countercultural icons such as members of Iron Butterfly, Peter Fonda, and the Doors' Jim Morrison, as well as various other "movie and rock stars, groupies, musicians, hippies, flower children, peaceniks, beatniks, freaks, and hordes of gawking tourists" who visited her North Hollywood shop, the Psychedelic Conspiracy (124). The Southern California Pleasure Faire takes its place in *Flower Child* alongside positive and negative psychedelic trips, the Diggers' crash pad, the Summer of Love, and rock-and-roll song lyrics in an impressionistic portrait of "flower power" (Sharan's preferred term). Describing the 1967 faire, she focuses on clothing as metonym of the faire's expressive potential:

> Caught up in light-hearted play, we skipped like children along one of the pathways, passing charming craft and food booths displaying colorful banners and flags. Women sashayed along the footpaths, showing off their luscious, jewel-red, sapphire-blue, royal-purple, and emerald-green velvet Renaissance dresses and robes, while the men cavorted in colorful silk and satin tunics, tights, high leather boots, and feather-plumed hats. Free to express creative joy, costumed children skipped, played, teased, and lighted as they raced around the Faire. Enchanted by the laughing faces, the brilliant outfits, and the medieval music, we merged into the revelry. (157)

After a Saturday at the faire that she describes as "magical," Sharan returned the very next day and planned to attend the next weekend as well (email). But the faire was canceled before she had a chance to return, following demands on the part of conservative activists (see chapter 1).

The same year Sharan attended the Southern California faire, filmmaker Pierre Sogol (likely not his real name) included a visit to the first Northern California faire in his early chronicle of hippie life in California, *Aquarius Rising*. The documentary's short segment at the faire immediately follows a sequence filmed at Gridley Wright's commune, Strawberry Fields, in which residents discuss philosophical questions related to the counterculture ("LSD is like a psychic vitamin"), including the definition of "free love." The shots at the faire picture a musician in Renaissance garb arriving to play, the words "Flower Power" stenciled on his guitar case.

Unlike this young musician, most performers, crafters, and volunteers at the faire did not *literally* have their hippie identity written on them. But the signifying was done in ways no less intelligible, with the result that the faire not only attracted visitors *of* that world; it also attracted visitors *to* that world. Farida Sharan recalls taking her "straight" neighbor to the Renaissance Pleasure Faire in 1967 and watching her initial reluctance give way as she "slowly tun[ed] in to the enchantment" (160). Wendy Newell, who was involved with the California faires for more than thirty years as a seamstress, musician, and dancer, sums it up as follows: visitors came to the faire precisely in order "to ogle the hippies—or join them!" (email).

One such "convert" declares that he knew the faire was "home" the moment he encountered it in Marin County in 1968. "What we now call hippies, whole families, were going about living out of doors, smells of exotic foods cooking, herds of children galloping about, fascinating garb and gear everywhere, and above all, people making things with their own hands," recalls the visitor, at the time a "very well educated" industrial designer. The faire, he explains, reached him at a time when he had "become disgusted with capitalism and determined to become an artisan, living. . . off the fruits of my own labor" (email). Marking his conversion by changing his name to "Rainbow," he became a successful woodworker who has participated in forty-three years' worth of Renaissance faires in Northern and Southern California, as well as the annual Dickens Christmas Fair.[1]

Lesbian activist Carolyn Weathers, who attended the Southern California Renaissance Pleasure Faire in Agoura Hills for the first time in 1970, writes in a reminiscence archived in the Mazer lesbian archives in West Hollywood, California, that the faire succeeded so well as conduit for the counterculture because it presented a well-thought-out version of "hippie heaven" ("Renaissance"). She fixes her time at the faire by recalling that it was the weekend before the Monday on which the Kent State shootings took place on May 4 and four months before the first Moratorium on Vietnam took place in September. "The types who went to the Moratorium were the types who went to the faire," Weathers explains. "If the faire had taken place one week later, it would have been a wake" because of Kent State (interview).

Weathers's recollections of her day at the faire center on the freedom she felt there as an "out" lesbian, walking around with her friends: four women constituting two couples. Weathers singles out two important incidents from her day at the faire to illustrate her overall feelings about the experience. The first of these centers on displays of affection between members of the two couples with whom she attended:

> It was hot as hell, and the beer gave Sharon a terrible headache. Brenda lit them both cigarettes and kissed Sharon before putting the lit cigarette in her mouth. The man behind them smiled broadly to watch two lesbians in love, as I snapped the photograph. . . .
>
> We moved on to an outdoor stage hung with brightly-colored banners. Groups of people sat outside under the oaks to watch Elizabethan farces. Beauty lay in Bubble Red's lap, and Bubble Red bent down and kissed Beauty passionately on her neck. Nobody cared. Someone took our pictures. The hippie chick on the top left and the straight man sitting behind Bubble Red, watching on benignly, in the fantasyland of the Faire. ("Renaissance")

The second moment Weathers describes had to do with figuring out how she, as a lesbian, would fit in to the faire's relative openness about female sexuality. To capture this, Weathers tells the story of an activity at the faire that involved soliciting fairegoers to roll down a hill in the arms of a woman calling herself, in common faire parlance, a wench. Weathers presents the woman in question as performing a degree of sexual aggression that was even less familiar in 1970 than it was when she wrote her recollection some three decades later:

> "Good my lords and good my ladies, gather round!" A man shouted from the side of a path, "Which of thee wouldst step up to have a roll in the hay with the most beauteous lusty wench?"
>
> A woman stood at the top of the hill, her bodice low and full, leering at the crowd, her hands on her hips.
>
> "I do!" I shouted and climbed over the low fence.
>
> The young woman posing as a wench looked at me as though she were unsure.
>
> "Well met, good lady," she said.

Fig. 4.1. 1970 Southern California Renaissance Pleasure Faire patron Carolyn Weathers (foreground, with jug) describes the faire as a safe place for "out" lesbians. (Photograph courtesy Carolyn Weathers)

"Yes, how now," I smiled.

The wench opened her arms, we embraced and lay us down on the ground. We pushed off and rolled over and over, faster and faster, down the bumpy, hay-sprinkled hill until till we came to a stop at the bottom.

People applauded. The wench bade me a good day. The man in pantaloons shouted, "Who wilt be next to roll in the hay with this most lusty wench?" ("Renaissance")

In explicating why that moment at the faire was so important to her, Weathers draws lines connecting what she saw as the general repression of female sexuality, her position as a recognizable lesbian, and the meaning of the word *wench*, which was—and remains—central to faire speak. Of the term, she says, "Today, it wouldn't bother me at all, because the American consciousness has been raised. Then, women's libbers were derided, although my history-loving self understood it. I love the term wench now—wench, tart, trollop" (interview). With wonderful literary style, Weathers bookends her reminiscence with two roads: the dirt road she and her friends walked on to reach the faire and the "revolutionary road" they walked on shortly thereafter as they took part in the first gay pride parade, the liberatory qualities of the faire having moved them in that direction ("Renaissance").

The early faire attendees and observers such as Weathers realized that the vision of the faire was a utopian and largely symbolic one, making the creation of a world so clearly bounded as "other" all the more poignant. David Ossman of the Firesign Theatre describes the importance of this experimental space: "In that day," he insists, it seemed like "there was no alternate universe at all. Suddenly, at the faire, it's a bright sunny day, everyone is going about gaily dressed" (interview). In both Weathers's and Ossman's recollections, the faire functioned as an "autonomous space" for both work and play in which history and identity are to some extent reimagined.

A 1972 exploitation movie, *California Fever* (also released as *Teenage Divorcee* and *Josie's Castle*) illustrates this principle of utopianism. In the movie, three couples have married quite young and, as a result, feel that they have missed out on the possibilities of the 1960s. They end their respective marriages, and half of each couple, two men and one woman, encounter each other and live communally for a while in a California house (the titular "castle"). During this time—and with mixed results— they explore new approaches to both sexual and nonsexual relationships. In a crucial if somewhat strange scene, the three host a party that is arranged to invoke the Renaissance faire. Guests and hosts play Renaissance-era music, speak in some degree of faire talk, dress in Renaissance faire garb—and move seamlessly from small talk and dancing into an orgy. As a movie, it is fair to say that *California Fever* has more historical interest than artistic—for instance, George Takei of *Star Trek* fame, who later came out as gay himself, plays a closeted gay character—and the "experiment" that includes the Rennied-up orgy does not end smoothly. But the film does make strong statements in favor of communalism, sexual liberation (especially for women and gay men), and nonconformism, emblematized by the sartorial.

California Dreams concludes with an (early) end to the 1960s, one in which the drugs have turned scary, the sex unrewarding, and the footloose lifestyle impossible to maintain. The main character sells her car, symbolically relinquishing mobility, and enrolls in college. But it is her countercultural experimentation that has allowed her to make these choices. In some ways, the development of the faire parallels the arc of this movie's narrative, as the same triumphs of the gleefully ad hoc collective that generated the first few faires served to facilitate its emergence as rationalized business endeavor and ultimately gave way to corporate pastime. With inexorable logic, it was the faire's success as "far-out" cultural production that made it impossible for it to remain such, both because of the spread of the new faires themselves and because of a broadening out of whom the faire was able to attract—whom it seemed most to be "for."

In the reckoning of many of the faire's first generation of participants, the history of the faire is best told as declension narrative: a utopian outpouring of countercultural creativity at its inception, conceived of as support for an important progressive institution, gradually overtaken by commercialism, rigidity, and corniness. In this light, the Renaissance faire's fate merely exemplifies the ripeness of the counterculture as a whole for commodification: its taming through co-optation, embodied for many people by Nixon's "sock-it-to-me" appearance on *Laugh-In* in 1968. Or, as Thomas Frank has thoroughly argued in his *Conquest of Cool: Business Culture, Counterculture, and the Rise of Hip Consumerism*, because the counterculture was always congenial to the logic of consumer capitalism's embrace of "rebellions" against previous generations of goods. In any event, some early attendees who readily identify themselves as being or having been "hippies" stopped attending altogether by the mid-1970s, as did some faire workers or volunteers. Some workers—crafters, "boothies," and performers alike—who also consider that the faire has somehow "fallen"—try to maintain as many aspects of the lifestyle that drew them in as possible, behind the scenes, on their own time.

The faire's primary audience (and its reputation) could not remain constant while so many things about the context and production of the faire changed. But if certain devotees stopped attending, disappointed at the turn away from its expressions of what many called "a hippie fair," others began increasingly to seek it out, finding opportunity there for their own cultural stagings. The most visible post-1970s faire attendees are less likely to consider themselves part of the *counter*culture than they are to call themselves part of a *sub*culture, and they tend to describe their time at the faire as a respite from the rest of their lives (albeit a much-treasured one), rather than something that can constitute active opposition to the "mainstream." Nonetheless, throughout the 1980s and 1990s, as the faire spread through a network of national business deals, a growing number of people still found liberation, if temporarily, in the faire community; these fairegoers continue to cherish its ability to recalibrate—or allow them to recalibrate—their experience of self.

The Birth of the Playtron

We are like church—not religion, but church.
—Steven Gillan, chief of Clan MacColin, Renaissance Pleasure Faire

As the Renaissance faire drew farther away in time and temperament from its hippie roots, it drew an ever-increasing number of what the faires' workers tend to call "mundanes," "normals," or—with slightly more of an edge—"tourists": families or couples attending the faire and hoping to have a good time, but without a particular investment in the activity. Some tourists enjoy the faire enough to come back the following year, and some of them do not and switch to another weekend activity. The visitors grouped together under this usage of "tourists," of course, comprise the wide range of people living near each faire site, and their composition reflects regional demographics.

More interesting for our purposes are the many dedicated attendees who return not only every year but generally every weekend the faire is open during its annual run. The visitors in this second category purchase season passes when they are offered by faire management. At some faires, they receive perks such as their own entrance gate, eliminating lines for them when the faire opens in the morning. They come in costumes, greet each other in "castle talk," become passionately attached to particular acts or pubs, develop friendships with others of their ilk, and—in the late twentieth and early twenty-first centuries—maintain and extend these friendships through Renaissance faire Internet communities. Although dedicated to their "home faire" (the standard term for the faire closest to where they live or to which they feel most connected), many of them travel—sometimes quite far—to attend faires in other areas. Evocatively, these visitors do not refer to "*the* faire"; instead, they say just "faire," as in "I met her at faire" or "I feel so comfortable at faire" or, when the season rolls around, "It's almost faire!" This change is, while simple—the only difference is a dropped article—a profound one, because the faire becomes, in this locution, a condition of being rather than an event. Combining the faire's particular usage of *play* with the more usual word *patron*, faire workers refer to these attendees as *playtrons*, acknowledging through the coinage the significance of these fans' involvements to the construction of the faire's meaning.

In some important ways, the stage was set for the development of Renaissance faire subcultures as distinct, particular to the faire's special offerings, rather than as an exuberant manifestation of countercultural energy, when the faire became settled and flourishing enough to be codified. This is backed up by the word choice of those I spoke to who tried hard to explain the difference between the early, more inchoate faires and the later ones. Of the early faires, more than one person tells me that "all you had to do was show up" or that "anything goes." "The vibe changed," says David Springhorn, who remains committed to the faire. "The interest grew in authenticity, and the faire became less hippielike. Some were too into [authenticity], and that became boring" (interview). But if the interest in authenticity and consistency—even keeping in mind that it is the *quest* for authenticity that is meaningful, rather than any real or imagined *content* of authenticity—alienated certain early fans of the faire, the rituals of performance that developed as a result of the new interest drew in other distinct groups of playtrons. In the faire's middle decades, there was a marked and surprising shift away from high-culture, Pacifica-supporter, educated, "arty" types. There was also a shift away from the dominance of youth culture that led mime Bill Irwin to remark that the early faire "was not a country for old men" (email). The latter cannot be simply explained by the aging of the faire's original devotees: so many new faires were springing up across the country without ever having the involvement of either California's legendary counterculture or the faire's original developers that the very idea of a faire audience had to change.

Class and Race at the Faire

Not surprisingly, playtrons seeking to create a sense of self particular to their time at the faire are not always able to greet a questioner with a lot of interest in dwelling on who they are and what they do in their "mundane" lives outside the faire gates. The response given to me by Renee Lebbling, a playtron at the Bristol Renaissance Faire in Wisconsin, when asked about her identity is exemplary: "Technically," she says, "I'm white, bisexual, an atheist, and working-class, but those sort of things don't come up very often and aren't important to who I am" (email). Still, to understand the fairegoers, it is necessary to recognize who constitutes the regularly attending fan group. Under the costumery that often—and deliberately—conceals or removes many usual markers of group identity, who, then, slowly but surely emerged as the largest group of playtrons in the faire's "posthippie" period? Who followed the hippies, the artists, hipsters, and avant-garde visionaries of the 1960s and 1970s? In the 2000s, the commonest pop-culture-purveyed stereotype of the faire enthusiast is a socially awkward role-playing gamer, who spends a lot of time in front of a computer. (Of course, spending time in front of a computer is no longer a particularly exclusive activity.) Certainly, this subgroup is present and, if their occasional sheepishness when self-identifying as such is any indicator, is well aware of the stereotype.

But going by numbers, it became plain, as I surveyed well over a hundred faire attendees in different parts of the country, that the largest subgroup of playtrons—in Massachusetts, Maryland, Texas, California, Georgia, and Wisconsin—identifies as blue collar.[2] Given time to compose their answers (as opposed to answering on the fly in the midst of faire activities), this identification was often articulated in ways that expressed a tension between faire identity and mundane identity. "*Outside* of faire, I am a white, brown-hair, hazel-eyed, straight, blue collar worker," answers Wally Sullivan (email; emphasis mine). "[I'm] straight white male working class with a splash of 'redneck' and avant garde," says Blake Chappell (email). "Can't you tell by my clothes?" teases Becca, before telling me that she was the first person in her family to go to college (interview). "I'm a retired caregiver, but you are probably talking to me because I am black at the faire," wryly comments "Marina" (interview). (See chapter 5 for a discussion of class as occasion for mockery of the faire.)

For working-class playtrons, faire activities not infrequently require financial planning and sacrifice. When I arrive in Houston to visit the Texas Renaissance Festival, "Andrea," the white, self-described "working, you know, working-middle-class" woman at the Advantage Rent-a-Car counter wants to talk about the faire when she ascertains my reason for coming to town. She tells me that she takes her grandchildren there every year, sewing garb for the whole family, out of thrift as much as artistic impulse, and buying such pieces as she could afford, bit by bit and year by year. She reveals that she was not able to visit the faire at all in 2008, because of the economic crisis; this was a huge disappointment to her (interview).

When I inquire about playtrons' jobs outside the faire, they promptly tell me but not infrequently point out that they are pleased with the fact that their jobs have no impact on the time they spend at the faire, with the possible exception of Randy, who remarks that his driving skills from his job as a trucker allow him and his wife to travel comfortably to other faires on weekend trips (interview). For instance, as I interview a group of volunteers at the Bristol Renaissance Faire in Wisconsin who almost all report having blue- (or pink-) collar jobs, Dextra, a secretary now on disability, wants me to know that there are also "fancier" folks in their organization, such as medical doctors and PhDs (interview); at this point, her group of friends hasten to call attention to the way faire participation levels the hierarchies of the outside world. Without the faire, they insist, they might never have been friends with each other at all, but now they constitute each other's relied-on support network. Further, comments "Holly," a web designer, the garb that playtrons wear at the faire serves to conceal certain class markers that people are used to "reading" in their everyday lives (interview).

Looking across economic class rather than at it, it is immediately plain that in all locations, the audience for the faires is mostly white—although racial composition of the faires' audience varies somewhat from region to region. At the Maryland Renaissance Festival, for instance, there are markedly more black attendees (including both playtrons and more casual visitors) than at King Richard's Faire in Massachusetts, and at the Texas Renaissance Festival, there is a visible Mexican American presence not found at either Maryland's or Massachusetts's faire. (The regional demographic is also acknowledged through food offerings such as tamales.) "Based on the thousands of people I see here every day, we definitely have our sprinklings of [nonwhite participants]," acknowledges a Maryland cast member, "But it's really white out here overall. . . . I wish it wasn't" (Wachtell interview).

In many cases, the faire's playtrons of color are determined to bring the question of race into their participation in the faire. They do this through some fledgling organizations for "Black Rennies," such as one formed through a page on the websites Myspace and tribe.net. But more consequential are the ways in which playtrons of color use their fan activities to make statements about history, particularly black history. Fascinatingly, whereas the notion of authenticity was used by several of my sources to explain the *lack* of significant nonwhite participation in the California faires' initial decades, pointing to the Anglocentrism that was part of the faire's attempts to cite concrete historical referents, some black and Asian playtrons have been able to use historical authenticity as a point of entry for their involvement.

Henry Hill, a thirty-seven-year-old African American, has been attending Renaissance faires for more than ten years and has traveled as long as four hours to get there. Like many patrons (as I will discuss shortly), Hill describes garbing up as liberating, as allowing him to be what he wants to be (email). But he also talks about dressing for the faire as a way simultaneously to educate white Americans and to develop a sense of pride among black Americans: "I play a Moor [at the faire]. It helps me keep things in perspective, as the Moors ruled over most of Spain for a very long time. It keeps me wanting to gain more knowledge so that I can share with more African Americans to tell them and show them that there is more to life and our history than being slaves" (email). The "faire name" that Hill created for the character he plays represents an effort to capture this sense of history and pride: he is Numair Numan, which he tells me means "panther blood" (a graceful allusion to the Black Panthers; email).

Allen, a thirty-year-old diesel mechanic originally from Senegal, also sees the Renaissance faire as a canvas for public exploration of questions of heritage. He drives from his home in Alabama to attend a number of southern faires, including ones in Florida and Georgia. Allen admires the faire's sense of whimsy, saying emphatically, "These are good people, *original* people." But he insists that what really attracted him to the faire, and keeps him deeply involved, is the chance he finds there to represent his home culture while living in the United States. "You don't see many Africans, dressed in African clothing, at the faire," he tells me. "That's what drew me in" (interview).

Among playtrons, efforts such as these to insert non-European history and culture into the faire are currently welcomed and even joined by many white patrons; starting in the 1960s, though, as the faire's participants began the process of continually sorting through the question of authenticity, the faire's relationship to Anglocentrism has remained a live issue. In particular, the fact that much of what is thought of as Renaissance literature (and science) is deeply indebted to the Islamic world, particularly the Muslim-ruled states on the Iberian Peninsula, has encouraged an expanding inclusion of performance, food, and visual statements from East, South, and West Asia, as well as North Africa.

Allen insists that people at the faire are interested in his culture to a greater degree than he finds in the larger population (interview). Indeed, some white playtrons are quite eager to think about the racial history of the Renaissance period and how that history can be mapped onto the faire's staging. Randy, for instance, a long-haul truck driver, tells me that the only person he had ever seen asked either to change what he was wearing or to leave the Maryland faire was dressed in "hard-core" BDSM chains.[3] Randy does not mention any visible racial markers of this person but tells me, "The way I see it, there would have been people in shackles and bonds during the Renaissance era. I have no problem with it, unless you hassle somebody. Once you get in here, it's all accepted" (interview). In other words, Randy is not simply making a statement in support of tolerance of sexual subcultures (though that is certainly part of his intent);

he is reading a historical dimension about race and power back into the ejected visitor's garb. Later that same day, I spotted an African American playtron making his way around the faire, shirtless and in shackles. The sharp nature of the commentary he was making through his garb was clearly making some people uncomfortable, and I was able to catch up with him long enough for him to tell me cordially that he fully intended to cause a certain amount of discomfort. I saw nobody holding it against him, exactly; it was as though they, too, acknowledged that there was some value in their being made uncomfortable. Attempts to inject racial consciousness into faire consciousness range from that playtron's confrontational strategy to Allen's and Henry Hill's idealistic educational impulse to the more lighthearted—but still serious—strategy of the African American playtron whose friend describes a day when he attended the faire wearing an entire court gown he had constructed out of kente cloth for the 2006 faire in Maryland (Gibson email).

If these playtrons of color wield historical details to bring the question of race into the faire, others employ a *counter*historical turn to use the faire to make their own historical arguments. Rather than using their garbed bodies to remind spectators of intentionally forgotten truths about European history, as does Henry Hill, these playtrons describe a delight in using their dress and their presence to imaginatively rewrite European history. An especially self-conscious example is Alice, a South Asian American college student in Texas. Alice asserts that her "third-world" presence is a reminder that at the historical moment being represented, if haphazardly by the faire, her family would have been considered savages to be ruled over. Of her garb, she declares,

> For me, I really love to wear garb at faire because I am creating a narrative that is counter to the way the colonial process really happened. For instance, today I was dressed as a wealthy merchant from London in the 1500s. That was my character today. I have other characters, and other garb, but this is really my favorite, and I have been working on it [the set of garb] for three years now. Now, as a woman of color, historically, this character would have been simply impossible. It happened the other way around: the English came to India and got rich. But dressing as though it was possible, and I might have been one, is just so great, I think. You know, you'll often

see white women, white Americans, wearing Indian clothing, or Mexican or whatever. Here, I get to do the appropriating. It makes me happy, and if it makes people who see me think about it, that makes me happy too. (Email)

Here Alice is advancing an argument similar to one articulated about the steampunk subculture[4]—which increasingly overlaps with the Renaissance faire playtron subculture—by a commentator calling himself anacronaut, a "half-Asian fashion designer" who explains that being a steampunk of color means "wearing the clothes of the imperialists, adopting their mannerisms, but retaining an identity in their hair and skin. There's an odd subjugation yet an ownership of the style in these old photos. Take the trappings of your enemy and wear them in your own way, use them against them" (qtd. in Jha).

Not everyone wearing a costume at the Renaissance faire intends to make such a pointed statement through it, but the donning of garb serves an important symbolic function nonetheless, because of the way it marks a deliberate act of nonconformity with norms of self-presentation. "My husband would never wear a skirt to work, but he wears a kilt in here every day," a woman dressed as a belly dancer (who works as veterinarian outside) tells me (Bowman interview). Through the comparison between what her husband wears to work with what he wears to the faire, she emphasizes the way garbing up defines ownership of her husband's time as his own, as opposed to his employer's. In this way, by dressing up, playtrons are simultaneously marking themselves as *insider*—associated with those who are most "in the know" at the faire—and *outsider*—enacting a sort of temporary "opting out" through clothing that breaks everyday rules. "The ones who hate their jobs wear really good costumes," writes Michael Ferrante of the 2010 Maryland Renaissance Festival in the *Johns Hopkins News-Letter* (Ferrante).

And an overwhelming majority of playtrons see themselves as consciously participating in an alternative culture (by their own conviction or design), if not an outsider culture (according to external forces of marginalization). One interaction with a group of playtrons at the Maryland faire functions as an elegant summary. "Excuse me," I say as I approach a knot of gorgeously arrayed friends talking together. (I am attracted to this group by their clothing.) "Are you regulars at this faire?" Promptly answers one of them, to general laughter, "No, we're not regulars. We're *irregulars!*" A version of this assessment was offered repeatedly; when I ask the large number of playtrons I surveyed to self-identity with any categories they find meaningful, those desiring to position themselves in *opposition* to the mainstream outnumber those who first gravitate to the more traditional categories about race, profession, and age. "I admit it: I'm a geek!" declares Kevin, a visitor at the Texas Renaissance Festival (Price interview). I have "a splash of avant-garde," says Blake, who attends faires in Maryland, Pennsylvania, and Virginia (Chappell interview). "I'm a mutt" is how Dakota, at the Maryland Renaissance Festival, describes his racial identity—well before Barack Obama caused a flurry by using the same term (Scott-Hoffman email). "A bit of a free spirit," admits Wally, a playtron at the Maryland Renaissance Festival (Sullivan email). "I'm of an 'alternative sexuality' myself," comments Allison, an attendee of the Bristol Renaissance Faire in Wisconsin (Villegas email); and "we all push the boundaries" is the assessment of Sean, at the Georgia Renaissance Festival (interview). "Most of the time, I am sort of an outcast," says MJ, who regularly attends several faires in California, matter-of-factly (Marcus interview). These comments are representative of dozens of similar ones; Renee, at the Bristol Renaissance Faire in Wisconsin, opines that the most important draw for playtrons is that the "faire is often a haven for those who are otherwise rejected in 'normal' society" (Lebbling email).

So what does the Renaissance faire offer to this grab bag of nonconformists? In the succinct words of Katrina Ranum, longtime attendee and current booth worker at the Maryland Renaissance Festival, the faire is "a place to be out." She means this in the most common sense, in reference to nonstandard sexuality—"You see couples who would never walk hand in hand in the street do it here," she tells me—but also in an extended sense, such that, as she puts it, "whoever you are, you can come here and find somebody who will make you feel normal" (interview). In fact, writer and New York Renaissance Faire choreographer Mark James Schryver connects these two senses of "a place to be out" in a piece on the faire published by, appropriately enough, *Out* magazine. "We put freaks, geeks, and outcasts on a pedestal" at the faire, Schryver states. "It's one of the reasons I think a lot of LGBT people come" (Moore).

Sex at the Faire

If you can't get your freak on at the faire, where can you?
—Manny, playtron

The notion of sexual acceptance is, to the faire's most devoted denizens, not just a passive construction, meaning merely that no one will bother playtrons for their sexual choices. Instead, those who have positioned themselves as faire insiders see the faire's embrace of the outsider as an opportunity or even an invitation. Manny, who drives three and a half hours from central New Jersey to the Maryland Renaissance Festival, says that not only does the faire community tolerate a variety of sexual orientations and expressions but the community believes that "the more variety [of sexual expression] the better" (email). A nineteen-year-old woman named Alison who has attended the Southern California Renaissance Pleasure Faire every year since she was fourteen tells me, "Sexuality in itself is a big part of being 'Faire Folk'" (Villegas email).

There is widespread acknowledgment that certain sexual subcultures feel particularly drawn to the faire—likely because they feel safe or welcome there. A blog post on *Lazy Gay News* reads, in its entirety, "I went to a Renaissance faire. Gay people loved it" (Becky), and *The Bear Handbook: A Comprehensive Guide for Those Who Are Husky, Hairy, and Homosexual and Those Who Love 'Em* has an entry on the faire claiming that "they are rife with Bears" (and adding, "The biggest queen will be the court jester) (Kampf 107). *Sex Tips from a Dominatrix* recommends shopping for the "wonderful items you can find at a Renaissance festival" (Payne 53), and *The Ethical Slut: A Guide to Infinite Sexual Possibilities* suggests that those who are interested in polyamorous relationships try the faire (Easton and Liszt 185).

But it would not be accurate to say that any sexual subgroup dominates. In *Bisexuality in the Lives of Men: Facts and Fictions*, Brett Beemyn and Erich W. Steinman use the faire as an example of a space wherein "the three sexual orientation communities—bi, gay, and het—come into contact with each other or intermix" (102). (Some faire adherents consider that there are more than three sexual orientation communities, but Beemyn and Steinman's point, which is accompanied by a map, is taken nonetheless.) Similarly, a contributor to the oral history collected in 2010's *Queer Twin Cities* describes the Minnesota Renaissance Festival as a "collection of disparate communities" (Twin Cities 127). A helpful respondent on an Internet discussion board advises a poster who inquires, "Is there a trick to finding kinky folk in vanilla settings?" with a short answer: "I believe the words you're looking for are 'Renaissance' and 'Faire,'" thereby assuring the original poster that all sorts of folk find their way to the faire (desjardins).

Piercing and tattoo artist and innovator Elayne Angel believes that the sexually open environment of the faire was responsible for her career. Born in 1960 in the San Fernando Valley, she found her way to the Southern California Renaissance Pleasure Faire in the 1980s; there, she encountered a male-female couple who both had nipple piercings. They both readily pulled up their shirts to show her the piercings—"and I don't think that sort of thing happens at the mall," she adds—and Angel soon sought out the place where they had the piercings done and had her own nipple pierced. Subsequently, Angel became manager and vice president of that business and had a shaping influence on the culture of body piercing in the United States: she is the author of *The Piercing Bible*, the first consumer guide to body piercing, and she is the first American tattoo artist to have a design (large wings on the back) copyrighted. Stating frankly that the faire was "a very sexualized atmosphere," Angel draws connections among "garbing up" for the faire, sexual openness, and her own artistic development: "I think wearing garb and being another character other than yourself allowed people to explore sides of themselves that they may not have confronted in regular life. I had many wonderful and enjoyable sexual encounters of many types at the faire. . . . It was the environment of the faire that led to the openness of them even demonstrating to me that they had pierced nipples" (interview).

Several attendees, when I asked them to describe the best experience they have ever had at the faire, responded with stories about sexual expression. According to Alison, a particularly moving faire experience came when she was "hugged after a flogging demonstration by another submissive for being someone who 'Got it'": "that was probably one of the most welcoming, as one of the best flogging demonstrations I've seen" (Villegas email). Dakota, who describes himself as having "settled on gay for now," insists, "Absolutely, judgments about sexuality are left at the door for most of the Ren Crowd. It is an open friendly and loving environment where no one has any hang ups about who sleeps with who." He describes his warmest faire memory as having taken place his first year at the faire, when he met "Howard, a cart driver": "He had on britches, a horse's tail and nipple rings. He let me brush his tail and then drove me around the village. That was a nice memory I keep in my heart. A 'worst thing' [at the faire] has not happened yet" (Scott-Hoffman email).

Because of the nonplaytron attendees at the faire, much of the sexual expression needs to happen sub rosa. In the faire's earliest countercultural days, even nudity was commonplace. Now, playtrons have gradually developed insider codes of expression. Allison explains, "We all have our own hidden expression—carrying floggers or handcuffs, the location of tails on a belt, certain favors on a costume all have their own meanings" (email). Katrina Ranum, of the Maryland faire, points out, "Each subgroup has its own chosen type of costuming. For example, [the clothing booth called] Noblesse Oblige is preferred by higher-end dom-sub," or those in dominant-submissive relationship pairings (interview). Ian Gibson, who has attended faires in Florida, Virginia, Colorado, and Pennsylvania as well as the Maryland faire, which he has attended every year for close to two decades, is very thoughtful about the different and sometimes contradictory mandates of sexual openness at the faire:

> Yes, sexuality is a large part of Faire. All are welcome and I have never encountered or heard of any negative incidents in all the years I have been going. With respect to expression . . . there is a line that is usually not crossed in that most of us are aware that there are many folks there from all walks of life. That is not to say that I (and my friends) are not afraid to show expression—we kiss, touch etc. and most of the straight guys give us big old kisses when they see us (which I think confuses some of the straight folks sometimes). That said we all push the boundaries but there is a level of appropriateness we all maintain. (I know that the Faire receives complaints every year as one of my friends is the senior lawyer for the owners and tells me stuff.) But MD [the Maryland Renaissance Festival] tries

to maintain a level of adult edginess along with the family Disneyfication (which they have tried to push over the last few years). (Email)

"Disneyfication" is a word I heard repeatedly from playtrons and employees alike in connection with the toning down of certain risqué performances, onstage and off. Although the word is implicitly critical, most playtrons seem to feel that there are—or can be—places and spaces for less restricted behavior. For instance, in Massachusetts, I was advised by several people that the last day of the faire was more open for adult expression than other days. In the words of James, who identifies as straight, "It is quite acceptable to express your sexuality [at the faire], within reason of course. The last day of Faire can sometimes go beyond such boundaries. That wouldn't be the ideal day to bring the children!" (LaRoche email). Returning that same year for the faire's final day, I could easily see what he meant. Performers gathered together on one of the stages and performed songs and skits they had written for the occasion. While most sexual innuendoes therein would still fly over children's heads, there was a great deal of extremely spirited performance of coming-out on stage, even by performers who would not call themselves gay offstage. The point really seemed to be gleefully—and, on this day, openly—to mark the space as "queer."

Along the same lines, a woman in Texas shared her fairegoing schedule with me while processing my rental car in the airport: bring the grandchildren (whose costumes she sews herself) in the morning and then drop them home and return without kids for the evening hours, when both performers and playtrons conduct themselves in a more risqué manner ("Andrea" interview). At some faires, particular stages or performances are marked with parental advisories, such as the "Rogues' Reef" stage in Southern California. (The "parental advisory" here is clearly articulated by one performing group, which announces upfront, "We say 'fuck.'" And indeed they do.) Many leather shops in faires around the country sell some fetish gear: restraints, whips, masks—a state of affairs that Marisa Meltzer, writing on the *Paris Review*'s online blog, finds "alarming." This is almost always kept behind the counter, hanging well above the eye level of children, and booth workers elide any questions about it posed by people who are not clearly asking from inside the

BDSM community. (Comedian Margaret Cho seems to have noticed some of this from the outside, wondering in her concert movie *Notorious C.H.O.*, "What's this weird connection between fans of . . . S&M and the Renaissance faire?")

But the many playtrons with whom I discussed sex at the faire seemed equally anxious to let me know that they are willing to behave "appropriately" in front of "tourists" or children and that doing this does not mean that they find the faire inhospitable to sexual expression. Becca, a twenty-year-old playtron at the Bristol Renaissance Faire in Wisconsin who hopes to get a job there eventually, comments, "This is the first place I ever kissed a girl. It's, like, it's hard to be ashamed in here." When I ask her why she thinks this is true, she answers, "Maybe it's because you're pretending to be someone else, you know? But it's someone else I would be if I could" (interview).

Becca's rather poignant comment hints at the two most common reasons playtrons give for what they think is most meaningful about the faire: that it gives them the opportunity to pretend to be someone else and that it gives them the opportunity to be who they really are. At first glance, this seems like a paradox, or at least a difference of opinion. But it is quite possible that both of these motivations can coexist in one playtron, and as such, they reveal a very important truth not only about Renaissance faire masquerade but also about the "outside" lives of many of its devotees: what passes for a person's "real" self is very likely to be an edited version, served up according to the mandates of normalcy. Pretending not to be that person might very well be an expression of who we really are. Renaissance faire playtrons would be far from the first people to put on a mask in order to reveal a truth.

Volunteers of Faire-America

For the "normals," the playtrons have increasingly become part of the show—a phenomenon that arguably began in the 1960s when enthusiasts like the teenage Howard Patterson (later of the Flying Karamazov Brothers) showed up and spontaneously performed for other attendees. (As I will show in the next chapter, mockery of the Renaissance faire has developed its own particular tropes; for these observers, playtrons are the most important part of the show.) Casual faire attendees often request photographs with particularly well-dressed playtrons. Playtrons, for their part, relish what they see as increased opportunity to interact with cast members and crafters; a large number of them list this among their motivations for not only coming in garb but creating entire personas to go along with the costumes. James LaRoche, who regularly attends King Richard's Faire in Massachusetts, explains, "When we're in costume, it just seems that the people who work at the Faire, almost always will interact with you," adding that one year, this interaction resulted in a prized invitation to a cast party (email).

And indeed, there has always been a fair amount of crossover between playtron and employee. Since the second day of the first faire, attendees who have been particularly devoted to the faire have returned to volunteer or work. Chris Springhorn calls herself the "oldest faire brat," a fond term used for someone who grows in the faire community or else joins it before the age of eighteen. She first attended the faire as a visitor in 1972, when she was seventeen. It was, she vividly recalls close to forty years later, "an indecent good time, . . . hot, dusty, and lots of fun." Being at the faire was like having "a two-week vacation in one day," she tells me, so she returned to work there and remains devoted to doing so (interview). Katrina Ranum, a farrier who works at the Maryland faire in a jewelry booth, tells me that she sought work at the faire in order to extend and enhance her experience as a fairegoer, not for the money. "I can make more money in an hour and a half outside than I do here in a twelve-hour day," she confesses (interview).

This crossover between visitor and worker is summed up with something approaching poeticism by a young booth worker named Billy selling jewelry at the Georgia Renaissance Festival. When I ask him if he and his wife (also a booth worker as well as a college instructor) work at any other faires, he tells me, "We go *on vacation* to other faires" (interview). Out of this dedicated involvement, several organizational structures have developed to give playtrons opportunities to contribute to the faire: Friends of the Faire groups at a number of faires and the faire guild system.

As an organization, Friends of the Faire does not require any special training to join: members are not even required to dress in garb or talk in period speak, although this is certainly encouraged. Memberships are sold each season and bring with them a number of perks. These benefits (which vary from faire to faire) might include a special area set aside on the faire set where members can socialize, rest, eat, and change clothes; discounts on official faire merchandise and admissions; prefaire classes if members wish to learn about accurate reenactment; a supply of cold water during the day; a special parking area. Volunteer opportunities are also available through Friends of the Faire, which many members see as an entrée to getting more formally involved with the faire.

But what most Friends of the Faire members say motivates them is the fellowship they feel as a result of their active participation. Many of them use the invented word "faire-mily" to describe the kinlike networks they develop. For instance, "Holly," who works in a clothing store and attends the Bristol Renaissance Faire on the border between Illinois and Wisconsin, remarks that all members of that faire's organization tend collectively to the groups' children. Further, Friends of the Faire members are quick to point out that certain rewarding friendships that happened through their organization would be less likely outside. They nurture these relationships (and prolong their fandom) during the off-season with events they organize, such as a winter feast, attended by more than one hundred members, to which many wear their garb. At a gigantic potluck dinner in 2009, in addition to all the dishes brought by members, the organization cooked and served 380 pounds of meat.

Similarly to the Friends of Faire organization, the guild system was created, according to Kevin Patterson (who was actively involved in the conception and establishment of the guilds at the California faires), as a way to accommodate the many patrons who wanted to volunteer to work at the faire and a way to organize them as their numbers began to grow overwhelming (interview). The guilds function as discrete performance troupes, generally (with some notable exceptions) exhibiting various aspects of Renaissance-era life. They tend to be organized around a particular ethnic culture (such as Scottish or Irish), a stratum of Elizabethan society (such as peasants or mongers), or a type of performance (such as parades or "fools"). The more than fifteen performing guilds at the Renaissance Pleasure Faire in Southern California currently include a peasants' guild, a parade guild, a military guild, a fools' guild, and a Puritans' guild.

The guilds are highly structured under guild masters (such as the "chief" of the Scottish guild). Requirements for joining vary from guild to guild; some require auditions, while others do not require any particular skill or talent—just dedication to the guild's goals. The level of commitment required to participate varies somewhat, too, though a certain amount of time and expense are expected. All guild members need to supply their own costumes, which must be approved as suiting the requirements of the particular guild, and to attend workshops before the faire opens on such subjects as language, performance, food, and history.

Many members value the guild system because it can be a pathway to a paying job at the faire. Owners and managers see guild participation as demonstrating seriousness of commitment, as well as ability to follow the particular faire's guidelines for costumes, language, and so forth. Liz Hoskinson, for instance, tells me that she became active in the Parade Guild at the Southern California Renaissance Pleasure Faire in 1977, when she was fourteen. At seventeen, she began dating the faire's stage manager, and when he stopped playing that role, she was able to step in. "I spent my twenty-first birthday at the twenty-first annual Pleasure Faire," she recalls. During her years at the faire, she went on to work in other departments as well (interview).

On the faire site, the guilds are assigned demarcated "home" areas where members congregate, socialize, and eat—all as part of the Renaissance faire show. They also wander through the faire interacting with each other and with attendees. Visitors might encounter members of the mongers' guild hawking "wares" such as fish or bread, those in the townsfolk guild preparing a meal using period-appropriate food and utensils, or Puritans hectoring people about sin and salvation.

The Guild of St. Andrews–Clan Mac Colin is a Scottish guild that performs music, traditional dances, and military formations and techniques. The "chief" of the guild, Steve Gillan, says that, unlike the professional faire performers, he takes "children, people who can't act" into the guild and teaches them the skills and historical knowledge they will need to take part. Gillan is a psychiatric technician with an art history degree; both of these, he jokes, are "good for this job" of guild chief (interview).

Gillan remembers attending the very first faire in 1963 with an English teacher from his Catholic high school. Since that time, the only years he has missed the faire are the two he spent in Vietnam in the army—and he still seems to feel regret for what he missed. When he returned to the United States, he found the Renaissance faire even more appealing than before he went to war. "The world turned funny while I was gone," comments Gillan, adding that as a result, many veterans found their way to the faire: those who had been in Vietnam, like himself, and veterans of other wars as well. The faire became precious to him because of its "broad-based view of the world"; indeed, confesses Gillan, when it came to needing the faire's expansive vision, "I was a male nurse—that was enough!" I pressed him for specifics of what he felt was welcome inside the faire's gates but not outside them, and he responded with a list: "Homosexuality, polyamory, prayer meetings, rigorous politics, crackpot religion, peculiar medicine. People were amazingly tolerant of everything, and there was plenty of intergenerational interaction. It was not part of my Eisenhower-era growing up, but here it was all OK" (interview). In words common among playtrons, Gillan calls the faire a "safe space to be" and a "family of choice" for devoted participants. Significantly, though, he also credits his own "intellectual curiosity" with deepening his involvement in the faire. Through his involvement, for instance, he became "pretty good" at Highland dance, for instance, and learned about both the design and construction of period costumes (interview).

Although faire guilds share a common structure, certain of them list more toward academically informed reenactment than other faire performers and participants. There are several military guilds, for instance, and these (as I will discuss shortly), are attentive to authenticity in representation. Likewise, a great deal of research and training is carried out by participants in other "demonstration" guilds, such as those representing ethnic groups or presenting household activities.

But despite the carefully organized structure of certain guilds, they still manage to carry out the anarchic nature of the faire. Crucial to the faire's destabilizing mission is the fools' guild, created in 1979 at the Northern California Renaissance Pleasure Faire and characterizing itself as "the Court of Misrule." Originally, the guild gathered up faire buskers who fit into the "court jester" mold—jugglers, mimes, clowns—into an improvisational performing troupe. The guild's original members then moved to Los Angeles, where they lived communally and hosted elaborate parties. Every year since 1981, the group, which calls itself a "disorganization," has crowned a "King of Fools," who can be either male or female, in a riotous public ceremony that usually takes place at the Southern California Renaissance Pleasure Faire. The "coronation" is preceded by a Parade of Fools, and the whole elaborate ceremony seeks to inhabit the spirit of upended hierarchy perhaps most famously exemplified by Shakespeare's Falstaff. (One of the earliest Kings was mime Billy Scudder, and David Springhorn was also crowned King of Fools—King Ignoramus I, to be exact—in 1981.)

At the Bristol Renaissance Faire, a "rogues' guild" likewise relies on fancy, not fact, to make its contribution to the faire's ambiance. The rogues roam the faire as a group, carrying a supply of flowers. From the crowd, they select a (generally) female visitor. If she has arrived with a companion, they pull that person aside to let him or her in on what they are about to do. Then, one by one, they approach their target, handing her a rose and making flowery declarations of admiration that are as humorous as they are sentimental. When I approach the rogues to ascertain that they are volunteers, not paid performers, one of them answers with directness while managing to stay in character: "Handing out the roses is payment enough," he tells me flamboyantly.

Dressing the Part

I consider sexual liberation to be a subset of fashion liberation.
—Wayne Koestenbaum

Many fairegoers, even casual ones, will don a small item of clothing in order to get into the spirit of things, even if just for the day. These casual attendees also have the option of renting costumes upon entering. But the playtrons are defined by their commitment to garb: if, in a rare instance, someone is seen on faire grounds outside of costume, friends will tease him or her about having showed up "naked."

For most people, acquiring the full set of clothing that distinguishes them from "tourists" is a gradual process. Many playtrons relate that a small item such as a leather mug or wristlet was their first purchase, around which they gradually built elaborate outfits, adding bit by bit over a period of years. Allison Villegas, a playtron in California, describes how her Renaissance faire clothing evolved along with her involvement in the faire:

> I have always attended the faire in costume. My first costume was a poor attempt at a merchant-class dress, made out of two or three dresses from a thrift store. Immediately after that horrible expedition into embarrassment, I went out and bought the Simplicity patterns for a bodice at my local craft store, and bought a cheap chemise and two skirts to go along with it, and that lasted me several years. This past season, since I was working, I bought a good quality bodice and chemise, several skirts, and over the course of the season (at two faires) probably over 25 accessories. (Email)

An impressive number of playtrons still make at least some of the things they wear, and judging by the conversations playtrons have among themselves about the craft of making costumes, the handmade, or Do-It-Thyself, is still valued in the faire's fifth decade. Ian Gibson estimates that as much as 70 to 80 percent of the garb worn by playtrons is homemade, and he adds that if he had the skill or the time, he would definitely make his own, because that would allow for greater creativity (email).

The number of Renaissance-festival-oriented clothing businesses, both at the faire and online, has increased steadily, making it easier for a more recent or casual visitor to the faire to acquire garb that is as elaborate as that worn by longtime playtrons or even by cast members. Costumers do a huge business at the faire, and a thriving clothing booth will contain hundreds of thousands of dollars worth of stock at a given time. The season-pass-holding playtrons spend a lot of money at these shops themselves, but as with any subculture that scorns "posers," they sometimes resent more casual visitors who, by virtue of spending a lot of money, can look the part of a playtron without committing to the community. Katrina Ranum has a long history of dedicated attendance at the Maryland faire, where she works simply out devotion to its community. Dropping a lot of money to acquire a full set of garb at once is, she considers, akin to a "microwaveable meal or saying, 'Here's money—make me creative!'" She feels as though this practice has contributed to making the faire's visual palette more homogeneous (interview).

Although some of the faire's earliest participants deplore the fact that *everyone* is not hand sewing *all* of their own clothing, what that means is not as clear-cut as it might seem. Those who think too much garb is bought or machine sewed might feel that there is more *personal* authenticity in the handmade and noncommercial, but others argue that there is often more *period* authenticity in garb that is professionally made. In Villegas's estimation, "Purists argue that homemade costumes are more accurate, but it really depends on the person doing the making and the person doing the buying—it is possible to find very accurate looking (though machine sewn) costumes for sale, and it's just as possible to make a very inaccurate costume at home" (email).

Villegas describes her clothing in loving detail that reveals how important the garb is to her faire fandom and that also indicates that her clothing is intended to signify on several different levels at once, conveying something about Renaissance-era social class, her new status at the faire as a booth worker, and the sexual subcultures in which she chooses to locate herself:

> My usual costume is that of a relatively rich peasant or very very poor merchant wife: I wear a burgundy bodice with tabs on the bottom edge, an off-white chemise with light embroidery, a green skirt of linen and a charcoal and gray striped skirt that feels like coarse woven flax or wool, and a saffron head kerchief. My belts are strung with bells, and carry my pouches (one for money and a phone, and one for a flask), wool-and-leather handcuffs, several fox tails (flea-furs, but they also denote marital status amongst faire folk), bells, a fan, a wooden tankard, and a small basket. My bodice is strewn (okay, covered) with faire favors, including those of a piece of tartan, several pewter pins, two "ticklers" made of feathers, and many trinkets given to me throughout the seasons. I wear yellow-and-black striped socks, because they match the booth I work at, and I jokingly say that they are reminder of where I'm supposed to go at the end of the day. (Email)

But almost everyone buys at least some portion of his or her garb, even if it is just an accessory or two. For many, it is a major expense, given priority in the discretionary portion of their budgets. Ian Gibson, for instance, readily divulges spending a great deal on garb and accessories and finds ways to extend his pleasure in the clothing by displaying it in his home and lending it to friends:

I spend about $1000 a year on clothing and have about $10,000 in jewelry that is only ever worn at Faire. (I lend many friends outfits as do most of my friends so that when non-Faire friends come they fit in and enjoy themselves more). I usually wear (top down) a hat (Tall Toad [a faire clothing shop] $100—own about 20 different types), Doublet (99% Noblesse Oblige [a faire clothing shop]—usually velvet and very ornate, about $700—own about 12), Lace cuff and neck chemise (about 10 of them), metal codpiece (about 6), leggings/tights (usually velvet with lace up the sides (about 20 in different matching colors), and boots (about 6 types). Sometimes a full matching cloak or sword cape (about 6) depending on the weather. I also have two kilts and one casual Scottish outfit and one full Prince Charlie black tie outfit, 6 different pirate coats with breeches and a whole bunch of other stuff. Some of the outfits are on rotating display on dress forms in our library throughout the year. (Email)

Gibson is decidedly on the high end when it comes to spending money on garb, but he also earns a higher salary than most. His spending is not out of line when it is calculated as a proportion of salary.

Manny defines himself as "creative class" and situates the expense of garb within a long period of being involved in, and devoted to, the faire; he makes the point that homemade garb might cost less in terms of money but requires additional resources in the form of time:

I have, over the course of my 24 years of Faire work and attendance, spent well in excess of $5K on garb, from $1200 mild steel plate mail armor to $800 boots, and a $1500 replica Henry VIII outfit ... to various other pieces from $15 to $200 each. I've probably spent another $1000 on materials for making other pieces, from a knee-length chain-mail shirt and coif, to kilts, baldrics, tunics, and accessories. No small amount of time was put into making those items as well. (Email)

Stephanie Hastings from Maryland is not uncommon in the way she carefully stretches the money she spends on garb: she acquired half of what she owns, she tells me, in one fell swoop by saving all her Christmas money and traveling to the New York State open house of Moresca, a popular faire clothing shop, which offers off-season deals (Hastings email).

Among devoted playtrons, men and women sew their own garb in equal numbers. Among newer participants, though, women tend to dress up first, and it is not uncommon to see a garbed-up woman accompanied by a man in street clothes. Through informal survey, I found some agreement among faire workers and other regular observers that the most macho, "straight" men who have some initial resistance to garb will wear kilts first. On some level, this seems contradictory, because a kilt in the American context is a kind of skirt. But the experience of wearing a kilt at the faire allows some men to work through an anxiety about masculinity in the context of dressing up, because the faire is stocked with jokes—verbal ones from performers, visual ones in the form of mirrors on the ground—about whether the wearer has anything on underneath. Still, even though kilt wearing allows for a steady flow of potentially comforting acknowledgments of the phallic, crises of masculinity are never entirely out of sight. "What Catholic school did you go to, little girl?" taunts the woman seated in the dunk tank in Maryland, here called Drench-a-Wench, as a man in a tartan kilt and a concert T-shirt passes by.

One thing is clear: men who regularly dress up for the faire are devoted to the practice and cherish the opportunity. Among the male playtrons, there is unanimous agreement that the costumery is a central part of the faire's pleasures. It often comes up when I talk to these men—especially, but not only, those holding working-class jobs—that there are very few chances for this kind of sartorial self-expression outside the faire. Indeed, when I ask them about their garb, male playtrons frequently refer to the strict patrolling of their clothing at work in particular. Perhaps the most striking example is Frank, a white playtron from Houston, Texas, in elaborate garb at the Texas Renaissance Festival in 2008. "I am headed back to base this week. I'm gonna be in uniform. This is my last chance," he tells me sincerely—then immediately requests I not identify him here by last name (interview).

Less explicitly linking "acceptable" male behavior with a uniform that scorns color, adornment, and individuality, but just as compelling and touching in its own way, is the testimony of Randy, a long-haul truck driver who has been present every weekend of the Maryland Renaissance Festival for seven years with his wife, both of whom attend in garb. An extraordinarily pleasant man, Randy is happy to spend his faire time talking at length with a stranger about why garbing up matters so much to him; occasionally, he remembers his faire persona and answers questions with "indeed" or "aye" instead of "yes," but mostly he seems too sincere about his pleasure even to maintain the beloved playacting while talking about it. "I have several full sets of clothing," he informs me, one of them a full set of plate armor that weighs forty pounds and is terribly hot in the Annapolis summertime. Like the majority of playtrons, Randy adds to his garb piece by piece, buying some things and making others. "Especially for men, there aren't many chances to get dressed up and go out," he explains. On this particular day, he is dressed all in vibrant green, which he says is his favorite color (interview).

Randy's insight about men's usual lack of access to the pleasure of self-adornment, in particular though color and frippery, is borne out by the playtrons' garb on display; the dramatic majority of male playtrons dress in nobles' costumes. Here, gorgeousness and elaboration reign supreme, completely outranking authenticity even among fairegoers who claim that an interest in history is one of the draws. (Randy, for his part, openly confesses that his clothing is probably "about a century too early"; interview). Dakota, whose "home faire" is also the Maryland Renaissance Festival, while discussing his love for garbing up, poignantly connects the limitations he perceives on what men can wear outside the faire to a suppression of sensory gratification. "I find men's clothes rather boring and plain shit in this time period. I prefer to wear fun, exciting, and comfortable clothes. When I costume at the faire, I know I will never get made fun of or persecuted. I can enjoy being . . . alive," he informs me (Scott-Hoffman email).

Female playtrons, on the other hand, are considerably more likely than men to dress in "peasant" garb, although here, too, the desire to participate in pageantry or even drag seems to be the draw. Playtrons tend liberally to apply the word *wench* to women dressed in "peasant" garb, and the term has a very particular meeting at the faire. The American Renaissance faire usage of *wench* smoothly incorporates the two (interestingly related) Renaissance-era meanings of the word: "servant, working or peasant girl" and "wanton or loose woman." For women dressed at the faire as "wenches," the term usually means sexually bold or otherwise unruly—as evidenced by the tradition of parades known as Wench Walks, in which participating women identify, approach, and mark likely looking men (and occasionally women) of their choosing, by kissing them while wearing bright, freshly applied lipstick. Crickett Lancaster appears proudly as her New York Renaissance faire sexually bold "wench" persona in the 2002 television documentary *Cleavage*, while Maryland playtron Stephanie Hastings writes, "I usually dress as a pirate, or as a wench, . . . sometimes as more middle-class but not too often—it's more fun to be a pirate or a wench" (email).

This difference between the commonest men's and women's garb hints that for many playtrons, the faire provides an opportunity to partake in that which is ordinarily denied: colorful, ornate clothing and primping for men, and sexual aggressiveness for women. Without having read Foucault (I asked), a playtron who attends the Maryland faire every weekend with her husband, muses,

> There are a lot of disciplines in outside society. Some people are afraid to let go of the rules and protocol, and [they think that] people who do must be undisciplined. If you don't follow those rules, out there, the response can get so negative that it can affect your job, your day-to-day life, your socializing. But at the faire, it is a very accepting group, because we have let go of those disciplines. (Bowman interview)

By giving expression through costume to socially forbidden pleasures, Renaissance faire garb functions as drag in the broadest sense of the word, as it refers to clothing carrying symbolic significance. Moreover, the pageantry and spectacle that constitute Renaissance faire participation call constant attention to the performativity and artifice of gender roles; this is accomplished not only through clothing but also through the elaborate enactment of flirtation and gallantry, turning putatively heteronormative situations into contrivance. For instance, Ian Gibson, who identifies as a white, gay professional, says that for many in his group of friends, the faire's draw is its ability to provide "an excuse to look completely fabulous and act with exaggerated manners and noblesse" (email). (Gibson's claim is echoed for me as I watch drag performer Dina Martina, in a New York City club in 2008, connect her own stage drag performance with Renaissance faire "drag": when an audience member tells her his name is Gavin, she coos, "Ooohhh, . . . are you from the Renaissance faire? Let's play damsel in distress!")

Drag happens at the faire in the more literal meaning, as well. Among playtrons in the faire (and among performers, too, for that matter) a fair amount of actual cross-dressing is always visible. (And a fair amount, I gradually learned, goes by largely undetected.) Numerous performers—some gay, some not—choose particularly traditionally masculine-appearing male audience members, call them onstage, and dress them up in drag for interactive parts of the show. They rarely choose playtrons in garb for this exercise. Events such as these are not perfectly correlated to the wearing of garb, but they do emphasize the deliberate blurring of gender and sexual roles that faire participation means for many fairegoers. Sir Larksalot the Bald, performing at the Maryland Renaissance Festival, chides his male volunteers to stand closer to each other, with the words, "There's no room for homophobia in this show." To encourage the volunteers, he holds their hands and leers at them; when the audience reacts to this, he puts his hands on his hips, looks at them, and declares, "What? With these tights, what did you think?"

For many women, a key aspect of the importance of garbing up—its "real gift to female playtrons," as one young woman puts it (Alicia)—stems from the reality that faire culture encompasses a much wider definition of what is beautiful than the advertising-driven beauty culture that exists outside the gates. This has the most striking implications when it comes to female body size. Many playtrons and faire workers were initially attracted to the faire, and remain deeply loyal to it, because of the way that larger women there are just as likely to display and adorn their bodies through garb as slender women are and are just as likely (or perhaps even more likely) to be considered beautiful. In fact, Aimee Boyle of the women's health website EmpowHer calls the Renaissance faire a safe zone because of its de facto encouragement of healthy body image through its tolerance of larger women and its deviation from what she refers to as the "styles and strivings" that serve "corporate agendas."

For many women, the question of female body size is the most radical and rare thing about the whole faire. Boyle, for instance, describes being made literally dizzy from the mere sight of larger women at the faire who adorn their bodies, act openly joyful, and most of all, are seen eating in public: "My mind was spinning faster than the wooden top my eight-year-old had in his possession and all the mead in the land wouldn't give me complete clarity; but I know this much, as I started the ignition and drove off, I felt I'd just left a happy, peaceful place, a place where breasts and hair and weight and laughter were all all right; where horses were important and people were, too." She muses that entering a space where women are supposed to enjoy food is "*shocking*, because in our current climate, women eating a lot of good food and getting round is aesthetically a hotbed of emotional, social and psychological turmoil" (italics added).

Large women who fall in love with the faire frequently use the language of trauma and healing to describe their experiences there. Jenna Dawn, a thirty-three-year-old American who writes for the Australian blog *Axis of Fat*, is blunt about the feelings of shame and inadequacy she has suffered over the years because of her size: "They've been damaging to my soul." Growing up in Southern California, Dawn first attended the nearby Renaissance Pleasure Faire with a high school drama group; she soon returned to work there during the summers. Dawn emphasizes that the faire is still "one of the few places that curvier women are celebrated, or actually seen as more beautiful" than their skinnier sisters. "I have never been thin—I am the same size I was in high school," she comments. "It's hard to grow up heavy! You're not attractive. You don't exist. It's hard to navigate" this as a young person. In contrast, Dawn cites the faire as the first place and time she "had a sexual identity." "It was amazing," she says of her visits to the faire as a young woman. "The garb really worked with my body. People would tell me I looked great. It was a heady experience—the first time I got any attention from men!" In Dawn's view, the most radical thing about the faire is what it has to teach participants about what is desirable: "It made me realize at eighteen that [the valuing of slenderness] is a cultural phenomenon," she says. "It was quite an awakening. It helped to save me" (interview).

Similarly, award-winning film and television actress Camryn Manheim writes movingly of finding her way to the Renaissance Pleasure Faire in Southern California as a teenager, in her memoir, *Wake Up, I'm Fat!* Manheim, born in 1961, first attended the faire at the age of sixteen, by which time she had already been made to feel inferior for years because of her size. She describes her first trip to the faire as almost painful because of the deep longing she experienced to be part of this "world that devoured curvy women and honored them with due respect" (21). She returned to work there the next summer, mostly hitchhiking from her parents' house to the faire site. Manheim openly cites the faire as the first place and time she felt beautiful and comfortable in her own skin:

> I worked at the Renaissance Faire for four summers. First as a court jester and then as a wench. It was my personal revolution. Sexual, emotional, and spiritual. I learned pretty much everything I'd ever need to know in the rolling hills of Agoura. . . . I was born in the summer of my sixteenth year. That summer and the three that followed, I celebrated my body. . . . In the four summers I worked at the Renaissance Faire, I learned how to walk around naked. I learned to love my body, and I learned to love that others loved my body. . . . Over those four glorious summers I did learn to fly. (31)

The Renaissance faire, writes Manheim, allowed her to "cast off the shackles of self-consciousness and self-loathing" (31). Similarly to Carolyn Weathers, who recounts in her memoir attending her first gay pride parade after attending the faire, Manheim describes her newfound confidence taking her on a direct path from the Renaissance Pleasure Faire in Southern California to activism with a radical feminist group in Santa Cruz called the Praying Mantis Brigade (32–37). The organization staged an annual event they called the "Myth California Pageant," which was timed to coincide with the Miss California beauty pageant, held every year in Santa Cruz. Manheim describes the Brigade's activists collecting blood donations from women who had been raped and pouring it on the stairs in the auditorium where the pageant took place, to call attention to the objectification of women in a "meat parade" (34).

Decades after Manheim's experience at the faire, she still rhapsodizes about the time she spent there: "It remains to this day—and I'm about to turn fifty—a very significant time in my life, friendship-wise, politically, socially, spiritually." She remarks, "I still feel exactly the same way. It's like if I hadn't spent those years at the Renaissance Faire, I never would have known what was possible, and I would have bought into the beauty myth much sooner and much more deeply" (interview).

Heavy women themselves are not the only ones who feel relief at the faire's broader palette of acceptable female body types. Randy, the long-haul trucker and dedicated playtron who had spoken to me at the Maryland Renaissance Festival of his own feelings about garbing up, brings up the subject of female body size without being asked. "I like a woman who is a little larger," he tells me, "and my wife, she is beautiful here. And larger women are beautiful here" (interview). Michelle, who works in the Heart's Delight clothing booth at King Richard's Faire in Massachusetts, confesses that her favorite part of the job is being able to fit women of all sizes. "A lot of larger ladies," she tells me, "when they are shopping outside these gate, they find that a lot of stores don't even carry things in their size, and if they do, [the selection is] very limited" (interview). Heather, a Friend of the Faire at the Bristol Renaissance Faire in Wisconsin, speaks of how important the faire is for a friend of hers who is a very popular member of their group, while in contrast, "the rest of society thinks everyone should be a size 2" (interview). Amy, a veterinarian whose "home faire" is the Maryland Renaissance Festival, comments, "Some of the ladies outside the gates maybe aren't looked on as so attractive; inside here, they are buxom beauties" (Bowman interview). Michelle, Heather, and Amy do not consider themselves overweight, but they all feel relief for their own sakes because the mandate to be thin or on a diet or both, they say, exerts a pressure on all women.

Amy Wachtell, a street performer who travels the circuit, posits a connection between the marginality of faire culture and its ability to foster a less narrow sense of female attractiveness:

This is a group of people that have looked beyond the mainstream to find what they really want to do. They don't say, "This is what people do, so I'm going to do it. I'm going to watch TV and watch sports and go to bars." . . . So, if you look beyond what people tell you you're supposed to like, you're going to look beyond what woman you're supposed to like. If every heterosexual man was able, was allowed, to look deep inside for what he really liked, every man would come up with a different ideal. Some men would want a short, fat woman. Some would want a huge, tall woman, an Amazon. I think everyone has their own idea. (Interview)

Wachtell adds that the act of garbing up is liberating from a variety of social strictures including but not limited to women's body size and that both men and women sometimes don, along with their costumes, an entire character with a name and, now and again, a different gender.

For many playtrons, then, garbing signifies more than just playing dress-up (which is not to diminish the fact that it is, profoundly and importantly, playing dress-up). It allows playtrons to experience their own identity as less fixed and more in their own control by developing and inhabiting a character. Steven, an oil-rig worker in Texas, travels from the coast to the Texas Renaissance Festival in Houston every year. He brings with him three complete sets of garb—and has developed three separate personas to go along with them. "Depending on what I am wearing on a given day, I am treated entirely differently" by other fairegoers, he reports (interview).

While acquiring Renaissance faire garb has become much easier (as long as you have the money, you can buy it at the faire), many longtime faire attendees find that the "outside" space to be nonconformist in dress has narrowed, if anything, since the days of the initial faires. But the more battering the outside world might seem, the more of a sanctuary the flamboyant, transgressive physicality of the festivals can be, and it is easy to see why longtime participants—workers as well as playtrons— worry about the consequences for this sanctuary if the space of the faire is to be "tidied up," in the words of performer David Springhorn, by its new corporate designers (interview). Anxiety over these changes is not new: writing in 1998, about the thirty-second annual Renaissance Pleasure Faire in Northern California, longtime faire worker David Templeton looks back over the history of the faire and tries to make sense of the changes in the faire's nature by placing them in historical context:

> These days, it seems that the great god Dionysus has been tamed by the unsmiling lords of common sense, commerciality, and fear of litigation.

The very bawdiness that gave the faire its reputation as the hottest party in town has been cropped back, censored, and tamed. Even a casual survey of faire workers—who prefer to remain anonymous—elicits a glum confirmation of the new Puritanism. "No more sex. No more drugs," whispers one veteran peasant. "This is now Disneyland."

Thus, although almost all of the hundreds of playtrons I surveyed state that the faire continues to provide them with important expressive opportunities, occasionally mentioning explicit strategies for working around and within the faire's increased commercialization, many of the faire's first, countercultural adherents worry that it has been too changed for them to recognize its early freedoms. However, both groups do share a protectiveness of the faire as a liberatory space, even if it now must host plural and sometimes collisional sets of meaning. I am reminded of the final words of the film documentary on the Cockettes, a psychedelic drag-queen performing troupe founded in San Francisco in the late 1960s that launched the careers of movie actor Divine and disco star Sylvester and, in its fusion of hippie culture with gay/drag culture, was kindred to the Renaissance faire in some important ways. In the scene, Cockettes alumnus Anton "Reggie" Hannigan is musing on the world of wars, corruption, and deception, looking out over the ocean and comparing his present life to his time in the troupe. "Give me a torn dress, a beach, and a hit of acid and that's enough," he says sadly. "That's a lot."

Military Maneuvers: Reenactment as Drag

In apparent contrast to playtrons who are attracted to the faire because of the opportunity that garbing up provides them to *break* rules, including those rules pertaining to gender roles, there is a contingent of enthusiasts who are drawn in by activities or values that resemble to some degree the hobby of military reenactment, a practice that seems on the face of it to be predicated on *following* rules, including those of gender, in the quest of ever-greater verisimilitude. Military reenactment in the United States is a pursuit that predates the faire by as much as a century, depending on what counts as reenactment. The first reenactments of Civil War battles took place before the war itself had even ended, as a way for soldiers to commemorate the fallen and to recruit new soldiers to the cause. Follow-ing the end of the Civil War, reenactment took place primarily as a part of a reconciliation effort; soldiers from the North and the South re-created battles they had been in, wearing their own uniforms.[5]

For the present purposes, though, hobbyist reenactment is more rel-evant. Cathy Stanton has introduced the term "avocational" to describe these reenactors, because while reenacting is a leisure activity for them, it nonetheless plays an important role in their sense of identity (vi). This practice developed in the United States simultaneously with the Renais-sance faire, beginning with the observance of the centennial of the Amer-ican Civil War. The political and emotional meaning of military reenact-ment was transformed, of course, when the reenactors were no longer former soldiers themselves, representing battles in which they had actu-ally fought, but rather hobbyists (no matter how serious or respectful they might be). It is no longer widely considered appropriate to reenact ongoing wars (though this does take place), and reenactment of certain historical wars, such as the Civil War or World War II, remains contro-versial as well because of possible implications about the racial politics involved. One could certainly argue that an "acceptable" form of reenact-ment of *all* American wars is now done cinematically, by professionals, in the form of war movies: these may depict, without challenge, actual battles of recent and ongoing wars as well as more historically distant ones—though recreational reenactors who face these challengers have been drawn on in the casting of war movies since at least the 1970s.

Military stagings at the Renaissance faire are seldom organized tightly around the precise presentation of actual historical battles the way "straight" military reenactments are, though particular historical figures might be represented among the faire's cast. Nonemployees more for-mally involved in exhibiting martial arts might belong to one of the faire's military-oriented volunteer performing guilds. At the Southern Califor-nia Renaissance Pleasure Faire, for instance, the Guild of St. Michael's operates as a sort of umbrella organization for various military compa-nies, maintaining instructional materials such as costume guides and cit-ing historical referents for the companies. The performers in these com-panies, such as Vietnam veteran and Scottish guild Clan Mac Colin chief Steven Gillan, are attentive to accurate depiction of military activities—

Fig. 4.2. Women at the faire frequently reframe the martial implications of chain mail, as do these two attendees of the Texas Renaissance Festival in 2004. (Photo by Paul Stout)

although they still temper this interest with the desire for performative achievement and inclusiveness. Outside the faire, Clan MacColin does participate in competitions against more strict reenacting groups. They sometimes are able to win over organizations with more resources, such as tanks or horses, Gillan explains, because "Renaissance faire weenies know how to entertain!" (interview). Gillan's words slyly indicate that a prizing of the performative and the inventive in reenactment extends beyond the faire, whether it is openly acknowledged or not.

Playtrons who are interested in military staging and possessing a more informal relationship to the faire often gravitate to fencing or jousting contests and their paraphernalia: armor, weapons, and shields. These contests are scripted and choreographed more often than not, which has the odd result of making them seem less "authentic" to some observers while at the same time bringing them more in line with traditional military reenactment because the results are predetermined. Blacksmiths are standard crafters at Renaissance faires, and in many cases, their booths (complete with furnaces for craft demonstrations) are located adjacent to the jousting ring. Here they display and sell different kinds of armor and custom-made weapons such as knives or swords. Further, certain playtrons make their own armor, especially chain mail (a time-consuming process to be sure, as thousands of metal links must be woven together). These fairegoers are willing to put up with an impressive amount of discomfort, walking around—sometimes in summer heat—wearing thirty pounds or more of metal.[6]

But most playtrons attracted to arms and armor at the faire do not bring this level of commitment. They might watch with interest the joust or the "battles" staged in the living chess game, but these often have a strong comic aspect that does not allow for too much seriousness of martial purpose. They buy and wear an item of clothing or a prop that, if not entirely functional, is more realistic than the wooden swords marketed to children, but they may not particularly care about learning how to use it correctly.

There is important countercultural precedence for this kind of adoption of military attire *as style* that is now commonplace at the faire. Hippies often wore fatigue jackets, not only to defang them but also to opt out of consumerism and to erase markers of class identity. Similarly, 1960s and 1970s dandies adapted military clothing—particularly jackets—as part of their finery, attempting to hijack its meaning and imbue the garments with less bellicose significance. Musician Jimi Hendrix is a useful example here: having enlisted in the U.S. military and subsequently come to oppose the country's escalating role in Vietnam, he sought out vintage military jackets to wear as flamboyant stage costumes.

While arms-and-armor playtrons are always visible at the faire in all regions of the country, I found no evidence that any major demographic group is particularly more attracted to this aspect of the faire than others. Self-termed "Dungeons and Dragons–playing geeks" from middle-class suburban families in Georgia describe making their own chain mail during their high school years, and a whole contingent of motorcyclists in Massachusetts add elements of mail or knives to the leathers they already wear. A group of "out" gay men in Maryland joke rambunctiously with each other for my benefit about the length of the blades that they sport along with the rest of their faire finery, and certain young women in California showily upend the whole idea of armor and its masculinist signification by adopting the faire's stylistic innovation of the chain-mail bikini top. (A series of fantasy novels, *Chicks in Chain Mail*, plays with that idea, posing several rhetorical questions: Who says women need to be rescued? Are our swords any less sharp?) The one generalization that does hold is that more men than women are attracted to armor, but there are enough exceptions to make it worthwhile for armorers to sell a range of items tailored to women's bodies, and plenty of women wear daggers of some kind at their waists or in their boots.

Not surprisingly, investment in the faire's more military looks ranges across a continuum of intentionality, a spectrum of realism. Some playtrons wearing martial garb are rather lighthearted about it: they like the way it looks or the attention "mundanes" pay them when they are wearing it. (Playtrons in armor are frequently photographed by more casual visitors.) Other playtrons consciously enjoy the idea of deliberately turning the aggressiveness of the martial into the fancy of make-believe; in Wisconsin, I witnessed an extreme version of this when a fairegoer presented a performer in his favorite act, the Sturdy Beggars Mud Show, with a condom made out of chain mail. And there are those whose interest in armor and weaponry more closely parallels the elaboration and attention to historical detail that preoccupy reenactors.

Even among the faire participants engaged in actual reenactment, says Gillan, that participants share a single identity position or ideological stripe "simply isn't so." He goes on to assert,

> To swab us all with the same brush [regarding motivation] is foolish. . . . We come in all colors and religions and races. Mostly, people do not do this for political attitudes. They are trying to understand the life of a soldier. . . . I am working in a period four hundred years ago. How patriotic could that be? Now, a proveteran sentiment I don't associate with being jingoistic. I have one officer who's a Quaker. He got out of the war as a conscientious objector. I'm a left-wing, working-class individual. I work with all kinds. As for the veterans [in the military guilds], most of us have PTSD to one degree or another. Oddly enough, this helps. (Interview)

Gillan strongly makes a case for the educational value of the faire's guild demonstrations. "What we're doing, even though it isn't academic, can make history come alive for those watching. If it's done well, it can have real value as a teaching thing," he declares. "We learn about the *doing* of things, by doing" (interview).

Ultimately, though, it is the coexistence or even commingling of motivations for the variously researched reenactment activities that proves to be the most instructive feature of the faire's military maneuvers. The way whimsy jostles against overt seriousness hints that the now-familiar category of "reenactment" has less to teach us about the faire than the faire has to teach us about reenactment. In other words, it might just be that instead of the faire being a kind of reenactment, or even an activity that resembles a reenactment, it is more useful to look at how the faire displaces our understanding of reenactment—revealing it to be, at least in its current incarnation, a kind of drag. Sometimes the drag is the cross-dressing kind, as when women reenactors impersonate historical women who dressed as men in order to fight in the war. But even when there is no cross-dressing—when male reenactors dress as male subjects, and traditionally masculine subjects to boot—there is still the same key highlighting of the distance between the "authentic" and the "constructed." The same truth holds when a drag queen puts on a wig and takes the stage or when a twenty-first-century man puts on a peaked hat and crouches in a field: it is not an impersonation that is meant to fool anyone. It is an impersonation meant to impress with the conscious knowledge of what a good impersonation it is.

Whether military reenactment has been cast as tribute or travesty, most commentators have pictured it as a different, more sober kind of masquerade than the kind of performance in drag-queen shows. To be sure, this is in part is because the reenactors' showy attention to historical verisimilitude, expressed in scorn or even hostility for the inauthentic (or "farby," in reenactors' parlance), gives a *sense* of realism, of being the opposite of fictive. But I would argue that it is also because muddy fatigues (gendered male) seem less frivolous than sequins and boas (gendered female), no matter what the biological sex of the person wearing them. We should be careful, then, not to take the stated values of reenactment too literally or too narrowly; we must be willing to probe more deeply the affinity that "period rush"—a term reenactors and scholars alike employ for the euphoria and freedom felt by reenactors in the emotional connection they feel to the place and time they are reenacting—might have to the sense of euphoria and freedom described by drag queens. After all, navigating bodily through the past, as Tavia Nyong'o reminds us in his examination of "affective transfers" in queer performance, may not be innately queer—but it is easily queered, accommodating as it does the "inserting [of] new subjectivities and new desires into familiar landscapes" (43).

The Renaissance faire's garb continuum, with velvet-and-lace frippery rubbing shoulders with medieval weapons reenactment and everything in between, reminds us that despite the scorn historians and professional filmmakers might be inclined to feel for history thus written by amateurs, the potential for amateur performance of history to be meaningful to its participants lies precisely in its ambiguity. "History marches on," writes Nyong'o, "but glitter sticks in its floorboards" (48).

5

"Every Day Is Gay Day Here"

Hating the Faire

Rennie: A renaissance festival hippie, often one who travels the circuit. Also sometimes "Festie." In conservative communities they are know by the public as "Long-haired-pot-smokin-daughter-stealin-rennie-hippy-freaks."
—*A Cross-Disciplinary Glossary of Terms for Historical Hobbyists*

Audience studies of American popular culture have, since at least the 1980s (with Janice Radway's important work on romance novels and Michael Denning's work on dime novels), paid careful attention to the centrality of cultural consumption and fandom in identity formation. Considerably less attention has been paid, however, to what Jonathan Gray calls antifandom—in other words, demonstratively hating a cultural artifact or experiences instead of loving it—which can be equally important to identity formation. The paradigm-creating work of Dick Hebdige and others has made *subculture* a familiar and useful analytical category for cultural historians. But scant energy has gone into theorizing or reading closely the significant meanings of active denigration of a recognized subculture. The one consistent exception has been historicist examination within popular cultural studies of what sociologist Stanley Cohen termed "moral panics": Elvis Presley's dancing, superhero comic books, backmasking record albums, certain video games. As language about a "hippie invasion" makes clear, the Renaissance faire from its earliest days has produced its share of narratives of moral panic. In its fifth decade, it still does: a scan of postings about the various faires on Internet review sites such as Yelp yields regular complaints about Satanic symbology. A reviewer named Kacey H., writing on Yelp about the Georgia Renaissance Festival, for instance, worries that "Wiccan, as well as satanic, symbolism was in nearly every gift shop."

Taking seriously the pleasures and rewards of cultural antipathy, or the social and cultural capital garnered through the activity captured by the slang formation "hating on" something, as a significant expression of self-definition, though, can be just as instructive as tracking what popular "moral panics" have to say about social constructions of "deviance" at a given historical moment. Consider, for instance, the lessons that the "disco sucks" movement in the 1970s has to teach us about the privileges of homophobia and racism, perhaps serving as a sort of consolation prize for working-class white Americans using a cultural form to pursue what David Roediger calls the "wages of whiteness," or what mockery of country music meant to strident nonfans as the genre's major producers and consumers were starting to leave behind the rural South, bringing the music with them.

By the same token, those who "hate on" the Renaissance faire need to be brought into its story for a full understanding of the faire as phenomenon. Not surprisingly, residents of areas adjoining faire sites mostly either love the faire (citing the jobs, attention, and business it brings to the area) or hate it (for the traffic and noise). This is the familiar double-edged sword of the tourism industry. But there have also been, since the faire's earliest years in Southern California, those who are deeply invested in expressing passionate opposition to the faire on the grounds of taste or fashion, so that ridiculing Renaissance faires very quickly became—and remains—itself a recognizable cultural trope. Indeed, as the faire itself has continuously evolved along with its historical content and changes in ownership, the terms on which it is commonly derided have been arguably the most steadfast expressions of the faire's social meaning. In other words, those who vocally hate the faire are using it to construct and circulate arguments about what sorts of cultural activities and individual behaviors should be considered acceptable, even as they make profound protestations about their own individual identity.

Organizers, workers, and visitors alike who attended the faire during its first decade stress that the faire presented a counterhegemonic vision, one that was at times, in the accounting of some informants, actively oppositional, as in the hiding of draft evaders on the faire site. Alicia Bay Laurel, author of back-to-the-land guide *Living on the Earth*, describes valuing the faire immediately as counterhegemonic suasion: "There and then I realized that how I wanted to live—out in nature, in a creative community with other artists," she says of her first visit to the Renaissance Pleasure Faire in 1964 (email). "It was a country," says performer David Springhorn, his word choice symbolically removing the faire from the geographies of the prevailing culture (interview). As I have discussed in chapter 4, several people who were involved with the early Renaissance Pleasure Faires in California, such as lesbian activist Carolyn Weathers and film and television actress Camryn Manheim, eagerly recount how the young faire, through its presentation of alternative values, played a role in getting them ready to take part in radical organized politics.

Defining faire society from 1963 to the present, participants and observers have used a variety of terminology to describe its ecosystem: counterculture, subculture, oppositional culture, alternative culture. Each of these must also be defined at least in part by the resistance it meets from the dominant culture. As the story of the right-wing attacks on the faires in the 1960s illustrates, public aversion to the faire has never been just a matter of personal preference: it has always operated as vehement backlash against perceived departures from the "normal." This resistance can take the form of incorporation, which of course is how hegemony works; for some participants, this is precisely what happened as the faires became commercial enterprises. Describing this process, David Templeton writes (in 1998), "If the early faires were an embodiment of the free-loving '60s, the new faire is a perfect reflection of the hyper-commercialized '90s. Customers are now met by banners proclaiming the joys of Miller Beer. ATMs are never far away, and even the street musicians are peddling their tapes and CDs." But despite what Templeton and others see as the faire's having been "cropped back, censored, and tamed," in its fifth decade, a surprisingly prominent and boisterous antifaire rhetoric continues to host a conversation about what sorts of minority practices should be tolerated (Templeton).

Indeed, as legacy of the reactions to the faire's originary association with both Pacifica radio and the bohemian enclave of Laurel Canyon, and also of its centrality in California's hippie counterculture, mockery of the faire is more familiar to some Americans today than the faire itself is; this is because the mockery is common among people who have never attended a Renaissance faire. Along the same lines, there are many people to whom Joe Pyne's name is currently unknown; what has been passed down to them, though, is his vilification of the faire—not just the fact of his negative feelings about it but the particularities of his condemnation. Much of the negativity is simple knee-jerk: several very thoughtful people who avidly volunteered to talk to me about their disdain of the faire began to look alarmed when I asked for specifics of what about the faire made them feel this way, as though, scrolling through their objections to it, their own critical faculties were suddenly catching up with received wisdom. Conventional wisdom will not necessarily provide an accurate or complete—or fair—picture of anything; nonetheless, it is almost always worth paying attention to for the truths it can reveal about prevailing attitudes.

Of course, Springhorn's Renaissance faire "country," with its insider cultures and its motivated eccentricity—even in its most mainstream manifestations—is not for everyone. That is a truism, and this kind of dislike is not what should occupy us here. Rather, I want to consider what it means when dislike of the Renaissance faire has a singular, directed edge to it, containing cultural, rather than personal, meaning—when the very existence of the Renaissance faire has the capacity to make some observers livid. Take, for instance, the statement of commentator Gage on a blog post about the faire: "I hate these stupid festivals of the subnormals so much that I actually feel angry." Or take television cult series *Mystery Science Theater* writer Kevin Murphy's explanation on the show's online fan site for the way that the show repeatedly turns the Renaissance faire into a punching bag—including one episode in which this is made literal, when the main character and his robot sidekicks encounter punching bags in the shape of playtrons in garb. "Many of us involved in the writing of the show," crows Murphy, "hate Renaissance festivals to the point that we have wished dire harm on their participants and patrons, written letters to wit, received court orders enjoining us from stalking around them, been incarcerated for lighting fires in the bazaar and hurling flaming dream-catchers at horrified festers."

Indeed, in some situations, loving the Renaissance festival gets the same reaction as hating the hometown baseball team—or hating Disneyland (despite the fact that acts have been recruited from the faire to Disneyland or that Disneyland's developers consulted with the Pattersons because they viewed the faire as such a successful event). Probing the reasons for this yields some useful insights about the way both the faire and ridiculing the faire function in tandem as collective social practice. Fascinatingly, if logically, the most frequent reasons for which the Renaissance faire are ridiculed are often the same reasons its fans find it so liberating.

In the twenty-first century, contempt for the faire falls almost exclusively into three major categories. The categories are so familiar to Rennies and anti-Rennies alike that many people in either group can list them off the top of their heads. One especially conversant detractor is Michael K., who shares a hotel elevator with me and three playtrons in garb one evening when I am on my way back to my room from the Renaissance Pleasure Faire in Southern California. When the playtrons leave the elevator before he and I do, he turns to me and scoffs, "Man, have you ever seen bigger weirdos?" He has the grace to laugh at himself when I inform him that I have come from the faire myself and am writing a book on the faire. When I insist that I really am interested in why people find it so tempting to make fun of the faire, he readily lists reasons: "Well, like I said, they're weird. And then there is what they wear. I mean, they have the right to wear whatever they want, but people are going to laugh at a man wearing tights, you know? And look at them. They need to stop eating those turkey legs. Especially if they are going to dress like that" (interview). Thus, in a tone hovering somewhere between belligerent and sheepish, Michael K. reels off several of what turn out to be the major ways in which passionate faire hecklers mock the faire: nonconformity, clothing, and body size. A poster on a discussion board on the website Democratic Underground touches on all the same points that Michael K.

does but in fewer words, summing up the faire as "fat middle-aged people in odd outfits acting weird" (uppityperson).

Tights Anxiety

A cloaking robe of elvenkind
Hangs in my wardrobe behind
All the things that mother said
Were proper for a boy
—Marcy Playground

Of the common terms on which the faire is publicly disdained, the commonest one of all is the fact that at these festivals, a visitor is going to encounter—to borrow the title of Mel Brooks's comedy about Robin Hood—"men in tights." Interestingly, the garment has always been important to both the faire's devotees and its detractors. Take two radio personalities who had things to say about the faire in the mid-1960s, talk-show host Joe Pyne and Pacifica broadcaster David Ossman, as flip-sides of the "tights" coin: Ossman rhapsodizes about going about "gaily dressed" with his "legs in tights" in order to capture what he found most joyful about the first faires, while Pyne, Phyllis Patterson recalls, cited male tights-wearing in his successful campaign for the faire to be shut down (see chapter 1).

The wearing of tights by men comes up in the majority of mocking accounts of the faire, the practice seemingly inspiring an outpouring of dread about what constitutes proper masculinity. The sheer frequency with which the specter of "men in tights" is invoked reveals that tights are operating as a sort of code or shorthand for transgressive male behavior, not unlike the wearing of long hair did in the 1960s and 1970s. This intense reaction, in the estimation of New York Renaissance Faire writer/ choreographer Mark James Schryver, "comes down to two things: masculinity and sexuality" (interview). To put it more simply, anxious discussions of male tights-wearing vis-à-vis the faire are frequently tied to what we now call homophobia. For example, the author of a blog called *I Am Guilty of Blogging* explicitly connects failed male heterosexuality with wearing tights when he sardonically proposes a new slogan for the faire:

"Renaissance Faire: Why meet women when you can wrestle with men in tights?" (Driscoll). Likewise, comic journalist Marty Beckerman writes of his trip to the faire, "Womenfolk's stockings on the 'men'! (I would vomit, but that would only make them feel better about their anti-social 'individuality')." Further examples of flamboyant lashing out at men in tights at the faire abound. In these depictions, male wearing of tights is taken to signal humiliation because of tights' current association with the realm of the female.

Frequently, the word *prancing* is used to describe what men in tights do at the faire. The word *prancing* is commonly used derogatorily about homosexual men, causing a controversy in 2010 when television personality Mika Brzezinski used it to describe the public celebration of the court decision overturning the ban on same-sex marriages in California. On writer Chuck Palahniuk's official website, a commentator challenged readers to use word in a sentence without sounding "all gay and stuff" (Parker).[1] Bradley Milam, head of the civil-rights organization Fairness West Virginia, included *prancing* in a list of antigay insinuations printed in the *Charleston Gazette*, recently used to discredit Commissioner of Culture and History Randall Reid-Smith. Reviewer Jeremy Witt, in fact, invents the term "Ren-Fair prancing" in his review of the heavy metal band Falconer's album *Armond*.

The connection between faire clothing, gender disobedience, and homosexuality is often direct and explicit. A clear example is a photographic post on the faire called "Losers as Art VII (Ye Olde Faire)," on a blog written under the self-aware name "Mr. Condescending." (Earlier posts in his series include photographs of poor people who live in trailers, fat people, people he supposes are drug addicts, and the mentally ill.) "Mr. Condescending" captions a photograph of a man in garb, including tights and a pattered tunic, with "The floral print vest and homo-erotic merriment was in full force in warwick [*sic*] forest today." In the comments to the post—and Mr. Condescending responds to every one—he further assays that "prancing around in fauntelroy [*sic*] costumes" is "disgusting." Along the same lines, a group-contribution website of "fake motivational posters" pictures two young men in tights at the faire, with the caption: "fantasies—Renaissance Faires have been helping the closeted gay man live them out for decades" ("Fantasies").

Bodily Eruptions

Above all, fat is female.
—Naomi Wolf

If "men in tights" operates as a kind of shorthand for gender disobedience in men, women at the Renaissance faire are most widely punished for departures from mainstream beauty culture in terms of body size. And as with men finding liberation in the opportunity to dress in garb, though they are ridiculed for it in some quarters, women commonly cherish the Renaissance faire as a place where larger women can be prized. Comedian Dan Bialek, for instance, has a sketch in which he ridicules heavy women in Renaissance faire bodices by comparing them to an airbrushed (or more likely Photoshopped) photograph of a slender model with silicone-inflated breasts (Bialek).

Along the same lines, blogger midgetmanofsteel posts a diagram to show how women's curves are visible outside constraints of their bodices at the faire (see fig. 5.1). The diagram both exemplifies and literalizes what critic Susan Bordo identifies as late twentieth-century fears of eruptions of female flesh, as tautness and firmness become at least as important as size to the dominant female body ideal. Midgetmanofsteel writes about women he deems too large to be in garb—or, it seems, in public—that "the real problem with this visual is that although they look all hot and bosomy up top, they are still big women." Finally, blogger demonbaby also resorts to the language of eruption to describe seeing at the faire "wrinkly old fat knockers squeezed out into plain sight."

When discussants on a tech-related Internet bulletin board criticize the bodies of Renaissance faire women, their phrasing betrays an eagerness to contain and discipline the sorts of bodily eruptions that the commentary of demonbaby, midgetmanofsteel, and Bialek (and many others) posit. In a thread titled "Wife dragging me to a Renaissance fair," a commentator who calls himself foghorn67 writes, "From what I know, the Renn Fair [sic] employees that camp there are a bunch of sluts." Commentator krunchykrome responds, "And the only guys that want them are the one's [sic] in capes and purple boots that camp with them." The original poster, by describing his wife as "dragging" him to the faire, seeks to show his resistance to the faire as feminized territory. His respondents reply with contempt for assertive female sexuality ("sluts") and demasculinized male expression ("capes and purple boots").

The same depiction of the faire as feminized terrain is expressed from the imagined point of view of the wife doing the "dragging" by a posting on Yahoo Voices (a community-generated source of information on a wide if somewhat unpredictable array of topics). In an article titled "Renaissance Fair: Persuading Your Husband to Dress Up in Period Costume," author Sophie S. recommends never to use the word "tights" but rather only to say "hose" in order to "ease your husband's embarrassment of wearing 'tights.'"

To be fair, all this anxiety about what the Renaissance faire does "to" gender expression and by extension gender roles has a basis in reality: the festival as a whole regularly and happily participates in, and brassily welcomes, a range of activities that can be lumped under the term *genderfuck*. The title of this chapter, for instance, "Every Day Is Gay Day Here!" was uttered from the stage by performer David Springhorn at the Southern California Renaissance Pleasure Faire. Springhorn's six words efficiently capture a great deal about faire attitudes concerning gender and sexuality. First, they are an acknowledgment that the faire's overall flamboyance— including costumes, ribaldry, elaborate speech, and the insistent performativity that comes from there being no "offstage"—gets coded as "gay" in much of the public mind whether any particular participants happen to be actually homosexual or not. Second, they recognize that this flamboyance makes some people nervous. Finally, they insist that playtrons and Rennies, Springhorn himself included, embrace this detour from the "straight." Springhorn's words, uttered in an exaggeratedly stentorian tone, are kindred in spirit to a pointed comment that the film actor Johnny Depp claims he made to a Disney executive who objected to the swishy flamboyance of the way Depp played the character of Captain Jack Sparrow in the four movies based on the Disney theme-park ride "Pirates of the Caribbean":

> "They couldn't stand him. They just couldn't stand him," Depp says of Disney's reaction to his controversial interpretation of Sparrow. "I think it was Michael Eisner, the head of Disney at the time, who was quoted as saying,

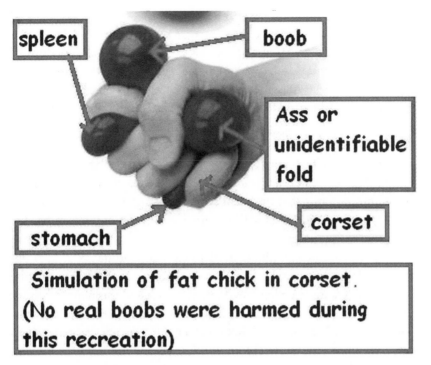

spleen

boob

Ass or unidentifiable fold

corset

stomach

Simulation of fat chick in corset. (No real boobs were harmed during this recreation)

Fig. 5.1. This drawing, posted on an Internet blog, expresses deep anxiety about the fact that larger women display their bodies at the faire.

'He's ruining the movie.'" Depp reveals to [musician Patti] Smith, however, that he remained unfazed by the studio's hysteria. "Upper-echelon Disney-ites, going, What's wrong with him? Is he, you know, like some kind of weird simpleton? Is he drunk? By the way, is he gay? . . . And so I actually told this woman who was the Disney-ite, . . . 'But didn't you know that all my characters are gay?' Which really made her nervous." (P. Smith)

Fittingly enough, in the years when movies in the *Pirates* franchise were released, dressing as Captain Jack Sparrow, as played by Depp, has very popular among garb-wearing playtrons.

Thus, while the Renaissance faire's playful tweaking of gender and sexual expression garners more mockery than anything else about it, the same practice is hailed by many of its adherents. A young couple features their wedding plans on the website Offbeat Bride under the heading of "Gender Neutral, LBGTQ-Friendly, Renaissance Festival Wedding"; the couple declares, "We both identify as genderqueer," so a Renaissance faire wedding (in garb) "was perfect for us!" ("Emmalyn"). A performer, dressed as a bishop, declares himself "the real Queen of the faire!" at the end of a season in Massachusetts, and those within earshot—all either playtrons or fellow performers—cheer. A cheerful couple in Georgia enter the faire wearing matching T-shirts; one declares, "Renaissance Fairs—Women in corsets—Men in tights—A bisexual's fantasy world," and the other, in the same typeface, says, "I Hit Boys with Sticks." Indeed, Tison Pugh, in his *Sexuality and Its Queer Discontents in Middle English Literature*, remarks that the mere semantic association of his academic field (he is a medievalist) with the American Renaissance faire has the potential to "queer [his] identity" (147).

Related to and sometimes overlapping with the question of properly gendered behavior, but not entirely the same, is the notion that the Renaissance faire is peopled by the unpopular and the nonconformist. The overlap is manifested clearly in a review by Bill Gibron on the website DVD Verdict; Gibran draws together the question of gender identity with the question of conformity when he criticizes a movie because a wizard character "looks more like a refugee from a drag show than a Renaissance faire." But the main way the accusation of being unpopular or untrendy is manifested at the faire is through application of the dismissive term *nerd*.

Illustrative of this trend, comedian Jesse Egan cracks that the Renaissance festival is "heaven for nerds" and that "mead" is "what nerds call beer." Similarly, the *Onion's* (generally nonparodic) popular culture website A.V. Club includes the Renaissance faire on a list it published as "The Knights Who Say 'Nerd': Twenty Pop Cultural Obsessions Even Geekier than Monty Python" (Bahn et al.). The faire is ranked on the list second in nerdiness only to *Star Trek* fandom. Comic singer "Weird Al" Yankovic in his song "White and Nerdy" rhymes, "I spend every weekend at the Renaissance faire" with "got my name on my underwear."

In fact, "Renaissance faire nerd" has become such a familiar putdown that faire adherents since the 1990s have taken up the term and used it self-referentially from the inside, in an example of the classic American strategy of sapping the hurt of insulting words by reframing them from within. As pertains to the faire, this whole dynamic is visible in a quiz, purporting to ascertain whether one is "victim or carrier of Faire Nerdism, or . . . just exhibiting slightly nerdish tendencies," that has made the rounds of faire-related Internet publications ("Are You").

The perception of "nerdiness" is enough to cause some people to be anxious to disassociate themselves from the faire. More than sixty years after the coinage of the word *nerd* for someone who is socially awkward, fifty years after the creation of "nerdy" superhero Spider Man, thirty-five years after the word *nerd* was popularized in the sitcom *Happy Days,* and twenty-five years after Bill Gates became a billionaire, it is time for a cultural critic to take up the theorizing of that category.[2] In the main, *nerd* seems to be an expression of anti-intellectualism, a relative of the *egghead,* since those in the category are generally presented as doing better academically than socially and tend to be imagined as wearing glasses, an emblem of intellectual orientation (as Aaron Lecklider has pointed out). The category *nerd* also seems to betray an anxiety about compulsory consumerism, since "nerds" are presented as not dressing according to what is in style or consuming the popular culture marketed to their demographic group. Finally, *nerd* (at least when used for boys or men) relates to the notion of proper masculinity that *men in tights* tackles, since male "nerds" are presented as effete, not able to participate in gendered activities such as dating or fighting; a staple trope in teen movies, books, or television shows is a high school "nerd" being shoved into lockers by his more masculine classmates and being unable to defend himself. Likewise, female "nerds" are most often presented as too studious to be considered sexually desirable. Both male and female "nerd" costumes can be purchased for Halloween; both versions feature mended glasses and unstylish, ill-fitting clothing (and in the circular logic of American capitalism, it is also easy to find a "sexy girl nerd" version). Some versions of the costume sport shorthand emblems of intelligence, such as a card with Einstein's relativity equation.

For the matter at hand—that is, cultural habits—the stereotype of *nerd* (and the related one of *geek*) is entrenched, and the cultural preferences that have attracted labeling as *nerdy* are well established, through jokes, name calling in books and videos, even "nerd day" at middle and high schools, reminding us regularly what qualifies. "Nerds" are comic book readers. They are science fiction fans. They do not like—or excel at—sports. They do like role-playing games. They do not care about fashion. They do care about computer programming. But until someone carefully tracks its application and the cultural "work" it does, probing the kinds of behaviors, attitudes, and values it seeks to contain and discipline, *nerd* will remain just that: a stereotype.

In reference to Renaissance faire participation, it is worth noting, the term *nerd* is used derogatorily and proudly in equal measure. (Though those who use it about themselves might well be preempting the label being directed at them from outside.) Young-adult author Heather Brewer touches simultaneously on both usages, dedicating her vampire series, *The Chronicles of Vladimir Tod*, to "the unpopular kids" and, in the biographical sketch at the back of the book, identifying herself as someone who loves to attend the Renaissance faire in garb. Mention the Renaissance faire, say playtrons, and it is common for people to repeatedly and defensively mock Renaissance faire "nerds" so that they will not be considered nerdy themselves. ("Wow! I'm back in high school!" sarcastically remarks one self-identified playtron at the Maryland Renaissance Festival in response to an article calling faire participants "nerds" [Mincher]). Stand-up comedian Dan Polydoris calls the scene at the Renaissance faire "mating season for social outcasts" and concludes that certain insufficiently masculine male attendees must be using a spell that "warded off women." Author Jala Pfaff, in her somewhat updated romance novel *Seducing the Rabbi*, finds "total weirdos and freakazoids" at the Colorado Renaissance Festival (21).

As with the question of gendered behavior, the application of *nerd* to playtrons does echo what the playtrons themselves often say about themselves—recall, for instance, the man who happily declares, "We're irregulars!" (quoted in chapter 4). When the *Washington Post*'s publication (both print and online) about arts and leisure in the DC area prints a mocking article about the Maryland Renaissance Festival, so many of its devoted participants reply in the comments section of the online version that it is hard to imagine the response is not part of an organized effort. The article, by reporter Robyn Mincher, touches on all three of the commonest areas of ridicule, referring both to men "prancing" around in garb and women's large erupting bodies, as well as calling participants "nerds." Much of the response, while angry, is quite savvy about what sort of critique is being enacted. A respondent named Lumpy, for example, makes explicit that the mandate to endorse certain "acceptable" activities requires the marginalization of others:

> It has always amazed me that rennies are called nerds, geeks and freaks yet someone who is a sports fanatic is an enthusiastic fan. I have friends who have mountains of trading cards, spent hundreds on replica jersies [*sic*], paint themselves up on gameday, spend hours tailgating, and pay thousands for season tickets. It just boggles my mind but at least you made yourself feel better by casting dispersions [*sic*] at something you obviously didn't get. I guess that's what we get for not being mainstream. (Mincher)

In response to the same article, another commenter chooses a different strategy—to resist the marginalization that has Lumpy so distressed, writing, "Remember that for many of us, we may be nerds (or geeks, et cetera), but we're also that person you go to work with every single day. We're parents and children, federal employees, Starbucks baristas, rocket scientists, retirees, students, and that guy you bumped into on the Metro" (Mincher).

The theme of "so nerdy that they can't get laid" coexists with a frequent accusation that the Renaissance festival is offensive because of the huge amount of sex and partying supposedly going on. (In some instances, this notion has been, and continues to be, raised as part of a "moral panic," but in the current moment, it is frequently the stuff of antifandom as well). Comedian Dan Bialek, for instance, refers to the faires as "super hippie orgies" in a move directly reminiscent of the rhetorical turn used to shut down the 1967 faire (Bialek). Los Angeles journalist Jeff Weiss blogs, under the headline "The Renaissance Faire Is Decadent and Depraved," that immediately upon arrival at the faire, he "realized one thing. The Renaissance Faire was about sex." One seasoned crafter, bodycaster Ann Curtis, keeps a cartoon hanging on her refrigerator in the back of her booth at the Maryland Renaissance Festival that neatly connects these two seemingly contradictory indictments; its caption reads, "Niche market pornography: Ren Faire Geek Sicko Shit." Once again, although such anxious speculation about debauchery at the faire is, of course, greatly exaggerated, there is nonetheless some truth underlying it, dating back to the faire's genitive role in the experimentation of the 1960s and

1970s counterculture. In the words of performer David Springhorn, for the Renaissance faire's first decade or so, the community hosted "every kind of sexual experiment that can be done" (interview).

The faire's post-1950s eagerness to look outside of traditional models of nuclear family has not entirely faded away; writer/choreographer Mark James Schryver comments of his own, more recent involvement with the faire, "I had never heard of polyamory, until I went to the Renaissance faire. I had never encountered a working 'open marriage,' until I went to the Renaissance faire" (interview). Largely for these reasons, Allison Villegas, a young and dedicated playtron who self-identifies as queer, opines, "Usually the people that hate [the Renaissance faire] so actively hate it because they are moralists or highly Christian, and I don't try to say that in a bad way" (email). She is not entirely wrong. A group called Renaissance Ministries is wholly devoted to attending Renaissance faires—in garb—in order to conduct a mission among the "pagans, wiccans, druids, witches, Satanists, palm readers, tarot card readers, new age channelers, and the like."

Despite the fact that Rennies and playtrons experience as open-mindedness and personal freedom the practices that have given rise to these negative stereotypes, the mockery rankles: in addition to the two women workers at the Maryland Renaissance Festival who declined to participate in my research out of fear that I would do damage by writing a scornful account, a playtron at the Georgia Renaissance Festival wrote me excitedly that she would love to contribute her perspective to a book on the faire and wanted to organize her close friends to participate too—but wanted to check first and make sure I intended to treat the subject respectfully. I sent her a brief outline, and because of my plan to include this chapter, on Renaissance faire "haters," she declined to communicate further with me.

The Renaissance Faire "haters" I approached in person, for their part, were generally quite eager to talk with me for this project, which supports the argument that antifandom provides real pleasures and rewards. But few of the antifans were aware that their antipathy to someone else's working at or attending the faire, which they experience as entirely "authentic" (to return to that vexed category), is descended in any way from the right-wing attempts to block the initial faires, even though both antifaire articulations cite sexual promiscuity, nonstandard dress and hair, and drug use.

Yet it is impossible to draw an arbitrary borderline through the historical record and to effectively claim that stances taken on one side of it have nothing to do with identical stances taken on the other side. For one thing, the historical precedents frequently surface in twenty-first-century faire bashing, as when someone (using the screen name geezer) writes on a message board, "Asking which is better: hippies at a hippie festival or Renaissance dorks at a Renaissance fair is like asking which is better: getting your genitals caught up in a meat grinder or farm equipment." In the 1960s, ridicule of the Renaissance faire's visual statements were recognizable as negative reactions to and against "hippie" clothing and long hair, reactions portrayed iconically, if problematically, in the 1969 movie *Easy Rider*. This censure continues to echo through current disparaging of the faire in a sort of sarcastic "return of the repressed"; a clear example is what commentator madtexter wrote on a blog post about the faire; by commenting, "Oh, gawwd. I would never go to a renaissance fair. Too many freaks," this commentator used the same name—"freaks"—that participants in the 1960s and 1970s counterculture gave themselves to distinguish themselves from the "squares."

As madtexter's semantic turn emblematizes, the same objections voiced against the earliest faires have been raised without interruption since: why would someone want to dress in such an "abnormal" way? Why would men wear their hair in such a feminine fashion? Is it unnatural, or just plain disgusting, to practice such "free love"? Does dressing like that mean you smoke marijuana? ("A lot of dudes there," Dan Bialek quips in his skit "Renaissance Fair(e) Myths," "looked like they sold weed professionally.") Is it anti-American to choose to live communally or, worse, outside of the nuclear family? (A message board commentator called lupi, who announces that he would rather shoot himself in the head than attend a faire, uses as his avatar the emblem of a hammer and sickle with a line through it, over the words "No Commies," while a defender of the faire, going by the name madmage, brazens it out on another board, admitting, "Here's one hint though: most rennies are very liberal . . . you can call them commies if you'd like to do so because a lot of them have the same ideals as 'communists' do.")

However, as the faire has evolved over four decades, and the composition of its audience along with it, one striking new grounds for opposition to it (or derision of it) has emerged. This has to do with the socioeconomic status (or, perhaps more to the point, the perceived socioeconomic status) of its attendees. Accounts of the faire in its first decade and a half largely agree that the most prominent audience group, those who really felt it was "for" them, tended to be youthful. By the end of the 1980s, this perception had started to shift, and as the twentieth century ended, a highly visible core audience demographic consisted of self-described blue-collar adults. This new demographic is reflected in a prominent line of satire focusing on class. "Most [playtrons] admit to having 'stupid' jobs" and come from "dull towns," dismissively writes Elizabeth Gilbert in *Spin* magazine in 1996 (106). On a blog called *Smart Sassy Mom*, the author titles a post "Renaissance Festival = Redneck Disneyland" (Stephanie). *Points in Case*, an online "college humor publication," refers to the faire as a "gathering of white trash dweebs" (Fugly Slut). Blogger Orlando "Winters" (the quotation marks are his), in a blog entry on how to spot rednecks, lists "the guy who plays town crier at your local renaissance fair." Humorous website Davezilla, in which readers are regularly asked to provide captions for posted photographs, hosted the following exchange in response to a picture of several ambiguously costumed adults:

> JOHN IN ANONMYITYVILLE: Looks like a white trash renaissance festival.
>
> CBATDUX: Is there any other kind of renaissance festival? ("Caption Time")

Commenter Dave_28, on a sports bulletin board, opines that "only the Texas Renaissance Festival surpasses the Crawfish Festival in density of white trash."

In the Internet era, class-based mockery of the faire exceeds antihippie mockery—though the two are certainly not mutually exclusive. As these examples indicate, most "hating on" the Renaissance festival has to do with feelings about those who people it: workers "on the circuit" are snubbed as migrant labor or hippies, while visitors in costume are faulted for having inappropriate gender expression or being too "low," "common," or crude because of their blue-collar status. Another important area in which the festivals are mocked has to do with the staging. For some casual visitors to the faire, as well as some people who have refused to attend a faire altogether, the idea of "no off-stage" is extremely upsetting. "I hide from the improvisational actors," writes Gilbert in *Spin*, of her first trip to the New York Renaissance Faire (102). As I discussed in chapter 3, scholars of immersion theater are not surprised at this resistance and even feel that pushing spectators outside of their comfort zone is the intent of a theatrical experience that breaks down the traditional division between stage and spectators' seats.

Occasionally, it is possible to see visitors to the faire become flustered and upset because performers have spoken to them directly. Getting them to talk about what has upset them yields probably more emotionally laden answers than they would give after they have had a chance to calm down; furthermore, it is tricky to talk to people who are angry and feel vulnerable without either contributing to their sense of exposure or getting shut down by them because they are annoyed about having been approached in the first place.[3] Furthermore, approaching people in situations such as this necessitated telling them, in essence, that I had been eavesdropping on them by way of introduction. This, coupled with the fact that many of the most virulent "haters" do not actually attend faires, meant that while most of the playtrons I spoke to were people I had introduced myself to at the actual festival, most of the "haters" were people I approached in other ways. But I did manage to speak to a handful of people at the faire following experiences in which they loudly rejected approaches by performers.

Tellingly, people who did not enjoy one-on-one encounters with performers tended to be angry about it, rather than condescending or indifferent. Their outrage generally indicated that they had a clear sense of the line between performer and spectator—and by walking up to them directly, the performer had crossed that line. One man in California tells me that he does not mind anything a performer does as long has he stays "out of [his] face"; a visitor at the Georgia Renaissance Festival snaps the same phrase at a performer there, who is teasing him about his "strange garments." (Plenty of people find this particular joke, which regularly crops up in video and literary representations of the faire, to be strained or corny, but it is also possible to see it as a barely coded reminder that "normal" is relative.) The phrase *in my face* implies that the issue was the space each person—performer, spectator—was supposed to occupy. Crossing the line between the two was unexpected and therefore unwelcome. The dismay from visitors who mind being directly approached supports Richard Schechner's claims that environmental theater can be profoundly discomfiting to spectators who have "learned" rules for audiencehood that are being subverted.

Almost all of the people who object to the faire after attending it mention that they did not like being addressed in faire speak, and almost everyone I spoke to who had an opinion about the faire without having attended it cited faire speak as a reason they did not want to attend. Examples of this reaction abound in online comments or reviews as well as in direct testimony: "They [fans of the faire] are easy to make fun of, because of the way they talk," a lawyer named "Sally," who has never attended the faire, tells me (interview). "I just don't like bad actors approaching me and talking in a terrible Old English accent and I'm supposed to play along," a blogger who calls himself Dr. Zibbs writes about the faire. In other words, "Sally" and Dr. Zibbs are made uncomfortable—one in practice, one in theory—by being directly addressed by someone in character. Moreover, performers and other faire workers who continue to refuse to break character even during a prolonged interaction (and this is by no means all performers) are seen as particularly irritating. Commentators also often refer to "bad English accents" (as opposed to English accents per se), though in general authenticity is not really a concern for these visitors.

Pioneers of environmental theater such as Richard Schechner and Sam Blazer are able feel successful when audience members are pushed outside their comfort zones by a performance that deliberately breaks down expectations for a theatergoing experience. For faire performers, it is trickier, as there are expectations across the board that visitors will have a lighthearted experience and, as part of that experience, will be inclined to tip performers, purchase food items or crafts, take souvenir photographs, and return for another visit. Thus, while many visitors do value encountering something challenging, innovative, or educational at the faire, others expect the experience to be comfortable above all else and resent any part of the experience that departs from that expectation.

Performers at the faire, particularly street performers, tend to describe such audience members as not wanting to "play" with them; they learn to recognize these patrons quickly and just as quickly to move on once they have ascertained that resistance is about to turn into hostility.

New York Renaissance Faire's Mark James Schryver is willing to share his strategy for smoothing things over when his elaborate and melodramatic flirtations with women anger male companions who are so socialized into the idea of competition for a woman's attention—and, he feels, a sense of ownership of the woman—that they cannot always see the flirtation for what it is: a performance, meant, among other things, to call attention to the constructedness and humorous potential of these gendered dances. He always has an immediate "out" in his back pocket, he says, a surefire way to diffuse any growing tension: he reveals to the man in question that he is gay. The man then immediately stops thinking of him as any kind of threat, and everyone is able to move on in good spirits. If the strategy is as successful as Schryver says, then he has pulled off something remarkable. He has used one of the commonest grounds for Renaissance faire ridicule as an escape hatch from another.

6

Hard Day's Knight

Faire Fictions

"Knights and swords and ladies in those beautiful gowns, it does have a certain appeal," Buffy admitted. "I thought maybe we could go."

"I don't know," Angel replied softly. "I try not to think too much about the past, even if it's further in the past than I can personally remember."
—Christopher Golden and Nancy Holder, *Child of th Hunt*

In *Child of the Hunt*—a fantasy spin-off novel based on the cult television series *Buffy the Vampire Slayer*—the title character and her friends (and allies in the fight against vampires and other supernatural threats to their small California town) try to sort out what it would mean if they were to attend the Renaissance faire that has come to Sunnydale. Although none of the young people has previously attended a faire, their discussions indicate that they each possess a strong sense of what one is like, acquired from the popular culture ether around them. The harassed heroine, Buffy, pictures it as romantic and gorgeous, a temporary escape from her grueling, unpleasant labor. The popular, fashion- and status-conscious Corde-lia sees the faire as mortifyingly nerdy. Giles, their adult mentor and school librarian, sees it as an educational opportunity despite the historical "mistakes" the producers are certain to make. As the group discuss attending the faire, they offer a sort of compendium of the various ways in which the faire is commonly depicted in literature, on screen, and in popular culture more generally.

Over the course of the faire's five decades, the frequency and location of its fictional representation has followed a trajectory similar to that of the faires themselves. Cropping up occasionally early on in nonfictional countercultural narratives (such as Malcolm Boyd's *Human Like Me, Jesus* in 1971), the faire then moved increasingly into the mainstream of genre fiction. These depictions in romance, mystery, fantasy, and young-adult books were followed by appearances in television, games, comics, and a few movies and "high" literary novels (i.e., non-genre-oriented works or, as they are sometimes referred to in the publishing industry, "hardback" novels.) Fascinatingly, the festivals rarely function simply as colorful backdrop in these depictions. Instead, they more often operate as a kind of cultural summary, used as an efficient invocation of various abstract qualities: liberation, imagination, and sensuality in some instances, and "geekiness," maladjustment, and embarrassing display in others.

This chapter considers the Renaissance faire as a fictional landscape, exploring the ways in which it is saturated with meaning by those who use it as a *device* rather than (only) a place. In some ways, this way of looking at the faire is categorically akin (and certainly indebted) to the way certain literary scholars have looked at fictional representations of real cities or places: James DeJongh's work on Harlem as a literary landscape in African American literature, for instance, or the way Katerina Clark has examined the constructions of St. Petersburg/Leningrad in Russian and Soviet literature.

Of course, faire fictions present as much divergence from those literary landscapes as similarity, and this divergence is worth pausing over. The faire is not "real" or organic in the way a city is; furthermore, it has multiple, nonidentical locations. Visiting it is a short-lived choice, and for the majority of people on-site, the faire is only seen during leisure time. Nonetheless, the way authors have used the faire as a place that is more than a place, a geography both literal and symbolic, an ecology of affect as well as physicality, makes these critical models both useful and relevant.

With that in mind, what I hope to shed light on here is some of the ways in which the faire has become available as a touchstone, a cultural high sign, that has proved durable enough to span decades, portable enough to accommodate a variety of contexts, and flexible enough to adapt to changes in form, time, and authorial intent.

Ripped Bodices and Shirtless Blacksmiths: The Renaissance Faire in the Romance Genre

That is a very good fantasy, one of my favorites. I especially like it when the bold knight tells me why they call him Sir Lance-a-Lot.
—Katie MacAlister, *Hard Day's Knight*

Examining works of literature from the perspective of genre, as Tzvetan Todorov reminds us, means seeking "a principle operative in a number of texts, rather than what is specific about each of them" (3). Surely, though, those readers devoted to particular genres of fiction— whether romance, science fiction, horror, or westerns—are gratified by both what is predictable about them (the generic conventions that define and endorse them for readers) and what is surprising (the small departures from the familiar that absorb the reader's attention and provide excitement). One could even argue that each entry in a genre of literature is in some ways in dialogue with every other entry, invoking previously established structures and commenting on them in some particular way; readers are, therefore required to bring a great deal of special literacy to these texts. To provide these simultaneous experiences of familiarity and novelty, successful genre fiction relies on a carefully maintained system of shorthand gestures as a way efficiently to saturate the text with the totemic and the original.

It is not surprising, then, that the Renaissance faire as a symbolic space is found far more often in genre or series fiction than in "high" or "literary" fiction. Thus, although many of these depictions of the faire are not realistic, in that they get many details of faire life "wrong," a great deal about the faire's cultural significance and meaning can be gleaned nonetheless through careful attention to what the faire is used to convey in these novels, whether its depiction is accurate or not.

Nowhere in fiction has the Renaissance faire been more attractive than to authors of romance novels, where it has cropped up regularly over the past three decades. Books in the romance genre tend to be quite short and follow a formula; in fact, some of the major publishers of romances offer would-be authors literal formulas in the shape of how-to guides, and dozens of popular books on how to write and publish romance novels have been issued since the modern, mass-market romance was introduced in the 1970s.[1] Meanwhile, more romance novels are published than books in any other genre. Because of the need for each new novel to distinguish itself quickly from so many others, romance novels rely especially heavily on codes and emblems to create narrative and emotional tension and to further character development. One way in which romances traditionally have quickly established generic "givens" and also created variation is through manipulation of setting, both geographical and temporal. In the many romance novels in which the Renaissance faire setting figures, it represents a manifest imaginary—a system of articulation—of the sensual and the sexual.

Not surprisingly, the Renaissance faire sometimes appears in romances as a convenient backdrop for elaborate and old-fashioned rituals of courtship and flirtation. In these instances, the faire provides fairy tale romantic fantasy and gorgeous clothing that is sexy without the negative connotations that attach in many circumstances to overt female sexuality. (Julie Beard, in her *Complete Idiot's Guide to Getting Your Romance Published* [2000], even recommends visiting "your local Renaissance fair [sic]" as a way to "get yourself in a medieval mood" before writing [166]). An example of this kind of usage of the faire is Suzanne Ellison's 1988 *Fair Play*, issued by the megapublisher Harlequin Books and introduced as written by a "devoted wife and mother" (2). The book's protagonist, Betsy Hanover, meets her soon-to-be lover when she volunteers to aid preparations for Ohio's Renaissance faire. Soon the pair are having dreams—literal and figurative—in which they come together, dressed in velvet, and speaking in a mixture of "castle talk" and quotations from Shakespeare about their union: "'Sir Geoffrey!' she pleaded in desperation. 'Oh, wilt thou leave me so unsatisfied?'" (112). The faire serves a similar purpose In Lori Wilde's *Zero Control*, copyrighted in 2009 to Lori

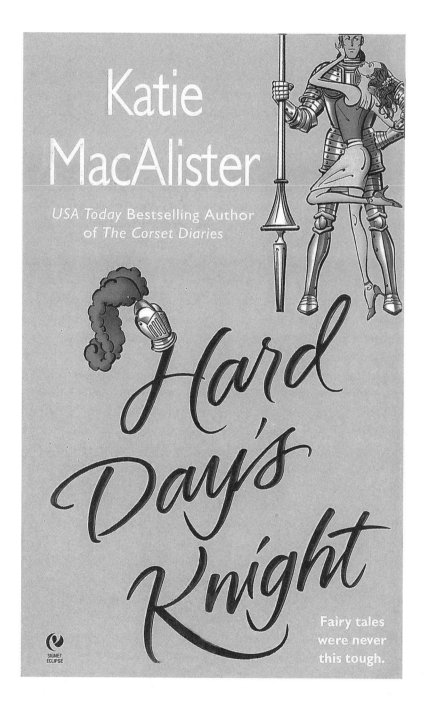

Fig. 6.1. Author Katie McAlister uses the Renaissance faire as the location of sexual possibility in her romance *Hard Day's Knight* (2005).

Vanzuri under Harlequin's Harlequin Blaze imprint. The Blaze series was designed to be more sexually explicit than other Harlequin product lines, with more sex scenes and somewhat fewer euphemisms for body parts, feelings, and acts; in *Zero Control*, the protagonist, Roxie Stanley, thinks vaguely, "Such a romantic epoch filled with great art and music and the concept of chivalry" (45).

But markedly more often, even in the commercially oriented, formula-driven production of scale that is the romance "series" industry, the faire is used to signify female sexual agency, some degree of sexual or corporeal freedom, and the attraction of stepping outside decorum, particularly regarding gender roles. In most of the faire-set romances published as part of mainstream series, this representation of the faire as empowering generally occurs within the structure of monogamous heterosexual relationships. However, in romances published outside of the largest publishing houses, as I discuss shortly, the faire provides an opportunity and normalizing context for sexual relationships that do not fit this mold.

In Clare Richards's novel *Renaissance Summer*, the protagonist, Pamela Stewart, seeks relief at the faire from her safe but uninspiring life as a grants administrator. As with many authors in romance series, Clare Richards is a pseudonym; the copyright of the book is registered to Carolyn Males and Louise Titchner. *Renaissance Summer* was published by Harlequin Enterprises, the Toronto-based company that is the most well-known and highest-earning publisher of romance novels. By 1985, when *Renaissance Summer* was issued, Harlequin was a growing international business and one of the most profitable publishers, with markets across Europe and North America and a variety of more specialized imprints focusing on different readerships, settings, and narrative tone.

Renaissance Summer was published during the height of what Stephen F. Hayward has called "the conservative counterrevolution," and that context is relevant to the novel's dual setting at the Maryland Renaissance Festival and Washington, DC's bureaucratic complex. The dual setting pits social and fiscal conservatism against personal fulfillment, found chiefly through nonconformity (in both choice of lover and personal deportment). The book's heroine is introduced in garb on the site of the faire, where she has taken the opportunity to sell muffins and cider for enjoyment rather than out of financial necessity. The first piece of information about the faire that the book offers is that Pamela has built her booth herself, with some help from crafters, and that she is very gratified by this (unusual for her) self-sufficiency. Predictably, she meets a man—and predictably, feels about him like she has never felt about a man before. The novel does, after all, follow the conventions of romance series.

But after Pamela has told the man, a performer at the faire, that they are too different and that they must not pursue their romantic entanglement, she is convinced to go to a Rennie party after the faire closes. At that party, food and wine are shared communally, and Pamela goes naked in front of a group for the first time: "If she had imagined that they would feel some discomfort about peeling off their clothes en masse, she found she was quite mistaken. . . . The shadowy figures of the celebrants, Rob among them, began discarding jeans, shirts, underwear and shoes. No one seemed the least self-conscious, and Pamela began to feel quite foolish about her own qualms" (109–110). Pamela's bodily empowerment leads her back to her romance with the faire and her actor-boyfriend. The book's final scene finds its protagonist working at the faire and bantering joyfully with her beloved "Rennie" friends.

A similar trajectory is traced in Penny McCall's mass-market paperback *The Bliss Factor*, published and marketed by Berkley Sensation—since 1996 an imprint of Penguin—as a novel of "romantic suspense." This novel (slightly more elaborate in plot and character development than the Harlequin romances but also hewing strongly to the conventions of romance fiction) offers a protagonist who has carefully constructed a conservative and conformist adult life after being raised by Rennies on the circuit:

> Rae had on a cream linen suit, the skirt a perfect inch above her knee, and bone-colored pumps with a sensible heel, and she was the one getting weird looks. But then she'd always felt out of place at these things, even as a kid wearing whatever getup her mother had dredged up out of her imagination—which could have been anything from a fairy costume, complete with gossamer wings, to the rags of a fourteenth-century beggar. The woman could have been a successful costume designer, but instead she chose to live in hell. (2)

The reader learns that Rae's given name is Sunshine—with the nick-name of "Sunny"—which she has dropped in favor of a more conventional moniker. Her mother regularly wonders aloud how her daughter could have chosen to be an accountant instead of traveling the Renaissance faire circuit, and she actively encourages her daughter to allow herself more pleasure—particularly, but not exclusively, sexual pleasure. "You should loosen up and enjoy yourself a little," Rae's mother tells her. "'Loose' being the operative word?" her less sexually adventurous daughter shoots back (101).

Though the vulnerability of crafters' life on the faire circuit is central to the story, overall the book comes down on the side of the idealistic parents. Rae gradually acknowledges that deep inside her, appreciation for what her parents have given her still dwells—as hinted, perhaps, by the fact that her chosen name, Rae, is not unrelated to her given name, Sunshine. She does not fully abandon the adult life she has constructed to return to the circuit of her childhood, but she does quit her accounting job in favor of a more exciting version in forensic accounting. More important to the novel's focus, she begins to allow herself more sensual pleasure, beginning a romance with Zach, a man she first encountered in the faire's blacksmith booth, forging metal while naked from the waist up.

The faire represents a legacy of creativity and nonconformity—including sexual nonconformity—in Kristin Hardy's novel *Bad Influence*, also published under Harlequin's Blaze imprint. This novel introduces its main character, the romance-formulaically named Paige Favreau, as being far too personally conservative—according to her outspoken best girlfriends—in sexual relationships. (This topic introduces itself in a discussion among these friends of the benefits of various sexual positions.) In short order, Paige falls for the grandson of her grandfather's next-door neighbor, despite the fact that their two grandparents are feuding over a burlesque museum that her new boyfriend's grandmother, a former burlesque star, wants to establish on her property, a move Paige's conservative grandfather believes would create a monument to vice. Three generations of Zach's family, as it turns out, share an "irreverent sense of the world and exasperation with the rules," and part of the expression this takes is the fact that Zach, like Rae Bliss-field, grew up on the Renaissance faire circuit with his Rennie parents:

"My parents were hippies. Still are, I suppose. You know, living outside of society's expectations, not getting married, all that. My mom makes stuff to sell on the Renaissance Fair [*sic*] circuit. We'd start traveling in April, go through October. All over the country . . . Winters we stayed at a commune in eastern Oregon" (89).

Anxiety about the faire and its meaning occasionally erupts in these romances, but interestingly, it is most often dispatched as *negative* indicator. For instance, in the opening of Diane Bernard's *Renaissance Man* (copyrighted in 1997 to Diane Levitt and published by Zebra Books), the protagonist's current boyfriend, Roger, refuses to "get into the spirit" (9) of the faire at the novel's opening and expresses contempt for people's garb. "I won't wear a pair of tights," he warns her, ultimately refusing to wear any pieces of costumery at all (10). In the end, Roger's attitude about the faire proves to be an early sign that he is not only an inappropriate lover but dishonest in his business dealings.

Romance novels set at the faire overwhelmingly feature a male-female couple on the cover, mostly picturing nothing at all that is particular to the novel except the heterosexual romance at its center. But there is also strong showing of Renaissance-faire-set romances that challenge heteronormativity, monogamy, and "standard" sexual practice. This is particularly true among the "insider" romances, which often reflect the openness to nonheteronormative relationships. Layle Black's 2011 sexually explicit *Faire Dreamer* is a novel that reveals itself to be penned by an "insider" through small touches, such as the hawking calls of "boothies," references to camping passes, and use of the word "mundane" for non-faire-specific clothing, thoughts, and concerns. *Faire Dreamer* is in the "erotic romance" subgenre; the book was issued by Siren Publishing, which markets both print and electronic romances under a variety of specialized imprints. This novel's protagonist has an experience not too far off from that of the story of Pamela in Harlequin's *Renaissance Summer*, who finds love and sheds inhibition at the faire—only in the case of *Faire Dreamer*'s Lindsey, she meets *two* men and ultimately sets up a household with both of them. But even before that happens, the faire has provided a haven for all three: the men from their childhood traumas and Lindsey from the self-hatred that she has acquired from a lifetime of people (including her mother and boyfriends) telling her that she is not skinny enough to be attractive. Amy Lane's 2010 novel *Making Promises*, published by Dreamspinner Press (which specializes in male-male romances), uses the faire to facilitate its protagonist's coming out as gay as well as his finding a romantic partner, a dancer at the faire. Ultimately, the faire is the location of both safety and redemption for Shane, his recovering-addict sister Kimmy, and his lover Mikhail.

With the ascension of electronic and relatively affordable print self-publishing options, self-published "insider" novels of the faire have proliferated as a means for writers and readers to engage and distribute representations of sexual or romantic relationships among those with preferences that do not find mainstream expression often. Trish Lamoree's self-published paranormal romance *Painting the Roses Red* (2009) depicts the Renaissance faire presence of the SMBD community (who run the leather booth) and offers up loving depictions of consensual sex acts with bondage elements. Along the same lines, *From the Ashes*, a 2002 fantasy-romance self-published by Renaissance faire performer Meghan Brunner, climaxes with the handfasting of its two protagonists, both female performers whose faire identity is not always neatly separated from their "mundane" identity. This blurring of *characters'* boundaries between the "lived" and the "performed" neatly parallels the blurring of *readers'* boundaries between the "experienced" and the "vicariously experienced."

In the ecosystem of the romance novel, sex and romance, the Renaissance faire, and the act of reading itself are all interconnected enactments of female desire. Because of this, Joyce Saricks tells us, readers of romance novels are "accustomed to being looked down upon" (145). Janice Radway, in her groundbreaking study of readers of romance novels (1984), argues that this broad cultural condescension to romance readers is evidence of their potential subversiveness. Like the romance novels themselves, their fictional faires represent a kind of question: what is female desire? Is it cause for celebration or shame? And who is in charge of it?

A Tiara and an Enchantment, Too! The Faire in the Fantasy Genre

Something about the Renaissance Faire beckoned to him like the sound
of a hundred sirens luring a lonely sailor from the sea.
—Karen J. Anderson and Rebecca Moesta, "Splinter"

It is not unusual, in romance novels about the faire, for female desire
to be facilitated by an abbreviated incidence of magic. In several of the
novels, the protagonist visits the faire only to be transported from the
faire to another time, where she encounters her destined romantic or sexual partner. Notably, the time travel that takes place is barely elaborated
(let alone explained) and, more important still, does not necessarily take
the heroine to the Renaissance period—even broadly defined, as some
faire participants do, to include the Middle Ages. In Diane Bernard's
Renaissance Man (1997), the protagonist is transported from the faire to
Renaissance-era England, but in Janeen O'Kerry's *Mistress of the Waters*
(1999), she is transported to pre-Christian Ireland. In Susan Sizemore's
My Own True Love (1994), she is transported to the year 1811. The only
logic at work here is that the faire is a place of magic.

These romance novelists are picking up on a sense of otherworldliness
that many observers have articulated as characterizing the faire. Descrip-
tions of actual faires—those given by visitors, by journalists, and in the
faire's own advertising—frequently employ a version of the phrase "Step
into another world." This notion that the faire is special for the way it
presents an alternate reality has made the actual (nonfictional) faire a
hospitable site to engage a sense of the fantastic since its inception in the
mid-1960s. In the faire's more recent decades, there is some talk that the
inclusion of these fantasy elements is inauthentic and therefore undesir-
able; nonetheless, it is still on the increase, as seen in costume pieces,
motifs in crafts for sale, special theme days at some of the faires, and
crossover of patrons and some workers in "scenes" such as FaerieCon, a
festival of music, art, and fandom organized entirely around the folkloric
and the mystical.

But these twenty-first-century incursions of fantasy into the Renaissance faire are far from new. By the mid-1960s, when the faire was

founded, the fiction of J. R. R. Tolkien had made a deep impression on the counterculture because the world he carefully constructed, the "Middle Earth" of his most important books, imparted a sense that another world was possible—or perhaps more important, believable. In *Ramparts* magazine, Warren Hinckle, describing Emmett Grogan of the Diggers, wrote in 1967,

> Except for the obvious fact that he wasn't covered with fur, you would have said to yourself that for sure there was old Frodo Baggins, crossing Haight Street. Frodo Baggins is the hero of the English antiquarian J. R. R. Tolkien's classic trilogy, *Lord of the Rings*, absolutely the favorite book of every hippie, about a race of little people called Hobbits who live somewhere in pre-history in a place called Middle Earth. (25)

While "every hippie" is, of course, a deliberately hyperbolic claim, Hinckle is right that Tolkien, who had had a steady American readership since *The Lord of the Rings* was first published in 1955, saw a dramatic and long-lasting spike in popularity beginning in 1965. "The Tolkien people may be less noisy than the LSD heads, but there are more of them," declared Henry Resnick in the *Saturday Evening Post* in 1966 (qtd. in Foster 14). The links that Hinckle and Resnick were making between Tolkien and the counterculture were increasingly joined by a variety of cultural commentators, who found that the books modeled relevant cultural, ecological, and political concerns. "Countercultural rebels longed for a world completely different from our own," write Joseph Heath and Andrew Potter of the romance with Tolkien in the 1960s (255). Heath and Potter's rather glib formulation does illustrate the root of the longstanding bridge between the Renaissance faire and fantasy writing: a yearning to imagine another reality, as an important part of expressing a critique of the actual one.[2]

Indeed, if, as Rosemary Jackson assumes in her seminal work on fantasy literature, the genre of fantasy is by nature subversive in that imagining another reality undercuts the current one, one could argue the same about the Renaissance faire. "What if sometimes the play is real, sometimes the magic is true?" asks a blurb at the front of Andre Norton and Jean Rabe's 2005 short-story collection *Renaissance Faire*. The point, of course, is that the play *is* real, not in the sense that magic exists or that the faire's patrons can actually "step back in time" but in the sense that play of the fantastic sort speaks *to* and *about* reality.

Because of the opportunities fantasy fiction provides authors (and readers) to imagine alternative societies, it has been an important location for literary decentering of social norms and assumptions, particularly regarding identity as we commonly construct it. Introduction of nonhuman characters, for instance, often operates as commentary on race and ethnicity, while fantasy's warring kingdoms speak about expansionism and empire, about the dangers of the will to power using weapons of mass destruction that inevitably turn even the best-intentioned into the very enemy they fight. Fantasy writing set at the Renaissance faire often explores questions of gender and sexuality, particularly, but certainly not exclusively, in fiction authored by women. Marion Zimmer Bradley's 1996 novel *Witchlight* and Esther Friesner's series of short-story collections beginning with 1995's *Chicks in Chainmail* use the faire not only to comment on traditional constructions of gender but also as occasion and permission to create an alternative cultural format in which women are the rescuers, of themselves and of men.

Bradley is one of the United States' best-known female writers of speculative fiction—and certainly one of the genre's most famous explicitly feminist writers. She is especially remembered for her *Mists of Avalon* series, a retelling of the story of King Arthur and Camelot from the point of view of its female characters. (In addition to fantasy fiction, she wrote, in the early 1960s, some pulp lesbian novels using pseudonyms that she protected for decades. At the time of publication, these books were considered pornographic.) In 1966, Bradley participated in founding and came up with the name for the Society for Creative Anachronism, a sort of philosophical sibling of the early Renaissance faire in its deliberately selective use of history as a way to construct an alternative cultural present (although there has always been both crossover and conflict between the two).

The protagonist of *Witchlight* is Winter Musgrave, a young woman who is suffering from amnesia induced either by madness or magic. She has some partial memories of herself working as a successful trader on Wall Street, but when she is menaced by a paranormal evil, she must gather the remnants of a magical "circle" she belonged to in college but does not quite remember in order to rescue herself and her old (male) lover. As memories return in fragments, Winter recalls a choice she had to make when she confronted an unplanned pregnancy: either return to the "straight" life her family wants for her, to work as a stockbroker, or travel the Renaissance faire circuit with her lover. The faire is never utilized as setting—Bradley assumes that the mere mention of it is enough to set up a dichotomous choice for her protagonist. Bradley implicitly privileges the messy, nonconforming world that includes the faire over the orderly, ordinary world that includes the stock market.

Esther Friesner's "Chicks" series brings together tongue-in-cheek stories by a range of writers featuring strong heroines in fantasy settings. The first of these collections, *Chicks in Chainmail*, was published in 1995; in short order, it was followed by four similar collections. Unlike Bradley, whose prose is so dead serious that it has been criticized as dull, Friesner has organized her series around playfully and punningly confronting stereotypes (and, in service of this, taking jabs at men who entertain notions of superiority). In particular, the series sets out to disable the portrayal of women in certain fantasy writing—and illustration—as male wish fulfillment. The packaging of the first book makes this goal plain, with the back cover blurb asking, "You think their swords won't cut, their clubs won't crush? You think they look *cute*?" (italics in original). The Renaissance faire occasionally appears in the stories, despite their having different authors: several of the heroines buy their armor (and weapons) and feel at home there. In other words, at the faire, they acquire the tools to both skewer and defend themselves against sexist constraints and constructions of womanhood.

J. A. Pitts's *Black Blade Blues* (2010), like the faire fantasies of Bradley and Friesner, is centered on questions of gender and sexuality. The book's woman protagonist, Sarah Beauhall, struggles to make ends meet by working two jobs that, taken together, articulate a bridge between fantasy fandom and faire fandom: during the day, she is a farrier and blacksmith at the Renaissance faire, and in the evenings, she works as props manager on the set of a fantasy movie. *Black Blade Blues* has an extended set piece at the faire that serves to reiterate, and then to knock down, preconceptions about the social meaning of "woman":

I was checking out a statuesque black Friesian named Pericles, owned by a strapping young knight in the group. He went by Sir Wenceslas, if you can believe it. He had a penchant for strutting around in a sleeveless cuirass so he could show off his bulging biceps.

I was pretty sure I could take him. (27)

The "young knight" loudly admires a woman walking by; when she returns to walk by again and again, he is certain that she is pleased by his admiration. But it turns out that she is walking by as part of her job on faire security, which becomes plain when she shortly dispatches—with a cudgel—a group of drunken attendees who try to grab her. Further, she is uninterested in any of her male admirers; instead, she becomes Sarah's girlfriend.

The matter-of-fact pursuit of nonstandard sexual arrangements is central to Mercedes Lackey and Ellen Guon's novels in the *Bedlam's Bard* series.[3] In these books, two Renaissance faire musicians, a man and a woman, set up a domestic and romantic arrangement with a third party, a male elf who ultimately joins them in performing at the faire. For much of the narrative arc, they are in hiding; it is this, rather than the nature of their sexual arrangement, that necessitates a certain amount of duplicity about the personal lives, though there a number of people (elves included here) who are aware that they sleep in one bed.

The *Bedlam's Bard* books reveal themselves as "insider" works through depictions of after-hours faire life and semicommunalism. They also return to the idea of the Renaissance faire as the location of an especially involved audience:

What was different about a Faire audience?

Finally, he decided that there was only one thing it could be. Attitude. The crowds on the Wharf were not looking for anything, they had no expectations, and they were not ready for the unusual. The travelers at the Faire were *expecting* things; expecting to be surprised, expecting to be entertained, expecting to enjoy themselves with something entirely new and different. (378–379)

The character's musing about the particularity of faire audiences echoes the musings of actual faire performers, but more important here, it can be read as a statement of desire regarding a prepared and "literate" readership that knows what to expect and hope for: from this novel in particular and from the fantasy genre in general. The faire, then, is not just setting: it is both model and emblem of artistic expression as a dialogic system, symbolically condensing and representing values and fantasies about art, sex, and their relationships to lived lives.

The fifteen original stories (by sixteen authors) in Norton and Rabe's 2005 collection can be taken as a collective musing on those values and fantasies. Ninety-three years old when the collection was published, Norton was a grande dame of American fantasy/science fiction who, among other innovations, was the first in American publishing to introduce a female protagonist into the genre, with her 1965 novel *Year of the Unicorn*. Norton died the year of *Renaissance Faire*'s publication; in her obituary, *New York Times* writer Christopher Lehmann-Haupt writes that her "central theme was the rite of passage to self-realization undertaken by misfits or displaced outsiders." The same, of course, has been said of the faire itself.

Taken together, the stories included in the anthology offer a full exploration of the faire's most familiar symbology. In the collection's first story, Elizabeth Ann Scarborough's "Jewels beyond Price," a jewelry maker at the faire discovers a wish-granting genie. On the story's last page, the (male) jeweler and the (male) genie, released from servitude by the jeweler, fall in love—thereby gently reminding readers what the faire's "magic" really is.

In John Maddox Roberts's "Girolamo and Mistress Willendorf," the faire promotes female power, sensual pleasure, and creative chaos over religious dogma and abstemiousness. The story's unlikeable protagonist is a magically awakened cleric who hates blasphemy, "crawling, disgusting life," and the very word "Renaissance" (61). Drawn to the "celebration of iniquity" (61) that is the faire, he encounters and argues with a fertility specialist there about life and salvation. The woman turns out to be more than human:

> "I am She who Always Was," proclaimed the woman. "I am she who quickens the earth and brings forth life. I am she who devours the dead and creates it all anew, every day." . . .

"Blasphemy! God and God alone brought forth all living things. God breathed into clay and created man!"

She chuckled. . . . "You'd like to believe that, wouldn't you? Isn't that the whole point of the Sistine ceiling? A male creating another male without having to deal with anything female first? It doesn't work that way, Girolamo. It never has." (68)

In another story in the collection, Robert E. Vardeman's "A Time for Steel," the faire's sense of freedom (embodied in a woman who gleefully rides naked through the faire as Lady Godiva) and magic (introduced in the persons of a fortune-teller who is actually Merlin and a blacksmith who forges King Arthur's sword) are set in contest with the policing of the outside world. (The cops lose that contest, but, won over by the faire, they do not mind.) In Steven Sullivan's "Renaissance Fear," a faire "hater" enumerates the reasons he dislikes the faire—all familiar ones:

Karl knew the faire circuit well, and there were plenty of things *not* to like about it: too many weirdos, too many aging hippies, too many "arts and crafts" booths, . . . too damn much strange (and overpriced) food, too many out-of-work actors, . . . too many dopers hiding out after the dissolution of the Grateful Dead, and *way* too many poseurs speaking with fake accents. (239; italics in original)

As the story's title foreshadows, the arrogant Karl gets his comeuppance.

Finally, in Rose Wolf's "A Dance of Seven Vales," the faire is the location for a struggle between the linked forces of nature and magic and the forces of profiteering and real estate development. A group of businesspeople are planning to destroy the faire site so they can put up a development called Greenman's Grove—echoing what happened to at least one site of the Renaissance Pleasure Faire in Northern California, wherein the faire site was turned into a development of new houses on streets bearing faire-inflected names. In this fantasy, though, magic prevents the takeover.

As with romance authors, Renaissance faire fans have made use of expanding opportunities for print self-publishing as well as online publishing to author their own faire fantasies.[4] In some important ways, self-published faire-set fictions share an impulse with fan fiction, the body of writing resulting from fan-authors writing about the characters and settings of television shows, movies, or published fiction. The authors generally do not expect to make money from their self-publication; instead, it stems from and expresses a devoted fandom and allows both writer and reader to extend their involvement with the faire beyond its annual season.

An especially clear example of this impulse is the short-story collection *Renaissance Festival Tales* (2009), edited by Eric T. Reynolds and Gerri Leen. The collection bills itself as a fictional antidote to the painful necessity of leaving the faire and returning to work; one story, Kim Vandervort's "Faire Aria," has a protagonist who ultimately uses magic to live at the faire forever. Similarly, Steve R. Romano's *Dreams of Betrayal* (2008) is based on the persona he has developed as a playtron at the faire, the punningly named Laktos the Intolerable. Meghan Brunner, a cast member at the Minnesota Renaissance Festival, has Rennies confronting "magick" on their faire site in *From the Ashes* (2002) and its sequels *Into the Storm* (2004) and *Towards the Fates* (2009). Debbie Fritter's *Joust in Time* (2008) follows the convention of time travel to and from the faire, establishing twin settings in fifteenth-century England and the twenty-first-century Bristol Renaissance Faire; similarly, Catherine Bybee's *Binding Vows* (2009) moves from the twenty-first-century California faire to fifteenth-century Scotland. David McLeod's web-published *Book of Heroes: George of Sedona I* (2011) also employs the time-travel convention to whisk a young man away from the faire and the gay baiting of his own world to a place where his love for men is literally magical; McLeod's faire fiction speaks (in unison with many others), as Rosemary Jackson insists the fantasy genre exists to do, "the language of desire, which seeks that which is experienced as absence and loss" (2).

Semiotics of the Mask: The Renaissance Faire in Mystery Novels

Was that just a disguise, or did it, too, have meaning?
—John Case, *The Murder Artist*

Mystery fiction, in which a novel represents a puzzle that literally needs to be "solved," constitutes a particularly self-conscious generic tradition. These books make explicit some of the central theoretical claims made by the "reader-response" school of literary criticism about the reader's role in creating the meaning of a text. As a distinct body of theory, "reader-response" is about the same age as the Renaissance faire: beginning in the 1960s, such critics as Norman Holland, Roland Barthes, Stanley Fish, and Wolfgang Iser have established that far from being a passive receptacle for authorial intent and ready-made meaning, the reader is instead an active agent whose observations and involvement with the text impart what Kant called "real existence" to the work and completes its meaning through interpretation. These critics contend that in the process of reading, readers of literature absorb pieces of textual "evidence" along the way and assemble meaning from them. In other words, readers carry out in every reading act what they know they are supposed to do when engaging a mystery story: take in clues, figure out what they mean, and develop some kind of reasonable conclusion based on those self-derived interpretations. For this reason, novelist and theoretician Umberto Eco, in his important 1983 novel *The Name of the Rose,* uses the process of solving murders as an extended metaphor for the experience of reading.

This significant turn away from envisioning a cultural transaction as unidirectional—a turn so central to the act of reading a mystery—parallels the stated objective of many Renaissance faire performers, who single out audience participation as the key ingredient of the faire's artistic raison d'être. For this reason, the critical approach of envisioning reader and author as engaged in a joint endeavor is not far away from the environmental theater's goal of turning spectator into actor. Indeed, literary critic Peter Kivy posits that literature should in fact be viewed as a performing art, one in which each reader creates her or his own performance in dialogue with the text.

A shared privileging of interpretation—reading a mystery with an eye to "solving" it, and visiting the faire with a mandate to become part of the show—accounts for part of the reason that the faire has been such an attractive location for authors of mystery novels to use as settings. One of the earliest literary representations of the faire, Marcia Blair's 1979 mystery novel *The Final Fair,* makes this interpretive mandate especially clear in its packaging. The murder at the book's heart takes place at the Northern California Renaissance Pleasure Faire, and the investigation also leads the book's amateur detective, Tory Baxter, to the annual Great Dickens Christmas Fair, also founded and produced by the Patterson family. The paperback's cover, which pictures a group of people in garb, announces the book as "The novel that lets you be the detective!" and asks, "Can you solve the crime by finding the clues in the story, on the cover, and in the illustrations—before you cut open the final, sealed chapter?"

This clarion call to the reader to work with textual clues is presented in the book as inextricable from the faire's call on patrons to take part by blurring the line between actor and spectator, as is evident in this early conversation between Tory and her friend Leanne at the faire:

"Did anyone stop you? Talk to you? Bump into you?"

"The purple monk!" Leanne cried. "That's right. The man in the fancy purple outfit!"

"What man? What did he look like?"

Leanne's face fell. "I don't know. A third of the people here have masks, and he was one of them." (11)

Figuring out who wore the purple monk costume is equivalent to solving the murder. Notably, the monk's garb does more than conceal its wearer's face. It also masks the wearer's sex—the "man in the fancy purple outfit" is actually a woman—thereby easily tricking everyone who comes in contact with the murderer at the faire.

Along the same lines, John Case's mystery *The Murder Artist* (2004) emphasizes Renaissance faire patrons' role in constructing the faire's "real meaning." The novel's first-person narrator, television news correspondent Alex Callahan, arrives at the Maryland Renaissance Festival outside Annapolis with his two young sons in tow, bringing a journalist's habit of assessing a scene for its "real," factual meaning. He is almost immediately frustrated in this endeavor: "The dividing line between imagination and reality is blurry, at best, with many of the fairgoers also in costume, some simple and homemade, some as elaborate as those of the actors—and probably rented from the shop near the entrance" (11). When Callahan's twin six-year-old sons disappear from the faire's jousting arena, however, he is forced to learn the rules and logic of the faire's reality and must figure out how to "read" its signs in order to find his children before they are hurt by a dangerous predator.

In *The Murder Artist*, a frightening villain has donned a costume in order to use the faire as his hunting ground. This is a common occurrence in mysteries set at the faire. In addition, in many of the novels, the detective (whether amateur or professional) dresses for the faire as a kind of undercover work, submerging her or his "outside" identity by putting on garb. For instance, in G. A. McKevett's *Sugar and Spite* (2000), the detective, Savannah Reid, and her compatriots garb up so that they will not "stand out like sore thumbs" in the faire's "tight-knit community," in which "everybody knows everybody" (149).

In McKevett's novel, as in many others, the detectives' garbing up is ostentatiously done, using character's over-the-top responses to call attention to the act. McKevett's books about Savannah Reid make a point about her refusal to curb her love of eating to conform with the cultural privileging of thinness; when she puts on a faire bodice, everyone comments on the way she looks in it, down to a gay friend who remarks, "We may be gay, but we aren't blind" (124). Her male partner, for his part, is made distinctly uncomfortable by the costumes and in particular does not want to wear tights. Characters in Joan Hess's mystery-series novel *Damsels in Distress* (2007) are similarly put off by the way traditional faire garb interferes with gender norms: "I'm gettin' tired of all these pretty boys prancing around," a faire patron tells his wife with barely concealed homophobia (128); the narrator's cop-boyfriend asks her, "How was your day at the fair, milady? Were you pursued by effeminate earls and fat, middle-aged barons?" (167).

The heroine of Nancy Atherton's mystery series, Lori Shepard, even uses the word "infiltrate" to describe what she is able to do at the faire by wearing garb. Atherton's 2009 faire-set novel *Aunt Dimity Slays the Dragon* is unusual in that it is set in a small English town. But the author, the character, and the faire are all distinctly American; the faire has been organized by a local man who discovered the faire in the United States and decided to bring the event—or, at least, its rowdy American version—back to England. When a series of potentially sinister events take place at the faire, Shepard puts on garb to investigate:

My progress was impeded by the crowds, but it was brought to a complete halt by a Cyrano de Bergerac clone, who waylaid me at the junction of Harmony Lane and Broad Street. . . . His utterly shameless flirtation attracted a small gathering of amused spectators who seemed to think I was in on the act. By the time he pressed his lips—and his oversized nose—to my hand, I was convinced that my disguise was working. With a little luck, and a little medieval attitude, I'd be able to infiltrate any part of the faire I chose. (139)

The way the mysteries call attention to the purposeful donning of garb immediately reminds the reader that everyone in costume at the faire is "going undercover" to some degree and in service of some agenda. In fact, in Atherton's book, both the narrator and her husband enjoy the way the garb allows them to dress more flamboyantly than they usually do and, especially in the case of the husband, frees them to behave more demonstratively as well.

Even more important, though, the garbing of detectives and villains reveals another reason that the faire has been so attractive to mystery writers: the semiotic potential of masquerade. Simply put, masquerade problematizes identity—whether the face is literally hidden, as it is in Blair's *Final Fair*, or whether other elements of costume conceal by presenting an altered "truth," which is what happens in Joyce and Jim Lavene's mystery novel *Ghastly Glass*. Published in 2009, *Ghastly Glass* is the second in a series of comic mysteries set at a Renaissance faire in South Carolina. In this novel (and the others in the series), the faire's masquerade is presented as disturbing several generally rigid identity-based categories. First, the novel's narrator, Jessie, approaches a masked and costumed dancer who had attracted her while he was onstage in order to tell him that she found him "hot"; much to her dismay, the sexy dancer turns out to be her twin brother, whom she failed to recognize in his costume (66). When the siblings then start to bicker about the uncomfortable situation, a nearby weapons maker insists that they settle their argument by fencing. Jessie wins the match but realizes that everyone is assuming she is a man because she is wearing male garb. Immediately thereafter, the actress playing the faire's queen—her brother's ex-girlfriend—starts to flirt heavily with her, also "reading" her as male because of what she is wearing. In short order, the faire's

Fig. 6.2. Mystery author Joan Hess finds the faire's structures of masquerade to be part of the puzzle her protagonist must solve in this faire-set entry in her popular mystery series (2007).

masquerade has obscured and upset familial identity, gender identity, and sexual identity, all as a matter of course.[5]

As Efrat Tseëlon points out in *Masquerade and Identities: Essays on Gender, Sexuality, and Marginality*, masquerade does not just make identity hard to ascertain: it calls into question the very "nature of identity" (3). Historically, there have been many ways that motivated masquerades have sought to trouble the waters of externally imposed identity in this way, with weighty social implications: race-based "passing" and cross-dressing are two significant examples. As I discussed in chapter 4, a large part of the faire's draw for many of its devoted playtrons is the ability to control aspects of their own identity (through creation of personas that are not in service of their outside identities) or presentations of that identity (through garb, bawdiness, or assertion of non-"straight" characteristics).

As a number of playtrons have observed, the faire's masquerade serves to conceal certain markers of identity, particularly class identity, thereby facilitating social interactions that class distinctions generally hinder outside the faire. Mystery novels, on the other hand, are by definition preoccupied with fixing identity: the key word in the nickname *whodunit* is *who*, as the story generally revolves around a person or persons presented with the task of figuring out the identity of a criminal, thus "solving" a crime. This preoccupation with the nature of identity is partly responsible for the prominence in American detective fiction of "identity"-based work in the past forty years, with the introduction of detectives whose character development is organized around the United States' most visible "identity" categories: African American detectives, female detectives, gay and lesbian detectives, Chicano/a detectives, Native American detectives, Asian American detectives, disabled detectives, Jewish American detectives, and more. To varying degrees, then, mystery fiction as a genre is invested in identity as a problem to solve, whether it is the kind of identity that attaches to individuals (who is the criminal?) or to groups (what does it mean to be a woman, an African American, a homosexual, or a disabled person in the United States now?)

If the mystery novels and the faires they depict are both obsessed with questions of identity, it is from opposite sides: the impulse and structure of the mystery are organized around pinning down who someone "is."

The faires, on the other hand, approach with identity as something to be deliberately hidden, blurred, or made fluid. For this reason, in mysteries set at the faire, the detectives and the festivals often end up at cross-purposes, and the mystery genre emerges as considerably less sympathetic of the faire than is other genre fiction (romance, fantasy, and young adult) set there. Even when mystery novels come to the faire, they by nature must represent and advocate for some version of law and order. But in these very books, the faire continues to hint—even after the mystery is solved and the questions have been answered—at unruliness and persistent disturbance of the "known."

Coming of Age at the Faire: Children's and Young-Adult Fiction

Maybe being anything other than average wasn't a total tragedy after all.
—Erin Dionne, *The Total Tragedy of a Girl Named Hamlet*

From the earliest years of the Renaissance faire, it always had a place for children—hardly surprising given that the faire was developed from a children's theater program and was organized by parents of young children. But its appearance in books intended for children and adolescents has come simultaneously with its transformation into a narrower notion of what "family friendly" means at the end of the twentieth century and into the twenty-first. Children's and young-adult fiction is somewhat unique in literature in that nearly all of it is written explicitly for one group of people by a distinctly other group of people. (Children's literature by children or young adults does exist; this small but fascinating body of literature is mostly ignored by nonchildren.) Because of this built-in imbalance of authority and voice, a great deal of children's literature—even the variety that strives to be especially respectful of its readership—is organized around either direct or indirect messages to young people about what they should be like or what they should know and act on.

One thing this means is that the books—especially the ones for younger readers—tend to have a pedantic orientation. Regarding representations of the Renaissance faire, in some cases what this means is that "educational" set pieces, generally about what Elizabethan culture and society were "really" like, are inserted. A particularly saccharine example for middle-grade readers is *Milady Alex!* Written by Diana G. Gallagher, *Milady Alex!* is a 1997 entry in a thirty-two-book series based on a show that aired on the children's television network Nickelodeon about a seventh-grade girl with telekinetic powers. The title character and her closest friends dress in approximations of garb and set out for the faire at the novel's opening. As they enter the gates, the children discuss in a stilted and thoroughly unrealistic way what is anachronistic about the faire and what is true to life:

> "Something sure smells good." Louis's face brightened as he sniffed the tantalizing aroma of freshly baked bread.
> "Another anachronism." Robyn nodded emphatically. "Back in the real Middle Ages everything was dirty and stank. And the peasants were not happy-go-lucky farmers living a simple carefree life, either."
> "She's right about that," Alex said sadly. "The kings gave land to the nobles and knights who helped them fight their wars. The serfs farmed it, but they didn't own anything, not even their crops." (5)

Here, the question of the faire's realism is taken up pointedly, despite the context of a main character who can shape-shift and read minds.

Likewise, several books in Wendelin Van Draanen's middle-grades mystery series about a junior high school girl named Sammy Keyes include discussions of the faire and a visit to the faire. After a teacher suggests to her class that they attend the faire and talk to the artists displaying their work there, Sammy's mentor, a kindly and wise elderly neighbor, gives her a minilecture on the kind of art she is supposed to value: "'The Renaissance faire? For art? Sammy, everything you're going to see there is going to be . . . how do I say this politely . . . B-grade, at best. You're not going to get any sense of true art at the Renaissance faire.' He shook his head and said, 'I'm surprised she didn't encourage you to go to L'Artiste or the Vault or someplace like that'" (12). The concerned neighbor then offers to take Sammy to a "real" art opening. In a striking if unintentional parallel to the faire's custom of garbing up, he instructs Sammy that she will have to change her clothes into something more appropriate, thereby raising the question of what really "counts" as drag, besides Renaissance faire garb.

More elaborate depictions of the faire in fiction for young people are found in young-adult literature, in which the faire provides a self-contained microcosm to act as setting and backdrop for an important coming-of-age experience. Young-adult fiction, commonly known as YA, is itself a fascinating formation. The conviction that young adults have particular reading requirements or taste, distinct from both younger children and full adults, emerged from publishers' marketing strategies to capture the emerging adolescent market that followed the recognition of the teenager as a distinct developmental stage—and consumer group—in the 1950s; the new category of readership was subsequently picked up by librarians in their classification of library books. Many accounts of the history of YA literature point to S. E. Hinton's important 1967 novel *The Outsiders* as an originator of the category, since it featured adolescent characters, was written while Hinton was still a teenager herself, and lacked the sentimental tone that characterized much fiction written by adults about children. YA literature generally features an adolescent as the protagonist. While it can be written in any genre, its most prominent form is the "problem" or "edgy" novel, in which the protagonist faces a conflict or situation that the young-adult reader is supposed to relate to.

Because YA fiction is written and published with a teenage readership (or more cynically a teenage market niche) in mind, a defining quality of these books is a mandate to create narratives that are respectful to their imagined readers. This does not mean that YA books do not share the didacticism of books for younger readers. But instead of the pressure to make the books "educational" in a scholastic sense, YA books are often organized around a kind of emotional didacticism, in which life lessons (about values, coping strategies, self-improvement, relationships, and the like) are imparted through characters' experiences. Mostly this focus on how young people should act means that the Renaissance faire is rarely mocked directly in YA fiction, although the fact that it is mocked is commonly portrayed. Instead, the faire tends to operate as a symbol or engine, first, of being true to oneself and embracing nonconformity (or rejecting peer pressure) and, second, of being kind to others whose interests or self-presentation is different from one's own, even if they seem to be "geeky" or outside of the pack. In short, YA books about the Renaissance faire are obsessed with the "normal."

For the kids in Paul Ruditis's 2008 novel *Show, Don't Tell*, in his YA series *Drama!*, the Renaissance faire operates as an almost magical realm of possibility and self-discovery, with the presence of high school prejudices and in some cases outright cruelty providing a picture of what the kids are escaping from as well as what they are escaping to. The former is a school-based hierarchy in which "popular" kids torment and even cyberbully the "weirder" kids, who are members of the school drama club, and the latter is the narrator's future as an uncloseted gay boy. With good humor if predictably, the emotional topography of the faire facilitates a kind of liberation from both the closet and the cruelty of high school cliquedom.

The book opens by establishing as a "given" that the faire is familiar to the narrator, Bryan, as an object of derision—and that it is likely to be familiar to the reader in the same way: "The Renaissance Faire has come to town. For those of you reading those words and groaning right now, I am so with you. Dressing up and staying in character all day with the 'thees' and 'thous?' That's too out there for even *this* Drama Geek" (1). Bryan agrees to attend the faire because it is important to his best friend, a girl named Sam, who is the daughter of Rennies and until high school traveled the circuit with her parents. Notably, he refuses to wear tights.

Once at the faire, Bryan, Sam, and their friend Hope are immediately and excitedly greeted by a startlingly voluble girl in garb. That girl turns out to be a boy named Marq who, in one of the book's early and most touching scenes, is allowed to play the role of Queen of the Faire for a day—something he has been hoping will happen for a long time— because the role's regular performer is up for a television role (a dead body in a medical show). When he leads the faire's parade as Queen Elizabeth, his parents rush out from their costume booth to watch him, forgetting in their haste to bring their camera. The moment is instructional for Bryan:

And let me tell you, this was a moment any father would be proud of.

Actually, he was. Daniel made it out beside his lovely wife—sans camera—and the pair were positively beaming when they saw their son as

Queen of the Faire. It was kind of nice. I was so busy watching the two of them watch their son that I totally forgot to take his picture. . . . As the crowd around us dispersed, several of the costumed folk came by to congratulate Sandy and Daniel on their son's accomplishment at making queen. It wasn't a surprise that the faire folk would be so accepting. These were a people who, by their very nature, embraced bravado and flamboyance. (31)

Before long, Bryan learns that Marq's parents joined the faire circuit full-time after Marq was beaten up by his high school's baseball team simply because he is, as he puts it, "Gay with a capital 'G'" (124).

Despite Bryan's growing admiration for the faire community, Marq disturbs him because Bryan senses, accurately, that the other boy knows his secret. By the novel's end, however, Bryan is not only able to accept a hug and "friendly kiss" from Marq, but he does not even mind that members of his school's popular clique have seen the kiss and, even more, have photographed it. In short, he is ready to come out at school. His friend Hope, meanwhile, kisses another girl at the faire and begins figuring out her place on the whole "spectrum of sexuality thing" (146).

Gillian Summers's YA series of faire-set novels—*The Tree Shepherd's Daughter* (2007), *Into the Wildewood* (2008), and *The Secret of the Dread Forest* (2009)—also focuses on the question of teenage conformity and newly developing romantic and sexual attraction. These books' teenage protagonist, a California "mall rat" named Keelie, undergoes a radical readjustment to the way she thinks about the faire when she must travel the circuit with her father, a woodcrafter, following the unexpected death of her mother. Gillian Summers is a joint pen name for Berta Placas and Michelle Roper, both of whom describe themselves as devoted participants in their local Renaissance faire.

Summers's faire-set novels are in the fantasy genre, and, like a fair number of fantasies set at the faire, these books make puns on "faire folk" (or "Rennies") and the "fair folk" of Celtic folklore. Keelie learns that while her mother was human, her father is not, and that this fact was responsible for her parents' separation. At the faire, Keelie finds in herself powers she never knew about; the books' use of magic here operates as a neat literalization of the self-discovery that comes with growing up. Moreover, she realizes that she can express herself through clothing and self-ornamentation without being conformist or—even more important—consumerist. Finally, Keelie continually learns that racial prejudice, figured, as is common for fantasy writing, through antipathy or superior attitudes among fairies, elves, humans, and especially in scorn for products of mixed pairings such as Keelie, is harmful to the collective as well as hurtful to individuals. Gradually Keelie, who initially is upset about living at such a "dorky" place as the faire and so far from the shopping malls she loved to frequent, becomes aware of the faire's gifts and its freedoms.

Ruditis's Bryan and Summers's Keelie, through their association with the faire, come to realize that "normal" is a kind of tyranny. So does Erin Dionne's eighth-grade heroine in *The Total Tragedy of a Girl Named Hamlet* (2010). Hamlet moves from being mortified by the fact that her Shakespeare-scholar parents bring her to work at the faire every summer and dress in garb year-round to appreciating that they have followed their passions and discovering a flair for Shakespeare (as an actor) in herself. But in Brad Barkley and Heather Hepler's *Scrambled Eggs at Midnight* (2007), the fourteen-year-old heroine, Calliope, wants nothing more than to stop traveling the circuit with her mother, a performer at the faire (and a bad one, in Calliope's estimation). Barkley and Hepler's novel is just as preoccupied with "normal" as the other YA novels are; it departs in that it prescribes "normal" as a necessary ingredient for adolescent happiness. In the case of Calliope, the need for "normal" is manifested mostly in the pain she feels in not having a permanent home base. In the end, Calliope and her boyfriend, Elliot, whose father runs a Christian weight-loss camp, must both sever their lives from those of their eccentric parents in order to be content.

Through Calliope's resentful voice, Barkley and Hepler critically assess the faire's attempts at historical accuracy (while, as it happens, themselves blithely sidestepping faire history by locating the oldest faire in Asheville, North Carolina, and having it run all summer for seven days a week). Their critique echoes the sections in books for younger children, in which the meaning of authenticity, so important in adults' discussions of the faire, is pondered in the language of children. In fiction for young people (written by adults with at least some degree of teacherly intent), this preoccupation with the meaning of authenticity runs the full gamut of familiar conclusions. Some authors condemn the faire as historically inauthentic (Barkley and Hepler, Van Draanen). Others find it to be *emotionally* real; a touching example is Lynn Hall's 1990 novel *Fair Maiden*, the earliest of the faire-set YA novels. At the book's opening, its teenage protagonist, Jennifer, muses: "This fair, this fantasy world, was her true setting. She had known that from her first visit here four years ago. This faire was more vividly real to Jennifer than her school or her home, more real than her friend Kelly and, please God, more real than her brother, Michael" (5).

Still other authors find that an important kind of authenticity is made possible by the faire's performativity and encouragement of self-creation (Ruditis, Dionne). In the end, what many participants have cited as the faire's central conceits—seriousness of play, consent to try out multiple versions of self, widespread questioning of what it means to follow or not to follow societal rules—serve these adolescent stories well, whether the fictional faire ultimately emerges in them as redemptive, damaging, or simply inconsequential fun.

Two Shakespeares, a Mended Heart, and the End of the World: The Renaissance Faire as Literary Motif

Thy drugs are quick.
—William Shakespeare, *Romeo and Juliet*

Unlike all of the romances, most of the mysteries, many of the fantasy works, and the majority of the YA books, Jess Winfield's 2008 debut novel *My Name Is Will: A Novel of Sex, Drugs, and Shakespeare* was reviewed in mainstream outlets as a novel of real literary merit. Donna Seaman, in the *Los Angeles Times*, called it "a cunningly witty, frolicsome, time-warping bildungsroman," adding, in an unconscious echo of what many commentators have said about the faire itself, that "serious business underlies the literary larkiness." It is not surprising that Winfield, himself a Renaissance faire performer (he cofounded the Reduced Shakespeare Company, likely the faire's most successful comic Shakespeare troupe), found the faire to be a compelling setting for a novel that alternates between narratives about William Shakespeare, playwright and secret Catholic, and

Willie Shakespeare Greenberg, lackadaisical graduate student and stoner. What is striking is that it took more than two decades after the first genre fiction about the faire appeared before "literary" fiction took it up as a subject in any significant way; clustered closely around Winfield's novel are Barbara Samuel's *No Place Like Home* (2002) and Darin Bradley's *Noise* (2010).

Before writing *No Place Like Home*, Barbara Samuel had a successful career as a writer of paperback series romances; *No Place Like Home* is her debut work of "hardcover" fiction. This novel, too, has a romance at its heart and shares certain strategies with the formula-driven romances. (Perhaps this represents an authorial habit of mind, and perhaps it is meant to appeal to her established audience, many of whom did follow her into this new category of fiction.) Her use of the faire, which is invoked rather than depicted, is in keeping with the "shorthand" function it often performs in the much-shorter genre fiction, too. It is used to quickly characterize the narrator's sister, a part-time Rennie. While the narrator, Jewel, is herself presented as maternal and nurturing despite a reputation for wildness, the sister, Jordan, is artistic and self-determined. Together with her husband, she makes pottery to sell at the faire, earning nearly enough in one season to live on all year. Jordan and her husband— whom she met at the faire—are "just not exactly on the same time continuum as the rest of society. They move in tune with an inner directive, or maybe just a natural one" (71). Echoing what many playtrons describe as a special quality of the faire, the narrator further describes Jordan as having the kind of figure that looks wonderful in a Renaissance-era gown, even though it departs from prevailing standards of slender female beauty, and as the prettiest one in the family.

Of the "high" literary depictions of the faire, Winfield's *My Name Is Will* is the most sustained and evinces by far the most insider knowledge. With the Reduced Shakespeare Company, Winfield worked the faires in California during the first half of the 1980s (subsequently taking the show to the traditional stage, in the United States and abroad). *My Name Is Will* draws on both the knowledge of Shakespeare that this gig yielded and the knowledge of the Northern California Renaissance Pleasure Faire. The novel's organizing device is that the two characters, separated by geography and time, have much more in common than their names. The historical Shakespeare writes and acts; the Shakespeare scholar quotes him aloud. The historical Shakespeare is shackled and tortured; the Shakespeare scholar is cuffed during sex play. The two Wills do meet, after a fashion, or at least glimpse each other unknowingly, during a parallel drug experience. The novel's final chapter is carefully written so that the reader cannot tell for sure which Shakespeare is being described, sitting in a bar, drafting a letter to a lover.

In both Winfield's stage career (with the Reduced Shakespeare Company) and his fiction, he draws on a healthy American tradition of desacralizing Shakespeare, beginning with the subtitle of his novel.[6] The major way he accomplishes this is by adopting a flippant tone throughout the novel, to which other authorial mandates, such as factual accuracy or narrative consistency, are subjugated. For instance, Willie Shakespeare Greenberg walks past a line of tables on the campus of the University of California at Berkeley, resulting in a parodic listing of student political clubs. One young woman is described as handing out copies of the *Daily Worker*, a newspaper that has not existed since 1956.

The tone of gleeful impiety does impart a palpable feeling of the faire, even if the book's one-note delivery has a sort of leveling effect so that all locations—the faire, the college campus, the boys school where William Shakespeare teaches, Willie's girlfriend's bedroom, a torture chamber, a pub—come across more than occasionally as fairly interchangeable, which has the effect of masking some of the faire's particularity. Nonetheless, it is the faire's upending of hierarchy that provides the attitude for the novel as whole or, more accurately perhaps, its diction.

When the Renaissance faire makes its appearance, Willie Greenberg has arrived there to deliver an enormous psychedelic mushroom to a buyer; since the buyer is the King of Fools (see discussion of the fools' guild in chapter 4), Willie dons a harlequin's outfit, enters through the employees' gate, and spends the night on-site. Winfield's portrait of the Renaissance faire mostly takes place after hours, among its performers and crafters. There Willie finds himself at an X-rated after-hours show (of the sort often mentioned by performers):

> Gertrude got hilariously, rippingly drunk watching Hamlet and Laertes trying to prick each other with blades dipped in LSD. In a gay porn takeoff,

Phuck squeezed the juice of a concupiscence-inducing flower into the eyes
of a foursome of Greek lovers, a fairy, and a guy named Bottom, in a Shake-
spearean donkey show.

    Wanna get high? Take it in the eye!

    Wanna have a blast? Do it with an ass! (215)

Along with these pieces of "insider" knowledge, Winfield makes use
of more familiar representational elements in the faire—a very friendly
orgy, a huge amount of drug use, and female sexual aggression:

"Truly, I am shocked, sir. Paying for thy kisses when thou couldst surely get
them free." He suspected she was just a paid Faire shill playing street theatre
with him, but when he moved toward her ever so slightly, smiled, and said,
"Verily a fool and peasant knave am I," she swooped right into his arms and
took his lips into hers in a passionate yet light-touched French kiss, running
her hands through the thick curls of hair around his shoulders.

    "Mmm," she said dreamily. "I *never* do that."

    "What, kiss a man?"

    "No, kiss a stranger." (30)

When the historical Shakespeare is arrested for his Catholicism, the
twentieth-century equivalent is Willie's being menaced by the DEA
under the Reagan administration's new mandatory jail time for first-time
drug users, making an implicit argument about what constitutes oppression and what constitutes a bald power play. The faire emerges as a lim-
inal space that has the potential to be liberatory. But that potential is
imperiled by the forces of outside policing.

While Winfield finds human and artistic potential in anarchy, a
potential threatened by too much external discipline, Darin Bradley, in
his novel *Noise*, asks what sorts of behaviors are permitted in order to
survive in a world that is terrifyingly without order. Bradley evokes the
Renaissance faire briefly but crucially as a model that the novel's two
protagonists draw on as they figure out how to survive an unspecified,
semiapocalyptic event by gathering companions, knowledge, and material necessities and leaving their Texas college town for their chosen
haven.

Bradley's book is densely layered and self-referential: the protagonists suggest that would-be survivors of what is called the Collapse or the Event must create their own narratives that justify the actions they wish to take. Presumably, *Noise* itself is such a narrative. The protagonists' experience with the faire is one thing that has given them an advantage in preparing to survive the Collapse:

> The Collapse was like a Renaissance faire. In my mind, they were the same. Some years before, my best friend Adam and I had gone together. Turkey legs, incense, cornets of roasted almonds . . . We bought swords at the Ren Faire. Unsharpened things that had to be peacebound while we stomped around the field in the mud, paying older kids to buy us beer. They were carbon steel, which was important. They would take an edge, but that would nullify the warranty. . . .
>
> We were running. We were several ages at once, the present and future-past. Stealing a bench grinder was many things at once—Ren Faires and running only two of the more obvious. (7–8)

Here, the faire's literal weapons (the swords) matter, but certainly not more than the figurative ones it has bestowed: time traveling and storytelling as ways to save oneself.

Visualizing the Faire: Screens, Comics, and Games

Gee, everyone seems to be playing the character that suits them!
—Larry Welz, *Cherry Meets the Renaissance Dude*

Darin Bradley's novel is both unsettling and sophisticated in its self-reflective musing on the nature of communication and its role in both the deconstruction and construction of social order. But the notion that the faire's narratives can save lives had already been made literal in a video game, "G.H.O.S.T. Chronicles: Phantom of the Renaissance Faire," released in 2009 by Aisle 5 Games. In the game, the player's avatar is a "ghost hunter" whose job is to investigate a supposed haunting at the faire. "Phantom of the Renaissance Faire" is a type of game called *hidden object game* (HOG). To win, players must solve puzzles located in the faire's various booths. The game is almost entirely nonviolent, but playing it does shed some light on Bradley's book, which, structured as it is around locating and acquiring useful objects, and ultimately making it alive to a final haven, is as much a literary video game as anything. Since Bradley works to introduce the cultural activities or "scenes" his narrator is involved in, naming the Renaissance faire and role-playing games such as Dungeons and Dragons, video gaming fits the portrait he is painting.

A card and activity game, "Ren Faire: Get Your Garb On" by Atlas Games, structures itself around the faire's breakdown of division between performer and audience. The object of the game is to be the first player to acquire a full set of garb; various pieces are won by completing performance challenges such as paraphrasing Shakespeare using puppets or juggling. The game requires players to be boisterous (there is a lot of shouting), indecorous, and mischievous. Two serious lessons do emerge, though: first, there is no way to take any of the gestures toward historicism "straight." Every pseudo-Elizabethan utterance, for instance, is self-mocking and tongue-in-cheek. This is instructive in terms of how to "read" these same gestures at the actual faire. Second, while the garb that players accumulate matches men's or women's garb at the faire, players who win items of clothing place them on their avatars regardless of sex. In the end, the winner and all the other players have been involved in at least some amount of symbolic cross-dressing.

Cross-dressing will almost certainly come about when children play with Mattel's Renaissance Faire Barbie doll, released in 2011. Of course, Mattel does not encourage cross-dressing the way the makers of "Ren Faire: Get Your Garb On" implicitly encourage it by the game's rules. To the contrary, Barbie has been at the center of an important cultural debate about construction of gender norms, particularly regarding appearance, for decades. Nonetheless, children at play go off script, and recollections of playing with Barbie dolls have always included switching clothing intended for Barbie and Ken, her male counterpart. The packaging of Renaissance Faire Barbie, who wears elaborate braids and a hoop-skirted gown, issues seemingly nonhumorous proclamations about knightly chivalry.

Pornographic treatments of the faire are organized around mocking the sort of sentiments that Mattel promotes through Renaissance Faire

Barbie almost as much as they are organized around sexual gratification. The association of the faire with sexual liberation, which so many of the romance novels with faire settings depict, has attracted a few pornographic treatments—as first seen in the 1967 photographic spread in *Adam* magazine (see chapter 4). It is outside the scope of this discussion to parse the continuum of liberation and exploitation in pornography; in any case, pornography does have a long tradition of being used for social and even political satire and has not infrequently taken an antibourgeois stance (that is, of course, complicated—as is any form of popular culture—by its enmeshment in a huge profit-driven industry). Further, pornography and the "adult" book and movie industries have long been linked to the struggle against censorship and the distribution of certain "outsider" art forms. As the feature in *Adam* illustrates, the earliest makers of Renaissance-faire-themed pornography seemed to expect viewers to be aware of the faire's reputation as both sexually free and antiestablishment. Too, it is important to note that these sexualized representations of the faire were among the earliest imaginative treatments of it.

Eight years after the *Adam* shoot was done on the faire site, and before the faire had found its way into fiction, a short (sixty minute) pornographic movie was filmed on-site (and after hours) in Southern California—called, simply and perhaps inevitably, *Pleasure Fair*. "There is pleasure for all at the Pleasure Fair," proclaimed the voice-over in a preview of the movie. Over Renaissance-era music, the preview promises that *Pleasure Fair* is "the intimate story of a boy and girl who operate a booth and become involved in strange goings-on backstage. There should be more fairs like this!" *Pleasure Fair* was made just as pornographic filmmaking was becoming semilegitimated, or at least was beginning to take advantage of a more liberal legal environment that followed a series of Supreme Court rulings in the 1960s. The movie was written and directed by Matt Rose and starred twenty-two-year-old Mike Ranger. Ranger was a relative unknown at the time, and *Pleasure Fair* was one of his first movies. In fact, his name did not appear on the extremely low-budget promotional poster for the movie. Ranger went on to become an industry star by about 1980, working with some of pornography's biggest stars (notably Kay Parker in the incest-themed series *Taboo*), though he exited the industry by the mid-1980s. With a less-than-feature-length running time,

Pleasure Fair was not released on videocassette; the production company, Zenith Productions, has disappeared without leaving much of a trace.[7] Some longtime faire workers do remember it being filmed, however, with one recalling in an online discussion that one scene involved a giant pickle (a staple of faire food).

The pornographic faire came to big-budget television in 2007, in an episode of the reality show about Hugh Hefner's Playboy mansion, *The Girls Next Door*. Perhaps it is inaccurate to call the episode, somewhat irrelevantly titled (via the name of a 1991 comedy album by Ray Stevens) "Surely, You Joust," a pornographic treatment of the faire; Hefner and his several "girlfriends" do visit the faire together in garb, but they all stay dressed during their visit. Leading up to the visit, there is plenty of nudity, with body parts blurred. The result is that the trip to the Renaissance faire comes across as poignantly innocent compared to the more ordinary time at the mansion, especially for Holly Madison, the girlfriend who has organized the outing out of her own love for the faire, complete with garb for all and tutorials in how to speak at the faire.

"God, I love the Renaissance faire! It's so . . . Elizabethan!" opens an "adult comic" in the Cherry Comics series by Larry Welz. For one page, the comic's main character, Cherry (previously known as Cherry Poptart until Kellogg's got wind of it), and her best friend discuss authenticity at the faire. Thereupon, kissing, groping, and disrobing begin. The story is called *Cherry Meets the Renaissance Dude*, and it was first printed in 1994. Various sexual permutations are pictured, including some mystical ones and some Shakespeare-influenced ones, but Cherry finds a "meaningful relationship" when she falls in love with a faire jeweler. Unfortunately, the object of her affections has, at the comic's end, left town to follow the circuit to the next faire. Interspersed with Welz's pornographic drawings are two full pages pleading for readers to support anticensorship activity, one under the caption "Fuck Censorship" and the other picturing the ghost of Joseph McCarthy rising from the grave.

Cartoon parody of a gentler sort characterizes episodes of four animated television series in which established characters visit the faire. Three of these are among the most popular adult-oriented animated shows on network television: *The Simpsons*, *Family Guy*, and *King of the Hill*. (The fourth, a 2004 episode of the kids' cartoon *Scooby Doo* called "Large Dragon at

Large," takes place in Scotland but follows the impulse of American children's books to point out the faire's shortcomings regarding authenticity.) All three adult shows aired on the Fox Broadcasting Network, and all three center on the experiences of a working-class family. In "Lisa's Wedding," an episode of *The Simpsons* that aired on March 19, 1995, the family visits a faire, and Lisa, the older daughter, has her fortune told. Through the device of the fortune-teller's predictions, most of the episode takes place in the future; Lisa's "seeing" her future like this allows her to learn important lessons about her family and her present life. In other words, the gift of the faire is its ability to speak to the future and the present—not the past. *Family Guy's* "Mr. Saturday Knight" recalls the history and reputation of the 1960s faire as a place where young people of countercultural bent experimented with LSD. In the episode, which aired on September 5, 2001, the titular family guy tries to fulfill his childhood ambition to be a jouster at the Renaissance faire; he acquired this ambition as a teenager when, during a bad acid trip at the faire, he jumped from a roof and was saved by a knight. Finally, in an episode of *King of the Hill* titled "Joust Like a Woman," which ran on February 24, 2002, the family's mother, Peggy, goes to work at the faire as a "cleaning wench" and must fight for equal pay for women workers—a worthwhile story to tell, even though no faire worker ever expressed that particular complaint to me (though certainly many workers, male and female, spoke of low pay generally).

If "Joust Like a Woman" uses the faire to argue—however humorously—for women's equality, several episodes of a live-action television series, *The Gilmore Girls*, use the faire to enforce the strict gender-based behavioral code the show established throughout its run. The show aired from October 2000 through May 2007 and received financial support from the conservative Family Friendly Programming Forum to develop its pilot episode. In its fifth season, the show contained a brief subplot in which Lorelei and her romantic interest and the male lead, Luke, spend time with his sister, who sells her jewelry at the faire, even traveling the circuit to do so. The details of faire life are presented particularly inaccurately, but accuracy is not the point of the portrayal. Instead, the *idea* of the faire is used to underscore the mainstream, acceptable gendering of the main characters, around which character and plot development are generally organized.

The male lead, Luke, dresses exclusively in jeans and a baseball cap and demonstrates his affection for women through home repairs. In his romantic life, he is depicted as possessive and angry, as when he destroys the car of his estranged wife's new boyfriend in a fit of jealous rage or later punches out his ex-girlfriend's new boyfriend (though these episodes are presented as funny rather than scary). In contrast, Lorelei, the female lead, is characterized by her trendiness and style; she calls Luke for help regularly, making jokes about the very idea of self-reliance. When, through Luke's sister, the Renaissance festival enters their lives, Luke and Lorelei's conversations about the faire are almost exclusively about the gender disobedience they find there. For men, this takes the familiar form of anxiety about tights wearing, which surfaces during a Rennie wedding. For women, the perceived lack of gender discipline at the faire takes the form of hairy legs: Lorelei cruelly intones, "Bathing suit season at the Renaissance festival is only enjoyed by the blind" ("A Messenger"). (The fact that women in period costume would have their legs covered underscores the fact that the hairy legs are a sort of symbol or shorthand for the gender disobedience, rather than a purportedly "realistic" observation.)

Compared to these and other television depictions, there has been much less attention to the faire on the big screen, particularly in mainstream, wide-release movies. An up-the-middle (bland, even) big-screen movie was filmed in 2009 at the Michigan Renaissance Festival. *All's Faire in Love* liberally borrows conventions from faire-set romance novels: Christina Ricci's lead character has quit her job as an investment banker to work at the faire, where she then finds romance. But this is a movie that just barely was made. Initially to star comic actor Jack Black and be titled *Ye Olde Times*, it was subsequently retooled as a romantic comedy after Black withdrew, costarring Owen Benjamin opposite Ricci. *All's Faire in Love* premiered on the grounds of the Michigan faire site but then disappeared for several years without much of a trace, finally eking out a very limited theatrical release in October 2011 and not making it to DVD until February 2012.

A much quirkier, almost equally under-the-radar movie about a version of the faire was made some three decades earlier: cult filmmaker George Romero's *Knightriders* (1981). One of Romero's few nongenre films, *Knightriders* stars Ed Harris and follows an idealistic troupe of jousters who travel and perform on motorcycles, setting up temporary Renaissance faires, complete with music and crafts, in successive towns. Along the way, the members of the troupe confront threats to their way of life that include commercialism, homophobia, corrupt policing, and the emotional and practical challenges of communalism. The movie ends sadly but not before giving more than a glimpse of how transcendent it can be to trust one's chosen companions and, using love and freedom as motivation, to write one's own stories.

Through *Knightriders'* exclusive focus on jousting, it represents the faire as a literal battlefield. But in all these fictional depictions, ranging from the pedantic to the pornographic, from the admiring to the appalled, the faire functions as a metaphorical battlefield for the writers and readers who recirculate and revise its decades' worth of accumulated meaning. All of these "faire fictions" are more than evaluative acts: they are post hoc attempts to define the faire—in some cases to contain it, in others to expand its reach. Scholars of popular culture use the term "textual poaching" to describe how active readers are able to interpret texts according to their own (not necessarily the authors') needs and values—a process Henry Jenkins calls an "impertinent raid on the literary preserve" (24). These versions of the faire, though, from children's toys to pornographic film, offer examples of poaching *through* textuality, rather than *of* it. Plundering the faire's coffers of meaning and setting the spoils to work in service of varied artistic, political, and commercial agendas, portrayers of the fictional faire, like its "actual" participants, are still finding opportunities within its gates.

Conclusion: Bohemian Rhapsody

Ron was the P. T. Barnum of the counterculture.
—Kevin Patterson

Ron Patterson, cofounder of the Renaissance Pleasure Faires in California, died on January 15, 2011, almost forty-eight years after the first Renaissance faire was held in North Hollywood, California. He was eighty years old. Although Patterson had not been directly involved with the faires for more than two decades, they nonetheless constitute a towering part

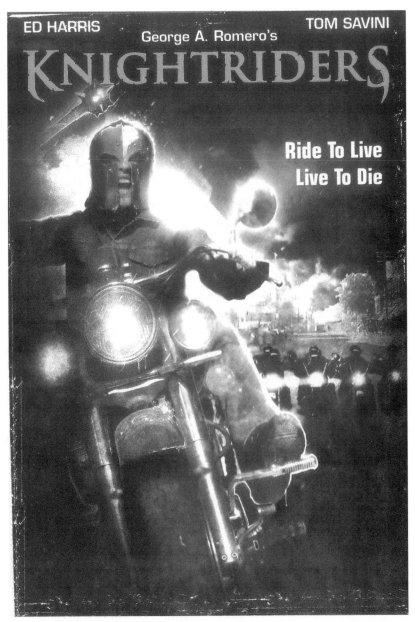

Fig. 6.3. George Romero's semiutopian 1981 movie *Knightriders* follows a communally living group who set up temporary Renaissance festivals, where they perform jousts on motorcycles.

of what he will be remembered for. This was immediately evidenced by the headlines of obituaries that ran nationwide, which referred without exception to the founding of the Renaissance faire; the piece that ran in the *New York Times*, by Margalit Fox, for instance, notes that the Pattersons' vision inspired a "thriving nationwide industry." Fox describes Ron Patterson's shaping influence on the faire both behind the scenes and in front of audiences: "An art director by training, Mr. Patterson was responsible for the look of the fair. He also cheerfully served as Master of the Revels—equal parts lord mayor, court jester and benevolent lout—heralding attractions in impeccable Elizabethan English."

But the lasting effect of Patterson on the faire and the faire on Patterson was witnessed much more dramatically—and personally—by Patterson's memorial, which his sons Kevin Patterson and Brian Patterson, along with a number of old friends, organized in San Francisco. The memorial was held on March 27, 2011, at the Julia Morgan Ballroom in San Francisco's Merchant's Exchange building and was attended by some three hundred family members, friends, and acquaintances from the Renaissance Pleasure Faires and Patterson's other projects, including the Great Dickens Christmas Fair. The memorial was a raucous and visually striking event. The invitation had specified that the dress should be "dapper to outlandish," and attendees obliged, arriving in a variety of attire that included Renaissance faire garb, Victorian and Edwardian costume, and more usual twenty-first-century clothing tweaked with embroidery, feathers, beads, bells, leathers, and velvets. The garb chosen by hundreds of people for this most serious of occasions illustrated yet again that the opportunity for nonconformist dress remains central to the faire's construction of meaning.

Still, as singular and even initially startling as the faire's visual palette has been to several generations of passionate adherents, perhaps it should not surprise us that the faire captured imaginations the way it did. American popular culture has always had a lot to do with dressing up *as such* (as opposed to the kind of professional theatrical performance in which the point is to forget that the performer is costumed). It was born in it, in fact: the first American popular entertainment was the minstrel show, bringing its self-conscious cross-dressing and blackface, its deliberate flouting of decorum, its overt racism, and (paradoxically) its acknowledgment of the richness of black culture to audiences from the 1830s onward (Lhamon). At the turn of the twentieth century, when minstrelsy had mostly disappeared, historical pageants became an elaborate civic ritual—and popular entertainment—in which thousands of nonprofessionals took part by dressing up across the country (Glassberg). During the same period, Wild West shows presented a heavily stylized vision of frontier life (Reddin). In the 1930s, thousands of nongay spectators flocked to New York's Bowery, Greenwich Village, and Harlem neighborhoods to gawk at the drag balls held there since the 1920s (Chauncey). As early as the turn of the seventeenth century, American cities in the South, most famously New Orleans, developed their own versions of participatory Mardi Gras masquerade. Yale University introduced the first costumed sports team mascot in 1889; the practice traveled over to professional sporting events from college sports in the 1960s (Daily). Convention-based fan culture (at science-fiction/fantasy conventions, comics conventions, or *Star Trek* conventions) is characterized through costuming (Bacon-Smith). Activities such as Burning Man, Live Action Role-Playing (LARP), and furry or anime fandom provide expanding opportunities for adults to costume themselves. Janine Fron et al. have usefully approached video games, in particular those in which players select, tailor, and outfit avatars, as an articulation of adult "dressing up" (Fron et al.).

Adult "dressing up" can be approached productively from a variety of analytic perspectives: psychological, historical, aesthetic, sexual. But—as Fron et al. point out—in U.S. culture, "dress-up" has generally been relegated in the public imagination to a pastime for girls, at least partially accounting for the gendered nature of much publicly articulated scorn for the faire. In the history of the faire, as I hope I have shown, the practice of dressing up has always existed in a dialectical relationship with assertions of Foucauldian discipline. In the faire's first, most avant-garde period, costumery functioned as visible statement of dissent against Cold War and consumerist demands for consensus. The experiences of Doris Karnes and other faire creators encapsulate the circumstance surrounding this dissent. Their creative activity shows that both the artistic and ideological roots of the faire ran deep in 1950s activism, but calling attention to themselves in this way elicited both heavy-handed and more culturally diffuse demands to embrace the relative safety of conventionality. A decade thereafter, during the faire's short but significant authenticity-oriented period, the same costumery was cleverly mobilized as part of an argument for the utility and integrity of the project on the heels of accusations that the faires were decadent hippie gatherings; in a way, the garb helped to form a case for the faire's respectability despite the fact that it had recently represented a kind of refusal of the functioning definitions of respectability. In the faire's corporate period, the notion of adults "playing dress-up," particularly when those adults are men, creates a marked anxiety—an anxiety often mobilized as a call to deride the impulse as improperly gendered.

Ron Patterson's flamboyantly garbed-up memorial lasted for hours; in large part, this was because his death was marked not only by eulogy and reminiscence but also by performance. The Pipe and Bowl morris team performed an opening dance and procession: the Abbots Bromley Horn Dance, an English folk dance featuring reindeer antlers and a hobbyhorse and dating to at least the sixteenth century. Singer Judy Kory, whose involvement with the faire began in 1963 when she played an apple seller at the first faire, performed several songs. The members of a capella group Oak, Ash, and Thorn sang several selections, at least one irreverently humorous. Chris Caswell, a Celtic musician who, in familiar Rennie tradition, describes his own music as "informed by Wales, the Middle East, Latin America, the French countryside," played the harp (Caswell). A New Orleans–style second line formed an exit processional. Taken together, the memorial's performances conveyed how capacious the faire's cultural ambitions and reach were.

These performances, and the commentary that accompanied them, served more than one purpose—especially taken along with various graphic arts presented at the memorial in the form of props, illustrations, and decorations. In addition to paying tribute to a man whom most of the people present considered an inventor of their life's pursuit, they formed a vivid, if anecdotal, portrait of the labor history of the faire. Because of the tight-knit nature of the faire community, the gratitude and idealization that are common at such events were strong here—but still, space was made for the particular kinds of ambivalence that can emerge from the fact of loving one's job despite that, necessarily, one feels underappreciated or even exploited sometimes. Perhaps a simpler way to express this contradiction is to think of the faire as a family business, involving a huge family with quite different levels of authority and remuneration. "We loved working at the faire," comments Ernie Fischbach about the faire as work environment, cheerfully adding, "The pay was dismal" (interview).

Thus, although the memorial was, unsurprisingly, heavily and movingly tinted with the romanticization of the eulogy, there were equally moving moments of refusal to idealize. One speaker, the actor and puppeteer Sandey Grinn (of the troupe Cock and Feathers), in a lovely list of things—the laughter of a child, the scent of cinnamon—that cause him to recall the faire no matter where he encounters them, included "when I go past a port-a-potty." He got a fond chuckle from his listeners—but he also said, to a large group of friends and colleagues, that smelling shit made him think of the faire. Besides making everyone laugh, his remark reminded them that even labors of love should be honored as labor. In a related rhetorical move, one speaker referred quite directly to Phyllis Patterson's reputation for rigidity, particularly when it came to organization, planning, and authenticity—as did many performers and crafters I interviewed along the way; about half the time, they added some version of "and that was a good thing for the faire."

By showing a group of people collectively coming to terms with their unusual working histories, the long recollections at Ron Patterson's memorial also gave a glimpse of the bittersweet insider attempts on the part of Rennies to preserve and tell their own oral histories, attempts that are gaining urgency as the first generation of Rennies has reached old age. (In addition to Ron Patterson's death, Phyllis Patterson, from whom he had been divorced since 1980, suffers from Alzheimer's disease.) A group of faire veterans have launched an enterprise called League of Extraordinary Historians to gather recollections; to digitize archives of programs, newsletters, and other faire-related paper archives in individuals' possessions; and to create a series of wiki pages about aspects of faire history. Another group, calling themselves Friends of Paramount Ranch, organizes annual picnics at the faire's former site in Agoura, California; the group also seeks to create a clearing house (posted on the group's website) for faire-related oral history, creative writing, art, and communication. In 2010, one of that group's regular participants, Jason Sarrow, produced a documentary called *Faire:*

An American Renaissance; what the film lacks in historical framing it makes up for with insider's perspective. These efforts at collective (and mostly nonprofessional) history express and pursue what David Glassberg calls a "sense of history"—which he defines as "the intersection between the intimate and the historical" (6).

Such attempts at preservation acknowledge, with the perspective of historical distance, that the faire's placeless, nonofficial invention of the past was a multifarious sociocultural formation and that the faire's earliest experiments are receding, even as the faire's current incarnation—with all its own particular cultural axes to grind (and throw)—remains indebted to it. Thus, old-timers' anxiety that the history of *their* faire is in danger of being lost underscores the fact that the faire now is quite a different animal from its countercultural ancestor. Of course, that the meaning of any cultural event changes over some fifty years is a truism. What I have called the "early faire," from its beginning in 1963 until it spread beyond California, formed an important early countercultural building block, providing, along with, say, the Greenwich Village coffeehouse scene and San Francisco's City Lights bookstore, one cultural bridge between Old Left and New Left cultural aspirations and institutions. Many of those idealistic early participants—including the faire's founders, Phyllis and Ronald Patterson—remained eagerly involved as the faire entered a new stage in its second decade, seeking to stake out new territory through focusing on the authentic and the educational as it became clear that the faire was going to grow and last. Some of these participants hailed the new emphasis, while others felt that the artistic possibilities of the early faire were sacrificed to an impossible aim of correctness. Finally, with corporate purchases of the large faires at the tail of the 1980s, in tandem with hundreds of small, less centralized faires springing up around the United States, the faire as an institution came, simultaneously, to represent homogenized "family" entertainment—and a haven from exactly that homogenization. Some of the faire's first participants have remained involved in the faire as it went through these changes, but more, such as mime Billy Scudder, have felt alienated, finding it has traveled too far from its original goals for them to enjoy. It is arguable that the faire has entered a fourth period, transformed, predictably, by the Internet; certainly, social networking and online platforms have extended and deepened both individuals' relationship to the faire and its corporate ownership's ability to brand and market it.

But absorbing the faire's lesson that play with the *past* is always about the seriousness of *now* raises the possibility that we must look outside the faire's front gates to learn what has changed most about it. There is, after all, a great deal of continuity in what has gone on at the faire since 1963; even the faire's most expressive detractors show, through the language they use about it, some awareness of its early roots. What the faire's practices have needed to speak to and about, though—what Raymond Williams called the "structures of feeling," the material circumstances that mold and determine how people experience the art that moves them and makes them feel—*that* has changed considerably. As Thomas Frank has conclusively demonstrated, the co-optation of the cultural manifestations of the "sixties" was accomplished early—and thoroughly—enough that the San Francisco Diggers felt moved to hold a mock funeral in 1967 for "Hippie, devoted son of mass media" (7). If the faire introduced a freshly imagined world through the lens of the past, that new code of conduct was appropriated by the marketplace pretty quickly. In the face of this swelling appropriation, it is not very surprising that by 1972 the faire was anxiously insisting on its own authenticity—or that "authenticity" should become the faire's watchword for the next decade. By the 1980s, "the sixties" was an idea, one that had become thoroughly commodified and its "vocabularies of transgression," as Frank puts it, overwhelmingly overtaken by popular-cultural representations of vague "rebelliousness" and glib sloganeering about sex, drugs, and rock-and-roll (x). Surely a portion of the faire's new opposition—enacted through ridicule now rather than organized politics—stemmed from embarrassment about that, an embarrassment that encompassed the political, social, and cultural ambitions these powerful marketing strategies had overtaken. (Indeed, writing in 1997, Frank uses the word "embarrassing" to describe contemporary commentators who were too uncritically idealistic about the counterculture.) In 2011, "hippie" is still being marketed, particularly through clothing and costume; arguably, the triumph of the word *hippie* itself, which youth counterculturalists did not use about themselves (though I have used it in this book for convenience) is evidence of the shaping influences of "the enthusiasm of corporations for youth culture in the sixties" (Frank ix).

Thus, it is worth considering that perhaps the enterprise of the faire represents *more* continuity than is always comfortable and that its reception, whether positive or negative, has always had to do with how its audiences are willing or able to understand "the sixties." History—even invented history—is a story of continuity much more than rupture, of each episode creating what comes next. Any careful historical account of the cultural politics of "the sixties" points to the counterculture's deep roots in the 1950s and earlier: as I hope I have shown, the Renaissance faire as case study leads directly back to 1930s radical theatrical experiments, 1940s (and earlier folk) revivals (in art and dance), 1950s Beatnik coffeehouses, various early American and European experiments in communal living, turn-of-the-twentieth-century immigrant music, and interest in early music that dates to the turn of the twentieth century—to name but a few of the faire's cultural antecedents. By the same token, looking forward from the faire's conception, although its demographic has aged and its management transformed, the faire still represents a location for sexual experimentation, the self-expression and gender fluidity of fancy dress, semicommunal living arrangements, and immersive theatrical performance. Most important, the faire's most devoted audiences found, and still find, that it expresses desire—a desire to inhabit, even if temporarily, a transformed world. Of course, the faire alone cannot fully *deliver* the desire—culture operates in a much more symbolic way—but its ability to *express* it has been cited as precious by hundreds of the participants I spoke to.

The line of historical continuity was appreciably present at Ronald Patterson's memorial but was nowhere more evident than in an oath that David Springhorn, the "Shakespeare" of this book's opening words, led the entire assembly in pledging. The oath was called "Captain Ron's Bohemian Oath," and hundreds of people of all ages rose to take it. The words were as much statement of purpose as statement of thanks:

I solemnly (but not too solemnly) swear
1. To walk through the world as if it were a music hall show and I, the chairman.
2. To love my family, be it blood or spirit.

3. To always dress with an eye toward theatrical and historical (if not hysterical) style.

4. To listen intently to the person I am conversing with as if they were the most amazing person in the world.

5. To laugh with every fiber of my being.

6. To grow old gracefully with dignity (but not toooooo much of that).

7. To flirt with shameless abandon and revel in the romantic sciences with complete abandon.

8. To elevate the taking of wine and spirits to an almost Olympian level, remembering that the god Dionysus need not be always worshiped on one's knees.

9. When tipsy to set a good example of good fellowship, bonhomie, and decorum.

10. To express myself artistically and theatrically with flair, style, and integrity, always remembering that the best shows are where you cannot tell the patrons from the performers.

11. To empower and inspire my fellow creatures to the fullest of their potential and join in praise of their triumphs (with Champagne whenever and wherever possible).

And lastly, to thoroughly commit myself to living in a perpetual state of wonder and delight, savoring my life to the fullest and to the best of my powers spread joy and magic wherever I go.

Captain Ron, we step forward to fill your shoes, because you unselfishly taught us how to live as Bohemians.

All those willing to commit to this arduous but delightful path signify by saying aye!

NOTES

Notes to the Introduction

1. Kevin Patterson is the oldest son of Ron and Phyllis Patterson, the founders of the faire. He was three years old when the first faire was held.

2. Vito Paulekas was a sculptor known for having the L.A. counterculture's first "crash pad" in his Laurel Canyon home and for dancing with his followers at early Mothers of Invention concerts.

Notes to Chapter 1

1. From here on, I use the last name "Patterson" to refer to Phyllis Patterson. For references to her husband, Ron Patterson, and her son, Kevin Patterson, I use both first and last names at all times.

2. Patterson refers ironically to the old saying that women only attended college to find husbands and then refers to her divorce from Ron Patterson in 1980.

3. California's state constitution still requires all state workers to sign a loyalty oath, and as recently as 2008, a Quaker was fired from one of the state colleges for refusing to sign the oath without inserting a provision that her defense of the state and country would be carried out nonviolently. She was reinstated shortly thereafter.

4. Bob Blauner details the physical ailments, severe drop in morale, and impaired work associated with the anxiety felt by professors at UCLA during the university's battles over the oath. Indeed, according to Blauner, a nurse at the university hospital was reported to have commented on the large number of "loyalty cases" coming in (128).

5. See Withington.

6. Here Lindholm is quoting Anna Louise Huxtable, taking her words from Gable and Handler (44).

7. See, for instance, Lewis and Bridger; Gilmore and Pine; and Bhargava.

8. Didion wrote about Laurel's piece in an article called "Alicia and the Underground Press," which was published in the *Saturday Evening Post* (13 January 1968, 14).

9. There are differing accounts, but no more than a two-week difference.

10. It is unclear whether the group of conservatives was actually organized by the Birch Society.

11. For more on Faire a la Carte, see Korol-Evans 38–42.

12. On the history of the Oregon Country Fair, see Suzi Prozanski's labor of love, *Fruit of the Sixties: The Founding of the Oregon Country Fair.*

Notes to Chapter 2

1. On the Arts and Crafts movement in the United States, see Kaplan.

2. Jelen's reference is to "psychological operations," which the U.S. Department of Defense defines as "the planned use of propaganda and other psychological actions having the primary purpose of influencing the opinions, emotions, attitudes, and behavior of hostile foreign groups in such a way as to support the achievement of national objectives" (D4).

Notes to Chapter 3

1. Cohen is describing the Northern California faire in 1981.

2. The group's sole record album was recorded in 1966 and was produced and arranged by David Gates, but its members went on to make lasting names for themselves: Royer and Gates founded the successful soft-rock group Bread in the 1970s, while Hallinan became a best-selling writer of mystery novels.

3. The *Buck and Mug* is the oldest of several self-published newsletters of the faire's employee community. It has come out of the California faires more or less biannually since 1978. Other Rennie publications have included *Uproots*, a newsletter produced out of the Michigan faire, and the *Rogues' Alternative Gazette*, or *RAG*, of the Maryland festival.

4. The term *ethnic-psych* is also used for music emerging from non-U.S. countries in the 1980s or later.

5. For a remarkably detailed account of the context in which Family Dog Productions organized its concerts, see Perry, *Haight-Ashbury.*

6. For an impressively full listing of shows organized by Family Dog Productions, see Ross Hannon and Corry Arnold's online compilation at http://www.chickenonaunicycle.com/FD%20Shows.htm.

7. First, the name invokes "Cantar de mio cid," or "The Song of My Lord," a medieval Spanish epic poem. Second, the name inverts the moniker of Symphony Sid, a hugely popular jazz DJ during the 1940s, 1950s, and 1960s. Finally, when the first two words are combined, the word "acid" obtains, referring to LSD and the music as a sort of sonic tripping.

8. There is no consensus about the origin in the United States of the term *belly dance* for Middle Eastern women's solo dance.

9. For more on pre-twentieth-century European klezmer, see Strom.

10. At issue is whether the form dates back further than the late fifteenth century. See Forrest.

11. Similarly to the historical plasticity of the Renaissance faire itself, *medieval folk rock* refers to music evidencing medieval, Renaissance, and baroque classical influences.

12. The San Francisco Mime Troupe's office website states, "The San Francisco Mime Troupe does not do pantomime. We mean 'mime' in the ancient sense: to mimic. We are satirists, seeking to make you laugh at the absurdities of contemporary life and at the same time, see their causes. We've done shows about most of the burning issues of our time, generally shows that debunked the official story. We perform everywhere from public parks to palaces of culture, aiming to reach the broadest possible audience."

13. On this and other differentiations, see Lust.

14. Trillin 115. Moschen—or at least his hands, which are swapped for David Bowie's—juggled in a mainstream feature movie, *Labyrinth*, in 1986, one year before the Flying Karamazovs juggled in a mainstream feature movie, *The Jewel of the Nile* (1987), which also starred Avner Eisenberg.

15. Loeffelbein notes four kinds of jousting. In the *tourney*, or *melee*, jousters compete in teams or as a free-for-all. In the *rider-to-rider* joust, two riders, wearing armor and armed with lances, charge at each other on horseback. *Riding at the quintain* has the jouster charge at a dummy that is rigged to strike back at the rider. Finally, in *riding at the rings*, the jouster must loop the target, a small ring, onto his or her lance.

16. One street performer I interviewed inquired whether I preferred she give the interview in character or out.

Notes to Chapter 4

1. The Dickens Christmas Fair is another event founded by the Pattersons, in 1970; it is currently run by Kevin Patterson. It is held during the Christmas season in Northern California. See chapter 1.

2. The term "working class" was used much less often than "blue collar." A considerable number of these patrons reported that they do not email or own computers.

3. I am referring to gear made for use in the range of sexual practices known as *bondage and discipline, submission and dominance*.

4. Definitions of *steampunk* vary, but in general, the term is used to refer to an aesthetic and sartorial subculture crafted around a subgenre of speculative fiction set in an anachronistic Victorian-era setting. In other words, it is the science fiction of an alternate past. Steampunk first came into prominence during the 1980s, when the term was devised as a variant of *cyberpunk*.

5. On Civil War reenactment, see Turner.

6. Of course, when it comes to weaponry, the faires necessarily discourage authenticity; for practical reasons, they either forbid weapons altogether or else require that they be "peace-tied" (fastened with a plastic cuff to the scabbard so that they cannot be drawn).

Notes to Chapter 5

1. Interestingly, the first respondent attempts to do so by crafting a sentence in black vernacular.

2. Linguist Mary Bucholtz, in performing a study on how high schoolers define the word *nerd*, comes to the conclusion that it is associated with what she calls "hyperwhiteness." The danger of her conclusion—which simply inverts centuries of American cultural constructions that have associated *cool* with blackness—is one that has sometimes troubled the field of whiteness studies: Bucholtz recenters whiteness while neatly sidelining the defining role African American culture has played in American popular culture broadly drawn (in other words, insisting on the primacy of *nerd* as white rather than exploring what it means in a context where black is cool). For more on Bucholtz's study, see Nugent.

3. Overall, it was fascinating to try to figure out how my own clothing would affect my ability to talk to various people at the faire. If I was not in garb, playtrons would tease me about being "naked." If I was in garb, people having a bad time would never speak to me, and some performers would treat me like a fan, which led to a different sort of conversation. If I wore "professor" clothing, people who identified as working class or blue collar would work hard to make sure I understood that there were other professional people at the faire.

Notes to Chapter 6

1. See, for instance, Kent and Shelton; Parv; Wainger; and Lanigan, to name just a few.

2. This yearning and critique were expressed in the slogan "Frodo Lives!" popular in the 1960s and 1970s.

3. The series includes eight books; all have Mercedes Lackey's name on them as either author or editor, and while they all take place in the same urban-fantasy "universe," some are novels and some are short-story collections. Many writers are involved.

4. Some of these opportunities are quite controversial and potentially exploitive "pay to publish" businesses.

5. Some scholars trace the importance of "solving" familial identity in mystery fiction all the way back to Sophocles's play *Oedipus Rex*, in which the title character questions several witnesses and ultimately pieces together the truth about his family relationships from what they tell him.

6. "Sacralization" is Lawrence Levine's term; for a discussion of the American history of both pious and impious approaches to Shakespeare, see his *Highbrow/ Lowbrow*.

7. A pornographic company named Zenith Pictures made gay male porn in from the 1950s to the 1970s and was known for poor record-keeping, slapdash marketing, inaccurate labeling, and operating under a variety of other names. I haven't been able to ascertain if this is the same production company. *Pleasure Fair* is heterosexual pornography, but it would not be unusual for a production company—or actors, for that matter—to occasionally cross over.

WORKS CITED

Abramson, Leslie, with Richard Flaste. *The Defense Is Ready: Life in the Trenches of Criminal Law*. New York: Simon and Schuster, 1997.

"Agoura Pleasure Fair Boosters, Foes Spar." *Los Angeles Times*, 19 April 1968. SF8.

Aksyonov, Vasily. *Non-Stop around the Clock: Impressions, Reflections, and Adventures*. 1976. Trans. Stephanie Sides. MA thesis, Monterey Institute of International Studies, 1983.

Alice. Email to author. 6 December 2008.

Alicia. Interview. 28 November 2009.

Allen. Interview. 24 April 2010.

All's Faire in Love. Dir. Scott Marshall. Patriot Pictures, 2009.

Alpert, Marco. Interview. 25 May 2011.

Anderson, Lesley. "New Finds: Mead That's a Cut Above the Renaissance Faire." *Chow*, 3 June 2009. http://www.chow.com/food-news/7700/new-finds-mead-thats-a-cut-above-the-renaissance-faire.

Anderson, Trent. Interview. 11 June 2011.

"Andrea." Interview. 28 November 2009.

Angel, Elayne. Interview. 22 March 2011.

Aquarius Rising. Dir. Pierre Sogol. Unreleased, 1967.

"Are You a Faire Nerd?" *Raven's LARP Resource Page*, 17 November 1997. http://www.shades-of-night.com/larp/fairnerd.html.

Atherton, Nancy. *Aunt Dimity Slays the Dragon*. New York: Viking, 2009.

Axmaker, Sean. "The Trip." In *The Scarecrow Video Movie Guide*. Seattle: Sasquatch Books, 2004.

Bacon-Smith, Camille. *Science Fiction Culture*. Philadelphia: University of Pennsylvania Press, 2000.

Bahn, Christopher, Steven Hyden, Josh Modell, Noel Murray, Keith Phipps, Tasha Robinson, Scott Tobias, and David Wolinsky. "The Knights Who Say 'Nerd': Twenty Popular Cultural Obsessions Even Geekier Than Monty Python." *A.V. Club*, 4 February 2008. http://www.avclub.com/articles/the-knights-who-say-nerd-20-popcultural-obsessions,2153/.

Baker, Tom, and Jonathan Simon. *Embracing Risk: The Changing Culture of Insurance and Responsibility*. Chicago: University of Chicago Press, 2002.

Bakhtin, Mikhail. *Rabelais and His World*. Trans. Helene Iwolsky. Bloomington: Indiana University Press, 1984.

Barber, Mary. "Artisans Mold Lives into New Forms." *Los Angeles Times*, 18 May 1972. SE1.

Barkley, Brad, and Heather Hepler. *Scrambled Eggs at Midnight*. New York: Speak, 2006.

Bart, Peter. "Madrigals Lull the Bohemians in California Meadow." *New York Times*, 9 May 1966. 41.

Beagle, Peter S. *Folk of the Air*. 1977. Reprint, London: Headline, 1987.

Beard, Julie. *Complete Idiot's Guide to Getting Your Romance Published*. Indianapolis: Alpha Books, 2000.

Bebergal, Peter. "Contemporary Psychedelia: From Transcendence to Immanence. *Zeek: A Jewish Journal of Thought and Culture*, June 2006. http://www.zeek. net/606music/.

Becca. Interview. 8 August 2010.

Beckerman, Marty. "Always Hate Gorks: My Visit to the Renaissance Fair." Marty Beckerman's website, 8 June 2000. http://martybeckerman.com/always-hate-gorks-my-visit-to-the-renaissance-fair/.

Becky. "Follow-Up." *Lazy Gay News* (blog), 24 September 2010. http://lazygaynews. blogspot.com/2010_09_01_archive.html.

Beemyn, Brett, and Erich W. Steinman. *Bisexuality in the Lives of Men: Facts and Fictions*. London: Routledge, 2001.

Bennett, Stephen. Interview. 28 September 2007.

Bernard, Diane. *Renaissance Man*. New York: Zebra Books, 1997.

Bhargava, Rohit. *Personality Not Included: Why Companies Lose Their Authenticity— and How Great Brands Get It Back*. New York: McGraw-Hill, 2008.

Bialek, Dan. "Renaissance Fair(e) Myths." *Dan Bialek Loves Kittens*, 1 May 2007. http://www.danbialekloveskittens.com/posts/renaissance-faire-myths.

Billy. Interview. 24 April 2010.

Birchard, John. "The Artful Bodger: One Man's Exploration of Early Country Woodcraft." *American Woodworker*, May–June 1989. 36–42.

Black, Layle. *Faire Dreamer*. Austin, TX: Siren, 2011.

Blair, Marcia. *The Final Fair*. New York: Zebra Books, 1979.

Blauner, Bob. *Resisting McCarthyism: To Sign or Not to Sign California's Loyalty Oath*. Stanford: Stanford University Press, 2009.

Blazer, Sam. "The Renaissance Pleasure Faire." American Theatre Issue, *Drama Review* 20, no. 2 (June 1976): 31–37.

Bowman, Amy. Interview. 13 October, 2007.

Boyd, Malcolm. *Human Like Me, Jesus*. 1971. Reprint, New York: Pyramid Family Library, 1973.

Boyle, Aimee. "Renaissance Faire Body Image." *EmpowHer*, 8 May 2010. http:// www.empowher.com/beauty/content/renaissance-faire-body-image?page=0,0.

Brackman, Jacob. "The Underground Press." *Playboy*, August 1987. 83.

Bradley, Darin. *Noise*. New York: Ballantine, 2010.

Bradley, Marion Zimmer. *Witchlight*. New York: Tor Books, 1996.

Breed, Allen G. "Not Just for Renaissance Fairs: Mead Producers Triple in 10 Years." *Huffington Post*, 28 December 2010. http://www.huffingtonpost.com/2010/12/30/not-just-for-renaissance-fairs-mead-producers-triple-in-10-years_n_802565.html.

Bromell, Nick. *Tomorrow Never Knows: Rock and Psychedelics in the 1960s*. Chicago: University of Chicago Press, 2002.

Brooks, Van Wyck. "On Creating a Useable Past" (1915). In *Van Wyck Brooks: The Early Years, 1908–1925*, ed. Claire Sprague, 219–226. New York: Northeastern University Press, 1968.

Brown, Don. "An Interview with Bob Thomas." *Buck and Mug* 2, no. 2 (1979).

Browne, David. *Dream Brother: The Lives and Music of Jeff and Tim Buckley*. New York: It Books, 2002.

Brunner, Meghan. *From the Ashes*. Bloomington, IN: AuthorHouse, 2002.

———. *Into the Storm*. Bloomington, IN: AuthorHouse, 2004.

———. *Towards the Fates*. Bloomington, IN: AuthorHouse, 2009.

Burleigh, Irv. "Plans for Fair to Be Protested." *Los Angeles Times*, 18 April 1968. SF1, 6.

Bybee, Catherine. *Binding Vows*. Adams Basin, NY: Wild Rose, 2009.

The Byrds. "Renaissance Fair." *Younger Than Yesterday*. Columbia, 1967.

California Fever (a.k.a. *Teenage Divorcee*, a.k.a. *Josie's Castle*). Dir. Lawrence E. Mascott. Producers Distributing Corporation, 1972.

Campbell, Patricia J. *Passing the Hat: Street Performers in America*. New York: Delacorte, 1981.

"Caption Time #108." *Davezilla*, 26 April 2006. http://www.davezilla.com/2006/04/26/caption-time-108/.

Case, John. *The Murder Artist*. New York: Ballantine Books, 2004.

Caswell, Chris. "About." Chris Caswell's home page. http://chriscaswell.net/page2/page2.html/.

Cather, Willa. *My Ántonia*. 1918. Reprint, New York: Oxford University Press, 2006.

Chace, Rebecca. *Chautauqua Summer: Adventures of a Late-Twentieth-Century Vaudevillian*. New York: Harcourt, Brace, 1993.

Chambers, Colin, ed. *Continuum Companion to Twentieth Century Theatre*. New York: Continuum, 2003.

Chappell, Blake. Email to author. 6 October 2008.

Chauncey, George. *Gay New York: Gender, Urban Culture, and the Making of the Gay Male World, 1890–1940*. New York: Basic Books, 1994.

Chiacos, Elias, ed. *Mountain Drive: Santa Barbara's Pioneer Bohemian Community*. Santa Barbara, CA: Shoreline, 1994.

Cioletti, Jeff. "Just Like Honey Mead Emerges from the Middle Ages." Redstone Meadery. http://redstonemeadery.com/store/catalog/Just-Like-Honey-Mead-emerges-from-the-Dark-Ages-sp-97.html.

Clark, Caleb John. "Hippie Marbling: An Art Form Rooted in the 1960s and a Look at One of Its Eccentric Pioneers." *No End Press*, April 2005. http://www.noend-press.com/caleb/marbling/.

Clark, Katerina. *Petersburg: Crucible of Cultural Revolution.* Cambridge: Harvard University Press, 1995.

Cleavage. Television documentary. Dir. Carl Hindmarch. World of Wonder, 2002.

The Cockettes. Dir. Bill Weber and David Weissman. Grandelusion, 2002.

Cohen, Abner. *Masquerade Politics: Explorations in the Structure of Urban Cultural Movements.* Berkeley: University of California Press, 1993.

Cohen, Robert. *Freedom's Orator: Mario Savio and the Radical Legacy of the 1960s.* New York: Oxford University Press, 2009.

Cohen, Stanley. *Folk Devils and Moral Panics.* St. Alban's, UK: Paladin, 1973.

Compton, John. Interview. 18 May 2011.

Conaway, Vince. Interview. 6 October 2008.

Copeland, Richard. Interview. 30 September 2008.

Coviello, Don. Interview. 3 February 2011.

Coyote, Peter. *Sleeping Where I Fall.* Washington, DC: Counterpoint, 1998.

Craven, Jerry. *Folk Pageants.* Vero Beach, FL: York, 1996.

Curtis, Ann. Interview. 28 September 2007.

Daily, Mary C. "Mascots: Performance and Fetishism in Sport Culture." *Platform: Journal of Media and Communication* 3, no. 1 (April 2011): 40–55.

Dallas, Paul. *Dallas in Wonderland: The Pacifica Approach to Free Radio.* Los Angeles: self-published, 1967.

Dave_28. Comment on "Texas Crawfish Festival." *ClutchFans*, 4 April 2010. http://bbs.clutchfans.net/archive/index.php/t-184906.html.

Dawidoff, Robert. Series foreword to Lasar vii–ix.

Dawn, Jenna. Interview. 23 November 2010.

DeJongh, James. *Vicious Modernism: Black Harlem and the Literary Imagination.* New York: Cambridge University Press, 1990.

Demonbaby. "Adventure Notes: Aquatic Humiliation, Renaissance Faires, Tyra Banks, and Hip-Hop Looney Toons." *Demonbaby* (blog), 14 September 2006. http://www.demonbaby.com/blog/2006/09/adventure-notes-aquatic-humilia-tion.html.

Denning, Michael. *Mechanic Accents: Dime Novels and Working-Class Culture in America.* New York: Verso, 1987.

DeRogatis, Jim. *Turn on Your Mind: Four Decades of Great Psychedelic Rock.* Milwaukee, WI: Hal Leonard, 2003.

desjardins. Comment on "How to Find Lovers Who Are into BDSM but Not in the Scene?" *Ask Metafilter: Querying the Hive Mind* (blog), 1 March 2010. http://ask. metafilter.com/147283/How-to-find-lovers-who-are-into-bdsm-but-not-in-the-scene.

Devantier, Alecia T., and Carol Turkington. *Extraordinary Jobs for Creative People.* New York: Infobase, 2006.

DeWitt, Mark F. *Cajun and Zydeco Dance Music in Northern California: Modern Pleasures in a Postmodern World.* Jackson: University Press of Mississippi, 2008.

"Dextra." Interview. 8 August 2010.

Dionne, Erin. *The Total Tragedy of a Girl Named Hamlet.* New York: Dial Books, 2010.

Draheim, Sue. "About Me." Sue Draheim's website, n.d. http://www.suedraheim. com/music/about.php.

Driscoll Web Development. "In Which I Lampoon the Renaissance Faire . . ." *I Am Guilty of Blogging* (blog), 13 August 2009. http://blog.iamguiltyof. com/2009/08/in-which-i-lampoon-renaissance-faire.html.

Drout, Michael D. C., ed. *J. R. R. Tolkien Encyclopedia: Scholarship and Critical Assessment.* New York: Routledge, 2007.

Dr. Zibbs. "When I Hear Renaissance Faire I Run for the Hills." *Dr. Zibbs: That Blue Yak* (blog), 20 September 2010. http://thatblueyak.blogspot.com/2010/09/ when-i-hear-renaissance-faire-i-run-for.html.

"Earth Mother's Wedding." *Rags* 3 (August 1970): 43–47.

Easton, Dossie, and Catherine A. Liszt. *The Ethical Slut: A Guide to Infinite Sexual Possibilities.* Emeryville, CA: Greenery, 1998.

Eco, Umberto. *The Name of the Rose.* San Diego, CA: Harcourt, 1983.

Egan, Jesse. "Jesse San at Ocean Beach Comedy." *YouTube,* 31 July 2009. http://www. youtube.com/watch?v=l9T3eVai7ZI.

"8th Annual Pleasure Faire Slated to Open in Agoura." *Van Nuys News,* 1 May 1970. 10A.

Eisenberg, Avner. Interview. 27 October 2011.

Ellison, Suzanne. *Fair Play.* New York: Harlequin Books, 1988.

"Emmalyn & Gavin's Gender-Neutral, LBGTQ-Friendly, Renaissance Festival Wedding." *Offbeat Bride,* 24 June 2010. http://offbeatbride.com/2010/06/arizona-renaissance-festival-wedding.

Faire: An American Renaissance. Dir. Doug Jacobson. J2F Productions, 2010.

"Fairest of the Faire." Produced and edited by David Ossman. Radio broadcast, KPFK, North Hollywood, CA. 25 August 1963.

"Fantasies." *Motifake,* N.d. http://www.demotivationalposters.org/tags/renaissance.

Ferrante, Michael. "Revelry Returns with the Renaissance Festival." *Johns Hopkins News-Letter,* 9 September 2010.

Fischbach, Deborah. Interview. 16 November 2010 and 23 February 2011.

Fischbach, Ernie. Interview. 24 December 2010.

Foghorn67. Comment on "Wife Dragging Me to a Renaissance Faire." *AnandTech Forums*, 2 August 2003. http://forums.anandtech.com/showthread. php?t=69506&page=4.

Foley, Charles. "Freep Gets the Bill." *Winnipeg Free Press*, 18 August 1971. 14.

Forrest, John. *The History of Morris Dancing, 1458–1750*. Toronto: University of Toronto Press, 1999.

Foster, Mike. "America in the 1960s: Reception of Tolkien." In Drout 14–15.

Fox, Johnny. Interview. 29 September and 17 November 2010.

———. Website home page. http://www.johnnyfox.com/.

Fox, Margalit. "Ron Patterson, Renaissance (Fair) Man, Dies at 80." *New York Times*, 2 February 2011. B18.

Frank. Interview. 30 November 2008.

Frank, Thomas. *The Conquest of Cool: Business Culture, Counterculture, and the Rise of Hip Consumerism*. Chicago: University of Chicago Press, 1998.

Franklin, Adrian. *Tourism: An Introduction*. London: Sage, 2003.

Friesner, Esther. *Chicks in Chainmail*. New York: Pocket Books, 1995.

Fritter, Debbie. *Joust in Time*. Casper, WY: Whiskey Creek, 2008.

Fron, Janine, Tracy Fullerton, Jacqueline Ford Morie, and Celia Pearce. "Playing Dress-Up: Costumes, Roleplay, and Imagination." Paper presented at Philosophy of Computer Games conference, Emilia-Romagna, Italy, 2007. http://www.lcc. gatech.edu/~cpearce3/PearcePubs/LudicaDress-Up.pdf.

Fugly Slut. "A Loose Interpretation of Twaticus Maximus." Ask Fugly Slut. *Points in Case*, 26 April 2010. http://www.pointsincase.com/columns/fugly-slut/loose-interpretation-twaticus-maximus.

Furst, Tim. Interview. 5 October 2010.

Gable, Eric, and Richard Handler. "After Authenticity at an American Heritage Site." *American Anthropologist* 98 (1996): 568–578.

Gage. Comment on "When I Hear Renaissance Faire I Run for the Hills." *Dr. Zibbs: That Blue Yak* (blog), 20 September 2010. http://thatblueyak.blogspot. com/2010/09/when-i-hear-renaissance-faire-i-run-for.html.

Gallagher, Diana G. *Milady Alex!* New York: Minstrel Books, 1997.

geezer. *Chautauquaamp.com*, 20 May 2008. http://www.chautauquaamp.com/index. php?content=forum&topic=Rod%20Welling?&page=forum.

Gellman, Michael J. Preface. In Scruggs and Gellman xi–xx.

Gibron, Bill. "Mystery Science Theatre 3000 Collection Volume 5." *DVD Verdict*, 14 April 2004. http://www.dvdverdict.com/reviews/mst3kcollvol5.php.

Gibson, Ian. Email to author. 1 October 2008.

Gilbert, Elizabeth. "Knight Fever." *Spin* 12, no. 9 (26 December 1996): 100–108, 161.

Gilkerson, William. Interview. 15 June 2011

Gillan, Steven. Interview. 14 May 2009 and 28 August 2011.

Gilmore, James H., and B. Joseph Pine II. *Authenticity: What Consumers Really Want.* Cambridge: Harvard Business School Press, 2007.

Glassberg, David. *Sense of History: The Place of the Past in American Life.* Amherst: University of Massachusetts Press, 2001.

Glessing, Robert J. *The Underground Press in America.* Bloomington: Indiana University Press, 1970.

Golden, Christopher, and Nancy Holder. *Buffy the Vampire Slayer: Child of the Hunt.* New York: Pocket Books, 1998.

Gousseff, James. *Street Mime.* Woodstock, IL: Dramatic, 1993.

Gray, Jonathan. "New Audiences, New Textualities: Anti-Fans and Non-Fans. *International Journal of Cultural Studies* 6, no. 3 (March 2003): 64–81.

Green, Martin. Introduction to Green and Swan xi–xvii.

Green, Martin, and John Swan. *The Triumph of Pierrot: The Commedia dell'Arte and the Modern Imagination.* New York: Macmillan, 1986.

Guida, Tony. Interview. 27 September 2008.

Gussow, Mel. *Theatre on the Edge: New Visions, New Voices.* New York: Applause Books, 1998.

Hairspray. Dir. John Waters. New Line Cinema, 1988.

Hall, Julie. *Tradition and Change: The New American Craftsman.* New York: E. P. Dutton, 1977.

Hall, Lynn. *Fair Maiden.* New York: Scribner, 1990.

Hamm, Trent. *1001 Ways to Make Money If You Dare.* Avon, CT: F&W Media, 2009.

Hardy, Kristin. *Bad Influence.* New York: Harlequin Books, 2006.

Harris, Lynnette. Interview with Mark Bell. *Gilded Serpent,* n.d. http://www.gilded-serpent.com/articles22/markbellspeaks1.htm.

Haskell, Harry. *The Early Music Revival: A History.* Mineola, NY: Dover, 1996.

Hastings, Stephanie. Email to author. 6 October 2008.

Hayward, Stephen F. *The Age of Reagan: The Conservative Counterrevolution, 1980–1989.* New York: Three Rivers, 2009.

Heath, Joseph, and Andrew Potter. *Nation of Rebels: Why Counterculture Became Consumer Culture.* New York: HarperCollins, 2004.

Heather. Interview. 8 August 2010.

Hebdige, Dick. *Subculture: The Meaning of Style.* London: Routledge, 1979.

Hendershot, Cora. Interview. 14 May 2009.

Hess, Joan. *Damsels in Distress.* New York: St. Martin's Minotaur, 2007.

"Hie Ye Back to Merrie Old England!" *San Mateo Times,* 23 August 1969. 2A.

Hill, Henry. Email to author. 24 August 2010.

Hinckle, Warren. "The Hippies." *Ramparts,* March 1967. 9–36.

Hinton, S. E. *The Outsiders*. New York: Dell, 1967.

Hobbs, Stuart. *The End of the Avant-Garde*. New York: NYU Press, 1997.

"Holly." Interview. 8 August 2009.

Hoskinson, Liz. Interview. 14 May 2009.

"How Alleged Reds Seized Youth Center Control Told." *Los Angeles Times*, 13 June 1961. 2, 26.

Hudert, Paul. Interview. 16 October 2008.

Irwin, Bill. Email to author. 23 March 2011.

Jackson, Rosemary. *Fantasy: The Literature of Subversion*. New York: Routledge, 1981.

"James." Interview. 28 September 2008.

Jelen, Peter. Email to author. 2 October 2009.

———. Interview. 18 January 2011.

Jenkins, Henry. *Textual Poachers: Television Fans and Participatory Culture*. New York: Routledge, 1992.

Jenkins, Ron. *Acrobats of the Soul: Comedy and Virtuosity in Contemporary American Theatre*. New York: Theatre Communications Group, 1988.

Jenner, C. Lee. "New Vaudeville." In Wilmeth 477–478.

Jezzard, Bill. Interview. 29 November 2008.

Jha. "The Intersection of Race and Steampunk: Colonialism's After-Effects & Other Stories, from a Steampunk of Colour's Perspective." *Racialicious*, 24 June 2009. http://www.racialicious.com/2009/06/24/the-intersection-of-race-and-steampunk-colonialisms-after-effects-other-stories-from-a-steampunk-of-colours-perspective-essay/.

"Joust Like a Woman." *King of the Hill* 112. Dir. Dominic Polcino. Orig. air date: 24 February 2002.

Joynson, Vernon. "Acid Symphony." In *Fuzz, Acid, and Flowers: A Comprehensive Guide to American Garage, Psychedelic, and Hippie Rock (1964–1975)*. London: Borderline Productions, 1999. 9.

K., Michael. Interview. 15 May 2009.

Kacey H. Review of Georgia Renaissance Festival. *Yelp*, 25 May 2010. http://www.yelp.com/filtered_reviews/eIR8NxVlO6VFk2JP8aopQ?fsid=rS9Gy6ktUeVioV HZoeX5Kg.

Kampf, Ray. *The Bear Handbook: A Comprehensive Guide for Those Who Are Husky, Hairy, and Homosexual and Those Who Love 'Em*. Binghamton, NY: Haworth, 2000.

Kant, Immanuel. *Critique of Pure Reason*. Translated by Paul Guyer and Allen Wood. Cambridge: Cambridge University Press, 1999.

Kaplan, Wendy. *"The Art That Is Life": The Arts and Crafts Movement in America, 1875–1920*. Boston: Little, Brown, 1987.

Keating, Jeanne Markham. "Currently Speaking." *Van Nuys News*, 9 May 1972. 2A.

Keith, Alan. Email to author. 15 March 2011.

Kelly, Thomas Forrest. *Early Music: A Very Short Introduction*. New York: Oxford University Press, 2011.

Kent, Jean, and Candace Shelton. *Romance Writer's Phrase Book*. New York: Perigree, 1984.

Kivy, Peter. *The Performance of Reading: An Essay in the Philosophy of Reading*. Malden, MA: Blackwell, 2006.

Knightriders. Dir. George A. Romero. United Film, 1981.

Knopf, Robert. *The Theater and Cinema of Buster Keaton*. Princeton: Princeton University Press, 1999.

Korol-Evans, Kimberly Tony. *Renaissance Festivals: Merrying the Past and Present*. Jefferson, NC: McFarland, 2009.

KPFK (radio station). *Folio* 5, no. 19 (30 March–26 April 1964).

Krunchykrome. Comment on "Wife Dragging Me to a Renaissance Faire." *AnandTech Forums*, 2 August 2003. http://forums.anandtech.com/showthread.php?t=69506&page=4.

Kunkin, Art. Interview. 2 April 2010.

Lackey, Mercedes, and Ellen Guon. *Bedlam's Bard*. Riverdale, NY: Baen Books, 1992.

Lamoree, Trish. *Painting the Roses Red*. Charleston, SC: CreateSpace, 2008.

Lane, Amy. *Making Promises*. Frisco, TX: Dreamspinner, 2010.

Lanigan, Catherine. *Writing the Great American Romance Novel*. New York: Allworth, 2006.

Lapin, Lynne, ed. *Craft Worker's Market: Where to Sell Your Crafts*. Cincinnati: Writer's Digest Books, 1979.

LaRoche, James. Email to author. 24 September 2007.

Larson, Linda. *Renaissance Thematic Unit*. TCR 580. New York: Teacher Created Resources, 1994.

Lasar, Matthew. *Pacifica Radio: The Rise of an Alternative Network*. Updated ed. Philadelphia: Temple University Press, 2000.

"Last Week Fights, This Week Tights." *Gilmore Girls* 86. Dir. Chris Long. Orig. air date: 11 May 2004.

Laurel, Alicia Bay. Email to author. 7 December 2009.

———. *Living on the Earth: Celebrations, Storm Warnings, Formulas, Recipes, Rumors, and Country Dances Harvested*. Berkeley, CA: Book Works, 1970.

Lavene, Joyce, and Jim Lavene. *Ghastly Glass*. New York: Berkley, 2009.

Lears, T. J. Jackson. *No Place of Grace: Antimodernism and the Transformation of American Culture*. Chicago: University of Chicago Press, 1981.

Lebbling, Renee. Email to author. 11 August 2010.

Lecklider, Aaron. *Brainpower: Intelligence in American Culture from Einstein to the Egghead*. Philadelphia: University of Pennsylvania Press, forthcoming.

Lehmann-Haupt, Christopher. "Andre Norton Dies at 93; A Master of Science Fiction." *New York Times*, 18 March 2005.

Levine, Lawrence W. *Highbrow/Lowbrow: The Emergence of Cultural Hierarchy in America*. Cambridge: Harvard University Press, 1988.

Lewis, David, and Darren Bridger. *The Soul of the New Consumer: Authenticity—What We Buy and Why in the New Economy*. London: Brealey, 2000.

Lhamon, W. T. *Raising Cain: Blackface Performance from Jim Crow to Hip Hop*. Cambridge: Harvard University Press, 1998.

Liberman, Lev. Interview. 20 May 2011.

———. Liner notes to *First Recordings 1977–1978*. Arhoolie Records, 1987.

Limerick, Patricia Nelson. *Something in the Soil: Legacies and Reckonings in the New West*. New York: Norton, 2000.

Lindholm, Charles. *Culture and Authenticity*. Malden, MA: Blackwell, 2003.

"Lisa's Wedding." *The Simpsons* 122. Dir. Jim Reardon. Orig. air date: 19 March 1995.

Littleton, Harvey. *Glassblowing: A Search for Form*. New York: Van Nostrand Reinhold, 1971.

Loeffelbein, Robert L. *Knight Life: Jousting in the United States*. Lexington Park, MD: Golden Owl, 1977.

Louie, Elaine. "Neighborhood Report: Lower East Side; A Man Who Lives by the Sword." *New York Times*, 6 June 1999.

Lundborg, Patrick. Interview with Joseph Pusey. *Lama Workshop*, 2002. http://lysergia_2.tripod.com/LamaWorkshop/lamaJosephPusey.htm.

lupi. Comment on "Wife Dragging Me to a Renaissance Faire." *AnandTech Forums*, 2 August 2003. http://forums.anandtech.com/showthread.php?t=69506&page=4.

Lust, Annette. *From the Greek Mimes to Marcel Marceau and Beyond: Mimes, Actors, Pierrots, and Clowns: A Chronicle of the Many Visages of the Mime in the Theatre*. Lanham, MD: Scarecrow, 2000.

Lynn, Cheryl. "Got to Be Real." *Cheryl Lynn*. Columbia, 1978.

MacAlister, Katie. *Hard Day's Knight*. New York: Signet Eclipse, 2005.

Macan, Edward. *Rocking the Classics: English Progressive Rock and the Counterculture*. New York: Oxford University Press, 1997.

Madmage. Comment on "The Seven Knightly Virtues." *IBRSC Public Forums*, 19 April 2008. http://forums.ibrsc.org/index.php/topic,7535.240.html.

Madtexter. Comment on "When I Hear Renaissance Faire I Run for the Hills." *Dr. Zibbs: That Blue Yak* (blog), 20 September 2010. http://thatblueyak.blogspot.com/2010/09/when-i-hear-renaissance-faire-i-run-for.html.

Manheim, Camryn. Interview. 18 January 2011.

———. *Wake Up, I'm Fat!* New York: Broadway Books, 1999.

Manny. Email to author. 4 November 2008.

Marcus, Greil. "The Firesign Theatre." In Marsh and Swenson, 175–176.

Marcus, MJ. Interview. 15 May 2009.

"Marina." Interview. 14 May 2009.

Marsh, Dave, and John Swenson, eds. *The New Rolling Stone Record Guide*. New York: Random House, 1983.

McCall, Penny. *The Bliss Factor*. New York: Berkley, 2010.

McCarthy, Justin. "1960s Brokaw: NBC Correspondent and 'Weekend Hippy.'" *Newsbusters: Exposing and Combating Liberal Media Bias*, 23 January 2008. http://newsbusters.org/blogs/justin-mccarthy/2008/01/23/1960s-brokaw-nbc-correspondent-weekend-hippy.

McKevett, G. A. *Sugar and Spite*. New York: Kensington Books, 2000.

McKinney, Joan. "A New Trip for a Child of the Earth." *Oakland Tribune*, 1 April 1971. 11K.

McLeod, David. *Book of Heroes: George of Sedona I. Gay Authors—Quality Gay Fiction Stories*, 17 January 2011. http://www.gayauthors.org/story/david-mcleod/bookofheroesgeorgeofsedonai.

Meltzer, Marissa. "Notes from a Renaissance Faire." *Paris Review Daily* (blog), 8 September 2010. http://www.theparisreview.org/blog/2010/09/08/notes-from-a-renaissance-faire/.

"A Messenger, Nothing More." *Gilmore Girls* 89. Dir. Daniel Palladino. Orig. air date: 28 September 2004.

Michelle. Interview. 10 September 2007.

Midgetmanofsteel. "Renaissance Redux." *Mental Poo* (blog), 1 October 2008. http://www.midgetmanofsteel.com/2008/10/renaissance-redux.html.

Mielnik, Michael. Email to author. 8 November 2010.

Milam, Bradley K. "Anti-Gay Language in Print Must Stop." *Charleston Gazette*, 12 June 2011. http://www.wvgazette.com/Opinion/OpEdCommentaries/201106120625.

Miller, Dustin. Liner notes to *A Cid Symphony*. Gear Fab Records, 1999.

Mincher, Robyn. "Deep-Fried Knights: Maryland Renaissance Festival." *Express Night Out*, 27 August 2008. http://www.expressnightout.com/content/2008/08/deepfried_knights_maryland_renaissance_f.php.

Moore, Chadwick. "The Gayer Side of the Ren Faire." *Out*, 16 August 2010. http://www.popnography.com/2010/08/the-gayer-side-of-the-ren-faire-.html#more.

Morgan, Edward P. *The Sixties Experience: Hard Lessons about Modern America*. Philadelphia: Temple University Press, 1991.

Mr. Condescending. "Losers as Art VII (Ye Olde Faire)." *Advice and Humor from Mr. Condescending* (blog), 9 July 2009. http://somanylosers.blogspot.com/2009/07/losers-as-art-vii-ye-olde-faire.html.

"Mr. Saturday Knight." *Family Guy* 37. Dir. Michael Dante DiMartino, Pete Michels, and Peter Shin. Orig. air date: 5 September 2001.

Murphy, Kevin. "Episode 703: Deathstalker and the Warriors from Hell." *Satellite News: The Official Mystery Science Theater 3000 Fan Site*, 2001. http://www.mst-3kinfo.com/guide/ep703.html.

Neiswender, Mary. "Hippie Press May Charge Crow." *Long Beach Independent*, 7 May 1968. B1.

Nelson, Marion. "Folk Art in Minnesota and the Case of the Norwegian American." In *Circles of Tradition: Folk Arts in Minnesota*, 24–44. Published in conjunction with an exhibition held at the University of Minnesota Art Museum. St. Paul: Minnesota Historical Society Press, 1989.

Newell, Wendy. Email to author. 14 July 2009.

"1975: Renaissance Festival." Rept. Margaret Moos. Radio broadcast, Minnesota Public Radio. 1975. Accessed at http://minnesota.publicradio.org/display/web/2010/09/22/1975-renaissance-festival/.

Noddy, Tom. "The Origin of New Vaudeville." Tom Noddy's website, n.d. http://www.tomnoddy.com/OriginofNewVaudeville.pdf.

Nordness, Lee. *Objects, USA*. New York: Viking, 1970.

Norton, Andre. *Year of the Unicorn*. New York: Ace Books, 1965.

Norton, Andre, and Jean Rabe, eds. *Renaissance Faire*. New York: Daw Books, 2005.

Notorious C.H.O. Dir. Lorene Machado. Cho Taussig Productions, 2002.

Nugent, Benjamin. "Who's a Nerd, Anyway?" *New York Times*, 29 July 2007. http://www.nytimes.com/2007/07/29/magazine/29wwln-idealab-t.html.

Nyong'o, Tavia. "Period Rush: Affective Transfers in Recent Queer Art and Performance." *Theatre History Studies* 28 (2008): 42–48.

Odom, Shane. Interview. 29 September 2007.

O'Kerry, Janeen. *Mistress of the Waters*. New York: Love Spell, 1999.

"Old Crafts Find New Hands." *Life*, 29 July 1966. 34–41.

Ossman, David. Interview. 30 October 2009.

———. "Pleasure Faire." *Los Angeles FM & Fine Arts*, May 1966. 3–5.

Overstreet, Stephen. Interview. 5 May 2009.

P., Ken. "Interview with Penn Jillette." *IGN.com*, 13 October 2003. http://movies.ign.com/articles/454/454422p1.html.

Paris Is Burning. Dir. Jennie Livingston. Miramax Films, 1990.

Parker, Nathaniel. "Use Prance in a Sentence without Sounding All Gay and Stuff." *Cult: The Official Website of Chuck Palahnuik*, 12 March 2011. http://chuckpalahniuk.net/forum/1000026/use-prance-in-a-sentence-without-it-sounding-all-gay-and-stuff.

Parv, Valerie. *The Art of Romance Writing*. Crows Nest, NSW: Allen and Unwin, 1993.

Patterson, Howard. Interview. 22 October 2010.

Patterson, Kevin. Interview. 10 and 11 August 2009.

Patterson, Phyllis. Interview. 11 August 2009.

Payne, Patricia. *Sex Tips from a Dominatrix.* New York: It Books, 1999.

Pearson, Rush. Interview. 11 November 2010.

Perry, Charles. *The Haight-Ashbury: A History.* New York: Wenner, 2005.

———. *Smokestack El Ropo's Bedside Reader: A Heavy-Duty Compendium of Fables, Lore, and Hot Dope Tales, from America's Only Rolling Newspaper.* San Francisco: Straight Arrow, 1972.

Peterson, Richard A. *Creating Country Music: Fabricating Authenticity.* Chicago: University of Chicago Press, 1997.

Pfaff, Jala. *Seducing the Rabbi.* Boulder, CO: Blue Flax, 2007.

Pine, Joseph, II, and James H. Gilmore. *The Experience Economy: Work Is Theatre and Every Business a Stage.* Cambridge: Harvard Business Press, 1999.

Pitts, J. A. *Black Blade Blues.* New York: Tor Books, 2010.

"Plastic Product Brochures." *PlasticLiving.com.* http://plasticliving.com/brochures/b.html.

Pleasure Fair (preview). Dir. Matt Rose. Zenith Productions, 1975. On *Quickie Graffiti: Snips and Clips, in Color, X-Rated.*

"Pleasure Faire on Today Despite Zone Board Delay." *Oxnard Press-Courier,* 4 May 1968. 10.

Polydoris, Dan. "Live at the Lincoln Lodge." *YouTube,* 2 March 2007. http://www.youtube.com/watch?gl=GB&hl=en-GB&v=4PBLtU83TN0.

Price, Kevin. Interview. 30 November 2008.

Prozanski, Suzi. *Fruit of the Sixties: The Founding of the Oregon County Fair.* Eugene, OR: Coincidental Communication, 2009.

Pugh, Tison. *Sexuality and Its Queer Discontents in Middle English Literature.* New York: Palgrave Macmillan, 2008.

Pycior, Julie Leininger. *LBJ and Mexican Americans: The Paradox of Power.* Austin: University of Texas Press, 1997.

Radway, Janice. *Reading the Romance: Women, Patriarchy, and Popular Literature.* Chapel Hill: University of North Carolina Press, 1984.

Rainbow. Email to author. 20 June 2012.

Randy. Interview. 14 October 2007.

Ranum, Katrina. Interview. 28 September 2007.

Rasmussen, Anne. "An Evening in the Orient: The Middle Eastern Nightclub in America." *Asian Music* 23, no. 2 (Spring–Summer 1992): 63–88.

Reddin, Paul. *Wild West Shows.* Urbana: University of Illinois Press, 1999.

Reid, James MacDonald. Email to author. 17 March 2011.

Renaissance Fair: Psychedelic Pop Culture Auctions. Home page. 2009. http://www.lysergia.com/RenaissanceFair/RenaissanceFair_main.htm.

Renaissance Men: The True Story of the Hanlon-Lees Action Theater. Dir. Kevin Leeser. 3 Alarm Carnival Productions, 2008.

Renaissance Ministries. *Logos Christian Fellowship,* n.d. http://www.logoschristian. org/renaissance.

Reynolds, Eric T., and Gerri Leen, eds. *Renaissance Festival Tales.* Overland Park, KS: Hadley Rille Books, 2009.

Richards, Clare. *Renaissance Summer.* New York: Silhouette Books, 1985.

Roberts, Cokie, and Steven V. Roberts. "Elizabeth Is Alive and Well and Living in Agoura, CA." *New York Times,* 7 May 1972. XX7.

Roberts, John Maddox. "Girolamo and Mistress Willendorf." In Norton and Rabe 60–72.

Robbins, Karen. Interview. 7 June 2011.

Rockwell, John. *Outsider: John Rockwell on the Arts, 1967–2006.* Pompton Plains, NJ: Limelight Editions, 2006.

Rodel, Kevin P., and Jonathan Binzen. *Arts and Crafts Furniture: From Classic to Contemporary.* Newtown, CT: Taunton, 2003.

Roediger, David. *The Wages of Whiteness: Race and the Making of the American Working Class.* New York: Verso, 1991.

Rogovy, Seth. "The Klezmorim: Left Coast Origins." *The Klezmorim,* n.d. http:// klezmo.com/bongo_origins_0.html.

Romano, Steve R. *Dreams of Betrayal.* Charleston, SC: CreateSpace, 2008.

Rook. "Arizona—What a Long Estranged Tweek It's Been." *Rogues' Alternative Gazette,* 2003. 37.

Rose, Barbara. "Crafts Ain't What They Used to Be." *New York,* 19 June 1972. 72–73.

Rosen, Jody. "Joanna Newson, the Changeling." *New York Times Magazine,* 7 March 2010. 4.

Rosenthal, Rachel. Email to author. 11 August 2010.

Rosenzweig, Roy. *Eight Hours for What We Will: Workers and Leisure in an Industrial City, 1870–1920.* New York: Cambridge University Press, 1985.

Rosenzweig, Roy, and David Thelen. *The Presence of the Past.* New York: Columbia University Press, 2000.

Rotsler, William. "Hippies' Mardi Gras: Hippie Flower People Frolic in Mad World of Middle Ages." *Adam* 11, no. 9 (September 1967): 22–25.

Rowland, Howard S., and Beatrice L. Rowland. *Guide to Adventure, Travel & Study, U.S.A., for High School and College Students.* New York: Quadrangle/New York Times Book Co., 1973.

Royer, Robb. Interview. 20 August 2010.

Ruditis, Paul. *Drama! Show, Don't Tell.* New York: Simon Pulse, 2008.

"Rumpelstiltskin." *Reading Rainbow* 42. Dir. Larry Lancit, Mark Mannucci, and Ed Wiseman. Orig. air date: August 1987.

S., Sophie. "Renaissance Fair: Persuading Your Husband to Dress Up in Period Costume." *Yahoo Voices*, 15 May 2008. http://voices.yahoo.com/renaissance-fair-persuading-husband-dress-1458679.html.

Sahm, Doug. "Be Real." Rec. 1970. *Best of Doug Sahm and the Sir Douglas Quintet.* Island Def Jam, 1990.

Salimpour, Jamila. "From Many Tribes: The Origins of Bal Anat." *Habbi* 17, no. 3 (1999): 16–19, 35–36.

"Sally." Interview. 28 June 2010.

Samuel, Barbara. *No Place Like Home.* New York: Ballantine Books, 2002.

Samuel, Raphael. *Theaters of Memory: Past and Present in Contemporary Culture.* London: Verso, 1994.

San Francisco Mime Troupe. Home page. http://www.sfmt.org/index.php.

Saricks, Joyce. *The Readers' Advisory Guide to Genre Fiction.* 2nd ed. Chicago: American Library Association Editions, 2009.

Scarborough, Elizabeth Ann. "Jewels beyond Price." In Norton and Rabe 4–27.

Schaffer, George. "'Pleasure Fair' Finds Home in Agoura." *Van Nuys News,* 22 February 1968. 38B.

Schechner, Richard. *Environmental Theater.* New York: Hawthorn Books, 1973.

Schryver, Mark James. Interview. 28 November 2010.

Schulps, John. Interview. 14 May 2009.

Scott-Hoffman, Dakota. Email to author. 2 October 2008.

Scruggs, Mary, and Michael J. Gellman. *Process: An Improviser's Journey.* Evanston, IL: Northwestern University Press, 2007.

Scudder, Billy. Interview. 20 June 2009.

Seaman, Donna. "Toil and Trouble." *Los Angeles Times,* 20 July 2008. http://http://articles.latimes.com/2008/jul/20/books/bk-winfield20.

Sean. Interview. 25 April 2010.

Seeger, Mike. Liner notes to *Berkeley Farms.* Folkways, 1967.

Seidenbaum, Art. "Attention Pasadena—Bohemia in Your Midst." *Los Angeles Times,* 31 December 1965. A7, A9.

Sellers-Young, Barbara. "Body, Image, Identity: American Tribal Belly Dance." In Shay and Sellers-Young 277–303.

Sharan, Farida. Email to author. 20 April 2011.

———. *Flower Child.* Boulder, CO: Wisdome, 2000.

Shay, Anthony, and Barbara Sellers-Young. *Belly Dance: Orientalism, Transnationalism, and Harem Fantasy.* Costa Mesa, CA: Mazda, 2005.

Shelton, Kent. Interview. 11 June 2011.

Shields, Robert. Interview. 29 June 2009.

———. *Mime in Our Time*. San Francisco: Get the Hook, 1972.

Shirey, David L. "Crafting Their Own World." *Newsweek*, 21 July 1969. 62–67.

Shteir, Rachel. "New Vaudeville." In Chambers 540–541.

Sieve, Mark. *Call Me Puke: A Life on the Dirt Circuit*. Minneapolis, MN: Two Harbors, 2009.

Simon, Jonathan. "Taking Risks: Extreme Sports and the Embrace of Risk in Advanced Liberal Societies." In Baker and Simon 177–208.

Sir Barchan. Interview. 28 September 2007.

Sizemore, Susan. *My Own True Love*. New York: HarperPaperbacks, 1984.

Slater, Dashka. "Is Jousting the Next Extreme Sport?" *New York Times*, 11 July 2010. MM24.

Smith, Brianna. Interview. 22 April 2009.

Smith, Jack. *Smith on Wry or, The Art of Coming Through*. Garden City, NY: Doubleday, 1970.

Smith, Patti. "The Crowded Mind of Johnny Depp." *Vanity Fair*, February 2011. http://www.vanityfair.com/hollywood/features/2011/01/johnny-depp-201101.

Smith, Victor. Interview. 28 September 2008.

Sneed, Richard. *The Faire: Photographs and History of the Renaissance Pleasure Faire from 1963 Onwards*. Santa Cruz, CA: Good Book, 1987.

Snow, Nancy. *Propaganda, Inc.: Selling America's Culture to the World*. 3rd ed. New York: Seven Stories, 2010.

Spacedsaviour. "A Cid Symphony." *Spaced2Saviour* (blog), July 2009. http://mod-adelic.blogspot.com/2009/07/cid-symphony.html.

Spires, Will. Interview. 28 March 2011.

———. "Robert D. Thomas Remembered in Word and Music." Paper presented at Sonoma County Museum, July 2005. Manuscript obtained from author.

Springhorn, Chris. Interview. 14 May 2009.

Springhorn, David. Interview. 14 May 2009.

Stanley, Owsley. "Bob Thomas." *The Bear*, n.d. (c. 1993). http://www.thebear.org/Bob_Thomas.html.

Stanton, Cathy. "Reenactors in the Parks: A Study of External Revolutionary War Reenactment Activity at National Parks." Boston: National Park Services and Heritage Partners, 1999. http://www.nps.gov/revwar/reenactors/intro.pdf.

Stephanie. "Renaissance Festival = Redneck Disneyland." *Smart Sassy Mom* (blog), 12 April 2010. http://smartsassymom.blogspot.com/2010/04/renaissance-festival-redneck-disneyland.html.

Steven. Interview. 29 November 2008.

St. Louis, Ray. *Road Dog Diary*. Booklocker.com, 2006.

Stone, Michael. *Contemporary American Woodworkers*. Salt Lake City, UT: G. M. Smith, 1986.

Strom, Yale. *The Book of Klezmer: The History, the Music, the Folklore*. Chicago: Chicago Review Press, 2002.

Sullivan, Stephen D. "Renaissance Fear." In Norton and Rabe 234–257.

Sullivan, Wally. Email to author. 16 October 2008.

Summers, Gillian. *Into the Wildewood*. Woodbury, MN: Flux, 2007.

———. *The Secret of the Dread Forest*. Woodbury, MN: Flux, 2009.

———. *The Tree Shepherd's Daughter*. Woodbury, MN: Flux, 2008.

"Surely, You Joust." *Girls Next Door* 44. Orig. air date: 26 August 2007.

Swihart, Stanton. "A Cid Symphony." *allmusic*, 1999. http://allmusic.com/album/a-cid-symphony-r430123/review.

Sylvester. "You Make Me Feel Mighty Real." Rec. 1978. *The Original Hits*. Fantasy Records, 1989.

Teller. Foreword. In Sieve xi–xiii.

Templeton, David. "Sex in the Shire: Debauchery a Lost Art at the Renaissance Pleasure Faire." *Sonoma County Independent*, 6 August 1998.

Thornley, Kerry. "Zenarchy—Chapter 1: Face of the Unborn." *IllumiNet Press and Impropaganda*, 1997. http://www.impropaganda.net/1997/zenarchy1.html.

Todorov, Tzvetan. *The Fantastic: A Structural Approach to a Literary Genre*. Trans. Richard Howard. Cleveland, OH: Press of Case Western Reserve University, 1973.

Trillin, Calvin. *American Stories*. New York: Ticknor and Fields, 1991.

Trilling, Lionel. *Sincerity and Authenticity*. New York: Harcourt, Brace, Jovanovich, 1971.

Tseëlon, Efrat. *Masquerade and Identities: Essays on Gender, Sexuality, and Marginality*. London: Routledge, 2001.

Turner, Rory. "The Play of History: Civil War Reenactments and Their Use of the Past." *Folklore Forum* 22, nos. 1–2 (1989): 54–61.

Twin Cities GLBT Oral History Project. *Queer Twin Cities*. Minneapolis: University of Minnesota Press, 2010.

Unterberger, Richie. *Urban Spacement and Wayfaring Strangers: Overlooked Innovators and Eccentric Visionaries of '60s Rock*. San Francisco: Miller Freeman Books, 2000.

uppityperson. Comment on "Got Back from the Renaissance Faire Tonight!" *Democratic Underground*, 23 October 2006. http://demopedia.democraticunderground.com/discuss/duboard.php?az=view_all&address=105x5761505.

U.S. Department of Defense. "United States Special Forces: Posture Statement." Darby, PA: Diane, 1993.

USIA (United States Information Agency). Home page. 1999. Archived at http://dosfan.lib.uic.edu/usia/.

Van Draanen, Wendelin. *Sammy Keyes and the Search for Snake Eyes*. New York: Yearling, 2008.

Vardeman, Robert E. "A Time for Steel." In Norton and Rabe 73–91.

Villegas, Allison. Email to author. 5 November 2007.

Wachtell, Amy. Interview. 28 September 2010.

Wainger, Leslie. *Writing a Romance Novel for Dummies*. Hoboken, NJ: Wiley, 2004.

Walker, Michael. *Laurel Canyon: The Inside Story of Rock-and-Roll's Legendary Neighborhood*. New York: Faber and Faber, 2006.

Walkowitz, Daniel. *City Folk: English Country Dance and the Politics of the Folk in Modern America*. New York: NYU Press, 2010.

Watts, Avery. Interview. 1 November 2010.

Weathers, Carolyn. Interview. 24 January 2010.

———. "Renaissance Pleasure Faire." *Mazer Lesbian Archives*, 2007. http://www.mazerlesbianarchives.org/index.php?option=com_content&view=article&id=62:renaissance-faire&catid=35:true-life-lesbian&Itemid=62.

Weaver, Derek. "From the Keyboard of the Editor." *Rogues' Alternative Gazette*, 2003. 4.

———. Interview. 29 September 2007.

Weiss, Jeff. "The Renaissance Faire Is Decadent and Depraved." *The Passion of the Weiss* (blog), 23 May 2006. http://passionweiss.com/2006/05/23/the-renaissance-faire-is-decadent-and-depraved/.

Weller, Sheila. *Girls Like Us: Carole King, Joni Mitchell, and Carly Simon—And the Journey of a Generation*. New York: Washington Square, 2008.

Welz, Larry. *Cherry Meets the Renaissance Dude*. Cherry Comics 16. Roswell, NM: Cherry Comics, 2000.

Whisnant, David. *All That Is Native and Fine: The Politics of Culture in an American Region*. Chapel Hill: University of North Carolina Press, 1983.

Wilde, Lori. *Zero Control*. New York: Harlequin Books, 2009.

Williams, Liza. "Come Buy My Magick." *Los Angeles FM & Fine Arts*, May 1966. 6–7.

Williams, Raymond. *Marxism and Literature*. New York: Oxford University Press, 1977.

Wilmeth, Don B., ed. *Cambridge Guide to American Theatre*. 2nd ed. Cambridge: Cambridge University Press, 2007.

Wilson, Jane. "Commerce in Hippieland." *Los Angeles Times*, 28 January 1968. B16–17, 19–21.

Winfield, Jess. *My Name Is Will: A Novel of Sex, Drugs, and Shakespeare*. New York: Twelve, 2008.

"Winters," Orlando. "A Lesson in Profiling." *Boy Writes Miami* (blog), 16 September 2010. http://boywritesmiami.com/2010/09/a-lesson-in-profiling/.

Witherup, R. R. "Pleasures of the Faire, Circa 1964." *Los Angeles FM & Fine Arts*, May 1965. 5–9.

Withington, Robert. *English Pageantry: An Historical Outline*. Vol. 2. Cambridge: Harvard University Press, 1920.

Witt, Jeremy. "Review of Falconer-Arnod." *Metal Review*, 4 July 2011. http://metalreview.com/reviews/6259/falconer-armod.

Witter, Bret, and Lorelei Sharkey. *Carnival Undercover*. New York: Plume/Penguin, 2003.

Wolf, Rose. "A Dance of Seven Vales." In Norton and Rabe 170–195.

World Crafts Council. Home page. n.d. http://www.worldcraftscouncil.org/home.

Yankovic, "Weird Al." "White and Nerdy." *Straight Outta Lynnwood*. Volcano, 2006.

Zekley, Mickie. "Adventures of a Street Musician, Part I." *Lark Camp*, 1995. http://www.larkcamp.com/adventures1.html.

———. Interview. 6 July 2009.

———. "Preston: Recollections of 19th- and 20th-Century Communal Life on Preston Ranch." *Lark Camp*, n.d. http://larkcamp.com/Preston/PrestonHistory.html.

INDEX

Page numbers in italics refer to illustrations.

ABOUT THE AUTHOR

Rachel Lee Rubin is Professor of American Studies at the University of Massachusetts, Boston. She is the author and editor of seven books, including *Immigration and American Popular Culture*, with Jeffrey Melnick (NYU Press, 2006), *Southern Radicalism since Reconstruction*, with Chris Green and James Smethurst (2006), *American Popular Music: New Approaches to the Twentieth Century*, with Jeffrey Melnick (2001), and *Jewish Gangsters of Modern Literature* (2000).